the enneagram, relationships, and intimacy

ENDORSEMENTS

David Daniels had a wonderful understanding of people, relationships, and the Enneagram. This book captures his wisdom and gentleness. Just like David, it's inspiring and enlightening. I put it right at the top of my recommended Enneagram books.

Jerome Wagner, PhD
Clinical Psychologist
Honorary Founder: International Enneagram Association

David presents a clear path for all of us and our relationships through the Enneagram and what he calls the path to "receptive consciousness"—which entails deep listening, kindness, and awareness of our reactivity and judgments. In David and Suzanne's book on the Enneagram and relationships, you will gain wisdom and learn to practice this beautiful form of being aware and receptive to others and to those you love deeply. David's great hope "to love better and live more fully" is revealed in the words of this book.

Russ Hudson
World-Renowned Enneagram Expert and Teacher

We are very grateful for the enormous contribution David Daniels MD made to the modern Enneagram movement as well as our own personal and professional growth paths. His book, *The Enneagram, Relationships, and Intimacy*, written with Suzanne Dion, showcases his deep insight into relationships, the Enneagram, and the human path of development.

Beatrice Chestnut, PhD and Uranio Paes
Founders of the Chestnut Paes Enneagram Academy
and Enneagram Experts, Authors, and Teachers

The Enneagram, Relationships, and Intimacy by David Daniels and Suzanne Dion is a book worth reading if you are interested in the most important aspect of developing meaningful, sustained relationships. Healthy relationships start with each of us exploring and working with ourselves so we are ready and able to have the kinds of relationships we most deeply desire.

Ginger Lapid-Bogda, PhD
Founder: The Enneagram in Business

David Daniels, MD, a well-loved, internationally known, and highly regarded pioneer in the Enneagram field always had a simple goal: to bring the Enneagram to the world. Through the training program he created with Helen Palmer and now maintained by The Narrative Enneagram—a nonprofit carrying forward his work—his dream is being realized.

This book shows David's brilliant understanding and keen insight into the joys and challenges of relationships. He and co-author, Suzanne Dion, offer useful suggestions and practices for how to create more loving relationships, including how to use the 5As in relationships. The 5As is a term used to refer to the Universal Growth Process (UGP) for Self-Mastery, a tool he and I created together. The UGP provides a simple yet powerful model for personal development.

Enjoy learning from one of the early visionaries through the richness of *The Enneagram, Relationships, and Intimacy.*

Terry Saracino, MA
Founding Executive Director: The Narrative Enneagram

Dr. David Daniels was such an important figure for many. Not only a professor of psychiatry, he was a psychiatrist who knew intimately the struggles of individuals, couples, and families and he brought his wisdom and healing to their care. David's brilliant mind and kind heart are reflected in his final book with co-author Suzanne Dion and provides encouragement and method for all who want to create more love in their relationships.

Peter O'Hanrahan
Core Faculty: The Narrative Enneagram
Peter studied and worked closely with David Daniels
from 1991 until his death in 2017

In my 30 years as a full-time Enneagram teacher throughout the world, I have always hoped a book such as this would exist someday. Accessible to all, it contains both David's experience and his delicacy. Besides Enneagram concepts, this book delivers precious data on emotional nurturing, spiritual development as well as the sexual experience of the nine types.

Eric Salmon
Director: Centre d'Études de l'Ennéagramme (France)

David wasn't only a wise teacher but a warm, compassionate presence who cared deeply about the power of the Enneagram and practice to cultivate wholeness and wellbeing. You're holding in your hands a book imbued with his voice, his presence, and his commitment to integrating research, daily practice, and compassionate mindfulness in our relationships.

Leslie Hershberger, MS
Transformational Consultant and Guide

David is one of the most relational people I have ever known. In this marvelous book, David will show you how the habits of your Enneagram type unconsciously run the tapes of intimate connection, and how to bust through the narratives you carry into a new way of relating from a deeper understanding of self and other, and setting the stage for something new to be birthed in partnership.

Barbara Whiteside
Whiteside Workshops
Enneagram and Family Constellations

Through his work, Dr. Daniels has helped countless couples navigate issues and find a path toward a healthier and more fulfilling relationship. His compassionate and insightful approach to couples therapy is truly inspiring, and his wisdom has the power to transform relationships and lives. Dr. Daniels' insights into the triggers of anger and the different sexual expressions of each type are invaluable for anyone looking to improve their relationship. This book is a must-read for anyone looking to deepen their understanding of themselves and their partner, and to create a more loving and harmonious relationship.

Gabriele Hilberg, PhD
Clinical Psychologist

This is a five-star resource on intimacy and relationships! Equal to having learned from these writers (Daniels and Dion) *in person* is having their words on paper in the same conversational, enlightening, and equipping way. This book has become a treasured companion and go-to resource for my work in training spiritual directors, coaches, and therapists in the Enneagram.

Rev. Clare Loughrige
Spiritual Director

David's genius and legacy lie in the brilliance of the nine Basic Propositions. If you don't know what they are, jump into this book and let your heart burst open with deep and abiding compassion. For me, the Basic Propositions are at the core of fully realizing relationships.

Anne Geary
Founder: The Enneagram Approach

This is a great book—comprehensive and unique in its own right—that covers attachment, temperamental nature by way of the Enneagram, the critical impacts of nurture, and how the developmental health of our personalities impacts our connection to ourselves, the fulfillment of our relationships, and potential of our lives.

Mark F. Schwartz, ScD
Clinical Director: Harmony Place Monterey

David Daniels' extraordinary book, co-authored with Suzanne Dion, is a powerful and inspiring roadmap that will help you delve deeper into the inner workings of the self and find meaning in loving, intimate, and sustained relationships. Through insightful questions, practices, case studies and reflections, the book seamlessly blends expert knowledge of interpersonal neurobiology with the teachings of the Enneagram to create the perfect guide on how to stay open, curious, and receptive toward ourselves and others. In following David's guidance, you will reclaim the gift of loving kindness that is innate in each one of us.

Suzette Fischer
Training Associate: The Narrative Enneagram (South Africa)

The unprecedented integrative depth and breadth of *The Enneagram: Relationships, and Intimacy* has been a hidden treasure in the Enneagram literature and community. The publication of this updated version should be celebrated around the globe for the impact that it will have on healing and transformation for self, others, and intimate relationships. Like the courageous body, heart, mind, and soul of Dr. David Daniels as he endlessly committed himself to developing compassion, love, and wisdom, so too this book—a legacy work of a lifetime—is courageous in spanning the breadth of the spectrum of the science to spirituality of the Enneagram in one book without watering either down. This book is a reflection of David and Suzanne's commitment to conveying the possibilities for physical, emotional, cognitive and spiritual wellbeing and development with ourselves and in relationships. our refined and evolutionary attention, caring, and dedication.

Jessica Dibb
Director of Inspiration Consciousness School
Founder and Host: The Shift Network Annual Enneagram Global Summit

the
enneagram,
relationships,
and intimacy

Understanding One Another
Leads to Loving Better
and Living More Fully

How to Bring Our Presence, Awareness,
and Authentic Selves to Relationships

DAVID N. DANIELS, MD, and **SUZANNE DION**

Foreword By Daniel J. Siegel, MD

NEW YORK

LONDON • NASHVILLE • MELBOURNE • VANCOUVER

the enneagram, relationships, and intimacy

Understanding One Another Leads to Loving Better
and Living More Fully

For more information about Dr. David Daniels and his work, please visit www.drdaviddaniels.com

Published in New York, New York, by Morgan James Publishing. Morgan James is a trademark of Morgan James, LLC. www.MorganJamesPublishing.com

Proudly distributed by Publishers Group West®

Morgan James BOGO™

A **FREE** ebook edition is available for you or a friend with the purchase of this print book.

CLEARLY SIGN YOUR NAME ABOVE

Instructions to claim your free ebook edition:
1. Visit MorganJamesBOGO.com
2. Sign your name CLEARLY in the space above
3. Complete the form and submit a photo of this entire page
4. You or your friend can download the ebook to your preferred device

ISBN 9781636985367 paperback
ISBN 9781636985374 ebook
Library of Congress Control Number:
2024941095

Cover Design by:
Suzanne Dion

Interior Design by:
Chris Treccani
www.3dogcreative.net

Morgan James is a proud partner of Habitat for Humanity Peninsula and Greater Williamsburg. Partners in building since 2006.

Get involved today! Visit: www.morgan-james-publishing.com/giving-back

"The understanding of
self and other
is the key
to my very personal,
societal, and
humanitarian dream."

— *David Daniels, M.D.*

DEDICATION

Dedicated to Judy

David's Beloved Sweetie

Dedicated to Love

CONTENTS

"Our qualities
of being
are what
we leave behind."

— David Daniels, M.D.

ACKNOWLEDGMENTS FROM SUZANNE

Gratitude

This is a very special book. Writing it has taken several years, multiple iterations, and a handful of extraordinary people, each of whom have loved a very special man very dearly.

This book is the long-held vision and heartfelt legacy of Dr. David Daniels. Three weeks before his unexpected passing, he excitedly turned over yet another working draft, and I had just begun to review his additions and changes when he left us. It was a longstanding promise made to David that I would finish this book on his behalf in the event he couldn't see it to the end.

Doing so has been nothing short of the most personally humbling and professionally challenging collaborations I've ever endeavored; notwithstanding, it's been the greatest of honors to complete this with him and for him, for his family, and for his global community.

David is the reason I came to the Enneagram. He's the reason I got certified as an Enneagram teacher and the reason I had the chance to become whom I'm becoming today. During a workshop David was leading for CEOs, I witnessed him give a tearful explanation of how the Enneagram fosters the development of profound compassion for ourselves and for one another. His heart was undefended and courageous. His passionate message to unsuspecting business leaders and tender delivery of far more than business-enhancing material opened my heart and changed my life forever.

An enormous thanks goes out to J. D. Daniels, PhD, and Denise Daniels, PhD, David's loving, devoted, and brilliant-in-their-own-right adult children who have been editing, guiding, and collaborating with me on David's last draft every step of the way. Seeing this project to completion would not have been possible without their immense support, dedication, and contribution.

All of us—myself, Denise, and J. D.—are enormously grateful to Morgan James Publishing for their guidance, belief in our book, and their editorial prowess to bring this updated 2025 edition to both online and traditional book sellers and bookstores worldwide. David's books have been published in numerous languages around the world and expanding the reach of this Enneagram book about relationships is now made possibly thanks to the vision of Karen Anderson and the expertise of our editor, Dr. Adéle Booysen.

A very special thanks to Dr. Dan Siegel, whose research, dedication to human consciousness and brilliance not only touched David but so many of us out here on the path to awareness and development. Those who get to read his insightful books can become empowered to take part in bringing his insights to individuals and families, to children, and to schools in order to contribute in our own unique ways to making a precious difference in this world.

To my indelible daughter, Britain: Thank you for the countless hours you spent smiling by my side down in my office all those years as this book was on my screen. And to my attuned and unconventional parents, Georges and Betty, who let me play as a child even for days on end—creatively, unencumbered, and uninterrupted. There aren't enough words to ever fully thank you for all you had gifted me as parents.

And to the extraordinary people in my life who have either shown up or stepped up with such immense love, talent, and support—editing, reading, commenting, caring, and postulating with me, I thank you. You've each played such a definitive part in this precious project and process, giving so much of yourselves—your time and your grace—to ensure we could see it through, as was David's passionate wish.

May this book live on as testimony to David's immense heart, vision, and countless contributions. On behalf of the people he loved, the personal development communities he touched, the Enneagram and its many applications to which he devoted his career, and to the world and its inhabitants, this book is written on behalf of his dream for us all.

May we come to see and be part of creating a more peaceful, loving humanity for which David had such hope and for which he worked tirelessly, passionately, and so lovingly.

FOREWORD BY DR. DANIEL J. SIEGEL

You have in your hands the wisdom of a renowned Enneagram teacher, the knowledge of over 40 years of therapy with individuals and couples, and the devotion of a man who dedicated his life to helping people improve their lives and relationships. David Daniels, MD, was an extraordinary individual with a deep interest and ability to be present, receptive, and embrace others for who they really are. Dr. Daniels' ability to connect with people, draw out of them what really mattered, and provide emotional integration and healing, were his tremendous gifts and what he practiced personally and professionally on a daily basis.

What made Dr. Daniels extraordinary is that he made relationships his number one priority in life. David believed that it is love, our relationships, and the love experienced in our relationships that feed our authentic inner self and provide the nourishment to lead fulfilling lives.

Dr. Daniels' ability to inspire receptivity (a kind of relational mindfulness in his view) through the lens of adult temperament opened a new level of my own understanding of the process of growing toward wholeness in life. I had known David for 15 years before he left us. We were two psychiatrists, each a bit off the mainstream path, and both steadfastly dedicated to the helping and healing profession and the integration of science and contemplative traditions.

We continued to meet, teach together, and learn from each other, being part of a working group we affectionately called the Brain Group (now referred to as the "Patterns of Developmental Processing" or PDP Group). Along with Laura Baker, PhD, Denise Daniels, PhD, and Jack Killen, MD, the Brain Group translates the language of an ancient emotional-motivational system called the Enneagram into modern scientific nomenclature and uses the lens of a field I work in, called interpersonal neurobiology, to look deeply at the interplay of inborn temperament and experiential neuroplasticity—how our brains are shaped by both genetic and interactive factors.

That work has influenced us both, and over those 15 years David and I supported each other as we integrated our knowledge of western psychiatry with the more contemplative practices of meditation and the experiences of mindfulness, open awareness, and the process of becoming whole.

In this book, The Enneagram, Relationships, and Intimacy: Understanding One Another Leads to Loving Better and Living More Fully, you are about to form a relationship with the words and advice of a dear scientist, practitioner, and relationship builder. David shares his wisdom of many years and wrote this book with Suzanne during the last seven years of his life, from ages 75 to 82.

I am also grateful to his co-author, Suzanne Dion, and his children Denise Daniels, PhD, and J. D. Daniels, PhD, that David's wish to bring this book to as many people as possible has all come to be. It is my wish as it was David's that this book and David and Suzanne's words bring you new insight, understanding, wholeness, and of course, more love in your life and in your relationships.

Take in these words from a modern sage and let David's light and love fill you with knowledge, skills, and inspiration to guide you on a journey to wholeness and well-being. Enjoy!

Daniel J. Siegel, MD
Mindsight Institute
Santa Monica California

PREFACE

We are living in a very interesting, very fascinating time. Gender is up for discussion, divorce is somewhat expected, nurture-dependent infants are left in daycare as early as six weeks old and with that, the potential for developmental neglect nearly normalized. Meanwhile, technology has far surpassed our wildest dreams, and individuals struggle to find a partner who can meet their needs, who can "make them happy." The level of disenchantment across our world is incredibly high as well as the level of progress, advancement, and fascination too.

I have spent six decades of my life caring deeply about the pain and disconnect as well as the growth, joy, and development of children, parents, families, and loved ones. My private practice was focused primarily on couples trying to get along, feel more loved and desired, and better understand each other.

Today, couples are struggling to make a living while keeping their families from dissolving. I also devoted much of my work to addressing issues of violence, including violence and defiance in teens. As a result, my work has directed me toward the development of non-violent communication and its impact on governance. So, for the last 35 years, I devoted my life to delivering one-on-one sessions, group workshops, intensives, and training programs grounded in the narrative and contemplative traditions that promote our living more fully in relation to one another.

How we get along seems to come up over and over again as we look for inner happiness. And relationships seem to be at the center of the joy we so often experience. Relationships affect how connected we feel to ourselves, to our purpose, and to finding meaning in life. And relationships seem to be the number one cause of the greatest suffering in our lives as well, over and over again.

At the center of much unhappiness, conflict, and despair even, I found our inability to relate to one another lovingly, or communicate honestly or effectively, or manage our emotional reactivity to be at the very heart of so many of our struggles.

I have often wondered if the strive-and-surpass, me-first, go-getter drive of American society might not be in line with our fundamental human nature and most basic of emotional needs. We need each other. We weren't designed to be isolated, swimming in riches.

It's that simple. We need each other and we need relationships—all kinds of relationships.

We do not fully develop, embody, or expand our sense of self without them. On our own, we equally lack the contact needed to gain an understanding of those outside of ourselves. When in isolation, starving for connection, we suffer. We may struggle socially, develop inadequately, and our ability to live with purpose and meaning may be hampered.

Research tells us that we are social creatures with a social brain. This means we are responsively co-regulating, completely interdependent, and we need to belong not only to thrive but also to experience ourselves wholly.

This book addresses the powerful need we have for one another, for love—physiologically, emotionally, and spiritually. Therefore, it's important to consider what keeps us from love, from experiencing it and cultivating it? And what is it that might keep us from loving one another? What might also keep us from what we call intimacy?

How we simultaneously ache for as well as diminish the love, intimacy, and connection possible in our lives is the goal of what we explore in these many pages. How we separate ourselves from love and how we resist it, even contract against it or sabotage it, these have been topics I've spent my life studying.

There are lots of books written about love and as many on relationships and how to make them better. Among those are some great books on the critical importance of something called secure attachment to relationships, and there's no doubt it plays an enormous part.

In these pages, we endeavored to add to these topics by drawing on my over 40 years of study as a private-practice psychiatrist (working primarily with couples), my 62 years of marriage, Suzanne's contrasting relational struggles and transformative learnings, and our deep and comprehensive understanding of human temperaments and personality proclivities, thanks to having studied something called the Enneagram.

Of all the treatment modalities I used and witnessed during my therapeutic career, nothing came close to helping couples heal their hearts and relax their defenses as much as learning the Enneagram.

Using a thoughtful and conscientious application of this system points us definitively and appreciatively at the internally organized differences found in human temperament that, as it happens, largely define each of the nine Enneagram types.

Why This Book?

While primarily exploring intimate relationships, this book is for all who want to "feel better within" and for those who want to feel more peace and acceptance when experiencing themselves when relating to others.

This is a book about love of self as well as love of others. It includes core practices for relationship development and offers hope for sustaining, flourishing intimacy.

This is a book that hopes to teach how to work with the key themes of our personality structure as well as with our own (and others') particular paths for growth.

Identifying and learning about our core personality structure (pattern, type, and propensities), we can more effectively free ourselves from the automatic and habitual cognitive-emotional perceptions and behaviors that create dissatisfaction in our lives and may not be serving us well as we relate to others.

Identifying our core Enneagram personality type can also free us from patterned reactions that bring either chaos or rigidity to our internal landscape and our experience of the world. Those are reactions and behaviors that may prevent us from sustaining relationships, from experiencing fulfilling intimacy, and, in general, from loving ourselves fully. This is what we hope to bring to light in these chapters.

I have wanted to write this book for a very long time, as my life's work focused on relationships, their importance, their quality, and the critical role they play in shaping our minds and hearts, as well as our lives.

While inclusive of in-use theories and some of the most relevant current research, this book is more of a guide, one to be used as a scientifically inspired provocation toward personal development. As such, it's a book we hope will motivate each of us to take seriously a practical application of reflective self-awareness training to cultivate self-observation, mindfulness, and the capacity for love and intimacy.

I have come to believe there is nothing more important to human life than two very simple things:

1. our relationship with ourselves, and
2. our relationships with others.

This seemingly simple discovery has shown up consistently across my years of study, experience, and research. From years of leading Enneagram narrative panels and many hours spent with hurting, struggling couples, I cannot emphasize enough the quality of our relational experiences.

Our relationship to ourselves is where we begin, as paradoxically, **it's our relationship to ourselves that determines the kind of relationships we will allow, engender, and cultivate with others**.

Understanding ourselves is what leads to understanding others. Intimacy with ourselves first, to a great degree, determines our capacity for true and lasting intimacy with another—psychologically, emotionally, physically, and spiritually.

The first question to consider is this: *How do we actually develop a relationship with ourselves?*

This might seem to some a very silly question. Isn't it already a given? "I talk to myself all the time," someone once said to me.

So, let me reword the question. *How do we develop a* quality *relationship with ourselves? The kind of relationship that yields an authentic felt experience of our cognitive-emotional inner world, of the truth of our innermost beingness, and our acceptance of it.*

And next: *How do we actually cultivate quality, loving, meaningful, expansive relationships with others? Relationships that are vulnerable and honest rather than defended and postured. Relationships that sustain us and nurture us rather than exhaust us and frustrate us.*

And the fundamental reason for writing this book at all is this: *How does this system called the Enneagram fit into the development of either of those kinds of relationships? Furthermore, can the Enneagram help us cultivate intimacy and more readily experience it?*

So, this is where we begin and where we hope to end up, too. This is what this book is about.

Over the years, I saw things that make a difference in relationships, and I saw what could bring about lasting change and far more fulfillment. This subject matter came to mean everything to me and to my work, and it is an honor to share what I've learned.

I hope to inspire in humanity our great need to care about this—to nurture, study, and commit to developing our capacity for quality relationships and deep intimacy. Quality relationships provide the most fundamental foundation for raising securely attached, beautifully adjusted children and for being a loving partner in pursuit of a love-driven life. Because this hope for fulfilling, meaningful, sustaining human relationships for us all is something I am deeply passionate about.

I've authored this book with the support and collaboration of my colleague, Enneagram teacher, coach, and writer Suzanne Dion. She has helped me to share my years of observations and the musings of our many conversations and work together over the years.

It is our earnest hope to have developed some useful and comprehensive insights as well as some working solutions and sustainable practices—ones that may enhance our *so* dear relationships, our lives, our communities, and our world.

"As we find ourselves, we find our way to others.

As we bond with ourselves, therein lies
the capacity to bond with others.

As we accept ourselves,
we can more readily accept others.

As we come to love ourselves, we come
to experience love and to truly love others. "

— *David Daniels, M.D. and Suzanne Dion*

INTRODUCTION

Love—the much-desired four-letter word. A matter of the heart that has toppled nations, driven individuals to commit murder, been the subject of art and song for centuries, and still takes top ranking in today's headlines. Part chemistry, part evolutionary instinct, part behavioral and part emotional—it's a non-negotiable on the way to spiritual fulfillment.

Our very survival-based need for love defines what it means to be human. With hundreds of years of fascination and analysis by some of the world's most celebrated thinkers and artists, why is love so treasured yet so seemingly difficult to find, understand, and sustain?

Many of us seek the silver bullet to a "happily ever after." Or perhaps there's an elixir that, given to Mr. or Ms. Right, will allow us to at last find the person of our dreams and ultimately beautify our lives. As we struggle to relate lovingly to important people in our lives, is it any wonder that the Internet is resplendent with articles and videos professing to help us interact more effectively with others, parent our children better, and yes, find true love for ourselves?

Despite all the how-to iterations, what we may have overlooked is that love is who we are and where we come from. Love is our essential nature. It's what we need most in order to develop and thrive and what we are capable of, intrinsically. It's already "there." Love comes from our being.

We can describe it emotionally and psychologically as well as scientifically or chemically. But what's most important and what I have come to realize is that we have to return to love, behave as if *love is what is*, stop diminishing and blocking it, and cease resisting it—cease resisting love.

So, what is love? We've read many a possible definition. Some are emotional. Some are biological. Some are experiential. Trying to define it in our own words for this book was quite the undertaking. And before you continue reading this paragraph, stop for a moment and see how you might *describe it in your own words*: What is love?

Defining Love

Love is a state of being and a way of relating. It is open and receptive; it is not judgmental and is not defended. It is unconditional, devotional, and reverent.

Love is at the very center of all of life itself and in its purest form, is imbued with free will. It's a force of some kind that carries in it a frequency so beautiful, so luminous, and so soothing.

Love is life-giving, caring, and sustaining. It's invaluable and immeasurable. Love is that unmistakable light that radiates in our eyes, and illuminates us with goodness, patience, and grace. It is love that expresses itself effortlessly as thoughtfulness, kindness, and gentleness. It is the driving force of our attunement and resonance, and to some incalculable degree, is brought further into being by our level of consciousness, awareness, and presence.

Love, after all, begins and ends as an inside job.

Love expresses the most fundamental of human needs and desires and is at the root of how we come to know ourselves, form bonds, and connect to each other. In fact, love is so vital to the survival and development of human beings that without it, we do not develop adequately, healthfully, coherently, or well, fully.

A lack of love in our lives can leave us impoverished cognitively, emotionally, physically, and even spiritually.

My Take on Love and Development

I do believe that all that we have of ultimate value is love. When one questions octogenarians, they don't usually say, "I wish I had *worked* more." Instead, you often hear, "I wish I had *loved* more." Or "I wish I would have taken more time to get to know others, be with my family, and appreciated more of the beauty and joy around me. I wish I had had more of a *heartfelt* purpose."

While this is so often shared, why didn't they do those things? What keeps us driven to make more money, garner more attention, or amass security beyond what's necessary, often bypassing our need for true love? I'd venture to say, could it be that love is the very thing most fundamental to our heart of hearts? Is it not what we're really seeking and trying to amass?

How do we know love, manifest love, and experience love? How do we know intimacy—true intimacy. And what is *intimacy*, anyway? Love and intimacy are very popular words, compelling concepts, but what exactly do they mean, and mean to our relationships? What does it mean to "be in relationship"? And who *am* I when I am in a relationship with another? And so importantly, what does it feel like, for me, to be in a relationship with myself?

These questions can be answered by taking a comprehensive look at both ourselves and our relationships. In both cases, we must address the whole individual and also each respective relational dynamic. I've thought a lot about how we actually create intimate, fulfilling relationships, ones that satisfy our mind, our heart, our body, and our spirit. Yet, in principle, **the material in these pages fundamentally applies to all meaningful, vital relationships, not just the romantic ones.**

This book hopes to help us understand how we came to be who we are and how it is that we show up in matters of love. And, importantly, what we can do about it.

While not a parenting book, what's shared herein will inadvertently impact your parenting. The development of self-understanding through mindfulness and mindful awareness practice, as discussed throughout this book, will impact the whole of your parent-child relationship(s) by influencing the quality of every emotional transaction you may have with your developing child(ren). God willing.

A large portion of this book speaks to the universal factors that govern all relationships, including those romantic in nature. Another section goes into depth about my favorite system for self-awareness development, the Enneagram, which I have come to believe is rooted in our evolution.

When studied comprehensively, the Enneagram will change the way you show up for and experience relationships by deepening your intimacy with yourself and with others forever—as it did for me, Suzanne, and countless others.

Attachment: Where Our Love Story Begins

So critical to our first few years of existence, love—expressed as a caring and attuned, safe and consistent bonding relationship between infant and parenting caregiver(s)—is where the foundation for our development begins. It not only creates the foundation; it potentiates our developmental growth.

Successful secure early attachment, as it's called, which refers to the quality of those first and primary caregiving relationships, is now understood to be necessary for our potentiated cognitive-emotional, psychological, and physical development.

How we experienced that early nurturance (attachment) influences how we come to express love—how we both give and receive love, and how capable we are of actually loving ourselves. Who we inevitably become as an adult in a romantic relationship is a direct expression of the quality of the attachment relationships we experienced early on. The basis for our "love potential," if you will, is put in place long before we had any conscious say in the matter.

How does this happen? While we enter the world "wired up for love"—ready to receive love and eventually to express love—the way our parenting caregivers interact with us as babies will determine our capacity for love later on. It will also, to a great degree, determine our foundational capacities for inner well-being as adults, including self-awareness and other-awareness too.

To quote Dr. Jaak Panksepp, the renowned affective neuroscientist as he speaks to what's triggered in both mother and infant when connected: **"Motherhood is the physiology of love."**

This means that the biochemistry of breastfeeding, attachment, bonding, touching, and nurturance that is generated in an infant in response to an attuned mother unleashes the same biochemical reactions as does the experience of love later in life.

While our capacity to love and to potentiate into knowing ourselves is inborn, it requires felt sense experience in order to develop. Loving transactions with the environment activate our innately wired capacity for love.

Implicit and Explicit Memory

Those first two to three years after birth—seemingly unremarkable in the grand scheme of things—happen to be among the most critical of developmental years, if not *the* most critical.

While *recalling* in the form of memory those earliest years is pretty much impossible (because our recall memory doesn't develop until a couple of years into our lives), something is, in fact, being remembered. Those very early, preverbal experiences are being recorded, but in a part of the brain called implicit memory. So, *what* is being recorded?

The emotional-somatic experiences are our limbic and central nervous system's responses to the environment of our early life. We don't *remember* those experiences later on, but one way or another, they are what we come to enduringly feel, act out, and express all across our lives. That is what's being laid down, and this is no small thing.

These early emotional-somatic experiences and responses are wired deeply into our very beings and lay the foundation for our developing and ongoing relationships to ourselves, to others, and to the world itself.

Implicit memory takes places approximately two years before our conscious memory, or explicit memory, comes online. Explicit recall memory is held in a different part of the brain, mainly in an area called the hippocampus.

Explicit memories are those we can call up at will. They are more like little movies or snapshots where we recall narratives and stories about the past as well as facts, data, events and other memorable details.

The impact of implicit memory has long been underestimated. Seemingly inconsequential, the early days of psychology tended to think what we can't explicitly remember can't hurt us, or those events must be rather meaningless. But we now know that's surely not the case.

For example, while we won't have an explicit memory of a terrifying experience of perceived abandonment that happened at 10 months old—one that left us screaming and painfully hungry in our crib for hours, alone and with no one responding—we *will* lay down an emotional memory of it.

The emotional experience of that terror will form a powerful emotional charge in the body's implicit memory system, especially if there was no relatively immediate nurturance to counteract it. Had that negative experience of terror been immediately met with nurturance once we were discovered in that state—one that would have soothed us back to emotional equilibrium—the intensity of the emotional charge, as registered in implicit memory, may have purportedly been lessened, even fully processed.

But without adequate recovery nurturance or the existence of many yet-to-be-understood factors, it's safe to say that our implicit memory most likely would have recorded that experience as non-ending terror, as hours of distress to an infant seem like an eternity.

As a result, I hypothesize that a resulting intrapersonal interpretation may herein begin to take form, as in, for example, a foundational sense that nobody cares. Or a deep despair that leads us to believe, *I am powerless.* Or believing, *the world does not respond to me, no matter what I do.* This detrimental interpretation can lead to what's called learned helplessness.

That type of early experience combined with how it is interpreted within us shapes our development and our sense of self in ways we are only now coming to more profoundly understand.

Likewise, implicit memory also records the emotional experiences of lying safely and cared for on our mother's chest at six months old. Feeling her breath on our cheek, hearing her heartbeat pulse in our ear for hours, and feeling her warmth all over our bodies are emotional experiences associated with what develops secure attachment and overall emotional well-being. Recordings of how we are loved and seen and held are just as impactful and long-lasting as those experiences that get recorded as more painful or traumatizing.

Getting Started: How We Came to Be Who We Are

Whether or not we remember is not what determines something's impact on us. **Our "behavior is the witness,"** Suzanne often shares. **Our internalized experience of ourselves also is a witness.**

Our outward behavior, particularly our reactivity and how readily it gets triggered, is the visible result of what might have happened to us early on. It is the evidence of what is driving us subconsciously—either holding us hostage or potentiating us beautifully.

What happened to us way back when is held deeply within our once infantile systems and is associated with the unwitting source of inordinate cognitive-emotional pain or the abundant, intrinsic love we feel within.

Emotional states of our early years become the states within us that come to be our internal experience of ourselves later on. Furthermore, while these are often states we can't exactly trace back with clarity nor locate specifically, they are foundational.

All this discussion points us back to our *developmental experience* of love itself. How we as individual beings experienced love early on is known to directly correlate with how we experience and express love in adulthood.

Looking at this fundamental premise through the lens of the nine personality structures of the Enneagram, we pose these questions:

Does the environment—our parenting caregivers, their way of handling us, their way of speaking to us, their way of correcting us or guiding us—impact each of us and our "love potential" in *the same way*? Or does the developmental environment impact different little ones—different dispositions—*differently*?

Early emotional experiences—and their consequential imprints—is *the place to start* and is what's required when understanding the complexity of who we are. Equal to that, then: What is it within us that *interacts with our early experiences*, particularly the experiences that affect our attachment security and relational transactions with others?

Is it just how we were cared for that made each of us who we are today? Or is there something else to consider? How do we account for the many differences found in siblings who shared the same household and same caregivers? Yes, there's the birth order consideration, and there's the state of being of the caregivers as each sibling was born. But it's hard to deny *there's still more* to it.

This is an important piece of the self-discovery puzzle and it's a part of the familiar and ongoing discussion of nature versus nurture. I'd like to approach the subject from a nature *with* nurture perspective, because I feel it's very important to marry the two.

The answer to our postulations is that it's our own innate biological disposition—or what Dr. Dan Siegel calls the neural propensities of our newly formed being—that is interacting with the environment to form the complex creatures that we are and that each of us becomes.

Our inherent nature is, in fact, what interacts with each emotional transaction and experience. It is, in turn, what reacts to the life and the people into which we are born. And that includes, critically, the so valuable experiences we have early on with our parenting caregivers. They are the most important aspect, bar none, of what we are calling "the environment."

What all this means is that the feelings, behaviors, and the cognitive-emotional level of developmental well-being each person expresses during their lifetime begin with some sort of initial and intrinsic organizing architecture.

With this intrinsic template in place, we respond to those interacting with us across developmental stages. Our unique experiences and reactions govern the flow of energy and information across our various psychodynamic systems. This template—our differentiating nature also referred to as *temperament*—is inherent and is the originating structure that deals with and is impacted by the environment from day one.

This book allows us to share with you why I have come to study, teach, and endorse the Enneagram with the fervor and passion that I have.

> "
>
> People do have neural propensities—called temperament—that may be somewhat but not fully changeable. No system of adult personality description that exists (except the Enneagram's contemporary version) identified an internally focused organization. That is, a view of how the internal architecture of mental functioning, not just behavior, is organized across developmental periods.
>
> ~ Daniel J. Siegel, MD
>
> "

Imagine now how useful it would have been to have learned our Enneagram type's propensity in order to recognize temperament when trying to figure ourselves out in high school. How about when it comes to raising children? Imagine how this understanding might assist us in better understanding and managing a subordinate in the workplace or a colleague we're collaborating with. And what about having this understanding in order to get along better with our beloved or when seeking a loving partner? Or when seeking someone with whom to have children?

The Enneagram—what a gem!

The Journey toward Self-Realization

This work—the work of personal development and self-realization—is not about self-disorientation, about rejecting parts of ourselves, or forcing ourselves into another temperament pattern, one we think we like better. It's not about becoming another Enneagram type, which is most likely biologically impossible anyway.

Our innate propensities and structural proclivities are themselves unlikely *to change*, not to mention that they are imbued with some of our greatest natural aptitudes. We don't want to negate those!

Likewise, when it comes to our relationships—including the relationship we have with each of our children—we are much better off working toward the growth of our beloved's or child's level of development and its potentiation than hoping to change aspects of their fundamental temperament, that is, their fundamental Enneagram type structure.

Personal development is nothing less than the desire to grow into the entire person we were potentiated to be from a developmental standpoint, as that's our divine birthright. It's to potentiate our neural propensities and to heal all that has infringed on our ideal development.

This includes coming in contact with our essential nature and our higher qualities of being. It also includes owning them unapologetically and honorably. It's about deconstructing and then easing the defenses, adaptive limitations, and negative conditioning imparted on us while growing up that may have impaired our intrapersonal development.

It's about getting present and taking on with great compassion and understanding the learned, in-response behaviors—the ones our particular neural propensities came up with as adaptive solutions—that may not be serving us that well. Those that have become maladaptive, emotionally limiting, self-distorting and destructive.

I am talking about deconstructing the conditioning that keeps us *feeling stuck*, makes us rigid in our ways or has us erupting out of control, or that which renders us unreceptive, distrustful, or unable to receive. Personal development is about "this" pursuit, where what needs to be excavated, dealt with, and finally, properly nurtured, gets its much-deserved day in the light of our conscious, compassionate awareness.

As we grow, mature, and find our way into adulthood, we begin our quest for a satisfying life, using the aptitudes, talents, and emotional well-being we have to work with to make this happen. In doing so, we pay attention to *who we really are and what we were designed to bring forth.*

There's no doubt that intimate adult relationships can be a great source of love and nurturance and can meet many of our needs for care and bonding. But there's a caveat here that begs for understanding. For those of us who may not have experienced good attachment relationships when young—ones with bonding, nurturance, and validation—the adult relationships we may seek can only do their best *to try* and meet our emotional and psychological, love, and nurturance needs.

Unfortunately, relationships often fall short. Why? Because as our internal make-up—based on our innate temperament, our neural propensities—meets with infancy and childhood experiences, our experience of love and relating, bonding and trusting, coping and caring is structured.

Enduring patterns have been formed, and our way of loving others and ourselves—and feeling loved by others as well as by ourselves—have been metaphorically turned on or off to varying degrees from infancy on up, depending on what's been processed (or not).

Our developmental processes are highly complex. Developmentally, we are as incredibly fragile as we are adaptively resilient. But it's the success of our developmental years that sets the foundation for relational stability, including the quality of the relationship we form with ourselves as well as the quality of relationships we'll be able to foster with others later on.

Depending on our early love and bonding experiences—ones that form our attachment style and capacities—we may or may not yet be able to adapt or receive, give or trust, love and accept adequately and flexibly, let alone fully.

When attachment systems fail us for reasons small and large, sensitivities to various attachment disturbances—and our adaptive responses to those disturbances—may be found to directly correlate with the neural proclivities and propensities we've come in with at birth. And those are fundamental to the organizing structure of each of the nine Enneagram types, something that is worth exploring further.

Sexual intimacy—or let's call it "interacting with a partner"—is in the end a palpable way to begin to experience connection and bonding. It can contribute to alleviating the discomfort of some of what may have been missing, damaged, or longed for in childhood.

Additionally, sexual experiences can foster physical gratification and a sense of affection or closeness, of course. But again, sexuality too can fall short if our receptors for affection, touch, and intimate, bonding experiences have not been sufficiently turned on, developed, or nurtured adequately when formatively young.

Self-realization is possible. We have a way to come to know ourselves intimately and to develop. And we can do so in adulthood.

We can study the Enneagram. We can study our childhood—attachment relationships and relational interactions. We can look at the emotional transactions in particular, studying them as we remember they happened or can be recalled as honestly and as compassionately as possible. We can unpack how we feel we were impacted, how we adapted to stay connected to those who mattered, and how those adaptations may have been internalized.

And as we do this, we start a presence process, a self-awareness mindfulness practice to lovingly guide ourselves into the self-accepting wholeness we deserve.

The Enneagram and Its Place in Personal Development

The Enneagram is a system that describes the human condition as it's organized, from the inside out. It's far more than a simple behavioral typology. It's a body of wisdom I stumbled on years ago of which I had no prior knowledge and one that profoundly changed my life once I understood it.

At first it was difficult for me to publicly own this remarkable knowledge for understanding myself and others because of its connections to spiritual life and the paucity of recognized research backing. Since I had come from a structured academic and medical background steeped in empirical science and its methodologies, I remained a closeted follower for a good 18 months before "coming out."

Besides this, I have found that the worlds of modern psychiatry and psychology tend to put people into rather negative-sounding, stereotypical personality groupings like paranoid, sociopathic, and narcissistic. I so disliked this way of categorizing people that I just refused to do it. Yet, because I found the Enneagram system to be so veracious, so deeply insightful, so life-enhancing and so *liberating*, I finally could not do anything else but own it publicly.

The Enneagram is the most profound self-knowing tool I've come across in my 50+ years as a doctor, therapist, professor, lecturer, teacher, and author. It so wisely teaches us about our collaborative commonalities as well as our valuable, contributory differences.

Studying the Enneagram helps us to build, enhance, and sustain amazing and loving, intimate and fulfilling relationships. It does this by spelling out to us in surprising detail, *why we are the way we are*, and *why we do what we do*, leaving us with a compassionate and profound understanding of ourselves and others.

It provides us with a coherent map that helps us deconstruct our defense mechanisms—how our type specifically behaves when reactive and threatened—and how to recognize our essential qualities of being, our gifts and aptitudes, and our talents and contributory proclivities.

Without this understanding, our relationships can sometimes be nothing short of a challenge.

> Partnership demonstrates the differences between us. Each can be telling the truth, yet each can have a different story to tell.
>
> ~ Helen Palmer

Those differences between us, when not understood, and those stories of individual truth, when not validated, can tear us apart. "What is wrong with you?" we may often say to a partner who has a different point of view and is insisting on it. But when acknowledged, shared, and held reverently, when understood and not feared, those differences instead can be recognized as an asset, not a detriment.

Our differences are designed to support our mutual survival and add to one another's lives; they are contributory all the way to just darn stimulating. Our differences are what allow us to live together far more effectively, productively, as well as supportively, interestingly, and to a great extent, more joyfully.

Loving Better and Living More Fully

As we embark on the pursuit of living a fuller and more loving life, an endeavor this book hopes to support, let's summarize by saying this concerning how we go about it. It's much more promising and effective to work to increase our own level of personal development—to increase our cognitive-emotional response flexibility and presence—than it is to attempt to change our foundational temperament (our personality's organizational propensities).

Within each of us is an individualized capacity to grow and expand, and with that comes the self-honoring development and self-generated healing we need and deserve for potentiation and fulfillment.

As we find ourselves, we find our way to others. As we bond with ourselves, therein lies the capacity to bond with others. As we accept ourselves, we can more readily accept others. As we come to love ourselves, we come to experience love and to truly love others.

Successful integration of the concepts and practices in this book offers the ability to more fully give and more openly receive love, in every aspect of our lives.

Perhaps, and as we reflect, *there is nothing more important in our lives than to take this developmental journey.* There is nothing more precious than to have developed our capacity to understand ourselves, to develop and sustain relationships, to love, and to have done so with willingness, hope, compassion, and tenacity.

May we all do this. Let's bring our love to ourselves and to one another—consciously, compassionately, and reverently. Let's bring our willingness to develop to our fullest, most-loving potential to our families, to our communities, to the world, and inevitably, to our planet.

PART 1

The Basics of Healthy Relationships and the Enneagram

" By learning
about ourselves
more deeply,
we can give others
the gift of our presence
and our full attention. "

—David Daniels, M.D.

CHAPTER 1

Content and Process:
The Basis of Sustainable Understanding,
Embodied Learning, and Change

I am big on content. I've been writing and creating it for the whole of my career. I enjoy working toward conclusions and coming up with solutions, especially those that can make a difference. With that said, as much as I do appreciate content, reading and learning theories alone do not cut it. There's something else we need to do as we take on this work of personal development—and that's process and practice.

If all we required was content, we could simply read one of the more prolific books on the Enneagram, relationships, love or intimacy development and we'd have it. But alas, time and again, we find that's not adequate to bring about actual growth and change.

Hameed Ali (going by the pen name A. H. Almaas) once shared in a 2014 episode of the *Sounds True* podcast that his observation was that as few as one person in 10,000 ". . . can find their way to personal development without a teacher."

Of course, what does a good teacher do for us? They make us practice.

It is challenging to bring about constructive expansion and change on our own without guidance or by simply reading, without the benefit of simulation or interaction. To be honest, doing this work alone or just reading about it never worked for me. What I know to be true is this: *What's needed in addition to mentally learning the content is a definitive process that embodies it.*

The implementation of an applied practice means the repeated installation of what we had learned in such a way that an impactful emotional experience is evoked. Over time, this implementation of mental, emotional, and somatic experience and practice will bring forth what we hope to change, grow into, and conquer.

3

Practice that involves our senses anchors and builds the neural pathways we need for new learning, deeper knowing, and desired adaptation. Practice allows content to be embodied, owned, and then lived.

Content and Process:
The Key to Growth and Development

Over the years, my approach has focused much on how to integrate what we can learn cognitively with what we can practice physically and emotionally. Designing practices and exercises is a near hobby of mine, and I can honestly say I don't see enough process being processed! We lack good methods for developing ourselves beyond our habitual patterns and stubborn defenses.

Process lets us take ourselves on, to struggle with the material. Process lets us try it out and feel its initial discomfort—even awkwardness—and to recognize that.

What we practice starts to become familiar, less uncomfortable, and more feasible with every try. I find good process missing in a lot of the self-help approaches of today. The emphasis is placed heavily on the cognitive study of theory. Don't get me wrong, we do have to start with the cognitive, with the educative piece. But despite so many great concepts, there is often too little opportunity structured to put the new cognition into embodied reality.

Actual change requires the implementation of repeated, practiced, worn-in experiences to impact our brains. Exercises. Daily implementations. This is what allows our central nervous system—or what I call our electrical railway—to experience ourselves in groundbreaking ways that can change us.

As Dr. Dan Siegel says, **"The way we use our minds can change our brains."**

With *intention* we can affect our *focus of attention* and bring about radical personal expansion. Even better, we can use our intention to consciously focus our attention in such a way that we begin to proactively sculpt new neural pathways in our own brains!

What we experience as we practice provides a myriad of benefits, anchoring us in the commitment to improve our own capacities. Practice also brings us face-to-face with our resistances—including any discomfort that arises in response to what's unfamiliar.

Practice with intention supports us to cultivate a more expansive, less narrowed view of our own and others' habitual patterns. Ultimately, a more expansive view will feel differently to us, and we'll want to register that difference. Our practice will bring forth experiential perspectives that we then need to acknowledge, accept, appreciate, support, and then commit to as we strive to further develop.

Change and development depend upon an interweaving of both *what we learn intellectually* with a practice that puts it in motion. The integration of both *content and process* is the unsung hero of sustainable development and expansion. Therefore, some years ago I developed a model with my colleague Terry Saracino, teacher and president of The Narrative Enneagram training school. (Throughout this book, we'll refer to this training school either by its full name or by the acronym, TNE.)

We named the model the Universal Growth Process for Self-Mastery, or UGP in short. This model consists of five fundamental steps to do in order:

A1: awareness,
A2: acceptance,
A3: appreciation,
A4: action, and
A5: adherence.

The 5As, when deployed rigorously, can impact our daily experiences and interactions for the better. Here's an incisive description of the 5As, the content you need first in order to practice them consciously.

Figure 1: The 5As of the Universal Growth Process for Self-mastery

This methodical five-step self-mastery model is referred to as the 5As (A1, A2, A3, A4, and A5). These 5As are fundamental for moment-by-moment transformation. They are the fundamental practice companion to learned content. It's the answer to "What to do with what I've read?"

A1 | Awareness

Awareness is a form of recognition; it's the state of becoming present. It's a state of becoming cognizant. Awareness is conscious and it is deliberate. It is the watching of information and energy within us, and of what is being stirred up within in response. Awareness is neutral. It has no opinion and has no preference; it just observes what is.

Awareness is an intentional kind of witnessing and noticing, and it censors nothing. It allows us to be with something extraordinary. It gives us access to reality as it actually is. Awareness is a capacity that allows us to separate our internal experience of ourselves into one that is watching and one that is being watched.

Awareness is cultivated through practice. A part of that practice connects us to the present-moment sensations of our body and our neutral observations of those sensations. Awareness helps us develop our level of receptivity (the allowance of various energies and information to come in and be received by us).

Awareness is a neutral witnessing of self and others, a capacity we need to cultivate in order *to observe* ourselves, and others, *reacting* or *responding*. Fundamental to cultivating awareness is the ability to acknowledge without being judgmental or negating what we find is real for us or others inside. (As an aside, we'll refer to being judgmental as *judgmentalness* from here on out.)

For example, during a breath practice we are training our awareness into being. To do so, we begin by focusing our attention on our breath. Let's say we're also aware that as we breathe, we feel physically relaxed and pleasant. In this case, we are *with the breath and aware of it*, and we are also aware of *how we feel as we breathe*.

We are with the breath and our relaxed state, in the present moment—and we are aware of both concurrently. There are no thoughts of yesterday, tomorrow, or anything else. We are just with what's happening right here and right now, conscious of the present moment and aware of ourselves. We are fully present.

Just as quickly, we can become aware that we are no longer focused on our breath. In fact, thanks to awareness, we can become aware that our thoughts have taken over and we've gotten distracted. We suddenly realize that we've somehow jumped ship and have been thinking about a problem at work and its possible impact on our bonus.

Our awareness might also become present to the fact that we *don't exactly know how long* we've been preoccupied with these other thoughts, and we're no longer present to ourselves in the present.

It's our awareness, though, that notices we have shifted. It's our awareness that observes we went from being aware and present to ourselves in the present moment, to thinking about something else that is not in the present moment.

The moment we notice that our attention ran away with us—that we were thinking about other things—we will also notice that our present-to-self breathing process is no longer on our radar. We left it behind and were no longer aware of it at all. We might now also become aware of how those thoughts about a problem at work changed our physical state from relaxed to tense and that our feeling state went from pleasantness to angst.

The four main categories of thought that occupy our minds are thinking, planning, remembering, and imagining. Enneagram expert Helen Palmer refers to these four categories as the "automatic tendencies of thought." As we become aware that we went on automatic into one of the categories of thought, we can *consciously* and *proactively* return to the present moment and place our attention again on our breathing and our bodily (somatic) sensations.

Self-awareness is our baseline and ideally it remains a constant. While remaining present to self, can we consciously place our attention on whatever else we may need to be aware of, whether inside of ourselves or in our immediate surroundings? This is the objective, but boy does it take practice!

Developing awareness includes becoming aware of our awareness. This would be referred to as meta-awareness. This means we are aware *that we are aware.* We are watching ourselves watching our internal self, and we know it. We know we've tuned in to observe while at the same time, we are watching neutrally that we're observing something.

Something is observing the observer observing. Who or what is it that observes that we are observing? Who or what is the observing self behind the habituated self? Who is this witness within us?

These are powerful questions to ponder and ones that can leave us excitably curious all the way to mystified. Shall we hypothesize it's our inner light, our spirit, our higher self, the godliness within us?

The answers to "Who is it?" are exploratory and perhaps divine in nature as we try to understand what constitutes and drives this powerful observing capability. Nevertheless, *it's ours* to access, be with, rein in, work with, practice, and come to rely on trustingly.

Developing self-witnessing capacities promotes our coming to know ourselves and developing both emotionally and spiritually. As my son, psychotherapist J. D. Daniels, says, **"We cannot possibly change or grow what we cannot see."** Such seeing begins with awareness.

Our entire personal development journey really does begin here, with a practice that develops this single yet immensely profound capacity.

Accurate Emotional Tracking: Sensate Awareness

For example, consider moments when we've felt—*truly felt*—angry, anxious, or sad. *How* did we feel it? Did we sense it in our bodies? And how did we recognize it for what it truly was? By noticing the sensate feeling of a primary emotion as it rises and takes hold in our physicality, after having successfully engaged our inner witness, we can next inquire with genuine curiosity about the internal process that triggered that authentic emotion to kick-off.

This is the activation of our *sensate* awareness.

Sensate awareness gives the self-aware observer, our bystanding witness, the opportunity to tune in to the primary (authentic) emotion being felt—sensed with neutrality and self-intimacy (truthful caring and understanding).

This allows the vulnerability within us to emerge and be recognized—which is *so* important—rather than the primary emotion running us over—and running away with us before we even know what has happened to us. Or before that emotion has us launching our defense system with a self-esteem cover-up that's mechanistic and a long way from being vulnerable or receptive.

Our primary emotional upheaval requires self-intimacy and vulnerability to access. Without access to it, sadness and hurt might be covered with sarcasm and rage, anxiety might get covered with irritation and impatience, and anger may get thwarted as avoidance or apathy.

Covered up emotional upheaval (though most often done unconsciously) takes us a long way from personal intimacy and takes us even farther from healthy and effective, vulnerably authentic communication and connection with any other.

If we come to activate and master nothing but a capacity for self-awareness, we've accomplished a lot. Witnessing ourselves and gaining awareness is the Holy Grail of any of the personal development steps we may ever engage with and hope to conquer.

A2 | Acceptance

Acceptance is allowing. It's allowing without being judgmental, without censoring, without sedating.

Acceptance makes room for whatever arises in the moment within us and what we subjectively perceive is arising in others. Acceptance is also validation, the neutral validation of what is. It's the skillful art of being with something *as it is,* without judging it.

Acceptance does not mean we like something, agree, or necessarily condone it. What we want and need to accept includes the truth of our sensate awareness, our feelings, and what's under our awareness of our reactivity—if that's what's showing up. Acceptance also allows our more positive expressions of self to be allowed, as in our excitement, animation, and our joy.

Acceptance is non-resistance. It's a neutral sobriety that allows the subjective material inside of us to be seen for what it is. It allows us to acceptingly receive the subjective experience, as we perceive it, of another.

Then, as we simply accept without resistance what *is,* we stand alongside it. We *are with,* and *we are OK.* Acceptance has no conditions and no interpretations. Acceptance, simple validation, is a critical component of our development. Without acceptance, a painful intolerance of what we become aware of may dissuade us from further development work.

I've seen this happen time and time again. When what we become aware of is not met with acceptance, it's just too hard to deal with. As important as acceptance fundamentally is to our development process, it's also something many believe they've readily cultivated but, in truth, they haven't.

I have to share the story of a certain Type 1 (Perfectionist) *whom we may all know too well . . .* When attending one of our conferences a good five years into her study, she finally understood the meaning of self-acceptance.

At that conference, Terry Saracino—my colleague, TNE founder, and Enneagram master facilitator—gave one of the opening presentations. During her program, Terry—an Enneagram Type 6 (also referred to as the Loyal Skeptic)—told a story of an incident that led her to greater self-acceptance. As her story increased in complexity, Terry described finding herself on the floor, rocking and crying in an utter fear-ignited, dysregulated state.

Terry recounted for the audience how upset she was with herself. "After all these years as an Enneagram teacher and all this work I've done on myself . . ." she said, "and I was on the floor, falling apart *again?*"

Berating herself for a good while, she finally stopped, relating to the audience. "And then I said, 'Yup Terry, that's really where you are,' and I accepted it, as well, true, and real. In that moment, the berating stopped and the compassion began."

"That's self-acceptance?" the Type 1 asked. "I've never, ever done that!" She went on to say, "To me, accepting myself has always meant *preventing myself from ever improving* and, well, that was out of the question!"

Until Terry's presentation, this Type 1 had assumed she was a highly self-accepting person. But, in fact, she discovered that up to that point she had only allowed acceptance for what she judgingly *permitted* for herself. *What she did not agree with or allow for herself was not accepted.* In her world, acceptance meant getting stuck as is. In truth, that's not self-acceptance at all.

Acceptance is not agreeing or disagreeing; it's not capitulating or condoning. And it's not anything that would ever prevent us from developing.

Acceptance is the art of first getting real, getting honest, and then getting down with what truly is. It's only from the honesty of the here and now that we can make this kind of progress. From here, we can consciously decide to either grow and change, if we so desire (or not).

A3 | Appreciation

Appreciation is a feel-good sensation that comes from recognizing what is good and positive in ourselves, in others, and in the world. Appreciation lets us take in the gifts presenting in all things (*there's always something),* even in what may feel challenging, disconnecting, or daunting.

Appreciation is the energetic ally of gratitude. Having appreciation is to give thanks for something, honoring the presence of it, even if it's something we'd rather resist. Appreciation requires that we seek out what's positive and worthwhile in whatever is showing up; it's the value-add that follows acceptance.

Referring back to Terry Saracino, once she accepted that she really was down on that floor in a messy, anxious heap, her self-attack stopped and her self-love kicked in. Declaring and then appreciating that she had, in truth, *noticed* her level of dysregulation, Terry's self-intimacy and self-vulnerability increased.

These sequential steps are what allowed her to tackle more deeply her own development work, that which she much enjoyed and from which she benefited greatly.

A4 | Action

You may have heard me say before, **"Awareness without action is not awareness at all."** By this I mean to say: what's the point of recognizing something—becoming aware of a pattern that's gripped us, perhaps one that's inhibiting our self-expression, damaging our connection to others, or hurting us—and doing nothing about it? Or just reacting habitually to it, once again?

Awareness is great. Cognition is great. And acceptance of and appreciation for what we find inside of ourselves or imagine in others is also great. But is that the end of it? I think not.

Action is what we *do* once we have the awareness, once we've collected and contained—but not suppressed—what has come up. Action is the step we take next, when we're ready to express what our awareness has cultivated and what we've consciously decided to do about it.

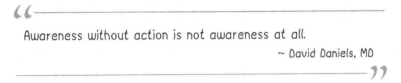

Awareness without action is not awareness at all.

~ David Daniels, MD

Conscientious action takes place when we are standing in self-efficacy, ready and able to *respond* rather than *react*. This is our chance *to choose how we show up* instead of defaulting to personality-automatic. For good discernment to occur, the action step requires a bit of on-the-spot self-inquiry—a skill we are developing with this work.

At this point, we are called upon to make sense of whatever content we're faced with as well as all the impulses, feelings, and reactions that may have arisen in the moment.

As we formulate the action called for, our type structure's key identifications, core beliefs, and associated deepest concerns and feelings will most surely show up for us. Here's where all our practice either goes out the window or gives us the grounding we need to sift through all of the information and energy flooding through us, including the emotional charge, if any, firing up within.

Can our practiced grounding in presence hold us long enough to respond lucidly and proactively so we can take action *consciously* rather than *reactively*? This takes training, concerted practice, and effort to master.

Surely, as we begin to take this on, holding and pausing may feel disorienting, even uncomfortable. We may even feel like a deer in the headlights as we thoughtfully and methodically take ourselves through the first three of the 5As.

"Hold on! I am running through the 5As!" I hear you, but it's not that easy, especially at first. The goal is to get us to the other side with an appropriate, conscious action at our disposal. But it's not always a clean, straight shot.

Patience, Obi-Wan Kenobi! We cannot reiterate enough how practice and more practice is the only way to attain any level of competency when interrupting our habitual patterns, especially those that fire off our defendedness and reactivity.

With time and diligence though, this process in its entirety can unpack in a matter of seconds and with less and less discomfort and struggle as well. Just wait—over time you'll find your way through the five steps in nanoseconds as they'll have become so experientially embodied, they're now second nature.

For instance, let's say we witness that we're feeling sorry for ourselves, perhaps we're even sulking that we're not getting something we want from another, for example attention, affection, time together, or space apart. We interpret this as the other not caring about us—and boy, that hurts.

I know, only a few of us do this, right? Through our awareness practice, let's say we recognize that we tend to blame the other whenever we hear in our head, *They don't care about us.* Blaming them happens spontaneously. But by slowing down and following the steps of the 5As, we come to terms with never having actually communicated to the other what we wanted. And though we may expect them to be, they're not mind readers. They may have no idea they didn't take care of a need of ours.

As we continue to self-observe, accept, and appreciate our internal exploration, we start to see that our hurt and anger, now directed at the other, was in truth self-generated. At this junction, we are primed to choose to express something different, to opt for a different outward behavior altogether. This is a conscious step.

As we free up the energy gripped by "others-blaming" interpretations that readily trigger our reactivity, that same life-force energy once used to contract against and sulk is now available to us—flowing freely—to show up for ourselves and respond to the other, but differently. Consciously. Communicatively. Even more playfully. Surely with far less sulking.

Responding more constructively, taking action rather than reacting habitually, becomes possible after the first three steps of the process of the 5As go into effect. It takes some "ego strength" as I like to call it. It takes courage to open ourselves up to realizing how our interpretations are, in fact, what often pull the trigger of our own reactivity.

This level of insight then opens the door for a deepening excavation of our own interiority, that which is ideally met with self-compassion. And self-compassion becomes the foundation, allowing access to how the hurt of various unmet needs originally came to be and how we may be acting out that hurt.

Self-intimacy and self-vulnerability are both products of the 5As process. And these traits consciously, thoughtfully, and effectively set us up for the action step. We'll go from sulking to perhaps asking the other for what we want in a sovereign, mature, and affirmative way (that is, using effective communication).

Self-compassion and self-intimacy also set us up for allowing compromise, being able to also accept another's needs responsibly. We may have more bandwidth and are more ready and able to do without, genuinely letting go of receiving a particular want or need from another at that time—even opting to meet their need instead. Having either of these capacities at our disposal leads to far more intrapersonal as well as relational success.

The action step also includes acting on what we've become aware of having an impact on our partner. How is feeling sorry for myself impacting them? How are they reacting to my reaction? There is a good chance sulking didn't make them feel good. And when we attack another, for example, for not meeting our needs, how do they respond? What action do they take? Do they distance themselves and withdraw? Do they get defensive? Do they counter-attack? Do they give us what we want, but begrudgingly?

As a part of our awareness-to-action process, notice how our habituated, automatic, reactive responses, those that get directed at our partner, rarely get us what we actually want (paradoxically). Perhaps now we've even made matters worse.

Let's take this scenario through the 5As. Centering ourselves into awareness, we become aware of what's happening. What is our sensate awareness telling us? Notice neutrally, receptively.

Then, compassionately accept what's coming forth, admitting, *Oh, this hurts.* We are aware that we are very uncomfortable in our own skin. The familiar thought kicks in: *My needs aren't being met.* And next comes the habitual interpretation: *They don't even care about me.*

Next, let's appreciate the fact that we've gotten this far by getting non-judgmentally real in our awareness process! *Great. Just great.* Some of these acknowledgments are hard to get honest about, so let's appreciate that.

Now it's time for action. What are we going to do about all this upheaval? Conscious action chosen: Let's set up a vulnerability share, which becomes an intimacy process for us both.

First, we ask our partner to sit down with us so we can share our sensitivity to whatever need we have that we perceive is not getting met. We tell them it brings up discomfort, and we describe the discomfort we've located. We then share what the need actually is, as in, "I've noticed that I could use some tender loving care, and I'm wondering when there's a good time for us to connect?"

By owning our feelings and sensitivities without the added interpretation of *They don't even care about me,* we save ourselves a lot of suffering. And by not blaming them, we don't put them on the defensive either.

A vulnerable share, our new action step, allows them to be open to our endearing and vulnerable ask. Our chances of getting our wants met go up significantly when we approach another with a more consciously chosen action. We win. They also win. We both win.

From following the steps of the 5As of the UGP, we become empowered to choose a new response to an old narrative and a familiar—and hurt-generating—dilemma. This, in turn, gives us the chance to navigate better in the future, which begins to change the dynamic of our lives.

The next time we find ourselves feeling a need or want that's not being met, let's take ourselves through the 5As. When we hit that pain of, *I'm feeling _____ again,* we see it, we accept it, and we appreciate it.

The goal is to learn to be aware right off the bat that there's pain here, and that pain wants something, it needs something. What it needs first and foremost is our own self-acknowledgment and care. It may be a long-held sensitivity. It may even be tender and shame ridden. Whatever it may be, put it through the 5As for a more loving, transformative experience.

The 5As keeps us from spiraling into a reactivity abyss. Instead, we can turn on the self-compassion as well as cultivate compassion for another—our partner—who also has needs and wants that may or may not coincide with ours at the exact same time.

Through repeated practice, the 5As bring us to a consciously actionable place, helping us over time to build the capacities needed for more thoughtful, intimate, conscious conduct that is self-loving, self-respecting, and others-respecting.

The action step is where the activation of our authentic power really lies. It's where the fueling of self-agency and our potentiation for greater response flexibility and greater fulfillment inevitably reside. This is a critical step and one not to be taken lightly.

This is the step where we consciously make a choice and act on it. Action is where we do something in conscious response to what's been insighted along the 5As path. This is self-mentorship in action, where we become our own most awesome inner coach—a coach that guides us into desired conscious conduct.

Actionable Conscious Conduct

Our internal mentoring coach is a resource we can cultivate to provide us with the support we need to attain integral self-agency and more rewarding conscious conduct. Conscious conduct includes two interrelated steps:

1.   the embodiment of acceptance, that which is fueled by receptive energy, and
2.   the deployment of a determined action that is respectful and honoring of ourselves, others, and the situation.

Acceptance is what clears the way for conscious conduct—conscious action—to occur. When acceptance wanes, check in. Most likely we'll find that we're resisting some unwanted aspect of reality as it actually is, sending us back on behavior-automatic.

With resistance, we may struggle to act on what's truly needed as we may be metaphorically tone deaf to what's best for all involved. A lack of acceptance almost always points at some form of resistance, which readily ignites reactivity and defendedness. And this, as we know, interferes with good choices and conscious conduct.

A5 | Adherence

Adherence is commitment. It's the agreement with ourselves to practice this process every day. This is a commitment to self-discipline. As J. D. Daniels shares with his clients in therapy, **"We're all in this together. We all have these patterns and a lot of them get in our way; it takes an over-time, active process to change them."**

That's what the adherence step is all about. Action taken only once won't cut it. I dare say this is where a lot of us drop off. We're all excited the first time we show up differently with the 5As in place and working! But then the novelty wears off and an old pattern works its way back in like old, comfy slippers. Soon we're sulking or brooding or frustrated again, over whatever. The old pattern is familiar and serves its legacy purpose.

Adopting and practicing the 5As are essential; it's akin to the tools in the toolkit of mindful awareness practices, also known as presence practices. The 5As are an easy-to-remember, methodical guide on how to implement the qualities of mindfulness that take on these concepts and result in rehearsing for change.

Changing our patterns takes continual practice, time, repetition, frequency, and commitment. Without the commitment driven by self-agency and proactive will, little will happen on the path toward less reactivity, more conscious conduct, enhanced presence, internal wholeness, and our fundamental capacity to love.

Adherence is an active process that builds the "neuroplasticity muscle." This is how we sustainably bring the changes we personally desire. Importantly, it's got to be a repeated process that allows us to deeply and unashamedly address our defendedness, our reactivity, and the many small and large ways we get upset, irritated, agitated, frustrated, and impatient as part of our day-to-day existence while riding the ups and downs of relationships.

It's our reactive, defended states of being that, when left to run amuck, destroy our experience of ourselves, harm those we love, and prevent us from the utter joy and relational fulfillment that are readily available to us. But it requires that we get out of our on-automatic ways!

Reach for it, for the essential *undefended us* within. As we do, we'll find those same essential qualities and much more reflected back to us in our external world.

Going from being a human on automatic to a human high on a fulfilling, integrated inner self, takes conscientious desire and the will to awaken to our essential qualities and gifts. It also requires that we get honest about our personality's liabilities and interior sufferings.

To do this, we start by educating ourselves cognitively and by practicing with ourselves committedly. This is the process that embodies our own aspired-for self-development. This is how we embody the growth we so desire for ourselves, and that each and every one of us deserves. This is what every single word in this book is about, from start to finish; this is, in truth, our sacred work.

Practice for Embodied Learning and Change

Practices are designed to help us embody the learning, awareness, and insights that eventually build new neural pathways in our brains, while embodiment is at the core of changing cognitive-emotional behavioral patterns.

Our practices will impact our levels of defensiveness, which arise from reactivity, either generated and triggered inside of ourselves (like negative self-talk), or in response to the environment. Reactivity causes discord and trouble, internal chaos, or immoveable rigidity.

New forms of awareness can interrupt the defensive eruption of habitual cognitive-emotional behavioral patterns that are not flexible or even relevant.

In developing new response options, we can practice responses that are more conducive to the kinds of emotional experiences we want to accelerate or bring into our lives, maybe even for the first time.

CHAPTER 2

What Is Mindfulness? How Does It Impact Me and My Relationships?

Let's address the now popular yet equally scientific term *mindfulness*. Mindfulness is a moment-by-moment conscious state of intentional awareness. It's an attainable state of being that stabilizes the patterned flow of energy and information coursing through us, enhancing the quality of our interpretations, perceptions, and reactions.

Mindfulness is fundamentally activated, sustained presence. It organizes the way we focus our attention with all of what that focus stimulates in us alongside all the sensory input we receive from the environment and those in it. And it does so simultaneously.

Mindfulness is a superpower.

Mindful awareness may begin with the information gathered by our senses, including the sounds, smells, tastes, textures, and visuals around us. Mindful awareness may include someone's tone, someone's gestures, someone's facial expression (a frown, perhaps) as well as our environmental observances, like a speeding taxi or a raging bar fight.

It's what creates the feeling that arises when we gaze at a puppy or spy people kissing. All of this translates into information—neurological data. Data of this nature in and of itself create energy within us. Mindful awareness allows us not only to pay attention to this formulating energy, but to recognize it. And because of mindful awareness, this happens consciously.

All sorts of energy are simultaneously generated and received by our internal systems. Energy-generating data are activated from within us and from without, and it's happening all the time. Coherently organizing these many energetic inputs received by our many receptive systems in a cohesive, stay-present-to-it, non-overwhelming way is the finest of developmental goals. We call this integration.

Definition Integration: To form, coordinate, or blend into a functioning or unified whole.

For an individual, when it comes to what we may call wholeness, integration is made visible by character qualities that include a calm abiding, thoughtfulness, kindness, and gentleness. Integration shows up as a genuine interest in others, response flexibility, and as compassion, care, and empathy.

Integration promotes healthy discernment and fosters cognitive cohesiveness. Integration allows for receptiveness as well as right action, and it engenders cognitive-emotional and behavioral coherency. It is where and how integrity happens. Integration weaves together the parts of ourselves we struggle with alongside the parts of ourselves we readily accept.

Integration is to the brain what just the right dressing is to a complicated salad. While each ingredient remains gently distinguishable and deliciously contributory, it makes it all come together as one great meal.

And integration is the ultimate goal of personal development. From it comes the "everything else" we are actually looking for, like love, joy, happiness, and purpose. Because in truth, that everything else is based and dependent on the way we're metaphorically organized and how well we function from the inside out.

Mindfulness—via mindful awareness—is the key that opens our developmental portal, building the skills needed to regulate and channel information and energetic flow in new, proactive, more integrative, more coherent, and more self-actualized ways.

By becoming aware of our internal processes—including our thoughts, attitudes, and feelings, our perceptions and interpretations, and our triggered or chosen reactions—we can proactively break lifelong, automatic patterns of thinking, feeling, and behaving; patterns that may be limiting us, destabilizing us emotionally, or making us downright miserable.

These automatic, habituated patterns may be inhibiting our ability to love and accept ourselves and love, receive, or accept others. Becoming aware of these habituated patterns—learning what being "on automatic" actually means— empowers us with the opportunity to develop new ways of interacting, loving, and being. These new ways can be profoundly liberating and can, ultimately and extraordinarily, change our lives.

Mindful awareness also puts us in conscious contact with those talents and qualities within us that we deserve to love about ourselves and need to express fully for a fulfilling life—those qualities of our own true nature we deserve to claim, own, hone, and fully develop.

>
> *Being mindful opens the doors not only to being aware of the moment in a fuller way, but by bringing the individual closer to a deep sense of his or her own inner world. It offers the opportunity to enhance compassion and empathy. Mindfulness is not 'self-indulgent,' it is actually a set of skills that enhances the capacity for caring relationships with others.*
>
> ~ Daniel J. Siegel, MD

Mindfulness as a state, and mindful awareness practices build the platform within us from which presence—physical embodiment also called *groundedness*, openhearted receptivity, and self-observation capacities—can develop, take form, and prosper.

Before we go any further, let's define a few of these commonly used concepts and terms, making sure we're all on the same page.

Presence: What Is It?

Few of us these days are strangers to the "get present" movement. It's all over the Internet, on our Facebook feeds, and tossed around over lunch as "the thing to be doing." We're being told it's a really good thing. But do we really know what we're supposed to be doing? What part of us, exactly, is supposed to get present? Going through these next steps will hopefully answer those questions.

I like to separate presence into three attainable experiences, and then follow up with a fourth that is also critically important.

1. Presence to ourselves: Getting grounded in our bodies
2. Presence to ourselves: Utilizing our breath as we focus our attention
3. Presence to what is: Recognition of what's discovered within when being present
4. Presence to the environment: Taking in the external world and those in it

We can first access an experience of presence by finding it in our breath and in the experience of breathing. Once accessing presence through a breathing practice, we can turn our attention toward our inner world. In doing so, we'll experience our capacity for presence within.

Cultivating presence within *is everything* to our having a full experience of ourselves and of our own true nature. Once we've achieved a presence within, we can cultivate a presence to our environment, which includes not only our surroundings but also the people with whom we may be relating at any given moment and those with whom we share much of our lives.

Getting Grounded in Our Bodies

Getting present starts with focusing on getting into our bodies by paying attention to what our bodies feel like, what sensations we have, and where they are located. Our bodies are where the sensate signals of *our truthful* inner states of being are expressed and where they are felt.

Our physical as well as cognitive, emotional, and even spiritual states are communicated to us via sensations. The body is the conduit of these many and various sensations, including the sensations of our emotional chemistries, each of which is part of a very powerful and rather complex biofeedback system of sorts, guiding us along all through our lives. Our physical system circulates information and energy that are interpreted into meaning. That is what drives our sense of self and our sense of others across the entirety of our lives.

Through the body, our "state" speaks to us all the time. But in truth, many of us have become diligent practitioners of tuning it out completely. While this helps us suppress or avoid all sorts of pain—be it cognitive, emotional, physical or spiritual—it contributes to our tuning out all sorts of other life-invigorating sensations too, like excitement, animated joy, and unconditional love.

When one part of our sensations-system is suppressed, in a way the whole system of emotional-sensory range gets suppressed too.

Getting Present to Ourselves

Let's start by tuning into how our body gets grounded in space. Are we sitting or standing? Do we feel our feet, whether on the floor or while lying down? Let's feel our body's weight, wherever it is being supported. Allow our shoulders to drop, and run our awareness down our spines, starting at the nape of our necks. Now, let's track our sensations. What are the sensations? And where are they located?

Utilizing Our Breath

Now that we're grounded, let's observe and focus on our breathing—our life-giving breath, the powerful inhale and the relieving exhale. Let's place our attention on our diaphragm, then our chest and feel ourselves "being breathed."

Take a deep breath. Inhale fully, then exhale fully. And before much of a gap, take the next breath. Again, inhale fully and exhale fully. Repeat the process several times.

The goal of this breathing awareness practice is to train our focus of attention, which is the training that cultivates our capacity for presence. As Russ Hudson, Enneagram thought leader and author, asks frequently, **"So, how much presence can we actually tolerate?"**

Tolerating presence is not necessarily a given. Why on earth is that? Because presence—while a superhero state of being in and of itself—can bring up a number of sensations inside us that we may find difficult to *be with*. To *sit still with*.

Presence may bring up physical, psychological, or emotional pain we don't understand or don't want to experience. It can bring up emotional residue we may not want to feel or remember, let alone accept. Presence can bring up a haunting loneliness that seems to have no origin or an angst, impatience, or deep frustration that starves for relief. No wonder there's a tendency to not be present much of the time!

That said, presence is where we do our finest development work, come to love ourselves more dearly, experience others more fully, and live our best lives.

So, on that fine note, here goes!

What Can We Do Once Present? The Recognition of What Is

The consciously held experience of presence takes us to something called recognition—*the identification and calling out of what really is.* In other words, once we get present to something, we can name it.

The kind of recognition we want to engage here requires openhearted (kind and accepting) receptivity (an active state of receiving). As such, recognition is a receptive and honest state where *what is* can be felt and honored without censorship or judgment, and then identified—called out—as is.

Recognition collaborates with a conscious inner observer—one that is a neutral and non-judgmental inner witness—to lucidly and humbly call out the truth *as it is.* It occurs in that moment we honor our innermost condition and name it. It's where we recognize our authentic emotions and our *physical* state, which then points us to our *feelings* state. Not necessarily the feelings we *want*, but the feelings that are really there.

We may all want, at times, to recognize internal states of utter bliss and lovingkindness when we do this practice. We may want to believe we're "so evolved," but that's not always what turns up. Instead, we may find a negative self-judgment, a ball of anxiety in our hearts, or we may witness a self-attack or an other-attack going on inside of our minds.

Some days, recognition may call out that we're on top of our game. Other days, honest recognition may call out that we are stuck, jealous, seething, pissed off, or deeply sad. It may even call out that we've been reactive, unfair, or hurtful to someone.

Recognition may be coupled with feelings of shame and self-hate, or it may be coupled with a genuine curiosity, even compassion. (Great!) The *what* we couple with our recognition is beyond critical to our development. Do we condemn what we have found, or do we rejoice because of our honesty?

How we treat ourselves once we recognize our truth—the truth of what's within—is vital to our ongoing processes. What we cannot see and identify we cannot work with or ameliorate.

But if we punish ourselves one way or another for what we see and recognize, we may never want to look again. This is where many well-intentioned humans start and stop their personal-growth initiatives. Full stop.

Recognition that is met with curiosity and then compassion moves us toward integration, while shame and self-attack do not. Claiming our truth while meeting it with interest and care—thanks to a committed and practiced, curiosity-driven recognition process—is where we simply *must* consciously and knowingly begin.

During the recognition process, we might hear ourselves in one of these ways:

- "Oh, I feel agitated. Hmmm, where is that coming from?" (Recognition of the inner state with curiosity.)
- "Why am I always so anxious? It's so annoying. I've had it with myself!" (Recognition of the inner state plus self-judgment and self-rejection.)
- "Oh, I am jealous again . . . I hate that about myself!" (Recognition of the inner state's feelings with self-rejection.)
- "I can't stand that guy! I am so irritated. I feel small in his presence, and that hurts." (Recognition of the inner state plus honest self-disclosure that is met with self-compassion.)

- "Gosh! There's such deep sadness here, I don't want to feel this way, but it is what is." (Recognition of the inner state with honesty and self-acceptance.)
- "Oh, I feel so at peace, so serene today . . . It's lovely to feel like this!" (Recognition of a state of well-being and self-acceptance.)
- Or how about this one: "I'm not good enough to take this on." (A judgment that hurts and sabotages.) Immediately followed by, "Ouch! No wonder I've been nervous all day." (Recognition coupled with self-compassion.)

In a state of recognition, we allow whatever is the truth of our condition to reveal itself. We receive it, and we accept it. We allow and acknowledge it. And we are kind and neutral toward it—*it* being whatever uncomfortable (or not) simple truth has surfaced. *What* we recognize and then accept when getting present to our inner selves *is the very presence* we are wanting to cultivate.

To be effective, observing ourselves must be a neutral act, and it needs to be kind. It needs to have no agenda. It just watches. It can be likened to the neutrality experienced watching a delivery person leave a package for your neighbor. You acknowledge seeing it without judging it because he's just the delivery person doing what he always does. It's nothing more, nothing less.

As presence leads to recognition, it must then be followed by acceptance. Recognition plus acceptance allows for us to have an honest—*precious*, actually—observance of our truthful inner condition, our truthful inner state of being. It's ours, after all. We deserve to meet with it and own it fully.

Whether recognition is generated from our *wholeness* (which might bring on love, peacefulness, and feelings of serenity) or from *woundedness* (which might bring on hurtful self-judgments or others-blaming that may lead to anxiety and anger), our presence to ourselves—being present to who we actually are at a given moment—is a profound step toward development. Recognition is a can't-skip-it part of the journey toward personal integration. It is necessary when pursuing far more fulfilling, enriched, intimate, and engaged lives.

Presence on the Inside Versus Presence to the Outside

Finally, let's discuss *our ability to be present to the external environment*. What does this mean? First, I'd like to call out an important distinction as *presence* is often confused with *taking notice*.

Being present to the fact that we're in a restaurant is *a type of noticing, a kind of awareness,* but it's not yet exactly *presence*. It's simply basic information gathering. But being present to the fact that we're in a restaurant and someone's just started yelling at the waiter is environment awareness and has possibly raised our level of vigilance.

Still, it is not the same as being fully present. I have seen this form of knowing what's going on around us being taken as the whole experience of presence, and in such a case, much is left out.

The presence we're talking about is the *inside job*—the presence to our innermost state of being along with that of others. Those inner states of being accompany what we're aware of and present to in the environment.

Presence to the environment means we are receptive and openhearted to both the *experience* of where we are and, critically, *how* what we're present to externally *is impacting our inner states of being,* as well as *how we or the environment may be impacting others.*

Examples: Am I present to the gorgeous sunset that's only a minute from disappearing? More importantly, how am I feeling as I gaze at that sunset? How am I impacted by it? What's going on inside of me as I take it in? And next, if I am with another, am I present to *them*? Am I present to their inner condition or perceived state of being as they stand beside me? And do I offer them my presence? Do I tune in to them as well as to myself as we take in the sunset?

You may be thinking, *Good heavens, those four aspects of presence are a lot to take in all at once!* Well, interestingly we are faced with and have all four of these steps at our disposal at all times. It's just that we aren't aware of nor practiced at cultivating presence on a regular basis. Nor have we—for the most part— established a conscious connection to it, to the experience of presence.

And while it's taken multiple paragraphs to explain it, *with practice* we can consciously cultivate presence on the fly and in no time at all.

Let's Talk About a Mindful Awareness Practice

As we begin this journey into a mindful awareness practice, let it take as long as it needs. Starting out, training our awareness can be awkward. It's sometimes irritating, even frustrating. We may find our minds going all over the place and keep having to start over. We may struggle to identify our inner state at all. Registering how we feel might even come up blank at first. Or we may not *want* to feel what is actually there, so we jump out of the state quickly and deflect our attention to something else.

There's only one response to any of these scenarios. Try again. And again. We do get a bit of traction with every single practice. There's no such thing as a wasted practice, ever. When we struggle with it and do the work, it gets easier. Just watch. It's worth it!

As mentioned, practice is fundamental to the observation of our habitual mental, emotional, and somatic (physical) states, whether we're wounded or openhearted. Each of our adaptive strategies and emotional states correlates with where our attention is focused and what energies that *focus of attention* ignites in us at any given moment.

Practicing and coming to access the subtleties of our internal experience and our internal states are how we track our inner condition. And as we do so, we can also track our thoughts and our feelings, and we can do so with honesty. Both our thoughts and our feelings are forms of very real stimulus, and this stimulus, so to speak, drives our sense of self as well as our behavior.

It's important to understand that the energy formed by a single thought or interpreted feeling generates an energetic kick, a biochemical response of some kind. This is critical to monitor. Neutral and curious observation will elucidate what thought or what interpreted feeling provokes what response in us.

Perhaps a thought of getting hurt provokes an edgy avoidance response, for example. Or did our thoughts or feelings create a stress response that made us want to argue? What thoughts or feelings provoke an anger response in us? An anxious response? A shame response? Or did we interpret someone's behavior to mean we're not important, which then flooded our system with a distress response? And so on and so on . . .

Observing our internal, energetic flow of information and interpretations may also show us an internal response that is perhaps a diversion from a not-so-pleasant thought form or interpretation, one that instead of dealing formidably catapults us into a more pleasurable fantasy. Or one that takes us out of presence and into excitation or anticipation, which then distracts us.

We may also see a grasping for answers that provokes frustration, or a whirring of doubt that elicits anxiety, or negative self-talk that induces a shunting of vital energy and feelings of shame and resignation.

We are wrought with "synaptic legacy" as Dr. Dan Siegel puts it. These are neural pathways that run themselves out of habit, thanks to the propensities and prior experiences that have shaped us. We can run these patterns and their energetic impacts (on ourselves and others) for the rest of our lives. But we also don't have to. It does take work, but we do have a choice.

A Presence Practice: Taking Our Development into Our Own Hands

The key to driving our lives far more consciously, from the inside out, is to release the grip of these habitual patterns through a presence practice. A mindful awareness presence practice is what develops life-changing reflective capacity (the ability to notice). It also develops self- and other-awareness.

Mindful awareness is the ability to notice, recognize and name it, to call it out honestly, and then learn to allow what we see appreciatively and acceptingly. Such practice brings forth a heightening of our response flexibility, which is what allows us to have more choices as to how we respond, not just react. From this, we can expect interpersonal adaptability, the ability to flow gently and organically with others, coupled with self-allowance and self-acceptance—all of which lead us to better self- and other-understanding.

Cultivating this level of conscious awareness enhances our potential for a more fulfilling experience of self, others, and of life in general. Change, growth, and development depend on cultivating awareness—awareness that is directed at our own inner life, first. A mindful awareness presence practice also readily provides a basis for reflection and the grounding in presence on the spot when challenge and distress may easily ignite our stress-making reactivity.

The same is true for cultivating presence in order to take in the richness and beauty of life as it unfolds right in front of us—and for us. Every spiritual tradition includes an awareness practice. Awareness that is cultivated through presence is what gifts us the hand-up for personal growth and much-deserved development.

And as seeker and dilettante Baron Payton says poignantly, "**Awareness is curative.**"

The Power of Awareness

Awareness allows us to witness and then recognize where we are inside of ourselves in each moment. And here's the kicker: it's to do so without denying what we notice, without censoring what we observe, and without trying to manipulate it into something else.

Yet we often experience not liking or wanting what we see or sense inside. Or we want to resist that nagging feeling or psychological anguish . . . again. Hence, self-rejection of this nature is unfortunately common.

We so don't want to be having this awareness, so we deny it. Or in the case where we want to be something different from what we truly are, we negate our truth, which means we negate ourselves as we are. For example, we want to be more enlightened, less hurting, less needy, less reactive, or more evolved than we really are, so we reject rather than accept what our awareness brings up. But then we struggle to make ourselves fit an outwardly formulated persona that's more desirable yet detached from our true feelings.

These negative inner responses to our truth are at the root of self-abandonment, self-neglect, and self-disregard. This is how and where the presentation of a non-authentic self—the showing up of a not-honest me—begins.

When we manipulate ourselves and deny what's really going on on the inside and avoid our shadow material (which is, in fact, such valuable interior data), we miss the opportunity for deep developmental self-awareness and consequential growth.

As we avoid or deny recognizing and feeling the truth of ourselves, we lose our capacity for truth altogether. We lose our authentic selves. We lose our ability to stay present, self-aware, and self-accepting. We lose the capacity to know ourselves. And we lose the chance to develop and grow. As a result, an honest and loving intimacy with our true selves, and subsequently with that of others, becomes impossible.

> Between stimulus and response there is a space. In that space is our power to choose our response. In our response lies our growth and our freedom.
>
> ~ Viktor Frankl, MD

The Pause

By the time we get to adulthood, we may be long practiced at self-denial, self-censorship, and the many automatic responses that just take over. Until we truly take on the work of personal mastery, we don't tend to notice any of this, let alone have a chance to be in control of it. Many of us aren't even aware this is happening!

However, there's a tiny little gap—a pause—we can crawl into. It's painful at first, but with practice it can make all the difference in the world to take advantage of this gap right inside our minds. It may only be a millisecond long, but it does, in fact, sit right there between stimulus and response. If only we would honor it. And this pause also sits between the observer (ourselves) and the object (the other), creating the space between what we do and what another does.

This pause, albeit tiny, is full of promise, hope, and power.

So, what is it exactly that's required to pause, to hang out there between what's been *ignited* thanks to stimulus and *the impulse* that incites a response? It's the ability to hold the impulse—the biochemical, energetic charge—of the response that's instantaneously running through us.

That is what's called for. (Oh, that little ol' gap!)

Michael Brown, the author of *The Presence Process*, calls this "containment." Containment is neither sedating nor suppressing or denying. Rather, it's training ourselves to gently contain the charge, to hold it.

We do this while acknowledging it, without resistance, and we do this with grace and love, whatever the content. All of this occurs during a momentary, cognitive emotional suspension. Once suspended, we can observe the response that's been ignited, and with compassion, we can understand it and honor it. By doing this, we are free and empowered to choose a response that is best for us, one that aligns with our desired right action and for the highest good of all.

Establishing a mindfulness practice helps us develop that gentle containment. (It's not always *easy*, but it is *gentle*.) This is our pause capacity. And this pause capacity is what opens up that critical split second so we can enact our awareness.

Awareness clears the field and in it, we find ourselves present. With practice we can not only *tolerate* this presence but also *stay with it*. Mindful awareness that holds us in presence is what heightens temporal integration. (Oh yay!)

Temporal integration is what happens when the brain's differentiated sources of energy and information flow—cognitive, emotional, and physical—become linked to each other and become collaborative.

Integration leads to personal integrity and coherence, which enable us to cope better, for example, with uncertainty, decision-making, conflict, threats, and problem-solving. It helps us alleviate the chronic stress of running out of time and, instead, allows us to flow and experience our impermanence as a natural, not-threatening, and manageable phenomenon.

Pause capacity makes room for awareness and presence, and it catalyzes integration. It thus allows us to go from the metaphorical turbulence of our ocean's surface to the calmer depths of our ocean's floor.

Neuroscience studies validate the importance of a mindful awareness practice. Practicing mindfulness in the long term results in the development of more integrative neurons in the prefrontal cortex (where cognition takes place).

Those who practice mindfulness for a long-term period demonstrate having developed abilities as identified in one of Dr. Dan Siegel's mnemonics: **FACES**. It stands for more **flexibility, adaptability, coherence, energy** (meaning freed-up energy), and **stability**.

Studies also show that practicing mindfulness over a shorter-term period increases concentration, well-being, mental clarity, the processing of distressful physical sensations, the delaying of impulsive actions, and the modulation of anxiety responses in the amygdala (the part of our brain that plays a key role in the regulation of emotions, particularly the aversive emotions designed to ensure our survival).

Perhaps above all, *our cultivation of awareness* and *our capacity for presence* just might be the two most important qualities of being that we could ever bring to ourselves, and to our relationships.

These qualities are the gateway to self-understanding, self-compassion, and self-knowing. They are what allow us to come back to a state of grounded, internal presence, which then allows us to experience ourselves and others with clarity, discernment, empathy, and openheartedness.

Dr. Dan Siegel, again, offers a mnemonic to help us remember to reflect on these desirable qualities. It's the word **COAL**, standing for **curiosity, openness, acceptance,** and **love**. These are some of the rewards we may come to embody as a result of practicing mindful awareness.

Getting Present with Breath

The breath is a great inner-reference point to come home to since it is always there with us. There is nothing better than deep breathing for an immediate remembrance of utter aliveness and equally so, of our fragility and vulnerability. Between 16,000 and 20,000 or more times a day, our life-giving breath ensures our existence.

Being present with our breath takes us away from all the yammering and clamoring of the five-senses reality and away from preoccupation with either the past or future. The breath is content-neutral and unassuming. It has no agenda except to provide life-giving oxygenated sustenance. What a feel-good gift it truly is for building personal awareness.

Even if there are no other benefits except furthering our physical existence, it's worth the time it takes to practice connecting with it on a regular basis. Our breath is the core of our fundamental capacity to receive (inhale) and to give back (exhale). It is deserving of much reverence.

Breath and Our Study of Ourselves

Importantly, breath practice provides the fundamental starting point of every aspect of general and type-specific, inner-exploring reflective work. It's the very first place we may come to access a sense of ourselves. Take note, it's our sense of self that creates our reality.

As we come to learn the Enneagram system and our Enneagram type, we'll be gifted with a whole lot of information about our habit of mind and our focus of attention—and that of others too. And we will recognize qualities of awareness that we share with all others of the same Enneagram type.

With our developing capacity for presence and the Enneagram's vast teachings, we have at our disposal a multifaceted companion alongside us that allows and supports us to track our thoughts, feelings, and behaviors, including our reactivity (what triggers it, and how it shows up).

For me as an Enneagram Type 6 (the Loyal Skeptic), a mindful awareness practice got me disciplined enough to start catching myself doubting someone. I started to see when I did this again and again, which then triggered an anxiety-response in me, which, in turn, took me away from having faith in that person. I found that pattern to be somewhat destabilizing.

Without my becoming present to this dynamic, I would have had no idea how much separation I was creating between myself and others as a matter of course. Gaining presence also allowed me to see my worst-case-scenario thinking as disruptive. It was occupying a heck of a lot of my time and energy and running up my adrenaline as well!

Once I tapped into what these patterns were doing to me—both how they were trying to assist me but also derailing me—I was able to begin hearing and listening to the impact I was having on others, which I was quite resistant to hearing about before.

Mindfulness with Presence, Pause, and Breath

A mindful awareness practice can be done individually, as a couple, or as a group. And it can be done for various lengths of time, for the purposes of moving from reflection to awareness, and several times a day.

Such a practice can be done anytime to center ourselves and reduce reactivity. As appropriate or desired, it can be done with our eyes open or closed. There is no such thing as a "bad practice," even when there's a great deal of distraction, frustration, or even incompletion. Every attempt counts.

Returning to our breath is especially useful in becoming a better observer and far more attuned listener, in reducing reactivity at times of frustration or stress, and eventually, in redirecting our attention at will.

A mindful awareness practice is essential in working with the Enneagram as we must become a good self-observer to begin noticing with neutrality our reactivity, our habit of mind—our focus of attention, and the driving emotional anguish of our respective type's structure. These are necessary coming-to-know-self categories of awareness that allow us to come to ourselves honestly, unpretentiously, and innocently.

With this level of acquired self-knowing at our disposal, we have the keys in our hands to accepting ourselves and others more reverently and compassionately, opening the doors of self to the love available to each one of us from deep within.

This is the sacred, self-driven work of personal development that is valuable, life-giving, and soul-shaping. And it's a big—*very big*—part of what we came here to take on.

CHAPTER 3

The Biology of Relationships: The Anatomy of Love

Pop culture tends to consider *love* as some kind of chemistry or as something that happens elusively, magically, or whimsically—if we're lucky enough—at first sight. But there's an astounding physiological architecture to the experience of love, one that's as complex as the magic of the feelings themselves. We're not only designed to experience love emotionally but physiologically as well; and our systems thrive when we do. In a way, we might say that *love is built in.* We are wired for it.

Mirror Neurons and Attachment

Some of the most exciting research of this century tells us that we are a social living species with social brains, brains that to some extent read each other; brains that are wired to mirror each other's experience. This ability is made possible by what is termed "mirror neurons."

We all have mirror neurons and, to the best of our knowledge, they are wired in the frontal and parietal (the side areas) of our brain's neocortex. The neocortex is the part of our brain involved in higher-order functions such as cognition, critical thinking, generation of motor commands, spatial reasoning, and language.

These mirror neurons then link up with other cortical areas and the limbic system (which is involved in our emotional regulation, instincts, and moods) through a central or midline area of brain circuits called the insula. The insula is involved in governing our subjective emotional experiences, social cues, morality, and our somatic sensations.

Thanks to all of this amazing limbic and neocortex circuitry, we are able to form an internal representation or map of our world as well as others' minds, their feeling states, and perspectives. Metaphorically and technically speaking, we are wired to be linked together.

Attachment

Importantly, the experience of attachment, of connection to others, largely occurs through our limbic systems. Let's consider the experience of sadness that elevates to emotional distress, the aversive emotional system we achingly find ourselves feeling when we lose attachment and connection.

Most of us have experienced a lost child's distress in a department store, or the expected distress or utter panic accompanying the sudden loss of a loved one. The underlying sadness and then grief in reaction to such a loss of critical attachment relationships are the emotions that let us know how much we care, how much connection means to us, and how vital these experiences are to the whole of our being and our developmental processes and lives.

Now, coming back to mirror neurons, it's thanks to these neurons, in part, that we are able *to empathize and resonate* with others as they experience and express sadness and grieving as well as panic and distress even—emotional loss to any degree.

Mirror neurons are part of the system that allows parents, for example, to immediately tune into the distress expressed in their children, and it's this same system that allows loved ones to feel each other's distress during a conversation or heated argument as much as they can feel their own (*as long as we are present enough to do so*, we should add. But more on this in a later chapter).

Nurturance: Wired for Closeness

What is nurturance? We all literally require it to grow, develop, and thrive. We could speak of nurturance as food because it's one form of it. But here, we're speaking more specifically to another kind of nurturance altogether—one that is neurologically mediated by our limbic system, our mammalian brain. This kind of nurturance is formally defined as the emotional and physical nourishment and care given to someone, as well as the ability to provide it.

We're talking about *emotional nurturance*. Emotional nurturance is to humans what water laced with Miracle-Gro™ is to a potted plant. Emotional nurturance is the vital, invisible food each of us needs not only to *survive*, but also to *thrive*—to grow healthfully, fully, and to potentiate. Emotional nurturance greatly contributes to successful parent-child attachment, to the successful development of our self-esteem, and is what nurtures and develops our limbic system.

Metaphorically, nurturance is the difference regularly adding mineral-rich water to a potted plant can make. While we may be confident about the pot we've provided and all the sunlight it gets—thanks to where we've successfully placed it—too much or too little water can greatly impact how it develops. Adding the Miracle-Gro may be a time-consuming step that takes patience, diligence, and care, but boy, does it ever make a difference over time!

If that plant is outdoors, we might *hope* it will rain enough to sustain survival because plants (we tell ourselves) are resilient and hardy, so we don't worry about it much. Or we might douse it with the garden hose on occasion thinking the dousing will last, because we don't have the time or patience to water and care for it more consistently.

Soon enough, we'll find the plant has been smothered and is suffering root rot. Or it might seem OK, but it isn't as strong, glorious, or colorful, as it could have been, let alone that it's not blooming as it should. Though it's *surviving*, it's surely not *thriving*. The plant is stunted, maybe even scraggly and wilted. It struggles to absorb the sunlight, hold water, and attain healthy and ongoing well-being. It simply *didn't potentiate*.

In truth, we humans are the same. We don't thrive either when the care necessary for our development such as emotional nurturance and validating care are spotty, random, unreliable, or nearly non-existent across our formative childhood years. Worse yet, when it's damaging or traumatizing.

While designed to survive at all costs, *humans suffer when our developmental needs are not met.* But unlike unnurtured plants that visibly display their struggle, humans deprived of emotional nurturance suffer most on the inside. The impact is not necessarily visible, and the lost potential is not easily measured. We are often none the wiser.

While as children we may look fine enough on the outside—height charts are within the norms and we are carrying on and keeping up with our peers—chaos and dysregulation or rigidity and inflexibility may be developing. Meanwhile, on the inside a loss of connection to our authentic selves is growing, and it's showing up as an inability to tolerate frustration, as struggles with focus and learning, and as an inability to self-soothe. These developmental reactions are only *some* of what's crystalizing within our character structure and our cognitive-emotional systems.

A lack of emotional nurturance—or worse yet, damaging and traumatizing events—leaves us as developing humans without the internal resources we will need later on to cope, let alone thrive. All the growth, learning, development, and stress we will encounter along the way depend greatly on the coherence and integrity of these internal resources, those that were developed (or not) when young.

Though fed well, babies that are never held often die. And even if that baby were to survive, the lack of emotional nurturance impedes developmental processes and ultimately potentiation. Knowing that, it's astounding to learn of feral or severely neglected children surviving the utmost of horrific circumstances. This is proof that we often can and do *survive* against all odds—even with far from adequate emotional nurturance and holding.

But, still, there are problems. Deficiencies arise in our emotional and attachment systems, and shortages become evident in the developmental processes of self. Full potentiation is challenged. Emotional dysregulation, problems with impulse control, an inability to adhere to or set appropriate boundaries, and an inability to cope with distress or self-regulate are just some of the symptoms that begin to show up in toddlers and up, manifesting well into adulthood, wreaking havoc in people's lives and all manner of their relationships.

Suffering when young developmentally leads to suffering cognitively and emotionally later. Adaptive strategies that were necessary in childhood can turn into maladaptive and sabotaging strategies in adulthood. And as a result of our suffering and trying to cope, those around us suffer and struggle to cope too.

> Why is it such a big deal when we suffer a loss of connection, when our attachment is threatened? Because we're wired for it.
>
> ~ Gabor Maté, MD

Emotional Nurturance, Attachment and Connection

We're wired to be connected to others. Wired for connection is a trait we share with all mammals, and it's also what makes us human. It's how we survive and then how we develop. In fact, **"... connection itself is anxiolytic,"** says Dr. Mark F. Schwartz, former director of the Masters and Johnson Institute. He goes on to say, "It's connection that soothes a non-hungry but crying baby. It's being held that assuages a baby's distress and agitation." Connection is an anxiety-soothing mechanism, and it's built right into us and our central nervous system.

As far as our *ability* to nurture, this is interesting too. For example, removing the neocortex (the "thinking brain") of a mother hamster still allows her to nurture her pups. But even *slight* limbic—feeling, emoting, empathizing brain—damage destroys mama hamster's ability to nurture her pups at all. The limbic system is central to attachment, care, bonding, emotional nourishment, and to all mammalian development.

This also highlights the longer-term impact on baby boys and girls—society's future fathers and mothers. With those who have suffered losses in emotional nurturance during infancy and early childhood, we see an impact on their developing limbic systems. This calls on us to recognize the impact on their capacities to respond and bond fully in emotionally nurturing, validating, and attuned ways to the emotional and attachment needs of their own babies later in life. And those children, in turn, grow up to be either hurting or thriving members of our society.

As mentioned previously, studies show that infant mammals that are fed well enough but not physically interacted with, suffer. Conclusively, it's reported that those babies often fail to survive, and if they do, they don't develop well.

It's a fact: we need contact. We need warmth. We need that feeling of being cared for. It's a biological and developmental imperative that we bond and attach, that we are nurtured and loved. Our fundamental needs are fully dependent on a profoundly systemic matrix of transacting, one that literally impacts our brains on a moment-to-moment basis across our earliest developmental years and beyond.

Studies using infant monkeys raised in isolation—meaning having *no contact* with each other until adulthood—led us to understand the detrimental impact of the isolation. Those monkeys grew up, but they did not even know how to reproduce and often couldn't at all function sexually. Consider now the impact of isolation on humans, and let's consider it beyond just the infancy and toddler years, which we now know are undisputedly critical.

Let's consider an outcast-type pre-teen youngster, growing up in today's immensely busy, competitive, Internet-driven society. Imagine two exhausted working parents who have little contact with that teen outcast because everyone's got their own needs to tend to. Dinners together are hit-and-miss, and the teen stays preoccupied with his computer a lot of the time, anyway. Meanwhile, this youngster is also lacking a couple of solid, close friends.

This youngster needs more than intermittent contact with his parents to traverse the teen years, let alone to help him foster the necessary development to grow into a normal, healthy, social, and sexual, society-participating person.

Ongoing studies—including and importantly Dr. Dan Siegel's groundbreaking work in the field of interpersonal neurobiology—reveal the undeniable importance of human contact, and the fact that ongoing, validating contact is needed through our childhood developmental years for our socialization and relational capacities to develop fully, and function fully.

Our Hearts

On that note, let's talk about our hearts for just a moment. Not from a physiological point of view as an organ snugged well within the chest cavity, but from a nurturance point of view. As a matter of course, our hearts are identifiably expressive of our need for contact.

Extending outward toward others—thanks to its divine proximity to our arms and then hands—our hearts symbolically reach for others. We reach for a hug. We extend ourselves to offer an embrace. One of the very first things babies do is reach, arms outstretched, to a parenting caregiver. While a hug seems so commonplace and ordinary, we may easily overlook the vast importance of this seemingly banal gesture to our fundamental needs and developmental survival.

Being held and holding another are the embrace that sustains human life itself; it's the first safe place we find ourselves in with our mothers/caregivers, and it's something throughout each of our lives that we can readily give to one another for comfort, for safety, for affection, and for assurance. Being held and holding another are vital to experience early on in life for each of us to be *turned on* to love, and to caring and nurturing ourselves and others later on in life.

Gestures of emotional nurturance that are expressed physically, like hugging and holding, are the foundation of our own emotional sense of safety and development and ultimately, fulfillment. It's been identified that *the intention to hug* can have an extraordinarily positive physiological effect on us; just the intention itself has been found to light up parts of our brain.

To further elucidate how much is going on within us as we relate to and connect with one another, it once astounded me to learn that the human heart (this time, the organ) has a way of coordinating beats when in another's presence. When we're in positive emotional connection with someone, our sensory-sensitive hearts begin beating coherently, synchronizing rhythmically. This then affects our entire body's well-being and does so in very positive ways.

Knowing this allows us to put ourselves intentionally in this kind of emotionally openhearted state with a special and receptive other. We can get there by focusing on our appreciation for what is positive and precious, in ourselves, the special other, and in the world. This is a state of mind we can conjure up willfully, and it's one that generates a particularly positive feeling state and sets off a coherent rhythm in our own hearts. This then synchronizes with and becomes congruently harmonious with that of another and with all of life itself.

When we experience this kind of heartfelt congruency, all bodily functions—both emotional and physical—prosper. We relax. We achieve. We radiate. We live more fully. And we live longer.

In this state, we release more dopamine, serotonin, oxytocin, and even endorphins—our bodies' feel-good, feel-connected neurotransmitting chemistry. Each of these creates well-being and are the same feelings (and chemistry) that are turned on when in the arms of a nursing (if possible), loving, attuned mother during infancy, and when these developmental experiences continue and persist all through childhood.

When we feel love in our hearts, when we allow ourselves to experience love toward ourselves, then the immense electromagnetic field around our heart radiates a feeling of love toward others. This makes us want—from a very genuine, unconditional place—to give to and receive from others. Herein lies the potentiated bliss of being human.

In that, by appreciating, being grateful, and by loving, we catalyze and enable a sense of nurturing love for others, which is what inevitably nurtures ourselves. This is the kind of loving communication we want to have all day long, flowing back and forth between us, integrating the feeling hearts in our chests and the processing whole of our minds.

This is what supports and enhances the well-being we need in order to nurture the many aspects of ourselves that drive the cognitive-emotional, physiological, and spiritual mechanisms that create and drive our growth and that sustain our lives. This is good news all the way around. And it's attainable.

When There's a Lack of Contact, There's a Lack of Heartfelt Experience

As we've been learning, human infants raised with little human contact do not develop properly—sometimes they even die. Without adequate emotional nurturance, connection, and bonding, a chronological six-month-old infant may physically and developmentally resemble a three-month-old. This happens even though the baby is given plenty of food and has a clean physical environment.

Instead of thriving, these infants become sickly and withdrawn, lose weight, and even die at rates over 40 times the expected rate. And if for some reason some of them do make it, the state of their limbic development—their capacity for love and bonding, for attachment and emotional regulation—may be severely diminished. This can lead to a life of suffering for this being as well as for anyone this individual might encounter, let alone try to love.

The prisons in the United States are filled with men and women who have grown up without what they sorely needed to potentiate fully. Hence, they stumble into a life of crime as a way to survive, the best one can do when dealing with utter internal chaos and immense levels of intrapersonal desperation.

Remember a time not so long ago when newborns were separated from their mothers at birth, kept in a sterilized hospital nursery so mother could rest and baby's exposure to dangerous germs could be limited? Gazing through a window at rows of babies was as close as a dad ever came to his newborn child for a good week or more.

Another example is that of premature infants at risk. Until recently, they were excluded from caring, physical contact for the first days, weeks, or months of their lives, depending on the severity of their case. And again, how ironic it is that this very practice of isolation in germ-free incubators increased the likelihood of the infant dying!

We have long been a part of the normalization of practices that are detrimental to the most critical component of an infant's survival and development, that which includes human contact, warmth, care and holding. Thankfully, policies have changed, and parents are encouraged to have direct and immediate physical contact with their newborn; mortality rates with these advancements in place have fortunately and expectedly decreased.

Mammals, Nursing, and Nurturance

To further stress our intricate need for connection and attachment, a newborn's eyesight is designed to see just about eight inches in front of itself for the first several months of life, just the distance needed to take in the mother's eyes and face when suckling at the breast.

Furthermore, the nursing mother and infant experience a shared awareness of each other; they co-create the positive emotional experience of care, which is a profound exchange that all mammals share in common and need for healthy development. Additionally, the newborn infant physiologically recognizes its mother and physiologically responds to her much differently than to a stranger.

It's amazing to consider this. How on earth does that newborn baby know the difference? But it does. It's an evolutionary adaptation for an infant to know its mother because its highly likely that *with her, safety and care are most surely promised.* This knowing ensures and promotes the infant's survival and development over time.

Psychologist Harry Harlow's experiments with Rhesus monkeys circa 1960 proved astounding to our understanding of attachment and the instinctual need for comforting care. Here's what happened: Given the chance to choose a hard, wiry-prickly surrogate mother with abundant milk available, the baby monkeys instead chose a soft, warm, cloth-carpet surrogate to cling to and cuddle, despite the fact that this surrogate had no milk. Furthermore, the monkeys that chose the cloth-carpet surrogate, when compared to those who had been forced to choose the hard, wiry-prickly one, developed better. Those baby monkeys who could not soothe themselves with the wire-frame surrogate, even though they had plenty of milk, did not develop well.

The innate desire for comforting physical closeness overrode the infant monkeys' desire to feed themselves readily. Soothing comfort alone proved surprisingly more important to their later-on developmental well-being as well.

Research of this kind has helped us tremendously in understanding our own developmental needs. From affective neuroscience and interpersonal neurobiology, we are coming to comprehend our profoundly sensitive developmental systems, which seek nourishment that is far beyond food and shelter.

Our fundamental wiring is geared and ready at birth to receive love, comforting nurturance, secure attachment, and bonding in order to potentiate. And our profound life-long need for connection to others is an undeniable aspect of our humanness and our unfolding well-being. These are the precious interactions that feed our brains, promote our emotional development, and nurture our spirits, enabling us to experience a life of fulfillment—one that is manageable, enjoyable, and worth living.

The Role of Attachment Theory

What is attachment theory? Thought-leading research gifted us by American-Canadian psychologist Mary Ainsworth and British psychologist John Bowlby led to the science of human bonding and connection, of the need for physical and emotional closeness, and of whether or not we feel secure in our attachments, in our significant caretaking relationships.

The study of attachment theory brings us to understanding secure attachment, which is defined as the successful bonding of children to caregivers. When adequate, it results in three fundamental requirements being met. And when they are not, a specific aversive survival emotion kicks in:

- **The Need to Be Autonomous, Dignified, and Have Self-Worth**
  This fundamental requirement is associated with the Enneagram's
  Gut/Body Center of Intelligence. The driving aversive emotion of this
  requirement, when not met, is anger all the way to rage.

- **The Need to Be Connected and Affirmed**
  This fundamental requirement is associated with the Enneagram's
  Heart Center of Intelligence. The driving aversive emotion of this
  requirement, when not met, is separation distress all the way to panic.
- **The Need to Be Acknowledged and Secure**
  This fundamental requirement is associated with the Enneagram's
  Head Center of Intelligence. The driving aversive emotion of this
  requirement, when not met, is fear all the way to terror.

Attachment theory helps us understand these three aversive emotional
systems and how they are triggered when our fundamental attachment needs are
not met.

Anger results when there's an obstruction to our sense of power or autonomy,
our sense of dignity and self-worth. It is expressed by our need to mobilize
energy in order to obtain whatever we feel is necessary to obtain, pursue, or
protect.

Distress occurs when there is a loss of recognition by, or connection to, the
primary people in our lives caring for us. This is often associated with neither
feeling encouraged nor attuned to, not approved of, or not cared for.

Fear is described as occurring when there is a loss of a safe and secure person
to rely on at times of perceived threat or danger, or when the caregivers
themselves are unpredictable or dangerous.

Ways We Attach (or Don't)

When the caregiver is sensitive and present to an infant's or child's three basic
developmental requirements, **secure attachment** results and the child prospers.
When the nurturing person, mother or other, does not respond to the child's
needs in reliable and sensitive ways, or ignores or detaches from the child,
avoidant attachment takes place, which is characterized by the child shying
away from connection.

When the nurturing person is inconsistent, altering between attunement
and insensitivity to the child's needs, **ambivalent (preoccupied) attachment**
occurs, in which case the child manifests insecurity, resulting in clinging due to
limbic distress.

Finally, when the nurturing person shows unpredictability, harmfulness, and is utterly deficient in attunement, **disorganized attachment** results, with the child not knowing what to expect at any given moment. In this case, attachment strategies and capacities simply collapse.

In limbic-system terms, all this relates to the three Rs—limbic **resonance**, limbic **regulation**, and limbic **revision**.

Resonance means presence and receptivity to another in such a way that we align with and come alongside. We hear the other as they are to themselves, with ourselves being in a state of neutrality and authenticity, without judgmentalness or capitulation. We listen openly and caringly to our child's, our partner's, or our dear friend's subjective experience, their expressed and emoted intrapersonal melody, so to speak, whatever its tune.

Regulation refers to the balancing and harmonizing of the connection to another and the ability to adapt appropriately within a range of responses. This is closely associated with the mirror neuron system referred to earlier. As a result, there is response flexibility, resilience, emotional modulation, and contingent—that is, reliant—communication.

Revision takes place when we embody both resonance and regulation, which allows for others to be influenced and impacted by us in positive ways. It means that we all have the capacity to affect each other, and we do. And remember, as this is really important: We have the greatest power to change each other for the better by being an example first. And by using ourselves first as the exemplars, others are impacted energetically and in real time.

So, what does all this mean to us? It means that developing a loving being or a loving experience takes love. It means that our relationships and our belonging to each other are experiences both based on love. To live a fulfilling life, we are best able to do so from a loving place. And it takes love to gift a developing human a chance to develop fully and potentiate.

We know that to experience love and felt-sense connections we are utterly dependent on our limbic system, whether at five years old or 50. So, **what can each of us do to contribute to creating a world that focuses on developing loving beings from the moment they enter the world to eventually entering society?** This is the most sacred of undertakings. It's a fundamental mission for the entire collective—for each of us—and for the highest good of all. It's one we hope we all come to take seriously for generations to come.

> Not every story has a happy ending... but the discoveries of science, the teaching of the heart, and the revelations of the soul all assure us that no human being is ever beyond redemption. The possibility of renewal exists so long as life exists. How to support that possibility in others and in ourselves is the ultimate question.
>
> ~ Gabor Maté, MD

What If I Didn't Get What I Needed When I was Young?

What if I didn't get my developmental needs met in childhood? What if I did not receive the emotional nurturance I really needed? As Dr. Gabor Maté often puts it, what if things were done to us that shouldn't have been, that have left us traumatized—either consciously or unconsciously? Or what if what needed to happen didn't happen? As in, what if we weren't nursed or we weren't held in a way we needed for optimal emotional development?

What if we never felt loved, seen, heard, or understood, as in, there was little attunement or resonance between us and our caregivers? What if our parents did the best they could, but we still spent a lot of time alone and there wasn't much closeness when we were little? What if, worse yet, we were consistently and regularly neglected? Emotionally or physically abused?

What if we don't remember our childhood, but for some reason we struggle getting close to anyone? Does it mean there's no hope for us? Or what if our basic needs seemed to be handled but our perception and resulting feelings are that they were *not*?

Re-Parenting Ourselves: Empowering Redemptive Healing

When we are tiny, we have no say and no control as to how we're treated, how we are parented, cared for, or spoken to. But we *do* have control once we become adults. There's no doubt we are gifted an immense head start when born to conscious, attuned, loving, non-stressed parents who take an utter delight in our existence, our growth, and our subjective experience of our unfolding life. Wow, right? Sign me up!

As creative catalyst, musician, and producer of the band Giant Leap, Jamie Catto says, **"Tuning into our woundedness provides a gateway to our creative gifts . . . ,"** and we can decide ". . . **to turn our shadow material into rocket fuel for our life."** What an empowering statement he makes.

This hopeful perspective is so encouraging, and it's equally catalyzing. It energizes us to vitalize our own will and self-agency toward our own healing. Understanding our wounds and our interpretations of them, coupled with learning their valuable lessons, can make a critical difference in how we live out, enjoy, and potentiate our life to its fullest—despite how we may have gotten started while utterly dependent on others.

Tuning into our woundedness, which inevitably gets us to the sabotaging core beliefs that resulted and now haunt us, is probably the most important and profound gift any single one of us could ever give ourselves. Our experience of ourselves—which then becomes our overarching experience of others and of the world—is indeed largely determined by the start we got early in life and our internal interpretation of it. But leaving our development to the luck of the draw by not taking it into our own hands (that is, leaving the results unattended to), makes little sense.

Settling for festering psychological pain, internalized misery, discontentment, hard-to-bare feelings, isolation, and loneliness is not what any of us desires or aspires to. But it happens as one of the possible impacts of early trauma and emotional wounding and is surely an unnecessary waste of personal potential and the loss of the life that is waiting to be deservedly well lived and loved.

Metacapacities for Healing

Psychotherapy and the understanding of our developmental brain have taken over a century to tackle, but scientific research has come a long way as of late in its understanding of our fundamental capacity to change, develop in new ways, and grow. Neuroplasticity tells us that we can form new neural pathways within the neural networks that govern our sovereignty. It tells us that we ourselves can develop our brain's limbic system and that we can develop metacapacities.

Metacapacity is the ability and developmental process by which we come to watch ourselves, to self-know and inevitably, proactively self-develop and even heal, if we so desire. We can consciously activate our ability to observe ourselves thinking, feeling, and somatically responding. We can become aware of the content of our thoughts (metacognition), or we can observe ourselves observing ourselves and become aware of our subjective, internal experience of the observing itself (meta-awareness).

What has now been proven is that we can, in fact, take it upon ourselves later in life to grow beyond our early negligences and childhood deficiencies. While those experiences that were out of our control are some of what shaped our cognitive-emotional realities and how we saw ourselves in it, that's not the end of the story. It's a commitment to take this on—the work of self-development—but it's surely more than possible and well worth pursuing.

The Potential to Self-Heal

Let's look at it this way—thanks to a perspective shared on *Sounds True* by aforementioned Jamie Catto: Our bodies are hardwired to self-mend. For example, if we cut ourselves, give it a Band-Aid and a week's time, and the damage disappears. We are self-healing creatures, and we can see it with our own eyes. We are biologically engineered to move toward wellness, when possible; that's the natural state of nature herself.

But it's not just the physical body that has the capacity to self-mend; our psychological, cognitive-emotional bodies can too. If given the nourishment needed, our emotional (and other) energetic bodies can also process and *practice themselves into more healed, more integrated, more progressed states and capacities.*

How do we do this? Step by step. By undergoing deep work associated with our etiology (the study of what happened to us). By setting a conscious and compassionate intention to self-understand (which is where the Enneagram comes in). By committing ourselves to self-development that includes bona fide healing and growth. And by developing a mindful awareness practice that enables and facilitates desired change to occur.

We Can Do It!

It is, in fact, simple, if you think about the steps detailed—they make sense, after all—but it's not easy. As author and teacher Gabrielle Roth says, **"It takes great discipline to become a free spirit."** We've got to work at it over time with practices and conscientiousness.

Conditioned patterns of thinking, *not* thinking or *over*thinking; feeling and *not* feeling; and behaving, whether acting out or going numb, take concerted effort to identify. It takes devotion, a deep commitment, and a readiness to practice and stumble, then practice again. We learn to facilitate the observations first, and then the changes we need, deserve, and desire will follow.

We have the power to heal ourselves, if we choose to exercise it. And it's a power that does not ultimately rest in the hands of our parenting caregivers. At a certain point, our parenting caregivers hit their "sell by date," meaning they pass the point in time when *they can fix it*—or even a point in time that we think they *could or should fix it*. (*It* being what harmed us in childhood.)

These harmful events can be excavated and examined. And if we want, we can consciously and thoughtfully give ourselves as adults what we *didn't get* in childhood. We do this by embarking on our own reparenting process. It's the process of becoming our own ideal parent.

Re-parenting is the process of understanding, attuning to, and nurturing ourselves in ways we were not emotionally nurtured as children. It's the process of reclaiming our authentic—genuinely feeling, sensing, and expressing—selves.

You may have heard it said, "Our trauma is not our fault, but our healing is our conscious choice and our responsibility."

This takes us back to relationships, as they too serve a critical process in all this healing-growing talk. While *the work of self-development is an inside job and no one can do this work for us*, loving relationships are a significant and contributory facet of an intentional developmental process. As the original damage was done relationally, the work of healing is also done relationally, and exponentially so.

Relationships when we were young are where we got hurt. Relationships in adulthood are a place we can heal. It starts with the relationship we begin to build with ourselves anew, and it culminates in the relationships we will then seek in others—including and allowing ourselves to consciously seek relationships that are, in fact, loving, supportive, reflective, emotionally nutritious, and growth-inducing.

Relationships can be healing. In the relationship with ourselves—one we compassionately learn to develop—we can become the source and champion of our own developmental healing. And as a result, we can then bring that more present, loving, aware self to our experiences with others.

Deciding to take responsibility for our own processes and consciously engaging with our inner world make possible critical differences in our experience of ourselves, of our relationships, and of our place in the world.

> We are 100% responsible for who we are in relationships. Our task is to free ourselves sufficiently so that we can respond in the present moment—not from past programming. That's what freedom is.
>
> ~ Gabor Maté, MD

Mindful Awareness Practice Results in the Qualities of Secure Attachment

Thanks to much astounding research these past many years, following the work of American professor and author Jon Kabot-Zinn and that which has been written about and expressed in Dr. Dan Siegel's *The Mindful Brain*, we now know that the established qualities of an adult presenting with secure attachment correlate directly with the developed qualities of being of someone who has adopted a consistent and successful mindful awareness practice! This is terrific news! (Sign me up for this too!)

Research now concludes that an over-time dedication to a mindful awareness practice yields the same nine fundamental qualities associated with an individual who exhibits secure attachment:

Self-Regulation: The ability to regulate the self without outside assistance or influence, including stepping back from and modulating the aversive emotional systems as needed for equanimity and to make good choices.

Attuned Communication: The ability to read the signals of others and resonate with their subjective experience and state of mind.

Emotional Balance: This includes a flexibility of affective (emotional) states, feelings, and their identifiable arousal.

Response Flexibility: The capacity to pause, contain the charge of any level of reactivity, and choose a consciously desired response appropriate to the stimulus.

Insight: The ability to connect the dots across the many stages of our life, including the formation of a cohesive narrative of the past, one that correlates with the present as well as with the unfolding future.

Empathy: The ability to sense into the mind, the subjective experience associated with the narrative of another being, and align with them as if being them, with neutrality and compassion.

Ability to Modulate Fear: A capacity that slows down the uptake of stress hormones, which then prevents us from overwhelm and chaos when needing to deal with potentially threatening situations.

Access to Intuition: This requires an internal stillness and a conscious awareness in order to recognize and heed what's being received.

Morality: Provides a compass for consciously acceptable, do-no-harm ethical behavior, one that has the higher good of all concerned in the forefront, alongside personal integrity.

Whether or not we were gifted with secure attachment in childhood, know that we can strive to foster the same powerful, integrated, developmental qualities in adulthood by engaging a devoted mindful awareness practice. (There is hope for us all!)

At any time in our adult lives—and in combination with a mindful awareness practice—we can develop our internalized *nurturing parent*, one that learns to self-nurture and re-parent us as we had originally needed. Conscious reparenting of self provides us with a way of gaining the nurturance necessary for development that may have been lacking when we were young.

In conjunction with reparenting of self and through mindful awareness development and practice, we have at our fingertips the chance to self-develop. Self-development is where we begin in order to create and sustain more fulfilling adult relationships. (Queue the Enneagram!)

We can also develop, at any time, better parenting awareness and parenting skills to ensure the adequate and beautiful development of our own children. Committed practice means gaining opportunities to reflect on and then bring forth the beneficial qualities of attuned nurturance as was discussed earlier, qualities that engender secure attachment in our babies and that which form the developmental platform for all the childhood development that follows.

We have the power as human beings to bring mindful awareness practices and our own subsequent, developmental healing to our grown-up selves first, and then to the ones we love, including our romantic partnerships, our extended families, and our precious developing children.

The Anatomy of Love for Healing Self and Relationships

We now know about our cognitive-emotional as well as physiological need to connect, our need to bond, and our critical social-brain capacity to resonate with one another and inspire, support, and even heal, side by side.

We urge you to give yourself time to reflect on this material, which includes the information shared about our neurobiology, what we know about attachment theory, and an understanding of how to approach our own self-mending capacities.

There is an exciting opportunity right in front of us to take our own self-knowing and developmental healing very seriously. It's precious, sacred work, and it rightfully belongs to each and every one of us.

We also have the opportunity to take our many relationships and the power of their possibility to their greatest potential. The effect on our lives could be incomprehensibly life-changing, because the quality of our relationships directly correlates with the quality of our lives.

It's our relationships—with ourselves and with others—that bring the most beauty, fulfillment, growth and magnificence to our existence and to our time spent here on earth.

Let's give it all we've got!

CHAPTER 4

Getting to Know Ourselves: Let's Start with the Enneagram System

Before I had encountered the Enneagram, it took me a long time in a therapeutic setting to calibrate someone's personality structure, formulate an assessment, and organize around the issues faced. It's hard to try to figure out on our own our defensiveness, triggers that launch our reactivity, and the ways we escape reality. And it takes commitment, energy, and immense patience to track with clarity how and why we focus our priorities, create our realities, and formulate our inner stories. If we are fortunate, we find our way to something conclusive thanks to heaps of soul-searching dedication.

It's challenging when we don't exactly know what we're looking at within ourselves, let alone have the wherewithal to recognize what's not really working. It's a complex labyrinth discerning our patterns of thinking, feeling, and acting out. Tracking how we're feeling and showing up—are we coherent (or not), connected (or not), growing (or not)—this is not easy terrain.

What gets in our way in the beginning is that defensiveness doesn't know it's defended, disharmonious doesn't know it's possibly sabotaging, and toxic self-shaming doesn't know what it is doing to us and our relationships over time. And it doesn't know how brutally separating and restricting it really is.

When we've always done something a certain way, reacted to things the way we do, or have lived with anxiety or frustration or loneliness, day in and day out, we don't know there's another way to exist—to be. *It's just me*, we are sure to believe. We might even get mad at ourselves when we keep doing "that thing" we know gets us in trouble. But we just can't seem to stop, because *it's just the way we've always been*.

When someone's different from us or responds opposite to how we'd respond, we often think, *What's wrong with them?* We might even spend inordinate amounts of time struggling to convince others that *our way is the way*. Why is it that others—our partner, our boss, our kids—just don't get it?

How Do We Begin to Know Ourselves?

I'd like to begin by sharing that we humans have a "categorizing brain." Our virtual, pattern-recognition machine of a brain enables us, for example, to open countless doorknobs all over the world effortlessly without having to learn anew how to open each one each time. Our brain also gives us the ability to recognize a friend from afar or from behind, to remember a person we've met only once, even if we can't see the whole person or exactly remember their face.

Recognizing patterns allows our brain with its 100 billion neurons and thousands of connections from one neuron to another to deal with the world moment to moment without short-circuiting overwhelm. Imagine life if every day was a rediscovery of everything in it, as if for the first time! We'd be utterly exhausted, not to mention utterly absorbed in a constant state of wonderment, fascination, and over-stimulation.

That is the daily experience of a crawling baby. (Wow! No wonder they sleep a lot!) We are designed to categorize, organize, and make sense of the world as we grow by formulating a recognizable and trustable reality in which we feel safe to exist—one data acquisition at a time.

Various Typologies

It's not surprising, then, to consider that the field of psychotherapy as well as various traditions, detailing various personality typologies, attempts to help us make quicker sense of ourselves. For instance, the Four Temperaments Theory—sanguine, phlegmatic, choleric, and melancholic personality types—is based on the ancient wisdom of humorism that suggests body fluids affect personality.

There's also the Blood Type Personality Theory, which offers a differentiation of personality proclivities according to blood type. Meanwhile, the 16 types outlined by the Myers-Briggs Type Indicator is based to some degree on Carl Jung's personality differentiations. And there's the *Diagnostic Statistical Manual,* an identification system of personality pathology and mental health issues.

Each of these systems is intended to assist us in recognizing distinctive patterns of human personality and human well-being as well as pathology. As a clinician, the system I've found to be voraciously on point is the Enneagram system. It's the one system I keep referring to. I have used this system in my professional work, in forming an understanding of the most enduring life-long patterns observed in my clients' lives, and in my own development and growth as well.

The Enneagram's wisdom has its roots in the world's great spiritual traditions and in Pythagorean mathematics. This suggests to me that the Enneagram spells out our basic human characteristics as they contribute to the collective, to the evolutionary requirements of our species as its own systemic entity.

Connection to these deep traditions and fundamentals gives the Enneagram its distinctive clinical utility and its incredible usefulness. The Enneagram teaches us about varying human perspectives and uniquely designed focuses of attention. We need these perspectives and the varying focuses of attention, because they lead to the varying talents of different types of people, each of which helps our highly intelligent, social species to evolutionarily survive.

The Enneagram and our Evolution

There are nine distinct and fundamentally different personality types in the Enneagram system. These different types are internally organized, temperamental structures. Each structure has its own particular focus of attention and priorities, which leads to its identifiable way of thinking, feeling, and behaving.

From an evolutionary standpoint, each of these structures brings its own special gift to the collective, gifts that I have no doubt contribute to the whole of our fundamental survival as a species. With nine different focuses of attention, we each bring forth an assembly of strengths and strategies, capacities and sensitivities that were, and still are, gravely needed for our survival, evolution, and sustainability.

For example, if the whole of the human tribe was focused on gathering food, who in the group would have been focused on preparing the food, creating warmth and protection from the elements, or warding off invaders? If each of us had been designed in the same way, with the same proclivities, focus of attention and talents, it would not have made much survival sense whatsoever.

What's so profound about this system is that it details for us how human nature is intricately comprised of fundamental propensities. Each of these propensities—including personality strengths, liabilities, and adaptive patterns—is organized in a particular way, and each has its own fundamental core belief system and perspective.

Research studies from Alexander Thomas and Stella Chess, circa 1990, have also recognized nine identifiable temperament categories in babies between three and 18 months. Each of their temperament categories has a predominant way in which it organizes its attention, and these nine ways correlate strikingly to the nine Enneagram types and their respective habits of mind, focus of attention, and way of interacting with the world.

The Enneagram System

Ennea simply means nine in Greek. As the Greek word *pentagon* means a five-sided figure, it's easy to follow that an *enneagon* would have nine sides. *Gramma* is the Greek word for drawing, or something written. Hence, the direct translation of the word *enneagram* is that of a nine-sided drawing or figure, as shown in Figure 2.

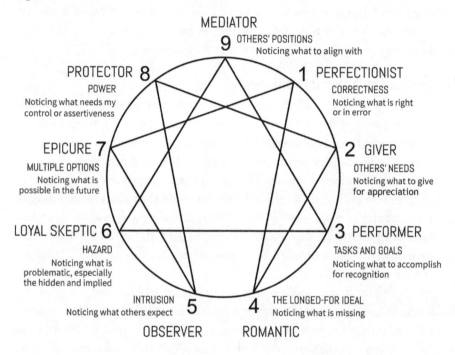

Figure 2: The Enneagram with Each Type's Focus of Attention

The Enneagram defines for us that there are nine distinctive and inherent ways of paying attention to reality, and each perspective drives certain identifiable thoughts, feelings, and ways of behaving *and* contributing to the world. Each of us tends to see a particular facet of reality in a given way, which means we do not individually see the full 360-degree view. We are, in fact, somewhat specialized.

As we were developing from infancy to adulthood, one of these nine ways of being and experiencing reality was supporting our development and driving much of how we interpret our experience. One of these nine cognitive filters and associated driving emotions set the patterning for the way the cells of our minds, hearts, and bodies adapted and strategized to express ourselves in the world.

These nine patterns are organized to protect us against psychological, emotional, and physical harm, and to cope with the pursuit of a safe, connected, and satisfying life. These cognitive filters and the associated driving emotions were also the exact same qualities we would use to protect core aspects of our essential selves in case of threat, abuse, neglect, or in the event we encountered devastating rejection by our caregivers in childhood.

However, the higher cognitive and emotional qualities within—and I do believe we come in with those—include our sense of self, our essential qualities, our particular aptitudes and strengths, and our higher qualities of personal hope, faith, and love.

The Fundamental Needs and Beliefs of Each Enneagram Type

Underneath each patterned set of attention-focused filters—the foundation of our Enneagram type structure—is something I have identified and named the **Basic Propositions**. It is a set of core beliefs that govern each type's existence and its beliefs around its survival, an agreement with self that dictates what it *must* and *must not be* in order to be its best self—a self that will be loved and accepted. The Basic Propositions are based on three critical, fundamental human needs:

The need for and a sense of dignity (self-worth), autonomy, and will (agency)

The need for love, bonding, and connection

The need for security and certainty

These underlying beliefs drive and further determine our focus of attention. In Enneagram terms, we call this focus of attention our "habit of mind." These underlying beliefs also drive how we direct much of our energy. In Enneagram terms, we call this the "driving emotion" of type.

While the development of the Basic Propositions is a foundational and very non-conscious process in our personality's development, these substantial patterns—along with their accompanying limiting qualities—are woven into our physiological fabric, which is the neural wiring of our very being and the driving emotional system of type.

All of this operates mostly non-consciously and automatically. Aspects of these patterns run themselves, even though they may no longer be what's called for in the present moment. Or even if they may be a relevant or appropriate response, they will still run habitually without much conscious awareness on our part.

Formed early on in our biological and environmental development, these patterns can keep us stuck in habitual responses and trigger reactivity that no longer serve us as useful or protective, even though they were originally intended to be just that and are some part of how we are driven to contribute to our species' evolutionary survival.

The Nine Enneagram Types Basic Propositions

Type 1 | The Perfectionist | The Basic Proposition
The original, undivided state of perfection in all things in each moment goes into the background in a world that Type 1s perceive judges and punishes bad behavior and impulses. Type 1s' disposition comes to believe that it gains worthiness and love by being good, correcting errors, and meeting the requirements of the critical mind. Concurrently, 1s develop resentment as a result of suppressing their anger or the guilt felt when responding organically to their impulses or when deeming their behavior—or themselves—as bad. Type 1s' attention is focused on errors and mistakes, unfairness, on taking responsibility, being dutiful and reliable, and by noting who is careless or wrong, or what needs fixing and improving.

Type 2 | The Giver | The Basic Proposition
The original state of personal freedom in which needs are met according to universal will and that of divine reciprocity goes into the background in a world that Type 2s have the propensity to perceive as, "I must give in order to receive." Type 2s' disposition comes to believe that they gain love and approval and can fulfill their personal needs only through their ability to give to others, care for others, and be unselfish and self-sacrificing. Concurrently, 2s develop a sense of being indispensable and become prideful when caring for others, believing they best know what others need. Type 2s' attention innately goes to others' needs and desires and often, are in denial of their own.

Type 3 | The Performer | The Basic Proposition
The original state of hope that trusts in the way things work according to universal law (which is not dependent on anyone's singular efforts) goes into the background in a world that Type 3s perceive rewards doing and performing, rather than being. Type 3s' disposition comes to believe that they can gain recognition, acceptance, and love through performance, doing and accomplishing, and success. Concurrently, 3s develop a go-ahead energy that includes self-deception

as they perform themselves into an image of some perceived success and approval. Type 3s' attention innately goes to tasks, goals, and performance, ensuring they succeed at *the image of the self* they desire and feel others desire or expect, and to succeed at the things they must accomplish in order to attain approval.

Type 4 | The Romantic | The Basic Proposition
The original ideal state of a deep and complete connection to oneself and to all things goes into the background in a world that Type 4s perceive won't accept them, abandons them, and leaves them feeling that *something of importance within it* is missing. Type 4s' disposition comes to believe that they can regain their connection, their lost "ideal state of love and beauty and union" by searching for the ultimate love or situation, one that is unique, ecstatic, special, meaningful and fulfilling. Concurrently, 4s develop an envy and a longing for what they idealize but that which always feels out of reach and unavailable, or is a something only others can attain. Type 4s' attention innately goes to *what could be* in conjunction with what is missing and lacking, which fundamentally leads to an ongoing relationship with disappointment, melancholy, frustration, defiance, or resignation.

Type 5 | The Observer | The Basic Proposition
The original omniscient state of direct knowing, the knowing of an existential energy that meets our fundamental needs, goes into the background in a world that Type 5s perceive demands too much and gives too little in return. Type 5s' disposition comes to believe that it needs protection from intrusions, from the threat of not having enough energy or capacity. It does this by assuring its life is lived through privacy and self-sufficiency, and by limiting its desires and by acquiring knowledge. Knowledge is the power needed to sustain the life force. Concurrently, 5s develop avarice for time, energy, knowledge, and specific possessions. Type 5s' attention innately goes to what is either physically or emotionally intrusive and then to detaching, to observe and figure it out on their own.

Type 6 | The Loyal Skeptic | The Basic Proposition
The original state of faith in self, others, and the world at large goes into the background in a world that Type 6s perceive is threatening, hazardous, unpredictable, and untrustworthy. Type 6s' disposition comes to believe that through vigilance, an active imagination, suspicion, and inquiry, it can assure a satisfying life of relative safety and certainty. Type 6s will either avoid what's fearful (the phobic stance), or they will face what's fearful head-on (the counter-

phobic stance). Type 6s are either escaping or battling perceived hazards and threats. Their attention innately goes to what could go wrong, potential hazards, worst-case scenarios—how to prepare for them and deal with them. Attention also focuses on safety, trust and betrayal, and on how to prevent helplessness and defenselessness that would leave it unable to rely on itself or cope with life.

Type 7 | The Epicure | The Basic Proposition
The original state of directed attention and concentration, also called constancy, which includes an ability to experience the full spectrum of life's many stimulating offerings attentively and freely, goes into the background in a world that Type 7s perceive to be frustrating and limiting. Type 7s use their capacities to redirect quickly to avoid pain and suffering, getting bored, or getting stuck. Type 7s' disposition comes to believe that they must escape frustration and boredom and assure a good life by seeking options, opportunities, new stimuli, and new adventures. Concurrently, 7s develop a "gluttony of the mind" for positive possibilities, anticipation of pleasures, multiple ideas, and future plans. Type 7s' attention innately goes to positive options, stimulation, deflection, and keeping life upbeat.

Type 8 | The Protector | The Basic Proposition
The original innocent state of knowing that truth is essentially the foundation of everything—and everyone—goes into the background in a world that Type 8s perceive as harsh, dominating, and unjust; where the powerful take advantage of the weak. Type 8s' disposition comes to believe that they can assure their personal sovereignty and gain respect and regard by becoming strong and powerful, by imposing their own personal truth, and by hiding their vulnerability. Concurrently, 8s are imbued with a robust, exuberant energy. Type 8s' attention innately goes to injustices, what's unfair, dishonest, and overpowering, and to what needs control, power, protection, and assertiveness.

Type 9 | The Mediator | The Basic Proposition
The original blissful state of unconditional love and union, in which everyone belongs equally and reverently, goes into the background in a world that Type 9s perceive requires accommodation and self-negation. Type 9s' disposition comes to believe they must blend in with others, not stand out nor make a fuss, and this accommodating stance becomes the substitute for its own sense of self-worth and belonging. Type 9s believe they can gain belonging and acceptance by aligning selflessly with others and merging with their lives and agendas. Concurrently,

9s often disperse its energy into nonessential activities and develop an inertia (self-forgetting) toward its own priorities, self-agency, and limitations. Type 9's attention innately goes to others' directives, other's agendas, and environmental claims that trigger the 9's participation in the world.

> Having read the Basic Propositions of each type, and having viewed the diagram of each Enneagram Type's Focus of Attention, what Enneagram type resonates most with you?

What Triggers Anger (and the Potential for Conflict) for Each Type?

The Reward and Punishment Systems of Type

The Enneagram, as it turns out, uniquely highlights how each type structure is wired to certain behaviors *that make it feel good*, that induce that type's sense of self and self-worthiness. In studying the Enneagram, we come to see quite clearly that each type structure demonstrates a particular set of behaviors that bring forth its own "feel good about itself" positive response. This is their internal reward system, one that is hooked up to all those powerful neurotransmitters (feel-good biochemistry, particularly dopamine), which may, in fact, be at the root of certain types readily and innately carrying out certain behaviors over others.

Furthermore, we can feel downright bad about ourselves and either self-punish or self-shame for doing something that doesn't hit the mark we've set for ourselves. Our sense of who we are—or *must be*—gets rattled when we say or do something that is in conflict with our type structure's core beliefs, those beliefs that govern what we believe *we must be or do* to be loved.

The way we cognitively-emotionally self-approve (reward) or self-disapprove (shame) is, in the end, what inevitably controls our relationship to ourselves and our subsequent behaviors. Our internal cheerleader rewards us for being a certain way, while at the same time, our inner critic punishes us for not being a certain way. And all of this is either driven by or affects our biochemistry.

Looking at this from a biological perspective, there is biochemistry behind each individual's thoughts, feelings, and behaviors. With this being the case, each Enneagram type's definitive structure controls how it likes and dislikes to show up.

Each Enneagram type structure's approval system is wired succinctly to endogenous (that is, we make it ourselves) feel-good chemicals. What does that mean? When we feel approved of by ourselves or someone else, we light up with dopamine and serotonin.

Dopamine is a neurotransmitter that gets us moving; it motivates us. It gets us up to feed ourselves, go get things, and do things. It leaves us feeling empowered and capable, and proud of ourselves in the world.

Serotonin, another neurotransmitter, is a mood regulator. It's what makes us feel that life is good, that we are good, that the world is good. It's the happiness generator and mood regulator. We generate both these neurotransmitters for all sorts of reasons, including when we behave accordingly and feel good about ourselves.

The same is true for each Enneagram type's disapproval system. It is biochemically driven too. For each Enneagram type, there's a different set of outcomes that will launch the disapproval system: the self-shaming, self-incrimination system.

Chemicals involved here might include a viscerally felt, life-force-draining slump due to self-shaming, brought on by the parasympathetic nervous system. And self-incrimination—dealt so harshly—can stir up internalized or externalized rage that then attacks the self from the inside or others on the outside.

Conversely, disapproval—from self or from others—can decrease both dopamine and serotonin. With that, a lot of that "feel good about ourselves" gets washed away, leaving us feeling awful. Bummed out. Depressed.

Once we get to the point of feeling anxiety-stricken, the brain sends a message to do something about the situation and secretes adrenaline. Still, we can feel utterly freaked out, even panicked. It all depends on how bad the disapproval was, how we interpret it (this is important), and how coherent we are in order to fundamentally process any of it—the discomfort of it all, that is.

Let's explore how this works.

Take an Enneagram Type 1, the Perfectionist, for example. This type tends to feel good—gets a high, if you will, a dopamine and serotonin rush—when they have everything under control, organized and in order, straightened up and lined up. I've often heard Type 1s tell me they get happy after cleaning their house or organizing their garage! And a not-so-emotionally-developed Type 1 can even admit to getting a bit high, *feeling good,* when scolding someone, pointing out an error, or calling someone out about an inappropriate behavior, insisting, "They should have known better!"

Type 1s reward themselves for doing good deeds, for seeing themselves as a good person, and when acting on that fundamental self-view that pushes them to be good and right in the world. Their disapproval system kicks in when they make mistakes, don't have the right answers, leave things unfinished, were not appropriate, or when they themselves or others have deemed them bad or wrong in some way.

A Type 2 for example, the Giver, gets a dopamine high for taking care of someone, for giving something away because someone else needed it, for seeing themselves as kind and loving people—the one to turn to for help, guidance, or love. Their personal disapproval system kicks in when they say no to someone in need, when they don't jump up to help, when they see themselves being selfish, or when they start to feel they haven't done enough for someone. And they can really crash emotionally when their giving has gone unnoticed and unappreciated.

> Consider for a moment, even if you are not yet certain of your Enneagram type:
> - What do you do in your own life that makes you feel good about yourself?
> - What do you often find yourself punishing or judging yourself for?
> - What are some of the things you do that leave you feeling disappointment in yourself or ashamed?

The Enneagram is based on an individual's systemic core beliefs, as described by the Basic Propositions. These beliefs are what shape each respective individual's pursuit of a satisfying life and an acceptable sense of self—a life worthy of love.

The Enneagram sheds light on—with fascinating accuracy—the way each type's attention is directed and focused (in Enneagram terms: habit of mind), and how that focus of attention directs and guides an individual's energy (the driving emotion of type).

As such, the Enneagram gifts us with a powerful and dynamic way to understand human personality. In particular, it allows us to recognize how each given personality type has a talent, a proclivity, for its attention to be drawn to particular aspects of the world around it and its relational interactions.

The focus of attention for each type tends to be seemingly effortless and rather automatic. It can and is often—if not always—associated with a person's aptitudes and readily available innate strengths and talents.

Know Your Enneagram Type as Key to Healthy Relationships

Before we embark on the Enneagram type structures themselves, remember that as human beings, we share in common having a structure—a type pattern—in place. There simply is no escaping typology since we have a categorizing brain that naturally puts virtually everything into groupings, categories, and compartments.

The way this is initially formulated is based on our innate temperament. But we can escape the stereotyping when working with typologies by becoming self-aware and conscious, sovereign, individuated human beings.

We need to remember there is great variation from one human being to another, even among people of the same Enneagram type structure (meaning, people of the same originating temperament and innate propensities). We are mysterious, spiritual beings with much to explore beyond our survival-organizing Enneagram structures.

In *so* many ways we are one of a kind, including our unique and precious ways of loving, our individual sexual expression, our creative forces, and our wide-ranging capacities for vulnerability and intimacy.

And as human beings, we can adapt and adjust under all sorts of circumstances, even though we have a core Enneagram type structure that we rely on daily. It allows those with whom we are in relationship to recognize us, know us, and appreciate us across time.

Working with the Enneagram system brings forth tremendous understanding and compassion for the self and for others of all ages, and is, in my view, the most effective path for personal, relational, and spiritual development. Bar none, it is one of the most profound studies available for the development of personal intimacy, and it is such intimacy with oneself that is engendered when self-awareness meets self-compassion. And self-intimacy is what allows us to experience any level of intimacy with another. That's a fundamental tenet you'll continue to come across as you read this book.

Studies reveal that the Enneagram's habit of mind shows up in our very own neurobiology. We know that our neurons operate according to an interwoven flow of information and energy. We have come to understand that this flow of information is not just happenstance but is organized internally by our personality's neural propensities—our temperament—driving our particular habit of mind and focus of attention.

So, what happens when we engage in personal development? We literally alter the interwoven flow of information and energy across neurons. We change and accept aspects of ourselves. This demonstrates how our minds can use the brain to create a new, healthier view of reality along with new, more fulfilling relationships and emotional experiences. These findings are tremendously hopeful.

We now know we have the power to create new neural pathways and enhance our ability to integrate the flow of information and attention across our cognitive, emotional, physical, and spiritual systems. And it all begins with our awareness of it.

Integration of our reactions to life and our experience of it results in better and more rewarding lives—for ourselves and for those we love. The promise of enhanced relationships and deeper intimacies exists and can be experienced by all of us, if we choose to pursue it.

CHAPTER 5

How We Are Structured: Three Centers of Intellience and Three Aversive Emotions

So, how do our personalities—and our relationships for that matter—relate directly to our neurobiology? And why is this important or relevant? To begin with, affective neuroscience and the work of Dr. Jaak Panksepp tell us that humans share in common various intelligent emotional systems with mammals.

In particular, three aversive (that is, ones that don't feel very good) emotional systems are shared and are in place to ensure survival. In accordance with how the Enneagram system is diagrammed and structured, these three aversive emotional systems correlate with the three specifically identified centers of human intelligence.

Not One but Three Processors

We've been acculturated to believe that our intelligence resides solely in our brains—in our heads, in that gray matter between our ears. So much so, that it can be surprising to learn that neuroscience has actually proven the existence of three locations from which we experience and perceive. There are at least three intelligences within us that formulate impressions and that are processing energy and information.

What scientists have come to learn is that energy and information travels from the gut and from the heart to the brain to be integrated and processed. This energy and information are processed in conjunction with the recognition, cognition, and perceptions of the many mental faculties of our minds. This is energy and information that are received and perceived from within ourselves, from other people, and from the world around us.

We are living in a time where scientific knowledge is catching up with the deeper insights found in esoteric and spiritual traditions, those that have been informing us for thousands of years, including insight about these three highly complex human intelligences.

Perhaps in most mammals, these centers may be considered rudimentary (well, as far as we've been able to measure), but in humans, these three centers are quite sophisticated. Behavioral modeling experts and authors Grant Sousalu and Marvin Oka penned *mBraining—Using Your Multiple Brains to Do Cool Stuff.* In it, they offer practical methodologies to better communicate with and access these three highly intelligent sources of human knowing, feeling, and sensing.

What is it that we've readily considered the location of our intelligence? This might seem like a silly question because it's easy to recall the definition we've been taught since grade school, but let's revisit this and consider *this* definition:

Intelligence is a masterful controller of a nervous system, a network of neurons that captures and processes information as some kind of meaningful data, and it intricately interacts with energy.

With this working definition, our consideration expands. While we well know of the processing center that's located in our mental capacities, two other such processing networks—networks of neurons—have been found to exist and are located in the body. One of these networks is in and around the heart. And the other of these neuronal networks is located in the intestines.

All three of these locations have highly sophisticated, intrinsic clusters of neurons and have very distinct roles. This explains the clash between what we *think* and what we often *feel*—the battle between our heads and our hearts. Add to that the gut instinct we might have that sometimes overrides both the head and the heart. Only by understanding these three intelligences—these three *networks*—can we come to understand ourselves and others as the highly sensory, vastly complex beings that we truly are. I tend to look at our extraordinary complexities with reverence, compassion, and awe.

To add to this, Western psychology and our education systems have elevated head/mental intelligence (cognition) to prominence as *the* location of human intelligence. Our school systems and respective curricula are geared toward head-centered learning—that is, cognitive processing.

When it comes to kids, some do OK and even thrive in this kind of learning environment, but others do not and can struggle miserably. The struggle some have might just alert us to the fact that learning is an individual process; it may also alert us to the possibility that learning may be driven more predominantly from one of the other two centers of intelligence. If so, those of us driving from one of the other networks would do better if the learning environment recognized this and could better accommodate it.

These other two centers of intelligence—clusters of processing neurons—are located in the heart (intelligence of connection, belonging, love, and acceptance) and the other deeper and lower in the body, in the gut (intelligence of sensations, of mobility, self-governance, spatial orientation, and arrangement).

The Enneagram also acknowledges these three centers—the Head, Heart, and Body—and recognizes that each one operates in each of us. Each is necessary for our survival. When integrated, three-centered awareness and three-centered intelligence are made possible, which gives us access to the gifts of all three centers at all times.

Three Centers of Intelligence

The Enneagram system recognizes these three centers of intelligence, also sometimes referred to as "domains of perception." How astounding it is that such knowledge was demonstrated in the Enneagram's wisdom long before the profound scientific advances of today had identified these three powerful neuronal networks in the body.

The Gut/Body Center | Enneagram Types 8, 9, 1
The Gut/Body Center is also called the Instinctual Center or the Sensing-Moving-Mobilizing Center. Here we locate our physical sensations and the sense of our own presence: "I am here, and I exist." Or "Where do I end and others begin?" Our gut system upholds the integrity of—and is the command center of—our immune system. The Gut/Body Center also upholds our sense of nobility, self-worthiness, and dignity: "I exist; therefore, I matter." It has a sense of what's fair and just, harmonious and appropriate, is at the center of self-governance, and drives our ability to mobilize, self-direct with agency, and activate.

The Heart Center | Enneagram Types 2, 3, 4
The Heart Center is also called the Emotional Center or the Connecting Center. This center's focus is on the interpretations of the emotional systems within us that are loaded with clues and sensitivities about ourselves as we interact with others. This center registers how we're relating to others—acceptance and recognition, connection and resonance, as well as processes feeling wanted and feeling valued. The Heart Center monitors the gaze of others, the quality of that gaze, the attention we garner and seek, and our overall experience of camaraderie, love, and bonding.

The Head Center | Enneagram Types 5, 6, 7

The Head Center is also called the Mental Center or the Thinking Center. This center includes processes such as thinking, perceiving, and cognition. It recognizes things and makes meaning of them, remembers facts and data and events, processes calculations and formulations, constructs theories, discernments, and judgments, generates ideas, envisions and fantasizes, creates narratives, and masters language.

Three Aversive Emotional Systems: Fear, Distress/Sadness, and Anger

The Enneagram's interpretation of these three centers, thanks to the work of the Brain Group, has identified them as potentially wired to the three big aversive (don't feel real good and can't ignore them) mammalian emotional systems.

As several of us in the Enneagram community became aware of affective neuroscience, we came to realize how research on mammalian emotional systems correlated with and validated the very structure of the Enneagram system—its three centers of intelligence and its fundamental wisdom.

To elucidate, aversive emotions are hard on our biological system. They are mostly unwanted because they only show up when we're in trouble, whether perceived or real. And they feel very unpleasant.

Those emotions are designed to get our attention, in primitive terms, to save our lives, to get us to respond to some perceived threat and as quickly as possible. Their chemical composition includes (but is not limited to) cortisol, adrenaline, and norepinephrine—the infamous stress hormones. These stress-responsive emotional systems invigorate us to the point that we must take some sort of action, whether that be:

Fight—assert, attack, launch defensiveness

Flight—take off, escape, turn away from or avoid

Freeze—don't move, don't deal, or deny

Or, thanks to more cerebral capacity:
Fawn—comply, capitulate, negotiate, or manipulate

While each of these emotional reactions is survival-critical, we don't do well in life if these are constantly charged up and running. These threat responses are pretty overwhelming—emotionally and physiologically—and if turned on constantly, they literally wear us out.

The biochemistry of our threat-response system—while providing intense levels of power and response capacity—is damaging to the body and the spirit if sustained over time. Aversiveness aside (they do not feel good), they do exist for good reason. Inadvertently, they are beneficial in function and have our best intentions at heart. They are intrinsically wired to protect and support our sense of self and well-being, and they're there to ensure we survive.

Evolutionarily speaking, neither we nor our mammalian counterparts would have made it for long had these systems not been put in place biologically. Fortuitously, these aversive emotions get activated when our fundamental survival needs are not met, are threatened, or are not to our personal liking.

The three aversive systems and the center of intelligence they correlate with, coupled with the fundamental needs associated with them, are as follows:

Frustration/Anger/Rage | Corresponds to the Gut/Body Center (Types 8, 9, 1): These reactions occur when we experience a threat to our dignity, a violation to how we believe we ought to be treated (according to us), and when we cannot get what we want, are enslaved, or when dominated. When something's in our way, our autonomy is threatened. This reaction is related to the Gut/Body Center of Intelligence, which is the center that senses what is wrong about the world around us and how we need to take action to correct it, fulfill ourselves, pursue our freedom, get what we want, and honor our sense of self-worth, our dignity.

Separation-Distress/Sadness/Panic | Corresponds to the Heart Center, (Types 2, 3, 4): These emotional responses occur when we experience the loss of our basic need for connection and bonding. Sadness, akin to loneliness, is the human's conscious experience of the loss of connection all the way to it spiraling into an escalated panic, as in that screaming-wailing child lost in a store when desperately separated from its mother. These emotional responses are related to the Heart Center of Intelligence, which is the center that informs us about the profound need we have for bonding, love, care, attachment, and relationship.

Anxiety/Fear/Terror | Corresponds to the Head Center (Types 5, 6, 7):
These emotional responses occur when we experience a threat, challenge, or danger to our basic need for security, certainty, and safety. These emotional responses are related to the Head Center of Intelligence, which is the center that figures out what makes life feel certain and predictable, safe, and secure for us.

These three fundamental emotions, coupled with the centers of intelligence in which they are activated, are very powerful. They are high-alert reaction generators, and we need them. When at their max, our entire being perceives a life-and-death situation, and these emotions are what can take us out of control into states of all-over chaos or lock-down rigidity.

Learning how to recognize, honor, and then modulate (tune and balance) these systems leads to the successful development of personal self-mastery, allowing us to handle the challenges, trials, and tribulations of ordinary life without it all causing undue amounts of intrapersonal stress that are not in line with the circumstances of the environment or situation.

For example, lack of modulation in these areas has us in abject terror when we don't feel prepared for our performance review. Or a state of utter panic overtakes us when our girlfriend wants to break up with us. Or we go into a fit of explosive rage when our wife says, "I'm upset, we need to talk."

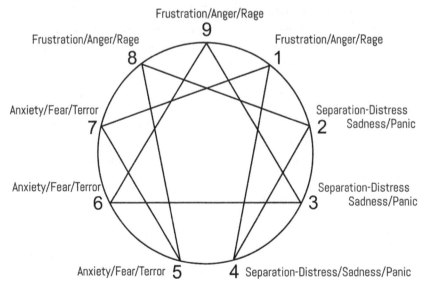

Figure 3: The Three Aversive Emotional Systems According to
Type and Center of Intelligence

> "
> Emotions [the basic aversive emotions] are complex, largely
> automated programs of actions concocted by evolution.
> Emotions are an integrated crown jewel of life regulation.
> ~ Antonio Damasio, PhD
> "

Working with Emotional Upheaval: Engaging with Our Reactivity

So, now we know what these big emotional systems are, what they do for us, and why we need them. But how do we deal with them? Here's what's critical to grasp. **While we may not want them, we do not want to circumvent them.** Our trying to avoid, suppress, sedate, or neglect these aversive emotions (fear, distress, and anger)—as so many of us do—is not what we want to do.

Avoiding and suppressing are not how to deal with them. Neither is repressing a healthy form of modulating aversive emotions. And sedating and neglecting also are *not* regulating. (Yes, all the time we confuse shutting them down with regulating.)

Not acknowledging the existence and upwelling of our aversive emotions across everyday life can hold us hostage and keep us from developing—both personally as well as in relationships. It also leads to the adaptation of an unprotected self, a self that has lost its necessary boundaries and self-caring limits, and a self that becomes disconnected from its authenticity. This encourages the formation of a non-authentic self—a self that manipulates itself into being something it's not but feels it should be. And then, it presents that contrived self instead to itself and to others.

But that's not to say these emotions do not have their proper place and purpose. We are not talking about *not* responding to the grizzly bear who enters our cabin at Yosemite National Park! *Drop the modulating and regulating and run!*

We're also not talking about the immense sadness and distress felt when losing a loved one, taking us to bouts of wailing or hysterical crying. *Leave the self-control at the door and allow ourselves to grieve fully the loss that needs to be expressed!*

Neither are we talking about controlling our rage when needing to defend ourselves from a dangerous other or when we've been threatened or violated due to assault or violence. *Forget relaxing into the anger, so as to not blow our tops—it's time to rage and save ourselves!*

Aside from those more extreme examples, not expressing healthfully our aversive emotions when they arise *can* and *does* lead to holding in place childhood-learned, no-longer-flexible adaptations as well as conditioned, negative core beliefs and subsequent reactivity—none of which serves us as we set out to conquer the world and build a fulfilling life.

It's because these visceral, aversive emotions can ignite habitual patterns of defensive thinking and acting that are driven from earlier conflicts or traumas and that are now—incongruous with reality as it may be—presenting itself. By adulthood, many of these highly reactive, aversive emotional defenses may have deeply embedded themselves in our structures and often (like, almost always) are not consciously understood and their origins not easily reaccessed.

Many of these habitual patterns of ours actually stir—even *ignite!*—a pot of inter- and intra-personal conflict that messes with our lives instead of effectively ensuring our imminent survival and fulfillment.

It's a worthy endeavor to devote ourselves to understanding, with great care and compassion, any and all of our aversive emotional systems when they've been activated. How much disturbance do they cause? Also called "affect dysregulation," studying these emotions and how often we are faced with them puts us on the road to self-development as well as thoughtful and appropriate emotional *stabilization—not suppression—*and leads to far less internal and external turmoil from unconsciously erupting in our lives.

Consciously and Proactively Coping with Aversive Emotions

What do we do now? Here's where the work of inquiry from a grounded (conscious sense of the self in the physical world), openhearted (present and receptive to our own and another's feeling states), and undefended (unassuming and curious) stance is the answer to all great questions.

In the grips of an aversive emotion siege, try genuinely asking, "Is this emotion telling me something of value? Is this feeling necessary right now to ensure my survival and well-being? Is avoiding this feeling and instead, becoming defensive or reactive, just 'old stuff' that is no longer working in my life or in this relationship?"

This process of inquiry, further discussed in Chapter 9, provides the path to freedom from the inadvertent tyranny and domination of old patterns and defenses, those based on *not wanting to feel* the discomfort of fear, separation, distress, or anger.

In learning to bring these powerful, rapidly erupting, reactive emotions to conscious awareness and allowing ourselves to question their authenticity in the moment, we can grow new cognitive-emotional structures in the form of new neural networks. Now we can modulate and regulate as necessary, as needed and deemed more beneficial, healthier responses for us and for those in our lives.

We Really Can Change

Why is a good process for self-inquiry important—inquiry that helps us engage with these aversive emotions more proactively? Because when this happens, we grow. We change. We have far more behavioral choices, many of which we'll find far more appropriate for the current moment or situation. With practice and repeated application, we can expand our neurobiological wiring to a varied, more flexible, and more nuanced repertoire of emotional and behavioral responses. The scientific term for this development process is *neuroplasticity*.

There is now abundant evidence that our brains can and do rewire—remain "plastic"—and are eminently capable of developmental flexibility and structural change throughout our lives. So, for all of us—wounded in childhood, battered or abused, neglected and traumatized, ignored and unattuned to—who find ourselves often swimming in aversive emotional upheavals, there is hope! There is definitive hope.

Integrating the Three Definitive Intelligences

The ability to recognize, value, and integrate all three of our centers of intelligence is crucial to attaining a fulfilling experience of ourselves and to cultivating relationships with others that thrive. It is vital to balance these within ourselves first, and then within our relationships. How we do that?

As it turns out, while each of us relies on all three centers to some degree, each one of the nine Enneagram types relies more heavily on *one* of the centers. Until, of course, we do the work of bringing all three equally online so to speak, which is a worthwhile pursuit and one we are certainly exposed to and encouraged to do as we continue to work with the Enneagram.

Discovering which center predominately drives each of us is of particular value, because knowing this is the gateway to bringing our dominant center of intelligence into balance with the other two centers.

For example, if in a relationship one of us leads with the Head Center and the other with the Gut/Body Center, we might want to ask ourselves, *Have I caringly acknowledged my partner today? How did I make them feel when I first greeted them? (That is, turning on the Heart Center of Intelligence.)* Or *Did I dismiss my partner's concern about the inappropriate and overpowering way he says his boss interacted with him during his morning meeting?* (That is, turning on the Gut/ Body Center of Intelligence.)

Leading with the Gut/Body Center: Types 8, 9, and 1

If we are leading with the Gut/Body Center of Intelligence, we tend to filter the world through an intelligence of our kinesthetic sense of movement, spatial acuity, our position in space and physical presence, our physical or somatic sensations, our sensate knowing, and our gut instincts. We use personal dignity and power to make life conform to the way it could be and should be and to get what we want. We tend to devise strategies that assure our place in the world, ensure our autonomy, and control those aspects of life to minimize discomfort.

All types depend upon the Gut/Body Center of Intelligence to develop the higher qualities of being that keep us in touch with the energy needed for action, to discern how much power to use in order to get what we want and value, and to supply a sense of being grounded in the world, as well as, how to be fair and correct.

In infancy, though not conscious of it, we are innately grounded in the present moment. Across our entire lives, it is the Gut/Body Center that has the wisdom within it to bring us back to the present. When we are truly grounded, we know who and where we are in time, space, and in our lives.

This center's intelligence is what we use to develop healthy personal boundaries, giving us our own sense of personhood from which we can move through life and move healthily toward constructive and dignified connections with others and our contributory purpose.

Effects on Our Lives

When we are driving from the Gut/Body Center of Intelligence, we can become indolent (self-forgetting and languid) at times. We can also become over-exerting, *push-too-hard* machines swept up in sensate experience. We may lack the perspective of thought and analysis (Head Center attributes) and may lack the perspective of our feelings, of our neediness, and of our need for bonding (Heart Center attributes).

What this tends to look like is someone who senses what's up in the moment and acts out accordingly—for better or for worse.

When driving from the Gut/Body Center, we can move impulsively or with a false and inappropriate sense of self-assurance. We may rush to judgment, believe we have agreement when we don't, or get overly critical about others' stances.

With insufficient balance from the Head and Heart Centers, our impact on others and the longer-term consequences of our actions may not be taken into account. Action needs to be balanced with thoughtful reflection (Head Center) and empathetic understanding (Heart Center).

Those of us who lead from the Gut/Body Center of Intelligence particularly need to learn to go against our natural grain to take action (or subdue), and instead pause. When pausing, we ground ourselves in the now and reflect on these potentially ineffective aspects of this center's style, making sure instead to integrate the qualities of both the Head and Heart Centers. The result of this integration can be surprisingly powerful.

> **Gut/Body Center** Key Words/Key Sensitivities: Dignity, self-worth, congruence, personal power, protection, comfort, taking action, justice and correction, harmonizing, and a sense of belonging. When we don't experience these qualities, we react with frustration, anger, or rage, as do all mammals, along with variations of anger particular to humans. Those include irritation, resentment, irritability, agitation, and impatience.

Case Story

Ross entered counseling expressing anger about how he experiences his partner, Xia's, off-the-wall accusations. Ross leads with the Gut/Body Center of Intelligence. Ross tends to sense things and respond sometimes quickly, sometimes slowly (since his gut reaction may take time to build), but often, without much forethought or analysis. This gets his partner, Xia, who leads with the Head Center, really upset. She tenses up, pulls away, and starts asking Ross challenging questions.

From Xia's perspective, she is just trying to figure out Ross's reaction, "What does that mean? How did you come up with that?" Xia loves Ross's grounded energy and ability to truly be present to her, yet she often reacts this way when he doesn't seem clear to her or when she just doesn't understand him. In turn, Ross feels demeaned and accused, leading to angry gut reactivity. Sometimes he sinks into a sulking withdrawal and at other times reacts with a sudden eruption rather than pausing and thoughtfully inquiring of himself what his gut hunch, reaction, is all about. This leads to a circle of escalating conflict, resulting in them both withdrawing.

In our work together, Ross came to better understand the strengths and challenges of his body-based intelligence, and he learned to pause before responding, do more analysis first, (a Head Center attribute), and realize and appreciate Xia's leading with head-based intelligence. As he became aware of his tendency to lead with body-based, gut intelligence and appreciated that Xia leads with her analytical, head-based intelligence, he began to work with his challenges. He was able to greatly reduce the repeated and disruptive episodes in their lives. While Xia never entered the counseling process, she did extensive reading about the Enneagram and the three centers of intelligence.

As a result of her study and Ross's changes, Xia greatly reduced her accusatory questioning and has been more forthcoming to apologize when needed for her over-questioning—at least, according to Ross. It's remarkable the changes that take place from understanding the function of the three centers of intelligence and how this functionality manifests in our thoughts, feelings, and actions and how they impact our transactions with one another.

Leading with the Heart Center: Types 2, 3, and 4

If we lead with the Heart Center of Intelligence, we tend to perceive the world through an intelligence that focuses on relating, connecting, bonding, feeling, and being felt. We are attuned to the mood and feeling states of others in order to meet our needs for acceptance, contact, affection, connection, and approval. We depend more than other types upon the recognition and admiration of others in order to support our self-esteem and fulfill our deep need for love and connection, as well as to feel and come to know our value.

To assure that we receive this approval and recognition, we tend to create an image of ourselves that will get others to desire and accept us, even see us as special. Furthermore, the power of this center is amplified by the positive emotion called *care*, the good feeling that comes from the bonds we experience through our relationships—an emotion and need also shared with all mammals. The mammalian mother-child bond exemplifies this magnificently. Every Enneagram type relies on connecting intelligence to experience and develop the higher qualities of the Heart Center, which include empathy, appreciation, understanding, caring-ness, compassion, and loving-kindness.

Effects on Our Lives

When we are driving from the Heart Center, we can lose the sense of grounding and perspective that the Gut/Body and Head Centers provide, and instead, find ourselves engulfed in seeking emotional responses from others that support our desired image of ourselves, and that we gain that desirable image in the eyes of others. We can pay too much attention to the bonds we have with others—their feelings toward us, which affects our own feelings about ourselves. And then, we defer back to *their feelings toward us* all over again.

This can lead to a submersion into the theme of "how we're getting along or getting liked or getting approved of (or not)" without sufficient task-orientation, cognitive analysis, or the maintenance of enough grounded presence within ourselves. This, in turn, can lead to a dependency on approval and the need for assurance—are we portraying a good, likable, desirable persona? What's called for, along with heartfelt feelings, is to have a balance of thoughtful reflection combined with a willingness to *engage objectively* when dealing with emotional as well as conflict-laden issues (Head Center attributes). It's also important to have the impetus to move forward appropriately and with integrity with timely decisions and actions (Gut/Body Center attributes).

Those of us dominated by the Heart Center of Intelligence particularly need to learn to go against our natural tendency and pause, ground the self in the now, and reflect on these potentially ineffective aspects of this center's style, making sure instead to integrate the qualities of both the Head and Gut/Body Centers as mentioned above. The result of this integration can be surprisingly pleasing, effective, and self-affirming.

Heart Center Key Words/Key Sensitivities: Love, connection, appreciation, affection, bonding, image, feeling, recognition, and approval. When we don't experience these qualities, we react with separation distress, sadness, or panic as do all mammals, along with variations of relational distress particular to humans such as yearning, longing, loneliness, and shame.

Case Story

Rosemary leads with the Heart Center of Intelligence. She wanted to experience what her partner, Peter, a Gut/Body Center type, *feels*, but not so much was Rosemary interested in what Peter *senses* and *does*. While she loves Peter's gutsy, forthright energy, and concern for Rosemary *getting what she wants*, she keeps longing for him to express his heartfelt feelings. She wants to be admired and appreciated, not just attended to.

Rosemary gets emotional, meaning expressive, emphatic, intense, and even tearful when Peter doesn't seem to approve of her—how she looks, what she feels, or what she longs for. He loves the taste of good food, but how it's presented doesn't matter to him like it does to Rosemary. She would welcome long conversations about relationships and what matters to her, saying, "I want you tuned into my feelings, my emotions!" But Peter expresses love with an energetic presence and with physical contact—hugs and sexuality, which Rosemary adores, but she says, "He never tells me he loves me. He never likes how I look, nor does he ever tell me how I make him feel."

This pattern, repeated over and over again, gradually resulted in a widening breach in their relationship. When they came upon the Enneagram and attended my seminar on the three centers of intelligence and relationships, they both became aware of the imbalance—where their respective focus of attention tended to go was not engendering compatibility. Regarding Rosemary, she almost immediately realized the way she experiences love was *just different* than Peter's.

Given her new awareness, Rosemary worked on noticing and better managing her rising emotional needs, their expression, and on her longing for recognition. She paused more to reflect on what really mattered and to appreciate the way Peter did express his care for her. She allowed time for thoughtful reflection (a Head Center attribute) and moved more readily into action (a Gut/Body Center attribute).

Peter, in embracing the Enneagram understandings and the vital importance of the three centers of intelligence, practiced bringing more attention to his Heart Center, asking himself what he is feeling, and importantly, expressing his love directly in words of care, admiration, and encouragement. As a result, their love thrived anew.

Leading with the Head Center: Types 5, 6, and 7

If we lead with the Head Center of Intelligence, we tend to filter the world through the mental faculties. The goals of this strategy are to minimize fear, to manage potentially painful situations ahead of time, to be prepared, and to gain a sense of certainty by employing thought processes of analyzing, envisioning, imagining, anticipating, preparing, and planning.

If we can figure out the world, understand and anticipate its requirements, we can gain security, plan and prepare, know the rules and abide, and assess risks. This requires anticipating the future—both positive and potentially threatening manifestations—and developing well-thought-out strategies to live by and resolve conflicts. All types depend upon mental intelligence to develop the higher qualities of the Head Center such as thoughtfulness, preparedness, anticipation, prediction, analysis, intellectualization, discernment, wisdom, comprehension, and higher knowing.

Effects on Our Lives

When we are enmeshed in the Head Center of Intelligence, we can lose contact with the vital instincts and the groundedness of our being (Gut/Body Center attributes), as well as nurturance from, and connection with, others (Heart Center attributes). For without sensations and feelings, we are unable to truly feel ourselves or to love fully. Some get frozen, paralyzed in the Head Center, figuring things out (analysis paralysis). Others can become overwhelmed with information and data, and simply check out. There can be too many ideas and not enough passion, fire, and expression of emotion to manifest a strong connection and bond with what we are doing or engaging with. We all need emotion and life-giving passion from our Heart and Gut/Body Centers to arise and ignite us, to love ourselves and others, and to participate fully in the world.

Those of us leading from the Head Center of Intelligence particularly need to learn to go against our natural inclinations and pause, ground ourselves in the now, bring attention to our heart and to our feelings, move into our power and our dignity. We need to reflect on these potentially ineffective aspects of this center's style while making sure instead to integrate the qualities of both the Heart and Gut/Body Centers as mentioned above. The result of this integration can be surprisingly effective, tenderizing, and mobilizing.

Head Center Key Words/Key Sensitivities: Security, safety, certainty, assurance, predictability, preparedness, thinking, anticipation, and opportunity. When we don't experience these qualities, we react with anxiety, fear, terror, as do all mammals, along with variations of these, particular to humans, such as angst, wariness, doubt, and apprehension.

Case Story

Bea, leading with the Head Center of Intelligence, came into counseling saying, "Juan just never stops to think. He just seems to go with whatever he is feeling." (Bea wasn't making any distinction between feelings and gut impulses). She wanted more careful analysis, wanted to prepare for both the best and worst that could happen, and wanted acknowledgment for her efforts to understand things. "It drives me crazy my having to cover all the bases, figure things out, and do all the meticulous planning." Bea had no awareness that she was owned by the Head Center of Intelligence, which was compounded by her worrying about the well-being of their two young children. Juan, who came into counseling with Bea, leads with the Heart Center of Intelligence.

It frustrated him that, "So much of our time together just goes into figuring things out, it feels unending." And he expressed this with much emotional intensity. While they clearly cared about each other, this *conflict of intelligences* had created a gulf in their relationship, pretty much ending the "honeymoon." Here it was the guy wanting more expression of feelings and longer and deeper conversations, and the gal wanting more intellectual analysis. In grasping the Enneagram's emphasis on three centers of intelligence, they could see how they each lead with predominantly different centers. This was a huge wakeup call for both of them.

Bea learned to pause when her mental pace picked up along with the anxiety and tension she regularly felt in her thorax and neck. This was common, she said, whenever she succumbed to her frenzied thinking pace. She calmed herself with slow and conscious breathing and put attention on asking herself what she was feeling in her heart and sensing in her body. She came to the awareness that she was over-analyzing things, believing this was the path to security. And Juan practiced calming his feelings by noticing them rising in his gut and heart areas. He came to appreciate Bea's Head Center point of view, as an expression of care for him and the children, and she for his Heart Center's feeling-based point of view, as Juan's way of caring for his family.

In a matter of a few weeks, the honeymoon was rekindled as they both came to putting more attention on the physical relationship, the Gut/Body Center being their least attended-to center. They had begun to successfully rediscover the critical closeness they needed to grow stronger together and stay committed.

While all three centers are essential to relationships, it's the Heart Center that tells us most about our bonds. It's our connection to others in the end that is most central to our experience of relationships. Understanding the neurobiology of bonding further validates the vital importance of our connections, of the love we receive and then cultivate in our lives. Our neurobiology is testimony to how we are wired for relationships. We all need to grasp the simple fundamentals of this wiring to truly appreciate how relationships are at the core of our development and our entire experience of belonging to one another, and to the whole of humanity.

Balancing the Three Centers of Intelligence

If you are new to the Enneagram, begin to think about what center of intelligence dominates your aptitudes and propensities and how there might be a different dominant center of intelligence operating for your significant other, family members, and co-workers.

If you find that the Head Center (analyzing) dominates and you tend to react with fear, anxiety, and questioning, your key will be learning to respond more consciously to Heart Center (feeling) and Gut/Body Center (sensing) types of people.

And if your Heart Center (feeling) dominates and you react with separation distress, sadness, and a yearning for connection, and find yourself readily approaching others to connect, your key will be learning to respond more consciously to Head Center (analyzing) and Gut/Body Center (sensing) types of people.

In the same vein, if your Gut/Body Center (sensing) dominates and you tend to react first with frustration, resentment, or outright anger and find yourself attempting to right perceived wrongs and injustices, your key will be learning to respond more thoughtfully and caringly to Head Center (analyzing) and Heart Center (feeling) types of people.

While we each possess each of the three centers of intelligence, one tends to be our leading or driving center, with the other two awaiting further development to greater or lesser degrees. Notably, our driving center is where we will find many of our innate proclivities and talents. It's also where we'll learn we have the most liabilities and blind spots as well.

Development that focuses on our driving center followed by conscious effort that brings our other two centers to the foreground brings us to a more balanced three-centered capacity—an "all cylinders online and contributing" capacity. And *that's* what's optimal.

CHAPTER 6

Self-Development Using the Enneagram

If you are new to the Enneagram or somewhat familiar but unsure about your Enneagram type, please take a moment and read *The Essential Enneagram* by David Daniels, MD and Virginia Price, PhD, as it includes an Enneagram test in the front. Or you can take the test online at narrativeenneagram.org. These tests are a good place to begin your inquiry.

You can also visit drdaviddaniels.com for more information on the Enneagram as well as a multitude of correlated teachings and information.

The Enneagram System: How to Work with It and Why It's So Incredibly Useful

As was shared in Chapter 4, the Enneagram points us at an intelligently organized hardwiring of neural propensities—a temperament—and a corresponding true nature or essence (qualities of being). These are the originating qualities of self that underline what we have to work with—lean into—as we start out in the world and first meet our parenting caregivers. All the resources we have available inside ourselves, that we serve up to deal with the kind of childhood and nurturance we receive and encounter (or not) become the foundation of our character structure's eventual and ongoing development.

Our different wiring is what accounts for our differences as siblings. For instance, one of us deals with mom's rage one way, while another sibling deals with it another way—*their temperament's way, their wiring's way.*

We each develop our own methods for coping and form definitive solutions for handling difficulty and adversity as well as for ensuring we can somehow be loved. We pull from our strengths—it's what we call up each time to best manage our developing selves. It's the organizing system within that responds and adapts to our parenting caregivers and to the world.

As we grow, we are laying down all of what gets conditioned or potentiated along the way, including our defense patterns, our innate as well as learned forms of self-expression and coping mechanisms, and our overall level of developmental well-being—all things said and done—takes shape.

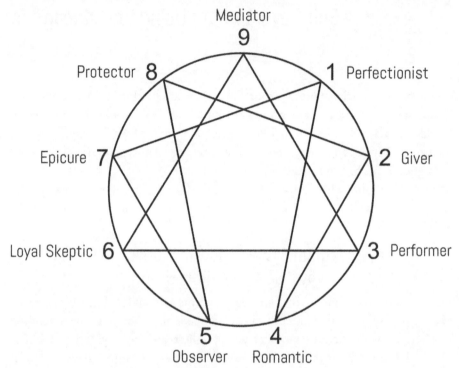

Figure 4: The Enneagram and the Nine Type Structures by Name

We Can Relate to All Types

Each of the nine type structures is part of a greater whole, which is represented by the circle you see in the diagram above. In fact, while we drive ourselves from one of these organizing structures more predominately (and will do so across our lives), we'll be able to see *a little bit (or a lot)* of each of the type's propensities in ourselves—some more than others.

Basically, we are all part of the greater soup of the human condition. The commonalities shared by one another allow us to understand and relate to each other successfully, collaboratively, and more definitively.

The Enneagram type structures of our parenting caregivers can also influence us, as do the two Enneagram types—called *wings*—that sit on either side of our own type on the diagrammed circle. Wings provide us with a few extra strategies, ones we'll use to carry out our core Enneagram type's purpose and aptitudes, beliefs and values. We'll tend to use one of our wings more often than the other. Consider the wing as giving your type structure a particular characteristic flavor—or a flair—and as such, it adds a "quality of being" and particular tendencies to your personality, if you will.

Starting Out on the Personal Development Path

Forget the complexities of the Enneagram for just a moment, as we don't need to understand it to simply get started. Let's look at ourselves in a way that we can all easily relate to: Each of us seems to have registered that we've got a "best self" and a "not-so-best" self. With zero personal development study whatsoever, we're all aware to some degree what these two selves are like. We're on top of the world when in our best self, and struggling to grasp that bottom rung when living out the other.

In our best self, we tend to feel good, confident, perhaps even upbeat, full of energy, and optimistic. We seem to know what we're doing and where we're going. We may have feelings of pride and dignity, satisfaction and strength, kindness and anticipation, and feel accomplished and worthy.

But when in our not-so-best self, the world can feel exhausting. We may be overwhelmed, feel burdened, insecure, or unworthy, or find ourselves complaining and whining about almost everything, or blaming and accusing, wondering why anyone likes us at all—or why we like anyone at all! We just want to crawl into a dark hole, as it all just feels like too much!

This is where we begin. We start with what we can see, with an acknowledgment of how our experience of ourselves can fluctuate. And the next question is, "Why is that?"

I don't know about you, but chances are you're like the rest of us, and time spent in our not-so-best selves sucks. I want to know how *not* to bring that onto myself, let alone onto my relationships. But this is exactly what happens when we don't know ourselves very well. These fluctuations between our best and worst selves pretty much do their thing and carry us along without our having much say or control over those fluctuations.

If we're interacting with others without knowing or understanding ourselves, then the best we'll be able to do, in truth, is show up one day as our best self, and the next day or so, as our not-so-best. And both we and our relationships just have to deal with it, and that's that.

We don't know any better, and in most cases, we are not tuned into the impact either. This cycle repeats itself for the entirety of our existence, across all our significant relationships, including those relationships we are having with our vulnerable, needs-us-so-much, developing children.

Ultimately, this cycle becomes the only experience of ourselves we and those who love us ever come to know. Many of these why-do-they-happen-to-me patterns don't actually work for us; they get in our way and can even hurt others and ourselves, over and over again. But we still run them, because *we don't know a way out.*

Trying to *will* them away with white knuckles and a fierce affirmation but without a clarity around their *systemic and originating emotional survival benefit*— let alone compassion for ourselves or understanding—is intensely hard work and (almost always) exhaustingly futile.

What the Enneagram brings us is a definitive way to map the best self and not-so-best self with amazingly incisive accuracy and insights, highlighting the profound complexities that make us who we are.

Once we learn the Enneagram—particularly, once we first land our own type structure accurately, *which is where we have the most developmental work to do and where our greatest aptitudes are found too*—a whole lot of information opens up for us. This can save eons of time otherwise spent on hit-and-miss, slow-going self-discovery and personalized postulation that may or may not bring forth a useful depth of understanding or a developmental path for growth.

The Enneagram system is, in my honest opinion, the *only typology* out there today that accounts for both our *unique differences* as well as our *commonalities,* which are all part of our evolutionary process and so cleverly designed for our collective survival.

Self-Discovery: Tracking Our Focus of Attention

Because the Enneagram sheds light on the way personalities are organized from the inside out, it gives us our type's particular slice of reality. Understanding this fuels a curiosity that fosters self-discovery, self-observation, and self-inquiry— the keys to coming to actually know ourselves *well.*

While it's interesting to consider the personality structures of those closest to us or ask someone else what type they think we are, *the discernment of our own type is fundamentally an inside job.* We have to look inside, into the interiority of our thoughts, feelings, and ways of behaving, and we have to get receptive and incisive about what triggers what.

After all of that, we must ask ourselves, "*Why?*"

How accurate we are at determining our type structure—especially when we first embark on this study—depends fully on *how honest we're capable of being with ourselves.* How capable are we at self-witnessing and how objectively can we do it?

It's worth asking ourselves, "Can I actually observe where my attention goes, as a matter of course? Can I track my thoughts? Can I track my many feelings as they are felt in my body, in my soma? And can I do so without editing them into something I can more readily accept? Can I watch my inner world of responses and meanderings, in action? Can I get honest about the mechanisms that guard my unmet needs and hurts, and how they may be running me, at any given time?"

This process is all about our *focus of attention.* But what does that even mean, and why's it so important? I developed a gentle inquiry process with several questions that will give us a guide as to *what* to notice in ourselves. (See Resources at the end of the book.)

Self-Discovery and Examination

On our path to self-discovery, some of what we find might not seem that big of a deal at first, but the fact that the nine Enneagram type structures *do not share the same focus of attention* is very important.

Each Enneagram type is extraordinarily, uniquely focused. An interesting way to look at it is by understanding the law of specialization. Specialization is when people specialize in one thing or another that they are good at. Specialization enables the accomplishment of otherwise unattainable goals.

> Specialization is when people specialize in one thing or another that they are good at. Specialization enables the accomplishment of otherwise unattainable goals.

We are, in fact, differentiated beings, specializing in a particular view of reality, and by focusing on some particular part of reality, we bring a particular perspective, talent, and aptitude to it as well. We get really good at our focus of attention, and we gift it to others as well as to ourselves. We gift it to the collective whole.

While you may be thinking this makes it hard for us to relate to one another, it's actually an extremely necessary aspect of our evolution. We are, as it turns out, architectured—not randomly but intelligently—to contribute in a certain way, and we do so *specifically.*

We are organized in such a way that our particular propensities contribute to a collective whole, one that has enabled the human race itself to survive and then thrive. Imagine again, as mentioned in an earlier chapter, what we'd overlook and fail to figure out if each of us focused on the exact same things, day in and day out? If we all tuned in to the detail and minutiae of building shelters and storing food, for example, who would be focused on tribal protection from warring enemies, the group dynamics of those out hunting, or laying down the rules and standards for civility and fairness?

Our various aptitudes, adaptive strategies, and focuses of attention are designed to coordinately contribute and to bring a benefit. That benefit is not only for ourselves, as it turns out, but is one that provides an incalculable benefit to one another. These definitive focuses of attention hope to ensure our existence and promote or delineate our possibilities.

Each of the nine personality structures is part of one larger organism (represented, if you remember, by the circle in the Enneagram symbol) that is greater than the sum of each of its nine distinctive, contributory parts. Without a doubt, each of the nine Enneagram structures—neural propensities/ temperaments—is something to reverently embrace, honor, and appreciatively cherish, because each serves a critical function to our collective experience and survival over time.

Eleven Basic Points About the Enneagram

As we continue to talk about the nine Enneagram type structures, here are important key points to keep in mind about the system itself:

1. **There are three energetic centers in the body.** In Enneagram-speak, human intelligence is categorized by identifying three energetic, neural-network centers of intelligence. These three centers are processing areas within us that receive and emit both energy and information that interact with both our inner worlds and our outer worlds. These centers are referred to as the Head Center, Heart Center, and Gut/Body Center.

2. **There are nine Enneagram type structures.** They are distinctive and reflect the unique qualities of differing temperaments.

3. **Each of the nine type structures is wired with valuable, contributory assets** to the survival of humanity, to the survival of the collective.

4. **It's important to take the time to decipher our own Enneagram type structure.** It's an intimate process and one that we can only, in the end, assess for ourselves. Doing so as honestly as possible allows us to more readily identify and own our essential qualities of being. The process of learning our type structure allows us to recognize our differentiating nature, our focus of attention, our talents and inherent

gifts, and our type structure's defense mechanisms, adaptive liabilities, and its weaknesses. Enneagram study also sheds light on our brand of emotional reactivity and how, when, and why it gets triggered.

5. **No Enneagram type is better than another**—or more advanced, more capable, more important than another. Nor are the Enneagram type numbers 1 to 9 hierarchical.

6. **Each Enneagram type is represented by a numeral.** While the number also has a name associated with it, we suggest we do not get hung up on the naming conventions assigned to each type, as they are only to be used as references. Think more of these type structures as dynamic energies that are imbued with aptitudes, sensitivities, and propensities.

7. **Each individual drives from one primary type structure,** although the system is complex and integrative. We do contain aspects of all nine type structures within our own framework, as we are designed to work together as well as relate to one another. We are, in fact, part and parcel of a whole in which we are dependent on each other as one collaborative humanity.

8. **Enneagram types are not gender-specific**—not in the typical sense.

9. **We do not change our driving center of intelligence during our lifetime.** However, this work of self-development allows us to bring all three centers of intelligence online—as fully operating energy and information processing centers—and into balance.

10. **We do not change our Enneagram type structure during our lifetime.** We are born with and will die with the same Enneagram type/neural propensity/temperament, but we *can* enhance our level of developmental well-being. And we do, in fact, have the capacity to change our level of mental health and emotional fitness—our response-flexibility and relational capacities, so to speak—which includes our level of presence and cognitive-emotional as well as spiritual well-being.

11. **Studying the Enneagram gives us a map to develop greater self-awareness and self-understanding.** It can greatly reduce the amount of time it takes to understand our personality, its gifts, and its liabilities. Because of that, the Enneagram can assist us to more readily progress our development and intrapersonal healing, allowing us the greatest chance to transform our lives and each and every one of our relationships for the better.

Levels of Developmental Well-Being

While there are nine personality type structures, there's also a need to calibrate *the state of that structure*, as in, its level of developmental well-being. *Developmental* refers to the process of development; the "how well" we cognitively and emotionally developed from infancy to adulthood. It's the development that happens as a result of direct experience, particularly, relational experience.

As we observe our own or another's Enneagram type, we also want to ask, "Is my own or another's personality structure in a *high* state of well-being?" or, "Does my level of developmental well-being or that of another exhibit qualities that are considered *lower*?"

This takes some fierce honesty to assess. *Remember: compassionate curiosity is a far cry from recrimination!* To keep this assessment very simple, the level of developmental well-being of a type, of a person, can rudimentarily be identified as follows:

High
Average
Low

What determines our level of developmental well-being, you might be asking? It's a critical question, and while this book is not a child-development book focused on etiology, there's surely a reason to mention child development again at this juncture.

There's no doubt that the kind of start we have with caregivers carries a significant weight when it comes to our level of developmental well-being. Developmental well-being begins with our early attachment bonds and experiences, that is, the *quality of attachment* we develop with our parenting caregivers.

In short, *secure attachment*, as it's understood, renders a *higher* level of developmental well-being while *disorganized attachment* can leave us suffering a much *lower* level of developmental well-being, which impacts us all along the way—and well into adulthood. (Chapter 3 covers attachment and its longer-term effects in some detail.)

For those of us who didn't have such a nurturing and bonding head start, we also now know through focused research that a securely attached individual expresses quite naturally the same seven to nine qualities of being as does an individual with a well-disciplined mindful awareness practice in place. Intention over time raises the level of presence and cognitive-emotional development and awareness. (This was discussed in Chapter 2. Remember: There is hope, because *we can change!*)

In 1995, the Centers for Disease Control and Prevention along with Kaiser Permanente studied 17,000 individuals regarding the impact of childhood trauma on adult well-being. The study was called the Adverse Childhood Experiences (ACEs) study. The results were overwhelmingly conclusive.

Our level of developmental well-being is, in fact, indisputably impacted by ACEs, and that include all forms of psychological, emotional, and physical adversity. These also include trauma, neglect, great losses as a child (as in divorce, death of a parenting caregiver, no parents or an incarcerated parent), or by suffering at the hands of parenting caregivers with one or more addictive disorders.

The ACEs study brought the impact of trauma and childhood adversity to the fore; it conclusively exposes the tremendous impact adversity has on the well-being of children and the ongoing suffering it eventuates in adulthood. And the ACEs study was sobering in that it brings the pain of childhood from the shadows of denial into the light of awareness. (What a tremendous study!)

Describing Low to High Developmental Well-Being

How much nurturance was available—all the time or only parts of the time— combined with a host of other complex factors that play into our overall development, shapes our level of developmental well-being. How we adapted depends too on how our particular temperament (Enneagram type) formulated its way of coping with the difficulties faced.

The level of developmental well-being helps us understand how defended, contracted, self-conscious, chronically anxious, belligerent, chronically frustrated, addicted, or defeated we are as we come out of childhood. There are four aspects to observe:

- How narrow is our window of tolerance (would say Dr. Dan Siegel) before we become emotionally dysregulated? A narrow window of tolerance tends to a low threshold for emotional arousal—meaning, we're easily and readily triggered.
- How frequently does it happen?

- To what intensity do we experience the dysregulation?
- How long does it take us to recover?

Understanding developmental well-being helps us identify traits suffered at lower levels, such as the ones just mentioned. Equally so, understanding varying levels of well-being also helps us to recognize how open, expansive, self-aware, self-confident and self-connected, response-flexible and adaptable, motivated and enthusiastic (about life) we are as well. These qualities more aptly describe a higher level of developmental well-being.

Higher Level of Developmental Well-Being

A *high* level of developmental well-being shows up as a mindful presence, an activated self-awareness, and with various differentiated parts of the self-system well integrated. High levels of well-being pave the way for more consistent access to both intrapersonal and interpersonal intimacy and vulnerability.

Emotional regulation and emotional stability are more the norm than not, and there's a skillful ability to self-soothe and self-connect as needed when facing challenges and upset. We are attentive, and we exhibit good response-flexibility. We are self-motivated, curious, empathetic, and sincere. We are thoughtful, kind, and gentle. We are accepting and loving, integral and respectful, discerning, self-sovereign, and self-honoring.

Lower Level of Developmental Well-Being

Perhaps we are somewhere on the spectrum toward a lower level of well-being. Lesser degrees of developmental well-being show up somewhere on an intensity scale regarding interpersonal and intrapersonal struggles. There's a tendency toward either cognitive-emotional rigidity or chaos—either of which can wreak havoc.

Mid to lower levels of well-being personalities tend to be more defended and *more often* defended, more controlling and less flexible, less honest and more reactive. Here we are prone to experiencing as well as expressing agitation, impatience, envy coupled with painful comparisons, varying levels of anxiety, depression, and apathy a lot of the time—or *almost all of the time.*

Poor impulse control, the inability to manage stress effectively, emotional dysregulation that is hard to relieve, defiance or conduct disorders may be prevalent. An inability to focus and concentrate—or sit still with oneself—may also plague us and result in childhood stress-induced attention-deficit/hyperactivity disorder, or ADHD.

With a *lower* level of developmental well-being, we struggle with life and struggle to soothe ourselves emotionally without assistance; we may turn to substances or various, addictive process disorders to alleviate psychological and emotional pain.

Average Level of Developmental Well-Being

And finally, an *average* level of developmental well-being contains expressions of both high and low, but there's a more stable experience of self with the ability to manage stress adequately enough. This assessment is dependent on the consideration of frequency and intensity, alongside the presence of consistent-enough self-soothing (or lack thereof) capacities.

These are among the more important differentiators in assessing where we're located on average and, most readily, developmentally. In this case, high-level attributes are intermittent, though sometimes experienced. Low-level attributes still plague one's experience of the world, of others, and of self when pushed hard enough, and cause discord.

We may struggle to stay present to ourselves, let alone others; we are a good way off from fully understanding our subconsciously deployed defense mechanisms, our full-on defendedness or reactivity, and often launch secondary, cover-up emotional reactions to protect against vulnerability and shame when triggered. We are unable to consistently interrupt these reactive patterns— sometimes we're more aware, sometimes we're not.

What Causes What

I tend to the growing understanding—and thanks again to the research of Thomas and Chess on identifying infant temperaments—that early trauma *is not* what determines our temperament, which infers that it does not *determine* our Enneagram type structure. That said, it sure can *shape* it.

Early attachment disturbances, trauma, and the whole of our upbringing— whether good or bad—*can* and *do directly impact* our level of developmental well-being. As we are for-survival structured beings, it's inevitable that we will rely on our organizing architecture (our temperament, our *nature*) to deal as adaptively best with the environment we're born into, be that one of trauma, neglect, and childhood emotional losses, or one of love and secure, loving attachment (that is, *nurture*.)

Our level of developmental well-being puts on display not *what's wrong or right with us*, but *what might have happened to us*, and how much development may have been hindered or potentiated along the way.

The Stories We Tell Ourselves

Beyond the set of facts of *what happened to us*, it's the stories we tell ourselves *as a result of what happened* that's the critical and perhaps even more important key to the long-term damage that results from adverse experiences—cognitively, emotionally, and spiritually.

As someone who loves recognizing patterns and studying them, I have found it quite interesting that *the stories we tell ourselves* as a result of any kind of childhood suffering tends *to tie back to those core propensities of cognition and emotion* over and over again, that which correlate with those core beliefs about the self, as is found in the nine Enneagram structures.

The Story and the Enneagram Type

The story a little Type 4 temperament will tell themselves when something goes wrong in their life, for example, will be a very *different story* than what a little Type 8 child will tell themselves when something goes wrong in their life, and so on. What we project onto a situation and how we interpret the same exact circumstances, type by type, are not often the same at all. And this is interesting. The why of this is calling for genuine curiosity, even further study.

All that being said, childhood trauma of all kinds and the corresponding emotional losses are a result of how it was *interpreted* by the suffering individual, which includes how it was *processed*, if at all.

Trauma's lasting effects, to a great degree, are what *contribute to* and perhaps greatly *determine* our adult self's level of developmental well-being.

One Enneagram Type, Three Possible Levels of Developmental Well-Being

As consideration of personality well-being comes online and into our awareness, we'll be able to see, for example, how three individuals of the same Enneagram type structure (and gender irrelative) may, in fact, be operating at three different levels of developmental well-being. They might feel to us and interact with us quite a bit differently from one another while still expressing the identifiable structure of a given Enneagram type, nonetheless.

Let's take Type 1, for example. One of those Type 1s may be operating at a highly present, highly integrated state of developmental well-being. This person will most likely feel open and approachable, thoughtful yet certain, receptive and kindly discerning.

Another Type 1 may be struggling at a lower level of well-being, which is where we'll see an intense level of rigidity, tension, perhaps high criticality, and an utter lack of presence. They seem to be *preaching at us* rather than *talking with us.*

And the third Type 1 may be operating somewhere in the middle (which is where a lot of us find ourselves having graduated a basic Western childhood), which may include moments of rigidity, then moments of presence, moments of discernment rather than judgment, then moments of judgment and criticality combined with moments of kindness and friendliness or coldness and avoidance—back and forth.

Our level of developmental well-being correlates directly with our level of self-awareness, cultivation of presence, and emotional stability. And if we didn't get our developmental needs met across childhood, don't be discouraged, *we can gift it to ourselves by embarking on a self-development process* now, one that includes a mindfulness practice!

Well-being is an important aspect of self- and other-understanding. Well-being serves as a barometer, if you will, of how we are and how cognitively-emotionally stable we are.

Developmental well-being has its critical place when looking at each of the nine Enneagram type structures and discerning how that type/person is showing up in the world and for themselves.

Well-being is how well our type structure functions to meet the demands of life, how well we feel inside of ourselves and with ourselves, as well as how we interact with others. It's foundational to building loving, sustainable relationships. Developmental well-being is the basis for how much we are able to potentiate the life we were born to live and enjoy.

The Higher Capacities and Path of Development for Each Enneagram Type

The following brief descriptions include a review of the core belief structures as formulated by each Enneagram type structure, with an emphasis on what's called the "Holy Idea" of each type. This, in essence, points at each type's higher self, their spiritual quality (the higher qualities it has to bring to the world). These type descriptions also include the consequential ways each type structure is organized around fundamental core beliefs and how those beliefs influence one's life.

Our type structures reveal relationship positives and hindrances. They also identify our original qualities of essence and the Holy Idea that goes into the background, to a greater or lesser degree, as our type structure's personality and level of well-being crystallize across our development.

Finally, we review key tips for each type's developmental growth in order to elevate our respective level of developmental well-being.

> As you read each of these Enneagram-type descriptions, try for a moment to identify with each of the types. Allow yourself to get a sense of each type's underlying perspective and way of being in the world. Appreciate what each type contributes. See which type tends to correlate with yourself as well as important others in your life.

The *process of development* for each of these nine type structures is fundamentally the same, as it turns out. **Although the process is simple, it is not always easy.** First, it requires we develop the ability to self-observe—to neutrally self-witness—and then cognitively and acceptingly recognize what we observe.

It requires that we train the capacity to get physically grounded so we can track our feelings and state of being as sensate experiences in our bodies—not deny what we sense or suppress it—and simply acknowledge what is present as well as its validity.

The process of development asks us to activate present-moment awareness. It asks that we consciously open ourselves to receptiveness, to focusing our attention on receiving energy and information from outside of ourselves and from within ourselves too, and without altering either.

It asks that we guide our hearts to becoming non-judgmental. And it asks that we engage a practice of self-inquiry, one that includes a genuine curiosity that enables us to discern what is in need of recognition, compassion, and acceptance. The process is simple but not easy.

Type 1 | The Perfectionist | Summary and Tips

There is an innate calling for and a sense of **perfection** in Type 1, that which is found in the original, undivided state of everything being exactly perfect in each moment, just as it is. It's the ideal experience found in the utterly accepting, nurturing, peace-giving, mother-infant relationship. For a Type 1, this essential state of perfection is what goes into the background in a world that we come to perceive as imperfect and flawed, one that needs improving and one that judges, condemns, and punishes bad behavior and uncontrolled impulses. We Type 1s have the propensity to align ourselves with the belief that to assure a good and satisfying life, we must be perfect ourselves. We must be good and right and not be wrong or below the mark in a world that we experience demands good behavior, and in one way or another, punishes bad behavior.

As a Type 1, we unsurprisingly and readily develop a judging-sorting mind that is governed by a strong inner critic, one that is fueled by a somewhat covert anger that seemingly protects us. It sets high standards to which we must fervently live in accordance with and abide. Our attention innately goes to what's wrong, incomplete, unfinished, not organized, or in disarray. We focus innately on that which strikes us as improper as well as on what needs to be improved, fixed, corrected or changed.

There's a deep care in Type 1 that is fueled by an energized frustration, that—if directed effectively—can bring forth (even catalyze) immense change, much-needed improvements, and necessary structure in the world. Subsequently, in our relationships we are conscientious, responsible, improvement-oriented, and generally self-controlled; however, we can also hinder our relationships by being critical, resentful, and judgmental, even scolding of ourselves and of others (particularly when not at a high level of developmental well-being).

We tend to be practical and diligent in regard to the tasks and responsibilities of daily life. Congruent with that anger—often in the form of tension, irritation, agitation, or frustration—resides our drive along with seemingly endless amounts of energy and conviction to do good.

Anger alerts us to what is incongruent with our definitive standards and with the ways we feel things could be and should be. This is all in accordance with our view of what's needed in the world and of our place in it. Anger, as it turns out, is the mobilizing force of a Type 1's relentless determination, care, and conviction.

Tips for Growth: As a Type 1, we need to notice and then give ourselves permission to reduce the power we give away to critical judgment. Instead, we need to learn to rely on thoughtful discernment. We can and will be safe without that critical voice so harshly running the show. Observe the tendency to self- and other-punish–judge, scold, or berate–when errors are made. This automatic dynamic can be hard on relationships, in particular, the relationship to ourselves can suffer under such scrutiny and incrimination and impact our availability to love and receive. Learn new ways of engaging with perceived error and interacting with more conducive-to-well-being solutions for improvement and correction.

Also, as Type 1s, we need to accept and integrate our personal desires and pleasures into our lives, alongside our conscientiousness, dutifulness, high standards, and commitment to responsibilities. This not only enhances our own lives, but the lives of all those who love us and interact with us. Becoming more tolerant is a virtue worth exploring and allowing, as it can ease much unnecessary tension held in the soma (body).

We will also want to learn to discern if what we judge to be errors or wrongdoings are actually, or more simply, differences, ones that come from our fundamentally different aptitudes and talents. Allow ourselves to see these differences appreciatively and with gratitude, instead with condemnation or frustration.

Type 2 | The Giver | Summary and Tips

There is **freedom** rooted in the natural flow of deciding to give and in opening to receive; this is the hallmark of divine reciprocity. There is an innate understanding of this in the core essence of Type 2. Freedom frees us up to give unconditionally and to receive appreciatively. We experience freedom when we *do not* have to act on every impulse to help, care for, or serve others. What brings forth this freedom is our own humility, which is what goes into the background in a world that we perceive requires us to give to others in order to be loved by others. In other words, we are compelled to believing we must *give* to *get*.

As Type 2s, we have the propensity to believe that to assure a good and satisfying life we must give fully to others and not be found useless or selfish. Therefore, we put a lot of energy into doing our best to fulfill others; we take care of their needs. We enjoy being the one that makes someone's day, and we enjoy being seen as a loving, caring, and giving person. This formula can lead us to becoming prideful and wanting to be indispensable. In the process, our attention naturally goes out toward others' needs and desires, solving others' problems and saving the day.

Consequently, in our relationships, we are caring, helpful, supportive, and relationship-oriented. But we can also hinder our relationships by being overly intrusive, prideful in our giving, and by demanding some kind of return for our efforts. We can get passive-aggressive all the way to downright angry when we are not appreciated, or when the reciprocity we've expected (covertly) never does take place (particularly when not at a high level of developmental well-being).

Hence, while having an almost innate empathic capacity and ability to attune to others, it can be hard for us to sense our own needs and desires until we are satisfying those same needs for others.

Tips for Growth: As a Type 2, we need to develop an individuated self–without feeling guilty for doing so–as very little attention goes to proactively fulfilling the needs of our own personhood. We can give ourselves permission to ward off the deeply felt repulsion of being deemed "selfish" when we do begin to take care of ourselves and put ourselves and the satisfaction of our own needs first, if necessary, and with self-agency, as is appropriate.

We can work toward overcoming the addiction–the high–we get when meeting the needs of important others, when never saying no, and when seeing ourselves as above others, as more altruistic and more caring. We can allow ourselves to see how we may overuse our own innately generous nature as a way to be loved, appreciated, and taken care of.

We can allow ourselves to explore our feelings when giving without conditions, when giving to ourselves without shame, and in learning to trust that others will love us, and come toward us, without us having to ingratiate ourselves to them first. We can hold the belief that love does and will come to us, organically, as we have brought it to others. As we come to trust in the *natural flow of love* coming our way, and in divine reciprocity, our ability to both give and receive freely flourishes. It also gives others the joy of giving to us freely and organically, without provocation or expectation.

Type 3 | The Performer | Summary and Tips

As a Type 3, we are intrinsically empowered; we strive toward capacity, self-agency, and the confidence to manifest. A can-do attitude is imbued with the hope that all can be pursued, acquired, and achieved. The original state of **hope**—which is felt when all possibilities are in front of us and attainable—is experienced when the life we desire is within reach and accomplishable. Hope is where manifestation organically unfolds in accordance to universal laws—it's just what we witness occurring in nature itself.

As a Type 3, hope is what goes into the background in a world that we perceive rewards effortful doing and accomplishing, not simply being. Subsequently, we have the propensity to believe that we have to gain love, recognition, and acceptance through performance, doing, and the attainment of some formulated definition of manifestable success.

We are defined by what we do and accomplish, what we are recognized for, and the respective status (acceptance) attained. Concurrently, we develop an enthusiastic go-ahead "we can do it" energy in order to align with an image that presents as successful—worthy of admiration and approval—as we've defined it. We therefore perceive that we must do something, become someone of value, and we must not fail.

As a Type 3, we develop a caring-through-doing orientation that impacts all that we do and how we bring ourselves to relationships. In the process, we veer from the veracity of our own true, heartfelt feelings. Instead, our attention specifically focuses on tasks, goals, and targets to accomplish toward some identified finish line that needs to be reached. Consequently, in our relationships, we are industrious, fast-paced, goal-focused, and efficiency-oriented.

But we can also hinder our relationships by being inattentive to feelings—others' and our own. We can become too focused on goals and can become impatient, applause-seeking, and inordinately image-driven (particularly when not at a high level of developmental well-being). Rather than feeling our own emotions, we have the tendency to channel our energy into performing well, daily productivity, and results.

Given our high, go-ahead energetic charge, it can be hard for us to actually sit still and not be moving things along that we want to accomplish. We may also push too hard for completion and skip necessary steps that others might feel are important.

Tips for Growth: As a Type 3, we need to slow our driving pace and allow ourselves to become receptive, which allows the space for our feelings to tenderly emerge, as is authentically needed. In the end, it is access to our feelings that ultimately guides our heart's true desires and our ability to connect with our divine purpose in the world. We need to integrate our authentic feelings and desires with how and where we might place ourselves in the world in order to have our own truly satisfying and fulfilling life.

This is important to ascertain, as we, Type 3s, can pretty much become anything we believe we ought to be as much as we can become what others want us to be. We can lose that honest connection with ourselves as a result of becoming something for others, without realizing that's what we've done. It's an authentic and honest connection to ourselves that allows us to determine what our own definitive, maybe even different direction might be, different from what others (society, culture, parents, loved ones, etc.) may have defined or wanted for us.

Welcome in and learn to appreciate our own feelings, and then those of others, and carefully observe our tendency to believe that feelings will only get in our way if we allow them to flood our awareness. Give ourselves permission to truly realize that love is a state of being; and that it is in truth, something we cultivate from the inside out.

As a Type 3, we need to embody the realization that love is not necessarily derived from doing and getting, but from something far more to do with developmental well-being and the quality of each emotional transaction experienced within ourselves and with others.

Our challenge is to know that our authentic value exists in how present we are—how present we are to ourselves and to others—and our having cultivated a knowing of ourselves and our true nature, rather than having our value come from our status in society, our monetary wealth, what's expected of us from certain significant others, or by how much we are admired or deemed acceptable by the world at large.

Type 4 | The Romantic | Summary and Tips

There is an innate resonance with the profound beauty of connection to **origin** in Type 4, that which is found in the original, undivided state of oneness and utter acceptance in all things in each moment, just as it is, and just as we are. It's the ideal experience of love itself, found in the deepest connection to the authentic self, to the fundamental preciousness of each unique aspect of ourselves and our fundamental acceptability. It's the fundamental acceptance of others and of our entire universe, just as they are and just as it is.

With a deep connection to our authentic true nature comes expressiveness, an ability to emote—to provoke and to respond—fully and with unabashed grandiosity or subtle tenderness. As a Type 4 in essence, we have an inherent attunement with our own true nature—our own true face—and with that of others as well.

For Type 4s, the original state of an ideal, deep, and complete connection to all things, where nothing of substance is missing or unacceptable for any reason—called *origin* in Enneagram terms—goes into the background in a world that we have the propensity to believe abandons us because of some sort of deficiency. It's a world that disconnects from us, leaving us bereft and with something of utter importance disappointedly missing.

We come to deduce that to assure a good and satisfying life, we must be special—something far beyond unacceptable-ness and beyond ordinariness. We must be some sort of ideal person, one who is not deficient and not less than, in a world that we experience otherwise would not love us as we are, perceived flaws and all. In the process, our attention focuses on what is disappointing, to what is missing or lacking from our ideal image of what makes a person—especially us—truly lovable and worth connecting to. In this construct, we are driven by a longing to become the internalized ideal.

This takes us far away from the emotional balance that comes with appreciating all that we are, as is, rather than identifying with all that we are not. An either-or polarization is often more the case, putting us above (superior), or below (inferior), back and forth, until we find we cannot land ourselves in any level of personal acceptance and equanimity. That extends to our experience of others as well.

Consequently, in our relationships, we are idealistic, deeply emotive, and as authentic as we can be—because we ideally want to be. But we also hinder our relationships by being overly dramatic and even self-absorbed (particularly when not at a high level of developmental well-being). We fret disappointment over what is missing in our lives, in ourselves, and in our relationships.

We can range from being very expressive and emotional to very quiet and withdrawn. Swinging back and forth from one extreme to the other is difficult intrapersonally and can be hard on our intimate relationships too.

Tips for Growth: As a Type 4, we need to overcome the longing for what we perceive is still missing, disappointing, or lacking in ourselves or in our surroundings, all while knowing that that something missing also happens to be that something we've decided is really important.

For us Type 4s, an attachment to disappointment and its resulting energy almost becomes an addiction, leading us to savor the melancholy we know so well and almost invite. It's a state of being that seems to ignite deep feelings of aliveness and intensity and specialness, ones that keep us from appreciating the ordinariness of the mundane, of the status quo.

It's important to learn to appreciate what is positive in our lives right now, just as is, and develop the gratitude that goes with putting attention on what's here, what's good about it, and what's real. In the process, we need to give ourselves permission to accept ourselves as lovable, as is. From here, we can receive our own "love-ability" with grace and kindness, humility, and a feeling of enough-ness.

Of equal importance is to allow ourselves to realize that a state of self- and other-acceptance is not dependent on being special, ideal, superior, or one-of-a-kind. It is simply so because we are who we are, and all is as it is.

Type 5 | The Observer | Summary and Tips

Type 5s are innately sensitized beings. Dare we say it's all felt. With an acutely responsive system, subtleties are perceived and are impacting. Stimuli of all kinds are abundant and can be overwhelming as there's a tender fragility and preciousness that is, in fact, what brings forth the sensitivity to detail, attention to nuance, refined postulation, and a delicacy that can be applied to thought, investigation, a good conversation, and the dedicated pursuit of learning and mastery.

There is an innate understanding of one's capacity for direct knowing in Type 5, that which is found in the original, undivided state of trusting that the information we need to survive and thrive is already a part of us, and we are an organic part of it. We are enough in each moment; we are potent enough and we know enough to exist and pursue our lives.

We are connected to our own divine wisdom, and we can access it on call. The original state of direct, or organic knowing—divine **omniscience**—is what goes into the background in a world that we have the propensity to read as demanding too much or giving too little, with us challenged by having to learn and know and figure it all out, at all times.

We lose contact with that abundant cosmic energy, the sense that, in fact, the universe *will* meet our needs, that we'll be OK, and that we are fortuitous enough to get through the life we were designed to live—without being overtaken and overwhelmed by all of what it takes to survive here.

Consequently, we come to insist that to assure a good and satisfying life we must be self-sufficient, all-knowing, and acquire copious amounts of knowledge in order to not become dependent on others, the world, and worse yet, energy-depleted by it all. The acquisition of knowledge, then, is what gives us the power we perceive we need in the world to survive. In the process, our attention naturally goes to emotional and physical intrusions—the claims and demands—being made upon our time, emotions, and life-force energy.

Infants exemplify nature's abundant flow of energy in and out of us, as infants exist in the present moment, without cognition and without the need to conserve their energy or resources. Energetically, we avidly prioritize for specific things we feel we cannot live without, as in private time, privacy, a place in which to retreat alone, and the time and space needed for the acquisition of knowledge.

Consequently, in our relationships, we are independence-seeking, non-demanding, analytical, thoughtful, and unobtrusive, but we can also hinder our relationships by being detached, overly private, self-protective, withholding, and withdrawn (particularly when not at a high level of developmental well-being).

Since we can also be highly sensitive to physical touch, personal intrusion, and over-stimulation, we have adapted by retracting away from experiencing the messiness and energetic ups and downs of our feelings in order to protect ourselves from short-circuiting uncomfortably, from being overwhelmed, or by being overtaken by the feelings and emotional needs of others.

Tips for Growth: As a Type 5, we need to learn to appreciate the abundant and sustaining flow of life-force energy, which is available to each of us, as it resides and is made available from within. We need to realize that withdrawal–from others, from life, from our desires–actually invites emotional loss as well as the potential for intrusion. It may also injure relationships over time, as in, when we are needed and wanted, we refuse to engage.

It's important to move into an experience of our feelings, a present-moment experience even better. Allow ourselves the time and disruption to engage with our feelings, accept them, and process them. Our feelings connect us to our humanity, to our spirit. Allow ourselves to learn to take time for feelings, spend time learning to cultivate access to them, and cherish them as we learn to articulate them to others, which is a very important developmental step.

As a Type 5, we need to learn to more fully participate in life's messy experiential possibilities. We need to engage with others and with our own need to express more of ourselves to those we love and who love us.

Allow an inner knowing, which is not necessarily from our schoolbooks' academic learnings, but that which comes from the experiences of life itself. Accept that participation in life–participation with others–actually leads to being energized, revitalized, and nurtured, rather than being drained and depleted. Allowing and exploring feelings reverses deeply held Type 5 fears that can cause our own brand of isolation and suffering.

Type 6 | The Loyal Skeptic | Summary and Tips

Type 6s are gifted with a system that is vigilant, alert, and with attention-span persistence. We scan the environment as a matter of course; it's a talent that is automatic, protective, and surroundings-aware.

Within our original, undivided state, we are trusting of the information we need to gather. Knowing and a sense of certainty are a part of us, and we are an organic part of a seemingly benevolent universe. Our observations and deductions are enough. We are safe enough and we know enough intrinsically to exist, to survive, and thrive in each moment, without second-guessing. It's the ideal experience found in a connection to faith—in our own wisdom, know-how, and sensory perceptions.

As we develop, the original state of **faith** in self, others, and the universe is what goes into the background in a world we have a propensity to perceive as hazardous, unpredictable, and potentially untrustworthy. Accordingly, we also come to believe that to assure a good and satisfying life, we must gain certainty and pursue security and not be rendered helpless and dependent on others or the world at large. In fact, in our estimation, the world is unpredictable all the way to frightful and downright untrustworthy.

We are innately wide awake, vigilant, and tend to miss nothing. In the process, our attention, if not monitored, more naturally goes to what we can't count on, what could be dangerous, what is not being said or is hidden between the lines, as well as to what could possibly lead to betrayal or danger. All possible scenarios are reviewed instantaneously. We are the masters at trying to prevent anything possibly harmful from happening—from existential concerns and worries to the prevention of emotional pain.

We prepare, rehearse and examine, observe and calculate, question and doubt, all of which keep us on our toes and in highly alert, adrenalized states of being. In the process, we disconnect from having faith, trusting in faith, in trusting in ourselves and in others. Consequently, in our relationships, we are trustworthy and loyal (sometimes to a fault) in the hopes that others will be too. We are good problem-solvers, devils' advocates, and troubleshooters. We are inquisitive and earnest.

But we can also hinder our relationships by being overly questioning to the extent we are accusatory, split quickly into black-and-white polarities, and can express our concerns sarcastically and sardonically. We can either become overly challenging (counter-phobic disposition) or avoidant of fearful situations (phobic disposition).

Our nervous system can be highly reactive and volatile, with flight, fight, or freeze mechanisms being easily triggered and readily activated—particularly when not at a high level of developmental well-being.

Tips for Growth: As a Type 6, we need to become aware of our preoccupation with what could go wrong, what's unsafe and untrustworthy, and the accompanying magnification of mishaps, potential danger or fault, all the way to perceived betrayals. There's a keen sensitivity to what could overpower and overtake us, what would render us helpless and out of control, and what could happen if we became dependent on unpredictable people or circumstances.

We are sensitive to discrepancies, inconsistencies, and double-binds. This sensitivity provides us with a tremendous sixth sense to sort through immense detail, incoherence in others or situations, and out-and-out lies that were intended to manipulate or confuse. It's critical that we learn to thoughtfully discern what really is hazardous and what we can let rest in good faith.

The whirring mind can be exhausting as it prepares and rehearses, checks and rechecks, doubts and reviews–over and over again. We can give ourselves permission to relax these processes and when we do, we build a new sense of resolve, a knowing that nothing bad will happen to us if we rest our over-doing mental processes.

Allow ourselves to realize that the whirring provides us with a sense of safety that alleviates the angst felt within, even for a short while. Try letting it go and feel our own authority rise as we do so, as we return to our essence's state of faith.

It's important to pay attention to what is already just fine, what has been fine in the past, and develop the courage to have greater trust and faith in ourselves and in others.

Type 7 | The Epicure | Summary and Tips

There is an innate responsiveness, excitability for life, for possibility, and an attraction to stimuli that are inherent to the Type 7 structure. Playfulness is natural and gifted to 7s. The world is to be explored, tasted, adventured, and lived fully. The seeking instinct is strong, leading us to new things, new directions, and new insights as a constant.

A felt resistance to the letdown of stagnancy—of getting stuck too long in one place—drives us 7s to continue seeking and pursuing, experiencing and sampling. Distractibility is high and so is our potential for discovery. As a Type 7, our original undivided state of excitation and delight, in each moment and in all things, is free and purposeful as it serves adaptability, desire, and inventiveness.

It's the ideal state of being as we marvel at life itself and all that which we are potentiated to experience. For a Type 7, this essential state of being is what goes into the background in a world that we come to perceive as limiting and restrictive.

The original state of focused yet exploratory, delight-driven purpose, called **"work"** or constancy, joins with the ability to live the entire spectrum of life fully and freely and without resistance. This fundamental aspect of essence goes into the background in a world that we have a propensity to experience as frustrating or inhibitory, fearing a world that will cause us pain and suffering if we allow it; we fear we will get stuck in it. Therefore, we possess a quick-moving talent to simply avoid it.

Accordingly, we come to believe that to assure a good and satisfying life, we must keep life stimulating and free, upbeat, and varietal. We do not want to be held back or trapped in such a way that we experience pain, distress-inducing boredom, or frightening restrictions.

We readily escape. We divert from the work of being truly present in the moment—to all that really is in the here-now—to instead finding ourselves future-focused and options-generating. In the process, our attention innately focuses on interesting, stimulating possibilities and opportunities so that we won't get mired in boredom, stagnancy, pain, or suffering.

And as 7s, we easily become an eager glutton for new experiences, new ideas, and postulations, and a variety of exciting, pleasurable adventures. We are adaptable and see possibility at every turn. Accordingly, in our relationships, we are optimistic, options-oriented, fascination-seeking, enrapturing, and adventurous.

But in the effort to avoid limitation and suffering, we can also hinder our relationships by being pain-avoidant, uncommitted, irresponsible, and self-serving (particularly when not at a high level of developmental well-being).

We tend to stay stimulated with ideas, anticipation, and activities and deliberately avoid sad or painful feelings, even though they may be what's called for in a given situation. Our energy tends to go up and out of ourselves and our current reality, which inevitably complicates our challenges, keeps us from adequate and purposeful constancy, and creates relationship struggles and disconnect.

Tips for Growth: As a Type 7, we need to recognize our propensity to engage in an excess of continual future planning and options-generation, which keeps us from experiencing the present moment and from dealing adequately with what's in front of us. Our desire for, and recognition of, new and stimulating experiences is a wonderful talent and attribute, but it can leave little room for the more mundane aspects of running a life and navigating obligations.

Learn to make lasting commitments, all the while, trusting in ourselves that these commitments and responsibilities will not confine us or enslave us. As a Type 7, we can learn how to ground our body in the present moment and release the grip of stimulation-hunting, future-tripping, and daydreaming.

Give ourselves permission to accept all of what life has to offer, because it's rich and meaningful to do so. That would include allowing any pain, fear, boredom, and limitations to be felt, without fearing that we will be trapped there forever. Experiencing the pleasures, joys, and vast array of options in life is a given for us.

We need not worry that we will ever lose these aptitudes and capacities as we allow ourselves to take on all of life, all of relationships, all of our feelings, and all of ourselves.

Type 8 | The Protector | Summary and Tips

There is an innate response-intensity, an exuberance, and force-of-nature quality to Type 8s. A sense of power and strength is imbued into our bodies and into our sense of being. We protect and we guard. We stand to be noticed, reckoned with, and experienced. We impact readily and as is needed. We hold space. We pursue justice. We stand for **truth**. These are qualities of our being.

The world is to be controlled, made fair, and life is to be lived lustfully and fully. Territorial instincts are strong, and a deep understanding of power and its deployment comes naturally. Who is in charge and what are they doing with that power? Where's the authority and what's it saying? The original state of innocence saw truth in everything. In truth we are protected, guarded, and dignified.

As a Type 8, our essential state of being, our innocence, is what goes into the background in a world that we come to perceive as harsh and unjust, a world where the powerful take advantage of others, of those that are weaker or more vulnerable. We readily see how truth when distorted leads to betrayal, a loss of trust, injustice and a chaotic and overpowering world.

Consequently, we come to believe that to assure a good and satisfying life, we must be strong and invulnerable. We cannot be innocent, let alone weak or powerless. In the process, our attention innately goes to power, control, our subjective perception of the truth, and to perceived injustices. We assert an endless supply of exuberant energy that is often felt by others as anger, dominance, short-temperedness and heated passion to assure our power, presence, and stance.

We can even become explosive with little to no prompting in order to regain control of a situation, which can be immensely intimidating or even terrifying to others. "Why are you so angry?" one might ask us as a Type 8, only to hear, "I'm not angry, I'm just frustrated. You haven't seen me angry!"

As a Type 8, we often do not calibrate our level of intensity accurately, let alone how it's impacting others. Our capacity to come freshly to each situation with an open mind atrophies as our insistence to control situations with our convictions dominates. Accordingly, in our relationships we are justice-seeking, direct, strong, somewhat innocently hopeful and tender, and very protective. We often radiate intensity and authority and are often sought for leadership and guidance.

But we can also hinder our relationships by being overly impactful, excessive, other-dismissing and impulsive. We are quick to the draw and get triggered and even angered with little provocation (particularly when not at a high level of developmental well-being). This can put immense pressure on our relationships, particularly those with significant others as well as those we work with or interact with on a daily basis.

Tips for Growth: As a Type 8, we need to become aware of our intensity, exuberance, bigger-than-life convictions, and ability to easily intimidate others. We can give ourselves permission to reduce our impulsivity, knowing it will not dull our enjoyment of and lust for life. Our task is to learn to appreciate vulnerability, tenderness, and receptivity as strengths rather than as weaknesses.

As 8s, allow ourselves to realize and moderate our impact on others, our ability to dismiss others, overpower others, and to rather stay present to others' reactions and responses to us, in real time. Can we adjust as we become more tuned in, reciprocal, and attentive? Can we take others in and listen to their perspectives? Can we allow receptivity? Keep in mind, receptivity does not mean we have lost ourselves or have gone soft on something important to us.

Challenge ourselves to come freshly to each situation, as our innate innocence knows how to do, and allow that innocence to be cultivated within us; if we inspire it to do so, it will return to us. In the process, we can allow ourselves to appreciate others' sense of truth, justice, and fairness. We can allow others to experience their need for power, as well as to express their own authentic power, in our presence.

Type 9 | The Mediator | Summary and Tips

There is an innate capacity for unconditional, pure beingness and a sense of others that is not separate from that of ourselves. We are one. As a Type 9, we feel inseparable from the greater environment and from others. Another's life, agenda, needs and wants become readily and easily that of our own.

Our vitality rises for the higher good of others, for the needs of our environment, and for the calling of our world. We are tireless, accepting, and devotedly attached to that which we have merged with and hold dear. Boundaries are penetrable and open. We are here and we are available. "Live and let live" takes us to states of **unconditional love** for all things, just as they are, just as they need to be.

The original, deeply blissful state of unconditional love and union in which everyone belongs equally, is loved and honored equally, is what goes into the background in a world that we come to feel makes us—or needs us to be—somewhat unimportant. It's a world where we tend to feel invisible, overlooked, even insignificant. Subsequently, we seek importance externally by blending in with others, showing up as a non-differentiated self, one that doesn't make a big deal of itself nor causes any trouble. In the process, our attention innately goes out to synching with others, matching and aligning, creating a non-conflicting, agreeable, almost boundary-less presence.

There is a capacity as well to blend and merge with the environment in a way that ensures harmony; yet as is often true, it's a contrived harmony. It's a "can't be, won't be disturbed" state that is comfy and peaceful, yet it's one that is an artificial state of purported well-being. Accordingly, we are prone to developing an energetic inertia that subversively disregards what is actually important to us, especially when it in any way conflicts with anything or anyone with which we are trying to harmonize, to sync up to.

Moreover, to truly take right action in our lives, day in and day out, we need to love and respect ourselves equally to the way we love and respect others. Consequently, in our relationships, we go along to get along, remain stand-out avoidant, seek to create harmonious energies and comforts and do so with great success. But we do so even when harmoniousness is not what's called for, and may provide a steady and consistent care for others that may not include ourselves too.

We can hinder our relationships by being self-neglecting and self-forgetting, conflict-avoidant, covertly defiant and downright stubborn (particularly when not at a high level of developmental well-being). Instead, what may be called for is allowing constructive anger and honest communication, by being willing to have our own biases, and by taking some personal risks via show-ourselves expressiveness.

Since we so easily merge (blend) with others as well as our surroundings, we have difficulty with setting and adhering to personal boundaries. We are highly sensitive to the tones, feelings, mood, and cadence of much of what is happening around us, all of which can lead to us shifting and adjusting and losing ourselves completely in order to align and accommodate.

Tips for Growth: As a Type 9, we need to pay attention to our own personhood and our own specific needs–to our own self-agency. It is important to determine our specific wants and priorities and take action with respect and self-honoring, accordingly. We need to learn to welcome the unavoidable discomforts of interacting with others, our innate need for differentiation, and the fact that showing up in our fullness allows others to rightfully show up in theirs.

We need to impact our world as our world impacts us. As we activate the power within us–that "familiar but readily suppressed" anger energy that is often numbed out and long repressed–that energy can instead be used to stand in the face of arising conflicts and the challenges that come with human relationships and life itself.

As 9s, we can meet our appropriate, self-respecting anger and navigate complex and contradictory objectives by giving ourselves permission to focus on what we want, rather than on what we don't want. This allows us to more actively pursue self-intimacy, which then engenders a more authentic intimacy with others. Self-intimacy locates our voice and activates its desire to be spoken and heard.

As we learn to love and respect ourselves equally to the love and respect we readily offer others, we regain our ability to feel and receive the unconditional love of our true nature, of our essential self. "I matter too."

The Enneagram, Relationships, and Freedom

Learning about each of these nine Enneagram type structures leads to immense understanding, compassion, and clarity about not only ourselves but also about our fellow human beings. It allows us to fear far less the thoughts, feelings, words, and actions of others when they are different from our own.

I've long known of the Enneagram's potential for powerful, effectual human development and potentiation. It's been my life's mission to bring this system to mainstream personal development as well as psychological teaching, coaching, and therapeutic work.

Our experience with the Enneagram Prison Project (EPP) is a beautiful case of this understanding. The EPP teaches the Enneagram in prisons and jails across the U.S. and Europe, often to lifers—those who will never be released, but who can cultivate a particular kind of intrapersonal freedom from the inside out.

By coming to know themselves, these men and women can be released from the grip of bad and harmful conditioning alongside the liabilities of their type structure, those they've in turn suffered for far too long and with no known way out.

The EPP is bringing this valuable system for personal development to the marginalized and incarcerated, to populations that tend to have little access nor the resources to pursue therapy or treatment centers for ongoing development and healing. It was an honor for both Suzanne and me to support the efforts of the EPP, both on the inside as teachers and organizationally.

For those of us that may have suffered harder than necessary beginnings, who may have left childhood with less-than-ideal levels of developmental well-being, the Enneagram, coupled with a method of practice like mindful awareness, brings us hope. It brings us a way to recognize and then compassionately understand ourselves and others. It offers a way forward to self-revelation, personal liberation, and life-changing development.

Case Story

When asked why and how the Enneagram had made such a difference in his life, former career criminal (as he was named by the system) Victor Soto encountered the Enneagram—thanks to the EPP—after nearly 20 years of incarceration. It took little time for him to explain to me:

"Told I was a piece of shit from the time I could remember, the Enneagram helped me come to terms with the fact that I *wasn't* just a piece of shit and a waste, but that I was also a good man, deep down. It taught me that I could reclaim myself, like my dignity. That I had goodness and qualities in my character that I could count on, that I could believe in. That single change in perspective changed my life forever."

Today, Victor is free. Free from incarceration and freeing himself daily from the childhood-induced self-hatred and narcotizing limits of his Type 9's self-complacency and self-sabotaging inertia. He is now liberating himself from all of which, including his limiting habits of mind, nearly cost him any hope for a loving relationship with himself, let alone a future he could call his own.

The Enneagram Frees Us

The Enneagram helps us to understand that we all have pre-existing biases—filters if you will—and talent-driven perspectives that affect the way in which we see and interact with the world, and the people in it. We wake up from our habits and biases. We also come to understand how we came to be who we are.

English empiricist John Locke, in *An Essay Concerning Human Understanding* (1689), argued that the human mind's initial template was akin to that of "white paper, void of all characters," with "all the materials of reason and knowledge" derived solely from experience. Referred to in psychological circles as a *tabula rasa*—a blank slate—this theory has been found to be untrue.

We now know that what makes us who we are is not solely the result of the environmental experiences into which we were born. Instead—and more complex than that—we come in with a central nervous system, a brain system that is wired up, so to speak, with particular neural propensities—an innate temperament—that governs to a certain degree, perhaps significantly, how we cope with the information and energy and interactions we have with the environment.

Add to that the possible unbeknownst to us impacts, the mystery of what the soul as well as the great spirit within us might be bringing to the table of our individuality. With all that said, we're downright extraordinary, fascinating mystical creatures, capable of so much—capable of love.

How we relate to ourselves inevitably is how we relate to others. Our self-love, which is in part our connection to our divinity, our essence, can be accessed and developed through self-awareness and self-acceptance practices. This is, in the end, what determines our capacity to love others and build solid, fulfilling, life-giving relationships. Healthy self-love helps us potentiate the life we were born to live, in a world in which we were designed to contribute, and through a self we came to explore and express.

PART 2

Understanding Each Other
and Practicing the 5As
for Healthy Relationships

"When we see defensiveness,
any kind of reactivity,
remember,
we are looking at
someone's pain. "

— *David Daniels, M.D.*

CHAPTER 7

Three Driving Instincts (Enneagram Subtypes) and Their Impact on Relationships

From the perspective of the Enneagram, we've learned that our human family consists of nine intelligent, non-randomly organized personality structures called Enneagram types. Each Enneagram type expresses itself uniquely, as in, has its own perspective, talents, and aptitudes, driven by its specific focus of attention, habits of mind, and emotionally charged interpretations.

Each type lends itself to particular liabilities too, which can get deeply ingrained and operate below our level of awareness—running on automatic. All these processes being in place all the time and, most often, running without our conscious awareness or recognition are what make us *us*.

This chapter takes us to another layer of personality understanding, in addition to the Enneagram type and its three centers of intelligence. Next is the study of three survival instincts and how these instincts are expressed by each of the nine Enneagram character structures.

These instincts play a role in the energetic expression of our personalities. You'll often hear these instincts referred to as Enneagram subtypes. What is an Enneagram subtype? Let's start by defining *instinct*.

> Instincts are non-learned, hardwired behaviors that enhance our ability to cope with vital environmental contingencies. Instincts are innate, typically fixed patterns of behavior engaged spontaneously upon exposure to specific stimuli.

Our instincts drive some of the non-conscious even intuitive ways we prioritize what's important in our lives. They impact our thinking, energy mobilization, and often are at the center of the content we tend to worry about most.

All animals are born with certain instincts. One way or another, these instincts help us survive. We may think humans have evolved beyond pre-programmed survival instincts, but this is not the case. For example, a newborn baby will instinctively hold its breath if placed under water and will readily suckle for milk if put to the breast. Neither of these behaviors were taught to the infant prior to them spontaneously responding as needed to survive or thrive.

Because these are for-survival spontaneous behaviors, we cannot ignore them when it comes to understanding our development as well as our personality peculiarities. These peculiarities focus our survival priorities—directing our time and energy—and they tend to have a significant impact on our lives and on the people with whom we're in relationship, whether in our personal or professional lives.

> In the best sense, our instinctual activity is how we express our life force and participate in the world. Each instinct has a special intuitive ability and the potential to excel in a particular area of instinctual life.
>
> ~ Peter O'Hanrahan

Now, let's tie this back to the Enneagram. There are three instinctual drives or subtypes that are critical to Enneagram teachings, and they are as follows:

1. The Self-Preservation Instinct
2. The Sexual (also called One-to-One) Instinct
3. The Social Instinct

Descriptions of the Three Instincts

These survival instincts—existential imperatives—are part of our body-based (mobilizing) intelligence, the Gut/Body Center. These instincts drive action, action that is deliberate and with an end-goal. They drive us to *do something*. They are wired within to ensure *we make it*. That we survive.

These drives are not passive but summoning. Their very nature provides us with insights into three imperatives we need for survival and that mobilize our energy—not only for physical survival, but also for the survival of our sense of self.

Although all of us are driven by all three of these as necessary—we deploy each of them to some degree—we most often express *one* of them more fervently than the other two. Which instinct in particular we dominantly express depends on various developmental experiences combined with our temperamental propensities. That said, as life's stressors and challenges arise and our survival systems are confronted in new ways, one of the lesser-used instincts could get pushed to the foreground of our prioritizing, changing our dominant instinctual tendency for a while.

For example, if our marriage is suddenly threatened by an affair, we may see the Sexual/One-to-One Instinct kick in to high gear, despite our dominant usually being that of Social. Or when we may unfortunately get laid off from work, the Self-Preservation Instinct may suddenly dominate the direction of our attention and energy, even if it's not usually our primary preoccupation.

Before we can effectively understand the characteristics of all three instincts, it's helpful to first understand their particular contribution to our survival strategies. From there, we can determine which one mobilizes us most passionately. Which one is it that drives its particular priorities most predominately? Here are the brief descriptions of the three instinctual drives and their most recognizable attributes:

Self-Preservation Instinct

Energetic Focus: The Self-Preservation Instinct is rooted in and mobilizes around more *existential concerns and needs*, including the protection of physical safety and comfort, and issues of security, including finances, food, warmth, shelter, and sustenance maintenance.

Identifiable Behaviors: The Self-Preservation Instinct focuses energy on the practical necessities of life, as in securing a home, paying bills, life-management tasks and upkeep, and investing in the future. Self-Preservation dominants strive to be self-sufficient, we can be disciplined and devoted to issues of security and practicality, and we're often focused on physical needs being satisfied, such as hunger, body temperature regulation, or a focus on our health. The Self-Preservation Instinct mobilizes us to ensure we are not lacking—stressed about or uncomfortably without—in the material world.

Challenges: Dominance in the Self-Preservation Instinct can lead to a preoccupation with security issues, money, logistics, and the practicalities of life, which can sometimes impede spontaneity, relating and connecting, and hamper appropriate and warranted risk-taking.

Sexual/One-to-One Instinct

Energetic Focus: The Sexual/One-to-One Instinct is rooted in and mobilizes around fueling personal vitality, sexuality and mating, intimate relationships, and interpersonal excitation and intensity. Fundamentally, it seeks viable possibilities for deeply felt experiences all the way to spiritual union.

Identifiable Behaviors: The Sexual Instinct focuses on the expression of passion and intensity, which is often directed at personal pursuits and the transmission of our desire to engage. This instinct is sensitive to mutual resonance, desirability, and attractiveness, and it values meaningful as well as purposeful, targeted personal connections, and professional pursuits.

Challenges: Dominance in this instinct can lead to focusing too heavily on pursuing relationships for a targeted purpose or for garnering interpersonal intensity. So much so, other interests, responsibilities, and needs may fall to the wayside. Pressures felt to be attractive and desirable can also be consuming—even distressing.

Social Instinct

Energetic Focus: The Social Instinct is rooted in and mobilizes what drives our tribal nature and our need for social structure; it is attuned to belonging, fitting in, social acceptance, and to adapting to others and group associations.

Identifiable Behaviors: The Social Instinct focuses on affiliations that promote survival. Community, group membership, and participation are sought; what gains importance is the seeking of a role or status, participation with others, companionship and fellowship, as well as camaraderie and team contribution.

Challenges: Dominance in this instinct can lead to a preoccupation with belonging and adapting ourselves to do so. Here we can lose our autonomy and individuality to the will and mores of a given group with which we're associated.

Development of Our Dominant Instinct

While in rudimentary form these three instincts are wired in by birth to some degree. It's theorized that our predominant instinct and its expression depend largely upon which period of early development was most difficult or most indulged. Too much adversity or too much protection either causes contraction (resistance) or fixation (preoccupation). Instead of supporting the personality and its corresponding needs in order to grow healthfully and organically, we postulate there's developmental infringement, of some sort, that sets us up to dominantly lead with one over the others.

It's also been theorized that these three instincts—Self-Preservation, Sexual, and Social—correlate with the first three chakras of the chakra system, a system that originated in India between 1500 and 500 BC. The word *chakra* is derived from the Sanskrit word meaning "wheel." Chakras are explained as energy centers that run along our spine, through which energy flows in our bodies.

There are seven main chakras, the first three being connected with one of the three instincts. The root chakra is associated with the Self-Preservation Instinct, the sacral chakra with the Sexual/One-to-One Instinct, and the solar plexus chakra with the Social Instinct. The other four main chakras are the heart, throat, third eye, and crown chakras.

As energy is either trapped or flowing freely across these "energy wheels," we are driven to overexpress or underexpress, to fret or vacillate over one or more aspects of our survival needs being met (or not). As such, the outward behaviors coordinated with each of these energy centers can be overdone, underdone, or misused.

What's interesting to note is how the properties of these three survival instincts as taught in the Enneagram system can be found similarly in another wisdom tradition and its teachings in another culture with its own contributory insights.

Cross-referencing between the Enneagram and teachings on chakras allows us to learn more as well as validate the many systems of understanding humans have been inspired to articulate and share across the centuries. How intriguing it is to access these varying wisdoms from across the world and recorded human history and compare it to our own learnings today.

To me, this is nothing short of fascinating—and potentially affirming.

Coming to recognize our own dominant instinct helps us better understand some of why we do what we do. The instincts clarify for us, for instance, what drives us to take care of *certain things*, what might frustrate the heck out of us if not dealt with, and what we tend to overlook completely that might drive others in our lives crazy.

Understanding the instinctual drives explains to us how we feel most comfortable (secure), purposeful (contributory), and engaged (fulfillment) with the world around us. Cultivating a working knowledge of our least-dominant instinct can also assist us to become more balanced, more self-supporting, and less frustrated, as this usually points to a neglected area of our lives, one that most likely needs more attention and care.

How Do These Instincts Impact Relationships?

If we are preoccupied with too much of one and too little of another of the instinctual drives, or over-compulsive with one and almost completely neglectful of another, we may come to find an imbalance (a big one!) and may see it having a significant impact on our lives and relationships. To make matters worse, when these behaviors are acted out more compulsively, we tend to not see them, and we may have little idea as to how this is affecting everything—and every*one*— around us.

Without awareness, we may not directly experience the out-of-balance challenges we're creating in our lives. Understanding where our energy is going, how *we are our energy*, as well as how it might be affecting others is worthwhile because as these instincts are played out, they can have a tremendous impact on our most intimate relationships. Unbeknownst to us and before we become aware, the different instinctual emphases may either bring balance to a relationship or literally polarize it.

Take, for example, "Sam" and "Rita," a young couple who had been dating for three years before getting engaged. As it turns out, both predominately drive from the Social Instinct. Dating one another was a huge success, as they spent most of their time socializing with friends, organizing parties at their place, and volunteering at their local Zen Buddhist center on the weekends, which is where they met.

Unfortunately, once married, neither was very gripped by the Self-Preservation Instinct. It took months to get furniture for their new place, they often opened the fridge to find it empty, and they spent an inordinate amount of money going to restaurants with friends instead of saving for a new car, which they sorely needed.

For all of us, these instincts also tend to greatly impact our way of expressing love to one another. That is where instincts and love languages absolutely overlap!

Take for example "Ryan," a Self-Preservation dominant married to a woman named "Susie," who first and foremost drives from the Sexual/One-to-One Instinct. Ryan works hard and brings home an ample salary that affords a beautiful home in the suburbs as well as a maid and a cook. Thanks to Ryan's efforts, Susie is supported and relieved of many standard household chores, leaving her free to pursue her own interests.

Susie, on the other hand, never sees Ryan because he works so much, sometimes 12 or more hours a day, and he travels frequently to secure new accounts. To Susie, who is often on her own and feels starved of romantic evenings, Ryan seems preoccupied and unavailable. Susie wants *lots* more face time with Ryan. But Ryan feels frustrated as he believes he's giving Susie *everything* that a man is supposed to give to his wife. To his dismay, Susie seems to just want more and more.

Conflicts tend to arise when intimates—whether partners, coworkers, family, or friends—have differing motivations, needs, and desires. The same is true when different instincts drive the energetic pulse of their lives, determining where they put their time and attention and how they express their love and care.

Ryan, in our example, so preoccupied with providing, expresses his love for Susie through duty—by providing comfort and security, shelter and support. He mobilizes his love and care energy through his Self-Preservation Instinct.

Susie, on the other hand, doesn't register Ryan's Self-Preservation priorities as love but instead feels neglected. The more Ryan predominately charges on with his Self-Preservation propensities, the more Susie feels unloved, and the more Ryan feels exasperated.

This couple may love each other dearly, but they're sorely missing the mark with one another. This could eventually cause a complete breakup.

In Sam and Rita's case (our Social-instinct-driven couple), they were happy as clams when dating, but when it came to building a life together, they found too much energy in one instinctual area and not enough in the others. This imbalance prevented them from fulfilling other necessary aspects of their lives together, like setting up their household.

As for Ryan and Susie with their differing dominant instincts, they couldn't understand the needs and grievances of the other, which resulted in discord, disappointment, and disconnecting resentments.

Neither of these cases is uncommon. This is what we'll come to see when studying how these three instincts can influence relationships and, specifically, our vital romantic partnerships. *Without understanding these differences in one another*, the jury's out as to whether or not our relationships are sustainable over time.

Additionally and importantly, we often rely *even more* on our dominant drive when conflicts arise in intimate relationships. You know, those moments where we feel threatened in some way or most vulnerable. Emotional conflict will surely trigger us, and to cope, we may find we actually amp up our dominant instinct—even if it's one of the causes of the conflict!

For example, rather than bring work into balance with intimate life, Ryan (our Self-Preservation dominant) may try to *work even harder* as a way to try to alleviate Susie's discontent with him. And Sam and Rita (our Social couple) may add *even more* outings to get relief from the stress of their challenged home life.

This is often the case; *we'll do more of what we are doing to fix what we're attempting to fix!* Of course, the solution again is awareness. It's bringing what's below our level of awareness into consciousness so we can actually work with it. Only *then* can we truly do something *different*.

It's also been said—and I tend to see this too—that people who share the same dominant instinct may be more likely to resolve these kinds of differences because their priorities are similar. They get each other more readily and without much explanation, as they tend to more readily condone the way each other spends their respective time and energy.

That said, when *our dominant instinct* is the least dominant in our partner, great irritation can result as our partner's priorities may seem unimportant all the way to being ridiculous or nonsensical, and vice versa.

A lot of hurt can build up and a lot of fights can follow when derogatory views of each other along with resentments pile up as a result of not understanding these three instinctual drives and how they play out on one another's choices. Mismatched priorities can lead to power struggles and ongoing difficulty and can, in the end, be polarizing. The key to our relational health and well-being lies in understanding each other before all this conflict happens.

The tendency to think there's something wrong with our partner when they have different priorities than ours is far too common and is destructive, not to mention disconnecting! Let's, however, consider is this: *We may actually benefit from partnering with someone who drives from a different predominant instinct than that of our own.*

Together, we can handle more, secure more, and even cover more *territory*— bringing to the table acumen one of us either may not have or may be neglecting. Understanding this gives us a much better chance at creating for-survival balance, harmony, and mutual respect, all of which alleviate conflict, frustration, and unwanted, disconnecting misunderstandings.

Coming to understand our own hierarchy of instincts along with that of our partner can set us up for far more teamwork and far less discourse. Understanding one another's instincts—and *their order of importance*—is critical, in our opinion, to longer-term relationship success.

And when we understand and respect one another, compassion is more apt to develop. Mutual understanding and respect come from learning about each other and then honoring each of our unique aptitudes and idiosyncrasies.

Understanding *how* and *why we're different* can take us from conflict and frustration to acceptance and even appreciation.

Our Enneagram Type and Our Instincts

To summarize, all three instincts are functions of each of us, but one tends to lead the way, hijacking more of our focus and energy than the other two. There is a hierarchy in the expression of the three. Some schools of thought call it "our stack," others call it instinctual prioritization.

What we have found to be true is that there is a dominant one (most prominent), a secondary one (intermediate in prominence), and tertiary (least prominent) instinct. In determining our predominate instinct, we need to pay attention to both type-specific expressions of it, as well as and usefully, its generic manifestations.

Given that we have nine Enneagram types and each of those types expresses each of the three instincts, we will resonate *with comforting familiarity*—regardless of our own type—with each of the other Enneagram types identifying with the same dominant instinct (generic expression) as ourselves. While not the same Enneagram type, sharing the same dominant instinct means that we will notably share much in common.

For example, a Self-Preservation Type 1 will likely see similar behavioral preoccupations as its own in a Self-Preservation Type 5, even though they will express these noted commonalities through the portal of their own respective Enneagram type with its core motivations and perceptions (type-specific expression).

As important as it is for us to determine our own Enneagram type with accuracy, it is equally important that we take the time to discover our dominant instinctual drive with accuracy. *A little confirmation:* Each of the instincts brings its own incalculable value and is survival-supportive; understand that one is not better or more desirable than the other. It's the *balance* that's ultimately desired.

Self-Preservation Instinct: Influence on Relationships

The instinct for self-preservation directs attention and energy to all things related to assuring adequate and comfortable physical survival. We prioritize and tend to satisfactory self-care, and we engender warmth and safety in relationships.

Preoccupations include questions like, "Does my work provide for us adequately? What about our children's future? Will they be safe? Will they obtain work that provides well?"

Family and friends as resources are also important. Those questions include, "Do we have a supportive and safe neighborhood? Am I safe to go on this trip? Do I have enough survival supplies—water, medicines, food, toiletries, clothing, etc.?"

Our Self-Preservation Instinct has its roots in our long, evolutionary history—plenty of natural disasters like droughts, floods, and famines or the horrors of war, disease, and pandemics have surely played their part! It's likely that greed, the sense of never having enough, or of not knowing when enough is enough, stems from the impacts of these historical challenges.

Since this instinctual drive tends to our most critical survival, when self-preservation needs are not being met or are being ignored it leads to distress, fear, and anger readily flaring up with partners and close others, with accusations such as these being tossed around: "You aren't supporting me." "You aren't taking care of us." "You don't do enough." "You don't work hard enough." "What if we're not gonna be OK?"

Big decisions—critical life decisions—are prioritized all the time around self-preservation basics, and this may very well promote a good foundation and a better life. *It's true.* But sometimes the self-survival focus can get to be *just too much*, and a "to hell with it" counter-reaction gets triggered.

Or there can be so much emphasis on *some* aspect of self-survival that other aspects are neglected, like when someone is working so much that their home maintenance falls to pieces. Excessive financial risks can be viewed as either an investment or as living beyond one's means. Both sides of the self-survival (prudent) and the counter-self-survival (taking risks) preoccupations can result in overpowering and preoccupying our lives, and indirectly, those in our lives too.

Just as a preoccupation with Self-Preservation can tend to our survival, a compulsive focus on Self-Preservation can lead to emotional and relational demise. When too much focus is placed on self-preserving and sustenance, our emotional-relational needs may be neglected.

Any out-of-balance, compulsive preoccupation with any *one* thing can draw attention away from what else truly nurtures vital relationships—like our spiritual development or our genuine interest in others. To foster a fuller, happier, well-rounded life, we need *more than one focus.*

Sexual/One-to-One Instinct: Influence on Relationships

For the Sexual/One-to-One Instinct, attention and energy focus more often on one person (one target) at a time, and it's based on passion attraction, energetic exchange, and the quality of the connection. This other-focused attention creates energetic intensity or heat. Bonding, closeness, intimacy, and union with special others are key to the drivers of this instinct. Relationships get infused with this instinct's vitality and passion, particular those that lead to deep emotional or physical intimacy.

This same intensity is initially felt and yearned for in the vital bond that becomes the relationship between mother and infant at birth, which unto itself is a true union and a first imprint. (We'll come back to this in a second.)

Sexual intimacy—mating—occurs in most all primary partnerships but may or may not happen based on an emotionally bonded, one-to-one relationship. Sex can occur within a variety of circumstances, as we know. And a deep bond may, in fact, be a sexual relationship's fundamental purpose and stance. If so, it will include a connective quality all the way to a desire for spiritual union. This can lead to an intensified emotional as well as sexual connection, both of which are capable of mirroring that first vital, blissful bond of utter undifferentiated union, as was once (hopefully) experienced in innocence (in infancy).

As we well know from studying attachment, one-to-one bonds that are formed early on between infants (then children) and caregivers are central to developmental well-being. Human beings have a long period of developmental dependence on caregivers. Our early helplessness sets us up for immensely intensified attachment experiences, as our very survival is dependent on so many countless transactions going right. For those leading with the Sexual/One-to-One Instinct, there's great sensitivity perhaps to bonding-related attachment disturbances early on, leaving an impression that this bond, in and of itself, is the most important aspect of our existence—and seeking it once more *is everything*.

Sexual expression itself is a biological imperative. Cultural and religious mores inherent to each society tend to regulate sexual expression and often foster the sublimation of the sexual instinct. Pair-bonding supports one-to-one relationships, as does the ongoing sexual receptivity of the human female throughout a given month. This is not the case for most mammals, where sexual receptivity is limited to a number of hours or days within a cycle.

In addition, if we look at the history of marriage, we'll see varying generational norms and attitudes when it comes to sexual desire and expression, and how and why we contractually partner/marry. Anger and distress rile up whenever pair-bonding conflicts with acceptable societal norms, and when cultural mores are threatened. And this goes for all of us worldwide, not only those driving from the Sexual/One-to-One instinct.

Some of the pitfalls of a Sexual/One-to-Ones' preoccupation with primary relationships can lead to a failure to fully develop a separate, individuated self. This may cause a predominant focus and subsequent preoccupation and desire to connect deeply and intensely with another, even beyond the desire to connect deeply with oneself.

This preoccupation can become consuming and can further lead to romantic fantasizing in order to generate feelings in the absence of the other, when disappointed with the other, or in the absence of a relationship altogether. To the other (if in a relationship), this intense preoccupation can feel like domination and smothering rather than intense love.

This level of consuming preoccupation may lead to the counter-expression of the instinct, wherein we instead insist on independence, thwart our neediness and relational vulnerabilities, and push away the intimacy of relationships.

Ultimately, Sexual-Instinct *preoccupation* (or its counter-expression), may lead to the neglect of self-surviving sustenance or of pursuing our role in society, or joining in with a desired group's purposes for our own development—even careers. This, of course, creates conflict and distress in our lives because it leaves us unfulfilled, which is ironically what turns us inside out and then impacts and disrupts our primary-partner relationships, and those we'll hope to have in the future too.

Social Instinct: Influence on Relationships

Here, attention and energy disperse into groups or affiliations, to adapting and belonging, because our tribal nature—our instinct to belong—is critical to our survival. We are not creatures designed to be on our own. Our very survival depends on belonging, a "we" existence, and group dynamics. There is a diffusion of energy here, which may foster a somewhat energetic coolness in relationships and coolness, perhaps, when connecting with others, unlike the more intense energetic quality of the Sexual/One-to-One Instinct.

The Social Instinct possesses a strong propensity to adapt and conform. To belong, we want to be and need to be deemed acceptable to others and the group in question. Conforming adaptiveness ensures that we succeed within a designated community, if possible.

Membership and contribution as well as belonging and fitting are survival themes. This instinctual drive is concerned with group cohesion, function, and effectiveness. Those leading with the Social Instinct more often indulge energy in *finding their tribe*—whether through religion, like-minded groups and causes, community issues, politics, and societal rather than individuated personal interests.

The Social Instinct drive tends to gather people for meals and sustenance, conversation, and events. They may take great care to provide group-sustaining activities, align with a shared purpose, and create opportunities for camaraderie that share experiences with like-minded others. The more the merrier!

We are a group-living—tribal—species, as mentioned earlier. Our collective survival over the millenniums depended upon different talents and points of view coming together as one functioning organism, if you will.

Evolutionarily speaking, in order to survive, we needed village members, for example, who had varying talents and perspectives. We needed an integrated system of contributory individuals to make it. We needed some who could take charge and some who could follow—carry out orders; some who cared about individual pursuits and others that cared for others; some that figured things out and some that could think ahead; some who focused on hunting and others on harvesting.

Some of the challenges faced by Social-instinct dominants involve anger that arises when other group members don't participate in the way we believe they should. Or when too much energy is spent pursuing social causes, striving in community organizations, and fighting for initiatives that paradoxically lead to the neglect of the family unit.

Group agendas can consume those who lead with the Social Instinct, even to the exclusion of self-preservation and intimate, relational needs. With their externalized focus, Social-instinct dominants can leave partners feeling forgotten and uncared for because, sadly, the Social dominant may find their intimate relationship not as compelling as the group and its needs—and this is felt by partners. Social Instinct individuals may not even notice they've left their beloveds behind in pursuit of their group-directed drivenness.

What we'll often see is that the Social-instinct dominant wants their intimates to join in and support the cause or activity as well. They want to share their externalized focus. This can lead to conflict and accusation, for example, "Why don't you just join in and be with me—and care about this with me?" And to a counter accusation, for example, "Why can't you just be happy here at home?"

You can see what a difficult impasse this is for couples who have not studied these instinctual drives.

Example of Counter-Expression: The Social Dominant

As mentioned earlier, counter-expressions exist—that is, counter-tendencies to each of the three instincts. This means we'll actually do the opposite, pushing against the intelligence of that instinct. And we do this for a number of interesting reasons.

We may source counter-tendencies back to our own unresolved issues, frustrations, even unhealed shadow material. For example, we might experience a preoccupation with joining a particular group but fail to act on it because of subconscious, sabotaging feelings of inadequacy. The critical word here is *preoccupation*. The preoccupation is what tells us what our dominant drive really is, whether we are acting on it (or not), expressing it (or not).

Or we may become overdosed and burned out, eventually withdrawing from a group due to sheer exhaustion. Yet we still think about it all the time, having a serious case of FOMO (a fear of missing out) on our hands! While having left the group may give us time to recover, it doesn't necessarily mean that our dominant drive has changed.

Again, the critical word is *preoccupation*. Both the dominant instinct as well as its counter-expression, when left unchecked, can result in driving our lives too much in one direction. Accurately calling out our dominant instinct or its counter-expression is very important to working with our own vital energies more consciously and more effectively.

Three Instinctual Drives Expressing Through Nine Enneagram Types

While we all express each of these three survival instincts at one time or another, each of them takes on its own twist when expressed by each of the nine Enneagram type structures. The way they're acted out is influenced to a great degree by each type's particular focus of attention, and how that focused acuity sees and interprets reality.

These instinctual drives are strong, dopamine-driven, and dopamine-promoting, and they are critical to our individual survival system as well as to that of the collective. Our instincts ultimately shape the way we go about getting our prioritized needs met, interact with others, and pursue our lives on a daily basis.

Let's look for a moment at how each Enneagram type's temperamental propensities affect how someone of a given type *feels* and *presents* energetically, regardless of the dominant instinct. After years of Enneagram study, this becomes more and more apparent and visible. It's fascinating, actually.

Over time, you'll come to see that *the expression of an Enneagram type lives in the entire body*. Type is not just a mental construct. Our Enneagram type shows up in our overall architecture—the way we move, our body language, our speech patterns, our facial expressions, and our gestures too.

It is significant how nine *focuses of attention* organize us in such a way that we can speak to nine energetic experiences of people particular to type. And these nine types come architectured with identifiable, valuable talents and aptitudes— ones that are seemingly natural and effortless for some types and far less natural and effortful for others.

So, to look at this in its entirety, we have nine type-differentiated focuses of attention, which delineate nine Enneagram type structures, each with their own energetic qualities. We also have three instinctual drives. This gives us nine specific Enneagram type structures, expressing in their own type-driven way, each of three instinctual drives.

For example, for an Enneagram Type 9, we'll see three expressions depending on what instinct is in the driver's seat. We'll have a Type 9 leading with the Self-Preservation Instinct, a Type 9 leading with the Social Instinct, and a Type 9 leading with the Sexual/One-to-One Instinct. So, we actually have *three expressions of Type 9* in our Enneagram system.

Likewise, depending on which instinct is dominant, we'll have three expressions of Type 2, three expressions of Type 1, Type 8, and so on. This renders nine Enneagram types multiplied by three instincts, which gives us a total of 27 focused and driven people-energies, each contributing to our collective survival as well as to our own ability to forge a satisfying life.

The Instincts Meet the Passions

Once an instinctual drive is dominating, it inevitably meets up with the type's driving emotional pattern—*their passion*. This is where a highly effective *survival drive* can become a downright liability. Because everything we do in moderation can serve its purpose. But anything overdone can potentially get us in trouble.

The passions of each Enneagram type with their volatility and protective defense system can push our instinctual behaviors to the limit. The key to this is *recognition*. Remember that aspect of self-awareness where once *aware* of something, we can *see it* and *name* it? Recognition, my friend, is the cat's meow when it comes to keeping our compulsions in check.

By doing our development work, we can invite ourselves to recognize that we are out of balance when we are—when we've overdone it, albeit very passionately perhaps and with great fervor—and to not ignore our loved ones when they start complaining. When we find ourselves becoming more compulsive or impulsive, it's time to identify if one of these instincts might be the culprit, running on overdrive.

Take inventory. Some of the signs that we're beyond a healthy expression of an instinctual drive might include exhaustion, alienation from family or friends, making too many errors, skipping steps, getting impatient when others give us unwanted feedback, and avoiding the truth of our neglect of loved ones or important others in our lives.

When our instincts are really out of balance, some part of our life might not be working at all (like it's malfunctioning). Another sure sign of an instinct dominating would be regular bouts of frustration and outbursts of anger. This is because our efforts do not match our desired outcome, yet it feels like we cannot let go. Can we stop, take a breath, and see what's happening to us?

Here are some examples: A Self-Preservation Type 4 fellow, "Frank," has been working 80-hour weeks to prove to his wife she's got the most special husband in town and that she'll have the finest of things. Frank might be shocked to learn that his wife is feeling so neglected that she's considering divorce.

Or a Social Instinct Type 7 mother, "Elizabeth," is so passionately devoted to the next presidential campaign that she chooses to miss her daughter's school play for the third time as it conflicts each month with local rallies. Elizabeth's lack of awareness doesn't let her realize that her daughter is now suppressing deep feelings of unimportance.

Differentiations: Instincts, Levels of Development, and Essence

There are a few differentiating components to always have on our radar when assessing the nine types. While persons of the same Enneagram type will have much in common, their dominant instinct may make them behave differently from one another.

The nine Enneagram types and the three instinctual drives direct the way each of us mobilizes a significant amount of our energy and impacts how each type spends our time or with what we get preoccupied. And while individuals may share the same dominant instinct, which means we'll mobilize priorities similarly, the way these priorities are expressed is dependent on each Enneagram type's structural dynamic.

Another quite critical, differentiating quality of personality assessment as to how others may experience a person of a given type is each person's level of developmental well-being (see Chapter 6).

Our level of developmental well-being can interfere with our ability to recognize our inherent type structure and may even confuse us about our partner's type too. Each Enneagram type has its own way for dealing with developmental challenges—we create our own solutions—which includes our responses to attachment disturbances and childhood trauma. Each type also has its own particular way of expressing our *higher* levels of developmental well-being too, which includes the way our higher self's qualities of being and the Enneagram's Holy Ideas of our divine nature are more frequently, readily, and visibly expressed.

Finally, there's another differentiator we'd like to mention—one that is far more complex to comprehend. As to all of what contributes to who we are, the possibility of a soul's impact merits mention. Consider for a moment the qualities of each individual's divine spirit and how that may also be informing our true nature. Does it have a say in our biological and psychological development as well? How might it be expressing itself through our driving instinctual energies and fundamental character structure?

When we talk about our essence and our essential qualities of being, are we pointing at the spirit within? And is our Enneagram type, in fact, some divinely organized reflection of this? Understanding the spirit within us—one of the great mysteries of human life and the focus of centuries of religious and philosophical postulation—is an undertaking that fills me with wonderment and reverence. While this book will not attempt to answer such enormous and extraordinary mystical musings, there's no doubt it's a fascinating something to explore and consider, and one that takes us into the realms of the divine.

As I've often sat marveling at one of our many panels in The Narrative Enneagram tradition, it always moved me to have, for example, a handful of Type 8s with all three dominant instincts represented sitting in front of me—so similar, yet so preciously different too. Always, *always*, it was clear that each was their own special *someone,* even though they were all Type 8s. They were unique unto themselves, precious, and light-filled-different from one another—each being their own cosmic mystery.

While still beyond our full grasp at this point, we cannot rule out the mystical when looking into each and every sentient being we encounter. This includes how we came in organized with a ready-to-be-developed character structure built on neural propensities and proclivities. And how we come to have the essential qualities we have within us, the ones we find so incredibly dear in each type and that we find so incredibly beautiful in the best of ourselves and in one another.

The source intelligence of it all is beyond magnificent to ponder.

The 27 Enneagram Subtypes Descriptions

So, here are each of the differentiations created by three instinctual drives, impacting each of the nine types—described and presented with affection.

Type 1 | The Perfectionist | Tension, Jealousness, or Inadaptability

As a Perfectionist, we have an innate sense of the correct way for sustaining our lives, and we vigilantly scan for standards that first, were never put into place, and second, that are being violated and that need to be restored and respected.

Anger, which can covertly show up as judgmentalness, frustration, agitation, irritability, or as feelings of guilt and resentment signal that, somewhere, some of our standards are being violated. Anger, resentment, and guilt get expressed by mobilizing to right wrongs, correct things, improve something, strive further, or to pursue the attainment of some sort of set standard for perfection. It's a quest toward the perception of—and a connection to—higher goodness.

We express and neutralize anger, resentment, or guilt by a dutiful push to fix what we deem to be broken, set things straight, make amends, clear the air, get above condemnation, adjust what's required, and, ultimately, strive to improve.

Self-Preservation 1 | Tension and Fretting

As a Perfectionist, we believe that our survival depends upon getting things right. We channel anger into perennial fretting and a form of unsettled frustration that drives us to do the right thing and not make mistakes. We've got to get above recrimination as that's where we'll be safe and above judgment.

This stance extends into our vital relationships. When we care about someone, they too must live up to certain standards (well, OK, *our* standards). We keep ourselves busy doing self-preservation tasks that reduce the fretting and frustration. These include cleaning, keeping things in order, and stocking up on provisions. We want and expect our partner and family to do the same.

We attempt to assert control and impose order over the natural world in these matters of shelter, existential safety, and self-survival. The best that we can hope for is some respite of relief, those moments in time that we may have scheduled sanctioned pleasure, but only when everything else is done. It's only *then* we finally stop and join in with others.

At our worst, this incessant drive can become limiting. The drive can create much inner tension, rigidity, a lack of spontaneity and a sense that others are indulgent, which leads to resentment. Feelings of this nature alongside the consequential resentments that build over time can greatly affect our relationships.

Sexual/One-to-One 1 | Jealousness/Heat
We guard intimate relationships and become vigilant and zealous about our conduct, our partner's conduct, and that of special others. We feel that nobody should violate our right to our passions or our desires—once we've finally earned them!

We express anger through fierce zealousness at the presumed violation of our self-set standards. Nobody should take what is rightfully ours, saying things like, "She shouldn't do what she's doing."

Special others must adhere to *our* view of correct behavior and acceptable protocols, reflected in statements such as, "You shouldn't . . . You're wrong." "You cannot possibly behave like that." "You can't possibly accept yourself *like that!*"

This zealousness encompasses the violation of anything we judge as important in the relationship, such as honoring sanctity and holding confidences, spending time together focused on one another, as well as expectations around truthfulness, integrity, and fidelity.

At our worst, we get totally heated up, possessive, intolerant, righteous, and scolding—monitoring situations and special others closely, even to the point of stalking. Perhaps, at times, we'll flame up in a caustic, punitive rage in order to impact a situation that to us feels out of control.

Social 1 | Inadaptability/Inflexibility
In the social domain, we channel our desire for rightness and higher good— along with its consequential tension and anger/frustrations—into correcting what we see in the world. We may take on particular roles to make a difference, joining groups or those organizations that have influence. We strive to make the system better, bring forth more integrity, more rightfulness, whatever is deemed necessary according to our particular standards. We become social reformers and crusaders, so to speak.

We become inadaptable or inflexible, insisting on our own views and implementations. We may screen out evidence that is contrary to our fervently held position. We are not only scanning for what is wrong with various other organizations or groups, causes and convictions, but we also see what is wrong about our own group or other's convictions. Our colleagues, associates, partner, and family must adhere to our standards. There is one right way, and they must support it.

At our worst, we can become possessed by righteous anger and dominated by black-and-white thinking, characterized by an inability to see differing viewpoints, agendas, or initiatives—all of which extend to our familial, community, and social relationships.

Type 2 | The Giver | Privilege, Seduction, or Ambition

As a Giver, the pride of fulfilling others' needs is a survival strategy that we believe will assure love and approval. This strategy manifests through the three instinctual drives, which serve to compensate for the loss of the original state of unconditional giving and unconditional receiving, the law of divine reciprocity. We believe that *we know best* what others need or desire—even before they know it themselves. It is reassuring to create the feeling of our own indispensability even though, in turn, it comes to feel like a burden that may harbor resentment in the end.

Self-Preservation 2 | Privilege

We assure our survival indirectly through earning privilege. This is accomplished by meeting the needs of others in our lives, especially our important relationships. Being nurturing and supportive of others propagates a deeply set feeling of entitlement. Pride then manifests as a sense that we ultimately and finally deserve to have our needs met too, after all that we've given. This shows up in statements such as: "I've given so much. When's it going to be my turn?"

We can get upset, even emotionally charged, when our relationships haven't honored us or given us the reciprocal, preferential treatment we've come to believe we've earned. This can be distressing to those in our lives who just want to give back on their own volition, not because they feel they have to, or that they owe us something. We staunchly protect all the way to defend our position as a selfless giver while hoping to assure that our own basic needs get met in return.

At our worst, however, we become preoccupied with—and demanding of—what we believe we need, even *deserve*, from others. This includes ways we want to be nurtured, pampered, loved, and appreciated—for our own personal survival. We can come to expect and demand reciprocity, to be attended to, to be escalated to that privileged position, expressly appreciated, and put first.

Sexual/One-to-One 2 | Seduction/Aggression

Here we cultivate personal pride by feeling needed and desired, being attuned to the other, and immensely empathetic. We feel that we can meet the needs and desires of a special other better than anyone else by gaining their approval and setting ourselves up to be their everything. For a partner, this is quite intoxicating. We seduce the other by attuning to their feelings, sensing into their needs and wants, and altering ourselves subtly to match our desired other's emotional state.

We seek attention and affection by giving what is needed first, using flattery and servitude, attentiveness and caring, thus building ourselves into a position of indispensability. Using our active energy assertively or aggressively, we captivate and capture the special other by taking on their interests, making them feel good, and matching exquisitely to what is required to win the other over. (When this Type 2 is your partner, the experience can be exceptionally intense.)

At our worst, we paradoxically become possessive and demanding, either overtly or covertly—becoming passive-aggressive when there's emotional upheaval—or we complain about our unfulfilled needs and desires to the point that it may potentially cause our partner to reject us.

As the "giving to get" dynamic is exposed, it's overwhelming and the relationship suffers as this can be especially distressing to a partner. This exposure may bring out our most protective defenses in order to deny it and attempt to recover our altruistic self-image.

Social 2 | Ambition

Our pride manifests itself in the social arena by giving to partners, family, and those in positions of power, thus assuring prominence, even indispensability, in the special group, family, or organization. Our pride shows up as ambition by pursuing stature and a positive public image through our alliances and alignment with our partner, mentors, authorities, and leaders.

We gain prominence through helper roles in visible social groups, work, or causes. Or we become the central figure, the hub of the family, the center of the team, the go-to person in our circle of friends. In all these settings, we look after the group's well-being, which bolsters our feeling lovable and hence worthy.

At our worst, however, we can disparage or reject and minimize others' inputs and contributions, believing that *only we* know what is really needed, and that *only we* are the ones, in the end, that make the critical difference.

We can also lose sight of our interpersonal relationship's unique needs while serving the demands and needs of the group we're devoted to, thus not recognizing our neglect in one area and our over-doing in another.

Type 3 | The Performer | Material Security, Masculine/Feminine Image, or Prestige

As a Performer, we believe that love and self-worth are based on other's perceptions of us. In this case, it's an *outside job*. Our value is placed on how we look and how we appear to others, what others think of us and how they approve of what we do and accomplish. Innate to this type's structure is the ability—talent if you will—to adjust on the fly, in the moment, and in response to what's wanted, what's admirable, and what's needed from us. We are able to alter our image, our energy, and our actions to produce a desired response, the response of affirmation and approval.

When this mostly non-conscious adaptive shape-shifting of our image works, we take on with relative ease the characteristics of the role, shifting our presentation accordingly to sustain that those we are in relationship with like us *like* us, *approve* of us, and *accept* us. In the process, we may have not only deceived or fooled others, but we have also inadvertently deceived ourselves, having lost our authentic self in the process—a common result of this sort of adaptation.

This talent—this powerful capacity—is one that causes us to lose ourselves for an adapted image and is the go-ahead emotional energy of deceit, that which can play itself out notably in the instinctual drives' behaviors and self-image-driven choices.

Self-Preservation 3 | Material Security

With the Self-Preservation Instinct of material security, our create-our-image energy often gets channeled into acquiring material things, positions in society, and possessions. Sometimes, this means endlessly working very hard to earn money for the family far beyond what the family may really need.

We inadvertently succumb to self-deception and deceit by identifying our self-survival with externals such as wealth, assets, our occupation, and even simply by doing and doing, which offers up an image of productivity, an "On it!" or "I sure have it all together" person.

We gain material status that we believe will assure survival and satisfaction for us and our vital relationships. A twist to this dynamic is how we define what success is. *It's specific to each Type 3's definition,* and it drives us to paint ourselves into becoming a wide variety of things deemed successful. This is what brings forth unique and diverse differences in each of these drives' expressions.

For instance, if success—what will gain adoration in one Type 3's community or family—is an image of frugality and practicality, we'll select an older, inexpensive, functional car because it's the right kind of automobile for *that* image. If success is defined by brand names and expensiveness, then a Porsche might be more suitable for that definition and corresponding image.

At our worst, there is no end to the activity directed at both acquiring the objects and completing the projects that we believe will bring security, love, and a sense of personal value. Others can become obstacles that incite our impatience and frustration if we come to feel they're in our way or impeding progress.

We may also come to feel that no matter how much we produce and achieve, our primary relationships seem to want *more* from us, including our time and attention—demands we may struggle to comply with as they only seem to slow us down.

Sexual/One-to-One 3 | Masculine/Feminine Image

As the Performer, in important relationships we formulate an "archetypical persona for our surroundings," that is, a masculine or feminine image that focuses on maximum star appeal. We manifest deceit by altering ourselves as necessary to look good, radiate competency, and wow the world with our charisma.

As a "human doing," we naturally perform the required role we've identified that gets us the results we desire. Our life depends upon winning the respect and adoration of others in vital business or love relationships, which is measured by the approval and personal attention we get for our image, our efforts, and our accomplishments.

We gain status in an intimate relationship by adopting a given role and by taking on the characteristics that we believe our partner is wanting and finds appealing. This may also result in uncertainty about our genuine feelings, our innate desires for self-expression, and even our unique sexual expression. At our worst, our significant others come to feel that we are disingenuous, disconnected, and that we care more about our image than their more vulnerable feelings or needs.

Social 3 | Prestige

With the Social Instinct of prestige, our success-oriented, striving energy is linked to our need for public recognition. We strive to receive honors, titles, influential connections, as well as be appreciated for what we accomplish, and we are compelled to look good in the process. We must be *somebody* in the eyes of others, or we're *nobody* in our eyes.

We get caught in the energy of self-deception by projecting the appropriate persona for the moment, for the group, or circumstance, and we take on the most desirable and appropriate thoughts and feelings for the *group's* situation rather than what might be true for *us*.

Whether genuine or only self-serving, our drive for recognition is directed toward winning the social approval of others and achieving a particular status, whether that be in government, religious organizations, businesses, or community groups. We can become quite political with people if that necessitates our end goals and boasts productivity.

We can come to believe that those we're in relationship with will love and respect us only if we achieve some rank of societal positioning. At our worst, our drive for recognition can be ruthless. It can be accompanied by outright dishonesty and manipulation, competitiveness that is scrupulous and that lacks awareness as to our impact on others, and inevitably, on our own starving-for-recognition reputation.

Our ability for self- and other-deceit and the alienation it creates is incredibly disturbing to our relationships—both our relationship to ourselves and the many relationships we are trying to cultivate with important others.

Type 4 | The Romantic | Dauntless, Competition, or Shame

As a Romantic, our mission is to regain the lost ideal love or circumstance, and at the most fundamental level, it's to reconnect with our own original essence itself—our own true and unique identity. Because of an endemic sense of fundamental loss, we struggle with an inner lacking, a deep and aching longing for unrequited fulfillment. Our self-esteem and well-being depend upon somehow compensating for these losses and inner lack. Through the emotional experience of envy and longing, and comparing ourselves hopelessly to others, we can too readily spiral into frustration and disappointment.

We compensate by seeking perceived authenticity, in this case by displaying emotional intensity as a way to express a unique and worthwhile self to the world that is over and above deficiency

Self-Preservation 4 | Reckless/Dauntless

How can being reckless and dauntless serve fundamental Self-Preservation survival? For the Romantic, to be ordinary, mundane, or mediocre is akin to death. Standing out is salvation. To survive, we *must be a special somebody* or *a special something.*

We achieve this by creating a very-different-from-others identity by seeking the bigger/richer/greater feelings and forms of expression and, above all else, by valuing authenticity (what's real and what's genuine). We seek this in others as well as in what we choose to do with our time and energy. Our contribution to the world is highly connected to what is meaningful to us personally and how closely we live our lives to our sense of meaning.

As Self-Preservation 4s, we assuage our envy by playing the edge and throwing caution to the wind, or by jumping into new situations, into whatever provides that sense of authenticity, intensity, and meaningfulness.

Paradoxically, we may neglect our basic survival needs. In this way, we feel enlivened and special. We are true to ourselves and refuse to submit otherwise. We have a reckless urgency to obtain those ultimate and uniquely elite, powerfully emotive experiences that make us feel alive and which quell our longing.

Determined to steer clear of the status quo, even seemingly ordinary life events are infused with a jazzed-up spin or dramatic flair. Perhaps we create a mini crisis with big feelings and just enough drama by threatening rejection or abandonment, or by breaking the rules.

Our close relationships can feel disturbed by what seems like unpredictability, way too much drama, and, at times, a neglect of basic needs that then falls on the shoulders of others to absorb. Others can also feel enticed by our adventuresome spirit—even enlivened by it.

At our worst, our self-absorption can become reckless, which paradoxically leads to disastrous outcomes. These include the reemergence of that nagging sense of inner lack and deficiency, which can grip us even more palpably, and that spiral of disappointment, or melancholic depression, can take us for a ride, again.

Sexual/One-to-One 4 | Competition/Hate

In relationships, envy and longing drive us to compete for that special position, partner, or mentor. This can make primary relationships feel special and wanted. This form of competition creates an invigorating energy, expressed as, "I'll show the world that I can get the special connection I deserve."

We use competition with others to overcome the often not-conscious feelings of inner deficiency. We fight for what is noteworthy, exquisite, aristocratic, and elegant. Identifying ourselves with items deemed superior or special elevates us, making us perceptively worthy and deserving.

As One-to-One 4s, we want to be treated as *a very special someone* by our partner or desired other. If necessary, a hateful streak can emerge, and we slam our opponents—imagined or actual. We compete not as much to win, though that's great, but rather not to lose.

Our self-esteem tends to rise and fall in comparison with others and as we fluctuate between the highs of superiority and the lows of inferiority. To intimates, this can feel like a roller coaster of ups and downs.

Rather than lose the painful comparison competition and the felt envy, which can lead to falling into a spiral of lack and deficiency, we may reject someone or something before being perceptively rejected ourselves. We abandon *first*. It's better to leave than to be left. In this way, we combat the envy suffered and abandonment feared in a sabotaging way.

This cycle is hard on our partner. Often, it's interpreted as *just not being enough*, leaving the partner feeling they're a disappointment and resigned to feeling that we just cannot be satisfied.

Paradoxically, at our worst we may end up destroying vital relationships. Trying to win the ultimate connection, we instead destroy it due to our lack of acceptance for what is really there.

We miss the point by not putting our energy into cultivating what is truly precious about the relationship and by not honoring and nurturing what we truly want and desire.

Social 4 | Shame/Counter-Shame

A Type 4 with a dominant Social Instinct more readily experiences shame when not measuring up to the group's expectations and feeling they're more of a misfit. This type of shame leads us to believe that our protective cover, our mask, is removed and that our deficiencies and shortcomings will be exposed publicly—right down to our so-unwanted mediocrity.

We mitigate our envy through subconsciously held shame. We strive to hide our defects and deficiencies, keep our fatal flaws from being detected, and avoid public and social disgrace.

Our shame, though, is what helps us design a viable approach when soliciting connection with others. This is expressed as, "I'm different, because . . ." Or "I don't fit in, but I like you." Or "Sorry I'm different, because that's real and that's me."

This can all begin to feel heavy-handed—even self-absorbed—to those we're in relationship with, those who see us as quite enough, as fine as we are, and who feel trapped in the loop of either having to offer chronic reassurance or ward off interpersonal defiance. Shame, particularly *toxic* shame, catalyzes a tremendous form of personal suffering inside of ourselves, and within our relationships too. Shame, however, when healthier, supports us and motivates us to shift gears as is necessary in order to better belong and fit in.

In the case of a Type 4, however, this can generate something called "counter-shame," which can ultimately drive us to create a new or updated image, reinforce a sense of pride around a created elitism or form of defiance, seek ways to look unique and special (or not), and find more pronounced ways to express our extraordinary individuality or heartfelt persona.

In short, counter-shame can elicit a sense of pride and arrogance for what we actually bring to, and do for, the group. Unfortunately, this can lead to our group (and its members) feeling that they are just not enough, thanks to our own projections of inner lack onto others, or onto the group at large.

At our worst, all forms of shame can lead to a retraction into self-absorption, melancholic rumination, and depression, qualities that are tiring and disturbing to intimates, to our groups, and to work relationships.

Type 5 | The Observer | Castle, Confidence, or Totems

As an Observer, we believe that to want or need puts us in jeopardy, lending us to dependency and depletion. We strive for self-sufficiency and independence as a protection from intrusion and a fear of exhaustion, of feeling depleted. We dread being drained, so we avariciously conserve our own energy supply by retracting into the sanctuary of our minds. When here, we can indulge in what we perceive that we can't live without, which primarily includes private time, personal space *that is private*, and the acquisition of knowledge and the time and energy to pursue it. This avarice, conservation of the self, plays out across various behaviors expressed by the three instinctual drives.

Self-Preservation 5 | Home/Castle

What better place to protect our boundaries and personhood than in the privacy of our own space? Through the sanctuary of our own mind and designated privatized world, we can keep others out, cleverly guarding their access to us. We avariciously protect and govern our own territorialized space, whether it's our mind, our room, our home office, or our castle. In this way, we can preserve our time and energy, acquire more knowledge, build a storehouse of necessary subsistence, and assure our survival.

As an Observer, we keep our precious independence by needing very little and hoarding what we think we need most. We don't intend to exclude our relationships or significant others; we are simply protecting our boundaries. We experience a kind of esteemed pleasure making do with less and often spurn possessions and luxuries.

We cling to whatever we believe assures us a satisfactory life and adequate relationships, including saving money, access to information or reading materials, conservation of energy, time for hobbies and collections, places to obtain needed supplies with ease, and plenty of private time to pursue our curiosities and interests. The positive for others is our live-and-let-live stance and our willingness to share our knowledge and know-how with genuinely interested others.

At our worst, we can become so retracted that we neglect our significant relationships, and they fall to the wayside. We often end up isolated and lonely, neglectful of our own emotional needs, and not socialized well enough to make those necessary connections—those that would otherwise support and nurture us and bring care and closeness into our lives.

Sexual/One-to-One 5 | Confidence

We bond to special others by sharing confidential information, sharing private and held-precious knowledge, and by giving up some of our much-conserved energy and even our feelings. In these sacred, primary relationships, we don't need as much to hide or guard our definitive boundaries, yet our avarice does still show. We still slip back into ourselves when there's a need for personal replenishment, which may include the time needed to assess a situation, treasure and more fully engage with the feelings just experienced in a personal encounter, or tinkering and postulating inside of our minds, as we so like to do.

By expressing a level of personal confidence, we are able to release the grip of our boundaries—those that guard our privacy—by allowing intense, mental encounters all the way to physically intimate ones with our partner or special other. Key disclosures are made and held sacred for a lifetime—recreated and ruminated over in our imaginations. These shared confidences assuage the loneliness that comes from isolating ourselves from our messier feelings and not-so-easy-to-control human interactions. We will do so, though, while maintaining as much as possible our autonomy and need for privacy.

At our worst, the intense one-to-one sharing can operate like an unpredictable on-off switch, to the dismay of special others who end up suffering unmet needs and a sensitivity to the rejection that can occur when it's time for the Type 5 to pull back and retreat.

Social 5 | Totems

We all need to belong, and we need to connect with fellow humans. As an Observer with an avarice and seeming gluttony for knowledge, private time, and energy conservation, belonging is not necessarily a prioritized pursuit. Our avarice manifests through cleaving to totems, which means grasping for the representation of things that a group shares and espouses, but that which is safely one step removed from ordinary involvement. Needing a knowledge-based role that buffers us from direct access, we are attracted to groups that share special knowledge, such as a field of study or systems, or a shared intellectual pursuit.

We have a hunger for and affiliate with people or groups that influence culture, events, and that seek greater knowledge through the power of the mind. In this way, we serve others and can be more generous with our time and knowledge.

As Social 5s, we align in the mental domain with leaders, movements, and systems where knowledge is valued and shared, such as historical researchers and philosophical groups, scientific and technical endeavors, sports expertise, or literary or artistic interests. Here we feel needed, contributory, comfortable, and a part of things. We attempt to obtain sufficiency through acquiring and sharing knowledge that befits the group.

At our worst, we use totems—whatever they might be—as a substitute for heartfelt human contact, paradoxically isolating ourselves from others and losing the capacity to cultivate connection, much to the dismay of our significant others and any of our relationships in general.

Type 6 | The Loyal Skeptic | Warmth, Beauty, or Duty

As a Loyal Skeptic, we believe the world is hazardous and unpredictable. Fear is felt energetically as angst, apprehension, and runs concurrently with hypervigilance and a readily alerted skepticism—all of which need channels for expression and relief. This is equally true for those of us that are counter-phobic, meaning, that we tend to most often confront fear head-on rather than allow it to overtake us. Counter-phobic 6s often report we are not necessarily deterred by fear and may often say we are fearless.

We tend to doubt and question others, read between the lines, and scan the environment for what could be problematic all the way to what is not on the up-and-up. We gather evidence, look for proof, and seek certainty. This doubting-scanning mind—with or without a consciousness of it being fear-driven—plays out in the instinctual behaviors. In a way, it is a compensatory reaction to the loss of faith in safety itself, in others, in the universe, and in the undefended, innocent self.

Self-Preservation 6 | Warmth/Friendliness

Driving with the Self-Preservation Instinct, we disarm others with our warmth and friendliness. By acting with kindness, thoughtfulness, and deference, the strategy is to endear ourselves to others to the point that they will find it hard to be angry with us or harm us.

We'll make friends and get those in our relationships to like us by pleasing, supporting, and aligning—in effect, by creating a safety zone populated with allies. This makes us feel safe and secure. We are loyal and supportive to our family and neighbors. This applies to the more counter-phobic 6s as well.

Avoiding risks and staying within well-known boundaries can abate the fears of the more phobic Type 6. Challenging and confronting what may be aggravatingly gnawing at us is the way the counter-phobic uses fear to ignite action and mobilization, which abates the agitation.

At our worst, we relinquish our authority and personal power, paradoxically making us more vulnerable, in that we wind up not tackling what really requires appropriate and necessary confrontation. Or we may over-confront and over-challenge as a way out of our angst, only to find we've unwittingly created more of it.

Sexual/One-to-One 6 | Strength/Beauty

Having power and influence with significant others counteract fears of aloneness and dependency. It is powerful to manifest connection and influence with our strength and beauty. These are intoxicating, appealing qualities that are less likely to create adversarial reactions than those of raw and overt power moves. Instead of craving reassurance and grappling for it, reassurance comes to us through the expression of and rewards garnered by our strength and beauty.

Knowing that we affect our vital relationships with our brilliant ideas, mental prowess, and physicality—our strength and beauty—we obtain desired assurance and confidence. Aesthetic qualities (creating beauty in our environment) and attractiveness command desire and allegiance from others, as does intellectual strength, which includes fiercely held ideological positions all the way to physical fitness, strength of will, and utter bravery.

Our fear (or angst) evaporates when we obtain the respect of associates or an intimate partner. While the preoccupation with strength and beauty in one-to-one relating is more common for counter-phobic Type 6s (because it is more congruent with their inherent propensity), it also shows up in phobic Type 6s as a subtler, more humbled expression of strength and downplayed beauty, all the way to a hesitancy in assertiveness and a subdued self-confidence.

At our worst, we can become possessed with the need to influence others and get them on our side, and we'll catalyze and evoke reactions in our partner and vital others by testing, provoking, contradicting, and challenging until we're satisfied.

Social 6 | Duty

In the Social domain, we assuage our fear through our loyal duty to a group or cause. We feel safer when bonded together with others in a common cause, where we understand the needs of the united group members and assure that a code of behavior is followed. We align with groups we trust through sharing mutual obligations and sacrifice, believing, "United we stand, divided we fall." We find power and hence safety in the group's authority. Knowing the rules and creating clear agreements with friends and colleagues are vital for overcoming our existential fear.

As a Loyal Skeptic, our tendency to project negative, disempowered power onto the world makes underdog causes particularly appealing. We align with the needy, the oppressed, and the persecuted. We work devotedly for the cause. The call to duty mobilizes us, but not overtly for personal gain, which would expose us.

At our worst, we give away our divine authority and authentic power. In our groups and organizations, this can result in having blind faith in something we believe is greater than ourselves, and negating all others who may disagree or want to challenge our loyalties.

Type 7 | The Epicure | Family, Fascination, or Ambition

As an Epicure, we cannot stand limitations. We pursue a good life, and our fundamental survival through a gluttony for interesting, interrelated ideas, fascinating future possibilities, intriguing stimulation, and scintillating adventures.

We express an outer-directed, upbeat, and energetic optimism and rationalize what we prefer to do in order to defiantly escape limitations. This gluttony plays itself out across all three instinctual drives, and in such a way that compensates for the tougher aspects of our lives—that which we must traverse, one way or another, as part of life's full spectrum.

That full spectrum includes developing the capacity to deal honestly and vulnerably with setbacks and limitations—without denial or resistance—and without fearing that if we do face it all, we'll be miserably trapped in it all.

Self-Preservation 7 | Like-minded Defenders/Family

As an Epicure, we feel secure when we identify with like-minded others, those who share our ideals, spontaneity, and willingness to keep it happening and light at all times. We find other deserving people to bond with, folks who mirror our buoyancy, pursuit of a great life, and bigger vision.

As Self-Preservation 7s, we form relationships with these deserving people, those that share our life view. Interestingly enough, they may only exist in our imagination as possibilities. Or they may be actual family members, friends, and associates who fit into part of our dream or grander scheme. In order to not be limited by or rejected in relationships, we seek individuals who support our way of being. Our gluttony plays out through these like-minded defenders who protect us from being trapped or limited, in what we otherwise fear could be a boring, unstimulating, limiting, and painful life.

We assure enjoyment in family-style gatherings, making sure we have lots of options and are living the good life. These individuals—our tribe—are like family to us, although often not connected biologically. We share pleasures such as fine dining, the-best-of-the-best of anything, globe-hopping, exploring, worldly adventures, new ventures, make-money schemes, and invigorating hobbies. As trusted fellow travelers, we brainstorm together to sustain and fortify each other's vision of a positive future.

At our worst, our claims on others to support our point of view or material desires can be highly demanding, self-centered, and thoughtless. And in the end, we may flee responsibility and any given situation to escape our perception of limitation.

Sexual/One-to-One 7 | Fascination/Suggestibility

When our upbeat energy and active imagination manifest in the One-to-One relationship, we connect by finding what fascinates and interests us. Our attention goes to what in the special other sparks our interest and imagination, that which will provide a channel for our energetically charged gluttony. We feel magnetized to this person and begin to idealize them.

We are likable, charming, and disarming—a great salesperson with intoxicating, stimulating propaganda. Our special others bask in our energy and get caught up in the rush of our ideas, plans, and possibilities.

When we lose some of the new-love buzz in a relationship or when the spark cools, someone else may easily catch our eye. We then find a way out, not realizing that we are breaking promises that, from our standpoint, we never really made to begin with, or weren't that serious about in the long run. Or we stick with it, ironically, finding ways through suggestibility and reframing denial to hold on to that shared vision of a positive future—even when the situation may be disastrous and not, in truth, in alignment with that vision at all.

Our innate half-glass-full optimism can prevent us from reading the dismal landscape with veracity. We just don't or won't see the negatives. At our worst, we lose focus and disperse our vibrant energy. We may rationalize our way out of seemingly committed relationships, responsibilities, and obligations when they lose their thrill, seem confining, or cease to be self-serving.

Social 7 | Sacrifice

As a Type 7 driving from the Social Instinct, we must rein in our gluttony for stimulating experiences or interesting ideas, plans, and projects. To function in the group or organization, we must sacrifice some of our own desires for the higher social cause. We can postpone our own gratification and accept limitations more willingly for the sake of group ideals or worthy endeavors with which we identify and enjoy. We participate with others who mirror our philosophy and our visions for a better world. If they don't get on board, we may ignore or denounce them.

Often, the hardest part of adhering to the norms and requirements of the group is in dealing with authority. We don't want to be told what to do or waste our precious time doing routine tasks. In this instance, sacrifice acquires a flavoring of martyrdom. We will, in this case, accept non-7-like suffering for the sake of the larger cause, while imagining an idealized future that equalizes authority and our defiance. We can feel ecstatic about the sacrifices we make for family and for our valued choices and pursuits.

At our worst, we overbook ourselves with too many social interests and activities, making it difficult to commit or participate fully in anything. We may also simply escape the situation if it gets to be too much, is not heading toward the outcome we want by design, or if it impedes our need for stimulation and limitlessness.

Type 8 | The Protector | Satisfactory Survival, Possession, or Social Causes

As a Protector, we move quickly from impulse into action, mobilizing rapidly in the face of opposition or obstacles, or when our sense of truth or justice is under siege. Our hearts are innocent and tender, and protecting that innocence is a constant priority. Our big, assertive, lustful, excessive energy drives an unremitting belief in our own truth, strength, and power. Simultaneously, we avoid weakness and vulnerability in ourselves, and do not accept it well in others either. Our lust-for-life exuberance, low tolerance for the weaknesses or needs of others, and insistence on a "my way or the highway" stance gets acted out through the three instinctual drives. Such that we don't even realize we are being excessive, intimidating, or overly impactful.

Self-Preservation 8 | Satisfactory Survival

We need adequate amounts of provisions and environmental security to assure satisfactory survival for ourselves, our intimates, and our associates. If we throw a party, for example, we may serve at least double the food and beverages that our guests could possibly consume.

As Self-Preservation 8s, we assert a large amount of control over our own survival needs and those we are charged to protect. Although we are generous with those we love and care for, they can often feel controlled, unfelt, and unheard. Our tendency toward excess shows up everywhere. We may not necessarily hoard things, but we want to make sure that what we need is readily available and in plenty; we surely do not want to be deprived, let alone dependent.

We exert control over our creature-comforts and physical environment. Our motto for satisfactory survival is, "Be ready and have enough." Taking charge of our material environment gives us the illusion that we are invulnerable and in control.

At our worst, this drives us to become preoccupied with never-ending demands for security and to obtain excessive control, even domination, over our physical environment and those in it—those with whom we identify, need to protect, or need to challenge to ensure our own truth and needs are met.

Sexual/One-to-One 8 | Possession/Surrender

As a Protector, our passionate exuberance wants to possess our intimate relationships, meaning, we want to know and control everything about that special other—mind, body, and soul. We want to protect them and be consulted in all significant matters.

We can be highly physical and highly sexual. We don't tend to think of our control as a negative, nor do we see that it is impacting or dominating. We're simply taking charge and providing our care and love for those special others who depend upon us.

Our vitality and verve infuse every molecule of our intimates—or so we hope. In business, this takes the form of a very commanding presence, a relentless competitiveness, and the power to do battle as necessary. Struggles over control let us know on whom we can count.

Possession in our personal lives and our potency with special others verify to us our power, strength, and efficacy. After we have tested an intimate's fettle and commitment, we can move to the polar opposite with our all-or-nothing style of interacting. We can, at times, surrender control and then we'll share a bit of our precious and tender hearts, but only when trusting that we will *not* be betrayed.

At our worst, our intense, energetic command can lead to dominating and controlling vital intimates with an all-or-nothing approach to relating—a stance that inevitably leads to disconnection, outright rejection, and mutual suffering.

Social 8 | Social Causes and Enduring Friendship

In the Social Instinct domain, our Type 8's robust, highly assertive, sometimes demanding, sometimes desirous energy (known as lust or life force) tests for and builds true friendships with individuals who share our values, sense of justice, and social causes.

As Social 8s, we develop camaraderie after we've tested the limits and have witnessed firsthand that others can meet us fully, stand for us, and that they'll match our stamina and fortitude. It's vital to us that others can be counted on honorably for directness and honest feedback.

We join activities, events, and social causes that take precedence over our personal needs. We are true, committed, and devoted to the group or organization and influence it according to our own sense of justice—giving our vital energy without hesitation.

Leadership seems to fall upon us. Together we struggle for justice and triumphs, all of which overcome any sense of powerlessness. We are like brothers and sisters in arms, sharing an "I've got your back" respect and common purpose. These affiliations even overcome our seemingly destined loner tendency.

At our worst, our intense absorption in social causes with committed friendships in community-building and in worthy projects can lead to an over-exuberance and conflictual interactions when others in the group don't comply with our version of what's expected. Furthermore, these affiliations can dominate our lives and short-change our vital relationships and intimate partnerships.

Type 9 |The Mediator | Appetite, Union, or Participation

As a Mediator, we have the natural propensity to merge into another, a way of engendering a non-differentiation between ourselves and others. We ourselves become a non-issue. We then seek externalized personal comforts to compensate for the loss of personal value and significance, that which is experienced when interacting with and subjugating ourselves to others.

We forget—or shall we say, disappear to ourselves—when it comes to recognizing our unique and important inner agenda, wants, needs, and independence. To manage this internal dynamic, we replace our autonomous identity with non-essential substitutes and activities, which might include numbing out to television, getting lost in books and in unimportant, long-winded, non-personal banter.

Our energy goes into becoming one with others and their perspectives and needs, deriving an accommodating stance that causes no trouble or extra effort and puts others at immediate ease—and in the driver's seat. This results in something referred to as an "energetic inertia" or sloth, in traditional Enneagram speak (calling out a laziness toward the self), which manifests itself through the three instinctual drives in specific ways.

Self-Preservation 9 | Appetite

In the Self-Preservation instinctual domain, our Type 9's energetic inertia flows into appetites and desires. We seek comfort through daily rhythms and by focusing on the little things, not realizing that the appetite or craving is a substitute for our more authentic needs calling out to us—those that have been numbed out, long repressed, or denied.

These little activities and distractions, interests in the external world that use up our energy and soothe us, actually take away from the time and energy that could be spent with ourselves (internally) and with our relationships (externally). These little desires or appetites for comforting distraction can feel vital, comforting, and right for us, and can even be used as a safe and satisfying replacement for actual intimacy and love.

We tend to like a tried-and-true structure and we-can-count-on-it daily routine that supports our lives and those in our circle. We can get lost in chores and errands, veg out in front of the TV, or start cleaning a closet that wasn't on our list, all as ways to stay away from the self and its autonomous, self-honoring needs.

Instead, we distractingly focus on something more pleasing and non-conflict-generating. We become engrossed in our familiar rhythms, in the agendas and viewpoints of others, or in a number of hobbies or tasks that will keep us gently and emotionally pacified.

Having lost touch with the innermost us, we attempt to reconnect through these substitutes, because in that time our discomfort with what's been suppressed temporarily abates. At our worst, we become stubbornly preoccupied with a myriad of inessentials such as small talk, ruminations about what we wanted to say but never did, errands and chores, even other people's dilemmas.

All of these ways of numbing out result in leaving no time to face, engage with, or embrace our own priorities, wants, and desires—let alone our impetus and purpose. Consequently, our ability to show up fully and connect honestly with our intimate relationships is stifled.

Sexual/One-to-One 9 | Union

In the Sexual/One-to-One arena, we seek comfort and belonging with special others. Our energetic self-inertia manifests by absorbing the other into ourselves and by being absorbed by another's point of view, their agendas, their responses to things, and to their feelings. We feel well insulated from rejection and seemingly whole in this union with our partner or special other, just as we do when alone in nature or sensing into the divine.

Our quietly held, hurtful experiences of being overlooked or disregarded evaporate as our identity merges into something other than ourselves. We are swept along, feeling, "I gain belonging, importance, and existence when merged and in tandem with something or someone else."

At our worst, since there's an energetic realization of there actually being a sovereign "us" inside—even though we are lost somewhere in the other—we can become quite resistive, passive-aggressive, and even counter-merging as our anger builds for having lost ourselves while the other is not noticing or seemingly not caring. In this case, we are not being present to either ourselves or the other. This can be both disconcerting and distressing to our special relationships as they've not known that a subversion of our authentic self was happening in the first place.

Social 9 | Participation

In the Social Instinct domain, we join a group or organization and channel our energetic inertia into comforting and pleasing group activities. Through participation, we feel included and inhabit a sense of belonging, even a sense of being loved. We can, without effort, overlook our own personal agenda as we fill ourselves up with social interactions, tasks, and functions, and a variety of group-serving activities.

In leadership, we can be quite selfless. We dispense and disperse our energy into timetables, procedures, roles, and goals. We promote the welfare of the group or community through our selfless participation, harmonizing approach to challenges, and our ability to mediate conflict between others. In these relationships, we find a comfortable niche and sense of belonging—a purpose. As Social 9s, we are busy and effective. Summarily, participation in groups and their defined activities keep us from experiencing the inertia that is happening toward ourselves.

At our worst, we can get swallowed up in the minutia of group activities and become preoccupied with fitting in, nailing it down, and getting along—at all costs. We don't always speak up when we know a better way or see something wrong because it's easier to go along to get along, to not make trouble, and just deal with it all later, if at all.

This can be distressing to those who count on us to lead the way, and very distressing to our intimate relationships, who may be relying on us to fully show up and take a stand or call a spade a spade.

Relationship Health and Compatibility: Know Your Enneagram Type and Subtype

Studying these three instinctual drives in detail as to how they are expressed by individuals of each of the nine Enneagram types provides us with an invaluable resource. The understanding of "why we do what we tend to do" cannot be underestimated as it pertains to being in a discerning relationship with ourselves first, and then, with another.

Asking "Why is my partner doing that? Why is *that* so important to them? Why is what's so important to me not important to them?" can lead to a relationship's dissolution because without this kind of study and understanding, we don't usually have an acceptable answer.

Our relationships suffer greatly when we do not understand ourselves, let alone, when we do not understand one another. That's why processing who we are and who our significant others are is such an intensely worthy endeavor. It allows us to get along with each other, replacing judgmentalness and fear with compassion and love as the splitting energies of judgmentalness and fear are a far cry from that of love and compassion. The impact of these energetic shifts alone is incalculable for all involved.

These instinctual drives most often govern how we tend to mobilize ourselves to action. It's what we routinely do and focus on. It's how we involve our significant others (or not). It's how much attention we have available to give others (or not). The more compulsively and unconsciously we find ourselves acting on these instincts, the more trouble and disconnect we may find in our relationships.

While we are often asked which Enneagram type should date which Enneagram type, my answer is always the same, **"Date a healthy one—any type with a high level of developmental well-being—as that's one of the most significant keys to relationship success, regardless of what type someone is."**

To that I should add that two developmentally sound individuals can still suffer quite a lot as a result of conflicting instinctual drives. These drives are at the root of many of our fundamental needs being met by one another. Watching our partner not prioritize things that are important to us can lead to hurt feelings and much misunderstanding—resentments can build fast.

The answer to this dilemma is first education. Learning about ourselves and others—our Enneagram type and our subtype, for example—promotes understanding. Add to this heartfelt back-and-forth communication.

What might have triggered a big fight in the past can become a good "instincts giggle" in the future. These understandings can free us up, removing the potential for unwarranted hurt, and instead leave all involved feeling more understood, connected, and accepted. This level of understanding gives us a secure base to respect one another mutually and unconditionally. It allows us to honor our unique, fundamental, highly contributory differences and motivations and that of our partners, our children, other family members, work colleagues, and close friends.

In our relationships, we can start by assessing ourselves first, starting with an inquiry around our predominant center of intelligence: "Am I dominated by the Head Center? The Heart Center? Or the Gut/Body Center?"

Next, take some time to identify our own Enneagram type, and then discuss and identify each other's Enneagram type with one another.

Finally—and not to be overlooked, particularly as the impact on coupleship is so great—learn to *identify* our dominant instinctual drive and that of our significant other, then *talk* about it. Discuss how the other two instincts stack up for each of us and pay attention to how they also impact our experience of one another.

All three of these specific identifications—center of intelligence, Enneagram type, and instinctual drives—provide us with a significant amount of incisive information that profoundly impacts how well we understand ourselves and one another, not to mention how we get along.

This learning provides us with a map, a masterful way to navigate a relationship as it brings a "relationship mindful awareness" to day-to-day interactions and to all ways of interrelating.

Yes, please!

I have found over the years that there is nothing more powerful than seeing a couple approach their relationship consciously, and it's so powerful when they do so in tandem. If only one-half of the partnership takes this on, and the other is not interested or not ready, the chances of this partnership surviving—let alone thriving—are dismal.

When one grows and the other doesn't, it's usually only a matter of time when relating to one another becomes more and more difficult. When each individual involved takes a committed interest in their personal understanding and development and then takes that same interest in the development of the other, success is on the horizon.

A commitment to the growth and development of each person—side-by-side, in cooperation with each other, and mutually supportive—is the greatest recipe for relationship success available to us. It's the secret to having and sustaining highly fulfilling relationships, partnerships, and in leading far more fulfilling lives overall.

Let the journey to self-development—to increasing our own developmental well-being—entice us, invite us, and call to us. And may we take the same interest in our partner's. May the development journey lead us and our relationships to far greater mutuality, mega happiness, and deep fulfillment.

CHAPTER 8

Gender, Masculine and Feminine Energies, and the Enneagram

Across my many years as an Enneagram system developer, teacher, and facilitator, I took note of people's responses to the system as they first encountered it. Determining with a good level of certainty which of the nine type structures we might be takes time and honesty. It's a process of self-discovery that requires a good deal of honest self-observation.

Something that comes up more frequently than not were people's reactions to the Enneagram types' naming conventions, as in, an Enneagram Type 1 is called the Perfectionist (or Reformer in other Enneagram schools), an Enneagram Type 2 is called the Giver (the Helper), Enneagram Type 3, the Performer (Achiever), and so on.

In an offsite workshop I was leading some years ago to Fortune 500 CEOs, one of the attendees struggled to accept his delineated Enneagram type because he could not accept the title "the Giver."

This man felt strongly he was an Enneagram Type 2 by the descriptions given, and my cross-referencing proved to me he was accurately self-assessing. But he was not comfortable. He was the CEO of a successful plumbing distribution company and didn't think a name like "the Giver" let alone "the Helper" suited his head-of-company, great-leader, take-charge image.

Those titles felt "too feminine, too nice," he said, even though he admitted to being "the guy who took care of things and his people."

In working with the EPP (the Enneagram Prison Project, as you may remember) on the inside of jails and prisons, the naming of the Enneagram Type 4, also called "the Romantic," did not sit that comfortably either with some (well, *many*) of the guys. Particularly former gang members were reluctant to self-identify when the type's title put on display their softer, more nostalgic emotionality and sensitivities.

While naming conventions such as "the Romantic," "the Boss," or "the Epicure" have been assigned to each Enneagram type by various Enneagram schools (and the names vary beyond that from one school to another), we'd like to propose we place a stronger focus on *the energetic quality* of the type—the essence and the characteristics that are expressed—thanks to the particular neural wiring and core beliefs, the how-to-live perspectives rather than getting hung up on any of the many monikers.

Enneagram teachers all over the world get the same questions about the system, and one of those questions is this: "Which type structures are categorized as male, and which as female?" As if finding ourselves in a type that we perceive is not fitting with gender-stereotypes would be awkward or embarrassing.

In Chapter 6, we stated that the Enneagram types are not gender specific. That means, we can have a male Enneagram Type 2 or a female Enneagram Type 2—or a non-binary Enneagram Type 2, for that matter.

But while not gender-specific, Enneagram types are, in fact, "energetic qualities and propensities" specific, which takes us back to our male CEO being apprehensive about placing himself in a type that possesses and espouses qualities of being that the American culture has feminized.

In 1955, sexologist John Money introduced us to his developing ideology, differentiating biological sex from gender. Money identified *gender* as an acculturated identity, a learned social construct derived from cultural norms. These learned rather than innate norms, he claimed, dictate to us what characteristics of our humanness are feminine and, therefore, female and which are masculine and, therefore, male.

So, here are some questions to consider: What qualities of being does your society feminize? What qualities of being have been masculinized? Where do each of us fit into those categorizations? (This has obviously become a very big topic as of late, so much so that we are watching society challenging the norms from the bottom up.) It's also worth asking where "personality" might fit into all of this.

In 1992, John Gray, PhD, wrote the bestseller, *Men Are from Mars, Women Are from Venus: How to Get What You Want in Your Relationship.* His book was written in the hopes of shedding light on some of the key differences between men and women. His argument assigned our differences in biology as gender differences and looked at how those differences impacted relationships.

While splitting our species in two is in line with the binary science of *biological sex,* splitting us into *two genders,* as did Dr. Gray, allowed for polarizing—though also useful, perhaps—understandings that may do nothing less than assist us in gaining compassion for those members of the opposite sex and for ourselves as well.

Furthermore, and importantly, without allowing ourselves to understand that "**Men and women are supposed to be different**," says John Gray, "**. . . it is such a temptation to insist we behave more similarly to one another, even complaining that men shouldn't be *that* way, or women shouldn't be *this or that* way.**"

What Dr. Gray alluded to way back then was that without the understanding of fundamental, biological differences, per his argument, as well as how we as a society have defined gender via the sexes and then programmed our responses to those definitions, we readily—and perhaps innocently—believe our intimate partner should be "a certain way," just like the stereotypes.

The number of arguments that arise between couples—of all combinations, for that matter—because there is little understanding of our much-needed, intelligently organized differences, is astronomical. This is true whether the difference between us be biological sex, gender-expected differences, temperamental character differences, or something else.

What happens when we want our partners to be something different than who they are innately? Gray's answer to that question covers it: It just may trigger in each other feelings of rejection, of "not enoughness," or "non-acceptableness."

It's clear where this not-so-wonderful spiral of non-acceptance is going to take us!

Honoring Our Differences, Celebrating Our Commonalities

What else then might we want to consider now, more than 30 years since Dr. Gray spelled out the relational and personality differences between biologically different men and women? Are there other considerations when moving toward greater compassion and understanding of one another, other than sex and gender differentiations? Well, yes . . . Because of the Enneagram and what it teaches us, we do, in fact, think there is more here to consider.

What we'd like to propose is this: Instead of splitting our species into two biological sexes that specify two genders (roles and identities), let's look at ourselves and our *qualities of being* from a broader perspective, one that comes from nine different angles.

An extraordinary amount of understanding and compassion for each other is to be had by looking at our *differences* and our *commonalities*, but from another perspective—from an energetic perspective, from nine Enneagram perspectives, nine neural propensities, from nine stunningly organized temperaments.

Each of those takes into account, one by one, those qualities of being that our respective society has feminized—sweetness, kindness, gentleness, softness, emotionality, receptiveness, patience, and sensuousness, for example. And those qualities in particular that the American society has masculinized—strength, assertiveness, protectiveness, leadership, fierceness, territorialization, authoritativeness, and aggressiveness.

What the Enneagram Brings to the Gender Discussion Table

The Enneagram is a highly complex system that takes us far beyond a simplified, categorizing personality typology. Its study includes a number of teachings around human energetic patterns, including how each type structure shows up in the world to build its life and relate to its environment. These varying ways energy is exerted and expressed within each type structure help us to understand, and make far more sense of why some males are thoughtfully gentle and tenderly withdrawn, and why some females are wonderfully aggressive and effectively authoritative.

Looking at behavior from a strictly gender-driven perspective, using only our society's gender-delineated traits can leave us, at times, scratching our heads. Looking at behavior from an energetic perspective—that which we'll garner from studying the Enneagram's complexities—will explain far better why countless men and women who have struggled for decades with stereotypical gender descriptions find immense comfort and immediate belonging when landing their Enneagram type.

How Each Type Expresses Traditional Western Gender Norms

Interestingly enough, each Enneagram type structure's innate, neural propensities do meet up with some of our more categorical biological sex as well as gender delineations, and that's worthy of acknowledging.

Keep in mind, archetypal energies—those that have been included across the centuries in folklore and mysticism as well as psychological study—foster an understanding of repeating energy patterns, those which also govern human society and the individuals in it. Feminine and masculine ideologies and qualities form and catalyze nature's much-needed energetic polarities, which are a great part of what drives, and has driven, our societal structures and evolutionary survival all along.

All things said and done, why then consider traditional definitions of gender when looking at the Enneagram types? How will this help us have more fulfilling relationships?

First, studying the Enneagram provides us with a deeper understanding of personality proclivities. As a result, it allows us to move past the singularity of traditional gender-delineated identifications into something more expansive; thus, allowing for our own energetic patterns to be witnessed, understood, and cherished, as well as those of our partners, notwithstanding those of others in general.

Through understanding comes the development of compassion, self-respect, and respect for others. An energetic study, if you will, also develops our capacity to work more deeply and concisely with our innate energetic structures and those of others rather than reject or dislike qualities of being that we, or others, may possess that don't necessarily fit stereotypical gender-delineated cultural expectations.

So, here goes!

Type 1 | The Perfectionist | Gender Norms

Type 1 is gender neutral with a leaning toward the masculine. They tend to be linear thinkers, organized, structured, and highly reasonable. Emotions are regulated and censored to comply with what's expected and what's appropriate. And they tend to follow the rules made by others if they've not made the rules themselves. Type 1s go by the book as long as the book is correct and fair *in their eyes*. Their standards are high, and they can be punitive when carrying them out and insist that others do the same.

With a strong inner critic and propensity for judgmentalness, 1s strive for correction, improvement, and higher good, often leading the way for moral and ethical excellence and adherence. Gender influences can be moderated or augmented depending largely on the content of the Perfectionist's internal standards.

Type 1s tend to choose duty and work over pleasure and play, which can feel patriarchal and authoritative. They are often promoted to leadership roles, thanks to their ability to regulate themselves and others and meet expectations.

In a relationship between two Type 1s, polarizing differences as to whatever standards have been set by either one of them can interfere with each other's sexual expression and their vulnerability with each other.

In a general way in both the female and male Type 1, splitting off impulses (driving pleasure and desire) in favor of what is right or more responsible can block or limit spontaneity as well as sexual desire and its expression.

Returning again for a moment to gender stereotypes, it is not necessarily expected from a man to suppress his anger, while it may be less acceptable for a woman to express hers. But Type 1s typically suppress or censor outright expressions of anger and, instead, express it as tightness and tension, rigidity, and resentment.

When 1s finally express their anger, it can come out toward a partner as a cause-and-effect, point-by-point prosecution of some sort. The result is a cool, mostly measured, calculated, and methodical being who may feel more machine-like than one that is emotional, vulnerable, and present.

Type 2 | The Giver | Gender Norms

Type 2 tends toward the gender-female stereotype. Type 2s are attentive to others' wants, wishes, needs, and desires (especially that of special others). They tend to be incredibly giving, self-sacrificing, loving, caring, and supportive. Type 2s are others-before-self responsive, and connection-oriented. For the female Type 2, these traits are relationship-oriented and are recognized as virtual mandates for women in many cultures.

There are few cultural restraints for Type 2 females to confidently act on their innate propensities, which correlate seamlessly with gender-typical female characteristics. With the coming in the USA of equal rights, Type 2 females were given a bit of permission to exert their often-well-hidden assertiveness more overtly and to consider their potential for more independence and less stereotypical caretaking if they so desire or yearn for it.

For the Type 2 male, the innate traits of this type tend to conflict with the male stereotype. Type 2s already have an assertive energy style, though often covertly expressed. But if expressed, it's directed at giving and caring rather than independence, competitiveness, and goal-setting.

Type 2 males often incorrectly self-identify as Type 3 as their expression of giving and caring, not saying no, and "relationships at all costs" are expressed through finances, providing material comforts and abundance, and spoiling their objects of desire demonstratively. Giving, caring, and nurturing are more recognizably female traits, and Type 2 guys miss recognizing these traits overtly because of the way they are expressing these kinds of impulses, tendencies, and aptitudes.

Both male and female 2s need to work on attending to their own needs and desires instead of getting their needs met through others who inadvertently get put on the hook to reciprocate one way or the other. Both need to learn to gain trust in the art of *proactive while unconditional giving*, and *proactive while not-resisted receiving*. This is the law of divine, organic reciprocity, and it is gender neutral.

Type 3 | The Performer | Gender Norms

Type 3 tends toward the gender-male stereotype. Types 3s are recognized for their assertiveness—even aggressiveness—externalized focus, linear approach, action-and-status orientation, goal-drivenness, competitiveness, and their somewhat feelings-avoidant yet connection-sensitive capacities. In the United States, Type 3 also represents the cultural slogans of "Just go do it," and the "Be your best self" rhetoric.

The Type 3 archetype is that of the hero, the winner, and the champion. The downside of this archetype is that there are no naturally occurring moderating influences. The Type 3 male often needs to become aware of his innate performance-bias when his significant relationships, in particular, are just not working out.

Those in relationship with either a male or female Type 3 speak to wanting more feelings, more authenticity, more receptivity, a slower pace (when possible), appropriate and more relationship orientation—as in time spent with one another.

A Type 3 female can find herself in an ambivalent situation as her gender-typical traits conflict with certain cultural norms and universal female-gender leanings. To adapt, she may modify or suppress her innate goal-focused assertiveness in order to live more in accordance with a more typical female image, the one that is expected of her. When she does, she can find herself doing and becoming so without realizing she's lost herself. This dynamic adaptation talent of Type 3 contributes readily to the personal self-deception proclivity they often suffer.

Both male and female Type 3s need to work at becoming more receptive. One way is to learn to take the time to truly listen to someone else. When necessary and called for, learn to allow pacing that's appropriate for all by slowing down and meeting others at their pace. Also allow and cultivate more presence—including and importantly, emotional presence—with themselves, their coworkers and friendships, their partners and, critically, with their children.

Type 4 | The Romantic | Gender Norms

Type 4 tends toward the gender-female stereotype. This type is largely congruent with female stereotypical qualities of feelings-orientation, relationships-orientation, emotional drama, peacocking, glamorizing, beautifying, meaning-making, sensitivity, depth, and a symbolic orientation to life. Additionally, the deep-feeling, romanticized, longing-for-connection traits of Type 4s fit the female gender bias.

Though highly empathetic, Type 4 females may also have a tendency toward self-orientation with a lot of attention being paid to their own inner world, which somewhat leads to the female gender-slighting moniker of drama queen. While this is not the same female gender bias of typified giving and nurturing, it's still within behavioral norms of what societies may deem acceptable and tolerable, even sarcastically *expected*, from females.

For the Type 4 male, however, there's an orientation toward deeply felt feelings, a longing for connection, meaning-making, moodiness, broodiness, nostalgia, and melancholy. Add to this occasional paralysis when needing to take action coupled with an internally focused self, and these traits all violate the male gender stereotype of an action-oriented, linear and logical, time-sensitive, decisive, goal-focused male figure.

Still, males of this type are often "closet 4s," so to speak, as they try to hide their sensitivity, their strong and emotive feelings, desire for peacocking and attention, and their longing for meaningful connection. Type 4s' natural propensities definitely fit the gender bias better for the females declaring as Type 4 rather than the males.

Both male and female 4s need to work on their tendency to focus on what is missing, lacking, and disappointing. By becoming aware of their submersion into feelings and how they more innately attend to themselves first rather than to another, relational experiences can begin to transform.

Both Type 4 sexes need to work on cultivating a genuine gratitude for what is present in their lives rather than feeling into what is not there, not up to par, or just not cutting it. This is some of what can leave Type 4 partners—male or female—feeling not enough and not acceptable, and in the end, not loved.

Type 5 | The Observer | Gender Norms

Type 5 tends toward the gender-male stereotype. Type 5s tend to represent the consummate "left brained" analytical, rational, dispassionate, knowledge-seeking type. Since 5s readily detach from their feelings, their behavior is congruent with the male stereotype of feelings-suppression all the way to holding them in abeyance. Consistent with what is often typified for males—that "men don't cry"—Type 5s move in and out of interpersonal contact and emotional connection without much fuss.

A Type 5 often shows care through analysis, information sharing, and factual advice. Both male and female 5s may also generously give, but it's usually when they know how much is being requested up front, and especially when it's for non-emotionally charged interactions, such as participating in problem-solving, handling finances and resources, and fixing things.

However, for Type 5s, thinking and analysis can replace doing. They are not usually highly competitive, overly aggressive, overly dominance-oriented, or overtly status-seeking. Type 5s are known as a more withdrawn type, retracting to the mind for solace, peace, mental tinkering, and rumination. They can have a gentle, thoughtful, non-intrusive demeanor, which in some circles, may be more attributed to more feminized gender traits.

A Type 5 female may conflict with cultural female gender norms. She may get viewed as distant, aloof, and not sufficiently feelings-oriented or expressive. She doesn't fit the female paradigm of sustained emotional connection, relationships-orientation, or nurturing caretaker. She may also be viewed as too analytic and over-mentalizing.

While the female 5 may experience herself as conflicted between her innate propensities and her culture's expectations of her, her female gender leanings and acculturation will urge her—somewhat expect her—to express qualities of empathy, compassion, and other-orientation, especially as she becomes a mother—qualities that may not come as naturally for her.

For both the male and female Type 5, development entails more sensitivity to feelings, more practice sustaining emotional connections with others, and more emotional and physical interaction with others. Learning to more openly and frequently express care, love, and intimate closeness is part of the growth path for Type 5s, both males and females.

Type 6 | The Loyal Skeptic | Gender Norms
Type 6 is gender neutral. As a result of the spectrum of phobic (fear) to counter-phobic (meet fear head-on) characteristics, 6s present as competitive and cooperative, goal- and process-oriented, as well as defiant and compliant.

That said, typical gender differentiations do not align with the phobic Type 6 male, but they do align with the counter-phobic male, as the counter-phobic style is far more in line with gender-typical masculine traits.

A counter-phobic Type 6 will confront or go against the fear and will often step forward before the fear is experienced. The aggressive, dominance-focused, controlling, and assertive-force orientations of the counter-phobic Type 6 have a gender-typical masculine orientation.

Expressions of warmth, feelings, and emotional connection, all found in Type 6—and particularly more readily expressed in phobic 6s—are considered to be more feminine characteristics and are most often associated with gender-typical feminine expression.

Typical gender differences in the Type 6 structure also prevail as they are inclined for the female to express beauty and the male to express strength, particularly with the Sexual/One-to-One subtype. This is indisputably one of the more specific ways our society encourages men and women to impact each other, and that's in order to attract a partner.

Interestingly, counter-phobic tendencies are often moderated, even subdued, by Type 6 females, while phobic tendencies are exacerbated. For Type 6 males, the reverse occurs. Since most 6s possess a variety of characteristics along the phobic to counter-phobic spectrum, we do find both Type 6 males and females expressing both of these divergent responses to fear. Gender expression in the Type 6 structure, though, does tend to be impacted more by the phobic and counter-phobic spectrum than by gender-typical expectations would dictate, per se.

For both, the path of development involves building trust in oneself and others while softening the tendency to magnify the negatives. Type 6s need to relax their tendency to see into the pessimistic side of things. Instead, they need to allow themselves to turn consciously toward optimism, despite what they may foresee.

The path of development for Type 6, while inclusive, needs to understand which style is more dominant. For development, counter-phobic Type 6 males would benefit from softening their protective mental shield to allow in and express their more emotive, tender feelings. This conflicts with the archetypal masculine as well as counter-phobic orientations.

Assuming more access to feelings and relationships-orientation, the counter-phobic Type 6 female may perhaps have fewer obstacles to development in this regard, as this would not conflict with the archetypal feminine.

Both the phobic Type 6 male and female, however, are encouraged to learn to more effectively face their fears and overcome surrendering their power to others. While these challenges are troubling for both male and female Type 6s, society seems more accepting of women who struggle with facing their fears than a man who does.

We also, as a society, seem to be more accepting of women who surrender their power to others—or some external authority—than we are of men surrendering theirs.

Type 7 | The Epicure | Gender Norms

Type 7 is gender neutral, with a leaning toward the masculine. Type 7s are highly charged by imagination, stimulating activities and options, and planning. They can take themselves and anyone else across an entire range of opportunities and options, and limitations are creatively avoided. Type 7s dynamically express the spectrum of both masculine and feminine gender-typical traits.

Neither Type 7 males nor females embrace the muddier, more painful feelings readily encountered in life, and neither want to be dragged down into suffering or limited by others. Both express themselves actively and assertively. And being a self-referencing type, both Type 7 males and females focus on their own needs and desires without much debilitating guilt or hesitation, which tends to be among the traits our society has masculinized.

Type 7s tend to lean toward the gender-male orientation as they more freely express themselves assertively, actively pursue life, and frequently dodge and divert limitation. The self-directed, self-referencing style of Type 7 gets further enhanced by the masculine, in that 7s lean toward a tendency for aggression, excitation and adventure, competitiveness, and their own defined version of success. They can also be inquisitively linear, approach-oriented, and assertively driven, which are more notably gender-typical male traits.

Compartmentalization and sublimation are typical Type 7 traits for both Type 7 males and females. Furthermore, the Type 7 male is likely to lean further into adventure and express even more active force, in comparison to a Type 7 female, who, in her own right, is adventurous and the type of person that more freely pursues her interests than women of the other types.

That said, in terms of gender bias, it may be safe to say that it's somewhat more difficult for a Type 7 male than a Type 7 female to create and allow a much-needed balance between assertive and receptive energies.

Again, the avoidance of limitation allows for a wide range of both masculine and feminine expression, resulting in a generally gender-neutral type. In terms of development, both Type 7 males and females need to moderate their activated, assertive, go-forward, I-gotta-be-stimulated energy, allow in a fuller range of feelings, and heighten their presence to, care of, and receptivity to others.

Type 8 | The Protector | Gender Norms

Type 8 is a gender-male stereotype. Type 8s possess aggressiveness, competitiveness, and "confrontative-ness" that are associated with power and control, and are action-oriented. While 8s make sense of "doing equals caring," the doing they choose with which to express their care might not necessarily be well thought out before they act. Type 8s operate with a "Fire! Ready? Aim" approach to life and tend to do things in that order—impulsively maybe, spontaneously for certain.

Type 8s are known for directness and crisscrossing easily—in and out of contact—with others. With their highly charged, exuberant energy and direct, confrontative style, 8s align synergistically with the archetypal masculine, gender-male stereotypical norm. It is OK to be a macho man as it's highly regarded in most cultures, but it's *not* so OK to be a macho woman in many cultures.

For the Type 8 male, there is little counterforce to either their habit of mind or external show of strength and power. Being a Gut/Body type, Type 8s operate more from a sensitivity to power, felt-sense impressions, and gut instinct than mental analysis and considerations over time. In the process, Type 8 males become experienced at being aggressive and dominating. They are sometimes even known to be emotionally unskillful, explosive, and even self-defeating.

The "school of hard knocks" and the notion of "tough love" tend to fit the Type 8 dynamic. Western culture, for one, tends to reward and accept many of Type 8's innate, more aggressive propensities—for males, in particular.

While the feminine archetype imbues the qualities of relationships-orientation, connection, feelings, and process-orientation, these are traits that will tend to moderate, sometimes frustrate, a Type 8 female. The life-force-intense, exuberantly energetic style of a Type 8 does not have much natural built-in counterforce, which can make life difficult for her.

Type 8 females struggle as society tries to force them to have their foot on the brake in order to comply more readily with stereotypical gender-female norms. This need for social compliance that pushes Type 8s to "tone it down" is expected far more from Type 8 females than from Type 8 males.

I've seen Type 8 females struggle to openly own the full expression of their Type 8's innate strategies and propensities until somewhere toward mid-life because they are so often chastised for being all of who they are. While they may suffer societally and personally, I have witnessed Type 8 females doing very well in leadership positions in the greater world, which is still to this day male dominated.

For both male and female Type 8s, it's important to notice as well as moderate their exuberant, all-in dominating energy so as to impact others more desirably and, at times, more appropriately. The all-or-nothing aggressive style can be limiting in the end. Growth comes from recognizing and allowing in the tender feelings, both of self and of others.

A new viewpoint for 8s is to see that vulnerability is powerful and weakness is sometimes what's real and what needs attending to. Others need to feel safe and heard in a Type 8's presence.

What an 8 sees as the truth may not be the only truth. Type 8s of either sex will benefit from allowing more range, tenderness, and by allowing others to express their tenderness and vulnerabilities, as well, as is appropriate. This will allow others in their lives to feel both safe and honored when interacting with them.

Type 9 | The Mediator | Gender Norms

Type 9 is gender neutral with a leaning toward the feminine. Type 9s possess characteristics that include other-awareness and concern, thoughtfulness, calmness, and approachableness. They also have characteristics that are typically expected and associated with that of females, including kindness and pleasantness, responsiveness, accommodation to other's needs, gentleness, supportiveness, conflict-avoidance, and relationships-orientation.

Both male and female 9s respond readily to others' needs and wants and do so in response to an innate gut instinct that immediately goes along without much visible resistance or hesitation.

Type 9s are responsive, accommodating, steady, and adaptable. They are known for their go-along-and-get-along energetic quality that promotes considerable flexibility and crosses gender-specific expectations. Type 9s of either sex can get stubborn and hold their ground when they really want to, though often non-consciously. It's innate and is their subtle, non-confrontational way of saying no more covertly, which ultimately protects their own sovereignty.

They generally relate comfortably to both sexes and are energetically neutral. Type 9 females are attentive to others' wants, wishes, needs, and desires. They can give readily when it comes to care and support, often without awareness of their own need for boundaries.

Type 9 females, in particular, but Type 9 males to a great extent too, have trouble saying no. This happens to the point that a female 9 often gets misidentified as a Type 2—the consummate female stereotype—that is focused on relationships and accommodating their partner's every need, often without even being asked to do so.

Female Type 9s who are less apt to satisfy another's needs of their own initiative (just like a Type 2), are generally comfortable with society's more typical gender-female mandates.

As for male Type 9s, they do have the capacity to be assertive and action-oriented, and they can make excellent leaders, though they tend to rise to the occasion when those assertive qualities are actively called for, demanded of them, or when given permission to step up. Type 9 males in positions of power aptly surround themselves with the talent necessary to get the job done. They are uncannily skilled at facilitation, mediation, and delegation.

Male Type 9s often experience themselves as and are viewed to be notably passive, slow to the punch, indecisive, and conciliatory—all of which are attributes that do not fit the gender-male stereotype, especially when present-moment, directive-assertive action is called for.

Not fitting the gender-male stereotype can be stressful for Type 9 males, as is the same for all males whose innate qualities include character traits that have been societally feminized.

Self-assertion, in-the-moment, "stand and deal with it" conflict resolution, forward-moving mobilization, and taking the lead despite other's opinions are qualities of being that Type 9 males can give themselves permission to develop and exercise despite their initial and internal reticence to do so.

All that said, I've found both Type 9 males and females relatively comfortable with their innate adaptability, slow-to-anger gentleness, and ability to resonate unconditionally and non-judgmentally with just about anyone, regardless of gender. Theirs is a gender-binary approach personified.

For development, while Type 9s are a gender-neutral Enneagram type, both female and male 9s need to give themselves permission to do the work of self-assertion and to give others the chance to experience their truth, their opinions, their needs, and their wants. Stepping up and differentiating themselves only to risk they're not agreed with or in sync with others, whether at work or at home, is what's called for and needed for growth.

Ultimately, "showing up" will gift not only their more intimate relationships but also all other relationships the chance to know them. Authenticity is desired and deserved as, ultimately, it's what makes way for actual connections—those that are real and felt (not contrived)—to happen.

The Enneagram, Self-Acceptance, and Gender

Without a doubt, there are many contributors to how we *see* ourselves as individuals, as romantic partners, as a gender in society, and as humans striving for our best life. But how do we *define* ourselves?

Across the seven or so years of this book's development, we witnessed massive societal changes as society's gender-typical programming came up for reevaluation. Biology surely cannot be overlooked, as it's the foundation of our hormonal systems as well as how we procreate, and those systems are in truth and for the most part, binary.

Our actual physical biology is a good place to start when seeking to accept ourselves as we were created, and it's a place to begin as well to review roles and identities and what that all means to each of us.

We humans have tremendous energetic capacities that range greatly and are highly complex. Whether we're born biologically male or female, we share much in common when it comes to the intelligences and aptitudes of our mental faculties, our emotional hearts, our instinctual gut/bodies, and the way it's all integrated—thanks to our minds and brains and the coherent cultivation of the capacities of awareness.

For those of us more innately aligned within range of a given culture's gender-delineated social constructs—and our having formed an identity consistent with those norms—we find ourselves met with societal acceptance. *Fortunate us*, as this more advantageously sets the stage for self-acceptance. But for those of us who do not innately fit society's gender-specific norms, there may be more of a struggle.

Societal non-acceptance surely exacerbates non-self-acceptance. Painfully, this can lead to varying degrees of self-consciousness, self-shaming and alienation, self-suppression, and countless levels of self-rejection, some of which may lead to outright gender confusion all the way to self-alteration, even mutilation.

Whenever there's a lack of self-acceptance, there's a much higher chance of isolation, relationships-apprehension, discord, and incalculable discomfort. As we struggle to *accept* ourselves, we struggle *to show* ourselves and, consequently, we may struggle with defending and protecting what's wanting to stay invulnerably in the shadows.

We may distort another's intentions, needs, or interpretations of us. And in turn, we may unconsciously shudder away from the vulnerabilities of intimacy, leaving us alienated and distanced from the most beautiful of experiences we may ever have with ourselves and with others.

Allowing ourselves to see the full spectrum of who we are—our nature-given biology combined with our personality aptitudes and talents, our feminine and our masculine traits, our expansive hearts and the way it so desires to express itself in the world—is of paramount importance.

Seeing into *all of ourselves* is what's made possible when we dare dive deeply, courageously, and inquisitively into our own temperamental psyches, emotionality, and embodied experience of our aliveness. The journey of self-development is our most divine calling. And it is the path, the only path, toward consciously developed self-acceptance. Self-acceptance is the path to attaining greater intimacy with oneself and with others. It is the path to more fulfilling relationships. And this, as it turns out, is the path to living the fullest experience of that thing called love—that which resides within us, desires to be received and felt, and yearns to be directed and expressed.

Perhaps the world would benefit from a more comprehensive understanding of the people in it. A more loving and educated understanding of the many contributory personalities is possible, and well, perhaps at this time in history, really necessary.

A broader approach would be sense-making and far more compassionate. I suggest we take on an Enneagram-based view of humanity, helping us better understand ourselves, understand identity, and understand personality itself. I suggest that we be open to a view where personality is *not* based solely *on sex-based gender*—where gender characteristics are defined so definitively on two biological sexes and ascribed and acceptable cultural norms.

This has not given us the entire picture. Gender-specific roles and expectations, to this point, have concerningly led to limiting stereotypes and the propensity for prejudices, harmful bullying, even the outright rejection of emotional and behavioral variances. It has also, concerningly, led to the outright rejection of one's own biological sex and one's own body when correlated with some notion of a gender that's deemed too limiting or misaligned.

Taking a compassionate view, we are all members of the same human tribe. Each of us is deserving of appreciation, compassion, and reverence, whether one of two sexes or one of nine types.

The Enneagram teaches us about energetic propensities and neural wiring, essential qualities of being, human emotional systems, and instinctual drives. Each of these ways of peering into our nature provides a much broader and more comprehensive, compassionate understanding of both ourselves and others.

Thanks to the extraordinary incisiveness of nine distinctive energetic possibilities and their unique complexities and contributions, human personality as revealed to us by studying the Enneagram is actually non-binary. All of who we are temperamentally is a vast and extraordinary frontier; the inner and outer terrain to be discovered and traversed cannot be left uncharted, let alone underestimated or limited.

We are much more than just a being from Mars or Venus.

Let's allow ourselves to take a broader view—an energetic view—of our human qualities and characteristics. There is much to add to this conversation. A nine-personalities view allows us to honor both our biological physicality in conjunction with our own extraordinary and complex character and how its organized itself adaptively, intelligently, and evolutionarily.

Learning there are actually more than two specified stereotypical *energies* when it comes to identifying and savoring differing human personalities, may we come to hold dear the flawless, error-free biological truth of being born physically male or female.

As we consider society's definitions of male and female gender and how those definitions have impacted us, the Enneagram gifts us a chance to consider not just gender delineations but "energetic patterns of being" delineations. These energetic patterns of being are the foundation of our personalities and how they develop. They are found and expressed in each of us across nine different Enneagram types, comprised of both biological males and females, irrespectively.

May the wisdom of the Enneagram serve us in a way that promotes self-understanding, self-allowance, and acceptance of self and others. This, in turn, leads to the unrestricted expression of love for self and others.

May our growing understandings ease tendencies to so tortuously self-reject and decrease the painful intolerances that cause so much unnecessary suffering and alienation within ourselves, across our relationships, and throughout the collective.

CHAPTER 9

Developing Mindfulness Awareness
Calls for a Methodical Process

While it is great to study theory and seek intellectual understanding, that is just a starting place. Intellectual understanding is not enough to do the work of personal development. We need to put the concepts into practice. And to do that, we need some kind of process. We need a practical, repeatable, skills-developing method that takes these concepts and embodies them into more integrated, intrapersonal neural pathways, ones that lead us to greater capacities.

Importantly, we need practices that develop **coherence**. Personal coherence is a developed capacity to integrate the many disparate parts of ourselves with one another. As such, coherence is a kind of glue. It allows us to connect honestly with ourselves as we remain genuinely openhearted and receptive, able to pause and contain impulses in order to compassionately make proactive choices—ones that are imbued with love, clarity, and right action.

Coherence allows us to develop beyond that knee-jerk reactivity that can hurt us and others, and it governs our ability to align our thoughts and feelings with our words and actions. Personal coherence fosters presence—being present to what's real on the inside of us, to what's going on around us, and to what we perceive is going on for others.

Next, we need **method** to develop our capacity for—and our level of—developmental well-being. Personal development that elevates our level of well-being is nothing less than opening up to all of ourselves—our unique and personal capacities and talents, our hopes and desires, our immense faculties, and to all that is love within us.

Personal development that leads to higher states of developmental well-being also connects us to—and then integrates us with—our shadow material, the parts of ourselves that we've perhaps exiled as unwanted, "reject-able," or shameful—any and all parts we may have deemed unlovable.

As it happens, these parts of ourselves are aspects of our Enneagram type's core beliefs, ones that we get compulsive about because we fear there's no love for us if we don't abide, if we don't comply with the mandates and drivers that support those core beliefs. Those mandates are often experienced as compulsively driven imperatives and are very much part of our humanness.

While we'd like our thoughts, feelings, and behaviors to be driven by our immense talents and aptitudes, they are, unfortunately, often driven by our most deeply held fears—including what's wrangling with our shame or covering over our hurt.

Instead of being led by triggered, emotional material that we may be unaware of, yet is limiting us—events that take us into reactive-automatic—personal development allows us to more consciously experience our lives from a higher state of awareness and deepen our developmental path. What a contrast! The stuff that's not even on our radar is what's actually in control . . . until we do the work. *This work.*

As my dearly respected colleague Russ Hudson—thought leader and author of *The Wisdom of the Enneagram*—says, **"The part of us that we cannot see** (are not aware of) **is running the whole show."**

Wow! Is that what any of us really wants? Probably not, but that's how we're structured until we do something about it, until we *decide we want to wake up* to it.

Until we decide to become more aware—more consciously, thoughtfully, and compassionately aware, mindfully aware—we can live out our entire lives simply responding to the impulses within us. We may never understand ourselves, let alone comprehend our own sometimes-sabotaging actions.

It really is a case of "what we haven't investigated, we'll know little to nothing about." It's a matter of us saying, "I am just the way I am."

That's all we know as we start out as young adults trying to build a good enough life. We start out by "doing our best with what we've got to work with," with an Enneagram type and a level of developmental well-being that was shaped across childhood, a lot of it long before we had any say in the matter. We became what we had to become.

A life that is lived with more conscious awareness is a life of proactive self-agency, self-love, and self-mastery, all of which then propagate the ability to relate to, be with, and love others and the world at large. It is what leads us to loving better and living more fully. A life that is fueled by conscious awareness allows us to navigate our hopes and desires, dreams, and purpose—consciously, courageously, and willfully.

Personal development is something not to fear nor resist but instead welcome and seek wholeheartedly as it leads to elevated, self-realized personal well-being.

It leads to far more fulfilled lives. And it leads to people from all walks of life and from all around the globe that are capable of love and of being loved.

For each and every one of us—for all of humanity—personal development is our ultimate vision and hope.

The Much-Needed Process: The Universal Growth Process

The Universal Growth Process (UGP) for Self-Mastery, introduced in Chapter 1, is the method I developed with my colleague Terry Saracino many years ago to begin building conscious *awareness* which, in turn, leads to eventual *self-mastery.*

The UGP is a remarkably practical, powerful, step-by-step process. Easy to follow, it gives us a way to do the work of personal development. It breaks down for us what to do first, what to focus on and look for, what to do with the awareness once we've garnered it, and how to continue working with it—over and over again.

Reading about mindful, conscious awareness is intriguing, right? It sounds wonderful. But how do we approach an effective self-awareness process?

To do so, we need a definitive plan, and the UGP's five steps—awareness, acceptance, appreciation, action, and adherence—are there to guide us and get us started.

But to become an aware person, what is it that we are supposed to be looking for or noticing? If we are reading this book as a first-time seeker, we may not have a lot of experience hanging out with our subjective inner world with any level of compassionate, non-judgmental engagement, let alone reverence. (As a matter of fact, we might not really like it in there at all.)

So, let's explore together. How many of us reading this book find self-punishment, negative self-talk, and self-attack—or heaps of anxiety about what or who we're *not*—as our experience of ourselves? What if *that's* what we find when we dare spend time alone inside of our own minds, inside our subjective inner world?

Our society's norms tend to point us *outside* of ourselves for answers, to look externally to find our value and pursue happiness. We're indoctrinated into thinking that life is found and lived in the activities we schedule, in the work we do, and with the people we either find ourselves with or seek out. While what's going on around us is surely an important part of our lives, it's how connected we are on the inside *in response to* the experience that we're having that's the truth and inevitable substance of our lives.

Our inner world experience is actually *everything*, but how much we tend to downgrade our subjective inner life is astounding. The subjective experience of ourselves is what we so often turn away from. Yet *that is our life!* Our lives are composed of our personal experience of everything. That's what carries meaning for us. It's the relationship we have with ourselves day in and day out that is what we eventually take with us in our hearts. Sadly though, we can literally miss it.

To be frank: how we lived life and felt it (experienced it) is what we'll come to terms with as our lives come to an end. Our emotional takeaways are what's left in our hearts and on our souls when all is said and done.

Witnessing ourselves from the inside out is not something regularly taught in the average American home or in most schools either. But it's the capacity to witness ourselves that relaxes our defenses, ignites our development, and promotes the integration of our spiritual qualities with our personality's proclivities—and our shadow material.

Yet witnessing ourselves as part of a mindful awareness practice is what readily and consequently brings higher qualities of being into our lives. It's what nurtures our developmental well-being, our sense of wholeness, and our fundamental constitution, which is fundamentally *love*.

A witnessing capacity is what leads us to developing self-awareness. The UGP is so useful because it provides *an actual method* for witnessing and engaging that is sequential and effective by using the 5As. As a refresher, they are:

A1: awareness,

A2: acceptance,

A3: appreciation,

A4: action, and

A5: adherence.

These 5As are easy-to-remember steps that can be—ought to be—applied readily at any moment of our daily "dallying."

For the most part, I have been teaching and practicing these steps for years but only organized them into this simple and life-changing format around 2007, after years of needing "more method" to bring to our students.

They are designed for the development of self-awareness and self-mastery, and are best done in order: A1 to A5. They foster the building of our capacity to *get present* and *stay present*, to show up for ourselves and make different choices as needed, and to gain the capacity to be less reactive and far more responsive—far more consistently.

The 5As' Unique Contribution

Awareness, acceptance, appreciation, and adherence (A1, A2, A3, and A5) are universal to many of the world's great traditions. For example, you'll find these concepts in centering prayer in the Christian tradition and in mindfulness meditation in the Buddhist tradition.

That said, the Enneagram's unique and powerful gift to the human development path, I believe, is in the action step (A4) of the UGP, which relies, of course, on pausing to reflect, recognize, and become aware—the awareness step—*first*. The action step though, takes awareness to the next level. It's at this point that we're primed to carry out a gentle and honest inquiry, one that allows us to discern what is, and then proactively choose the most lucid, constructive form of conscious conduct for ourselves and for the situation.

When woven together, conscious, receptive awareness that's met with an acknowledgment of what has just shown up within, coupled with non-judgmental **acceptance** and then **appreciation**, constitutes the great emulsifier. Let's call it the "great emotional stabilizer."

Once emotionally in check, we are able to view coherently what's needed for ourselves and for the situation, and we can do so with grace, humility, and self-efficacy. These are the steps that then allow for some sort of appropriate **action**. The action step completes the loop.

The action step is the outward expression of our awareness, the allowed-for acceptance, the pausing, and then the choosing of the proactive, decided-on response. The action step puts in motion our personality's capacity for presence, leading to its having met with and acted on its higher essential (spiritual) qualities of being.

As a reminder, the good news is that neuroplasticity exists! We possess the ability to form new neural pathways, new ways of being. As long as we live, we can learn, which means we can grow. And because we can grow, we can change. We can desirably and proactively grow and change.

This happens when we combine mindful self-observation with practice—over and over. Practice allows us to experience a new way to do things, a new way to be.

The long-term acquisition (ownership) of a new way of doing or being requires that it is first *enacted*, then *remembered*, and then, through *repetition*, the new gets firmly embodied. Repetition is made possible thanks to practice. (If you're wondering where **adherence** comes into play, keep reading.)

A Few Important Points About Practice

And now a definitive word about practice, because it's the critical piece of our personal development work, and we'd like to give it the attention it truly deserves. Practice is best done as often as possible, of course. That said, when is the best time? And how do we do it? While practicing when we are stressed and threatened is noble. (Baptism by fire has its merits!) It is best to also practice when *not* stressed or threatened.

For instance, it's best to learn how to swim and practice our strokes for life-saving competency before we get in a boat and find it's sinking. Most likely, our not-yet-perfected strokes will fail us if we hadn't really embodied them beforehand in a swimming pool. It's tough to do anything new well—let alone when stress and massive reactivity take over in moments of utter threat.

So, practice that builds self-mastery is needed daily, and it's best done when relaxed, when we're able to patiently and gently self-witness, recognize, and become **aware** of our thoughts, feelings, and drives. It's best done at those times when we can **accept** and **appreciate** ourselves and others, after which we can consciously and proactively move into the fourth A of **action**.

It's when we're at our more emotionally stabilized best that we want to discipline ourselves to rehearse—if you will—new, developmentally healthier ways to respond. It's this kind of conscious, not-when-stressed practice that enables us to build familiarity with the sensations, competencies, and skills of mindful awareness. Over time, the familiarity of the newer pathways gets embedded and embodied. Soon enough, we'll be able to get there with ease and at will.

Then, once we find ourselves under siege, the new, embodied learnings are right there to support us. And *that* is what we want. It is different from coming under siege only to find ourselves scrambling to defend ourselves yet again with habituated, ingrained patterns and all-too-familiar reactivity, neither of which worked too well in the past, and surely won't again.

The practice of getting grounded and focusing our attention on our breath—and hence, on our bodies and our somatic experience—is how we train ourselves to access and identify our deepest feelings and our automatic reactions. And this kind of developmental practice is best done when we are not preoccupied with everyday life either, let alone when being threatened or stressed.

Concerted practice allows us to build new neural pathways over time and in the long run, and in doing so, change habitual and ingrained non-choice patterns of conditioning that previously limited us and our response flexibility.

The Universal Growth Process and Self-Intimacy

One of the fundamental and indisputable gifts of the UGP is also one of the ultimate goals of this book: the development of self-intimacy. It's that important because **self-intimacy is the definitive gateway to intimacy with others**.

This means, *the degree of intimacy developed with ourselves is the foundation for the intimacy we are able to foster across all of our relationships, and in particular, our romantic ones.*

While the UGP is, no doubt, an instrumental and methodical tool for developing self-awareness—which leads to overall mindful awareness—it is also an extraordinary tool for developing a more *intimate working relationship with ourselves*, that which develops self-engagement and authentic self-understanding.

I say a "working relationship" as it's a process that over time takes us step by step into our inner landscape in a way that expands our inner life and our self-vulnerability. The UGP helps us get engaged with ourselves *neutrally, vulnerably,* and *repeatedly.*

These steps begin to build a system within for self-connecting. It's a way for the self to check in with the self and find out—with compassion, non-judgmentalness, care, and receptivity—what's going on.

The five steps of the UGP train us to reach for that personalized experience of our subjective internal world as it promotes our capacity to be more deeply and thoughtfully sensitive to our inner self, the vulnerable truth of us. Once we get ourselves here, our ability to be sensitive to our outer world and the people in it increases and deepens dramatically as well.

Steps to Self-Intimacy

Self-intimacy begins by developing the ability to be lovingly yet radically honest with ourselves. Self-intimacy is the practice of truthful intrapersonal encounters—many of them—each of which needs to be nourished with self-compassion and self-acceptance in order to be *tolerable*, in order to be *translatable*, and to be *honored* both neutrally and consciously.

Using the Enneagram as a non-judgmental, de-shaming self-discovery map, we can begin to foster an understanding of ourselves, which lends itself to developing self-vulnerability (and all the hurtful tender stuff we'd rather hide), which is the cornerstone of self-intimacy.

Starting with the easier, know-myself stuff first, begin by deciphering our *primary center of intelligence,* whether we're a Head type, a Heart type, or a Gut/Body type.

Next, we need to take the time to determine our *Enneagram type structure.* Self-knowing that gets us closer to self-intimacy is further garnered by figuring out our *subtype,* that is, which of the three *driving instincts* is our primary, and then, in which order do we express the other two.

Understanding our center of intelligence, our Enneagram type, and our primary instinct—also called our dominant instinct—gives us permission to look at ourselves far more objectively, less shamefully, and more lovingly than we may have ever looked at ourselves before. This is necessary because self-development work that brings forth sensitivities and personal vulnerabilities, for example, can be challenging all the way to unwanted if we don't first build a good foundation to support us across the tougher discoveries and developmental challenges that may surface. (Thank you, Enneagram!)

Next, we can develop self-intimacy by looking more closely at how our gender identity correlates with our Enneagram type. The Enneagram and its vast understandings of how we're organized from the inside out offer up an insightful understanding of our energetic qualities of being, of various so-called masculine and feminine personality characteristics, and how these are innately and overtly expressed across the nine Enneagram types.

As we turn to societal definitions of who we are and how we're "supposed to be" according to cultural gender norms, we may find that we either fit the norms or we don't. The Enneagram provides a thoughtful understanding of why this may be so. While fitting to the norms causes little trouble, *not* fitting can be problematic—even shame-inducing.

What the Enneagram reveals helps us see into ourselves beyond the potentially limiting constructs of a binary system for self-identification, one that is based on only two definitive biological sexes and the stereotypical qualities culturally associated with each.

Overall, self-intimacy can be initiated and fostered by good self-inquiry. On that note, it can be catalyzed by answering each of the questions posed throughout this book and especially in the accompanying workbook (see daviddaniels.com). It's our way to help us start a self-intimacy process. We've called these questions "prompts."

These prompts are designed for gentle yet poignant self-examination and are intended to be met with genuine curiosity. Curiosity fosters a nonjudgmental wonderment of sorts that opens the door to knowing ourselves better and more deeply. This is what self-intimacy is all about.

Self-intimacy is not necessarily a given. For many, it might be brand-new territory. So, on that note, it's important to add a method that engages us in self-intimacy development—found in the UGP. Utilizing the five steps of the UGP every day for every situation puts into practice a tangible, proactive, count-on-it protocol to locate the honesty and vulnerability within ourselves in real time, in the here and now. The UGP is a method for getting intimate with ourselves, one step of the 5As at a time.

The journey we take daily with an accepted, loved, and honored, "I want to hear from you" self, is a journey *so* worth taking. It's a journey of observing and recognizing, accepting, and then appreciating, followed by taking appropriate action—conscious, thoughtful, and for the higher good of all. This is the journey of personal development and, ultimately, the journey toward self-mastery.

Finally, self-intimacy is what deepens personal caring and then personal dedication, as it nurtures the safe emergence of the authentic self. Self-caring provides the foundation for personal dedication that is driven by our authentic relationship to ourselves. This tenet of self is honored by the implementation of **adherence**.

The adherence step is a grand step toward expressing ongoing self-care and self-love. It says, "I am committed to me." Adherence is an outwardly demonstrated act of self-worth and self-honoring, one that asks a lot of us over time, because it requires discipline, devotion, and dedication.

This is the work of personal mastery, as this is one of the process steps that must align with, and brought to bear alongside, all the concepts understood. With this step comes a practical working model, one wrapped around the word *adherence*. The adherence step is an identifiable outward expression of self-love.

The Universal Growth Process Work: Unblocking and Practicing

What I've found interesting over the years is not the immense capacity we have to learn or take on new material in order to develop or change. I have observed—with great compassion—our ongoing struggle to adopt new patterns and ways of being, even though we may desire to do so.

What prevents us from embodying new insights, from letting go of what's not working, even when knowing how beneficial it would be for us?

I've tended to see less resistance to *accepting* new material than to *implementing* it. Why is that? My answer over time circulated around the word *benefit*. Any living organism first and foremost does what it does to survive. Next, it hopes to have a satisfying life. Everything we do—what we think, what we feel and act out—has its purpose, its benefit. And all our activities contribute to our survival in one way or another and strive to get our needs met—either real or perceived.

Despite some or all of our activities also having become liabilities—having turned into compulsions that are now highly detrimental—there is still some sort of benefit in place for some critical reason. And for us to do something *differently,* we need to understand cognitively, emotionally, and spiritually what that benefit is.

But we have built up immense defenses to protect how we feel or to ensure that we get what we need at the deepest levels—which we perceive to be critical to our emotional and/or physical survival. These defenses are powerful, and they are deeply ingrained. They form the blocks we come up against along the personal development path. They literally block us from growing much or changing at all.

So much of what we act out in the form of defensiveness or resistance was conditioned into us very early on and throughout childhood. Adaptations that were once necessary were either learned, modeled, or expected of us. Fundamental aspects of our personality structure were with us from the start and were driven by our innate disposition—our neural propensities and central nervous system wiring.

Our innate wiring and our adaptations are key to understanding how we *now* show up in the world, how we feel about ourselves, and have come to be who we are. Our Enneagram type (pointing at our temperament) combined with how we've been raised (nurtured and conditioned) makes us who we become. To a great extent, it governs how we react to life, feel about life, and pursue our lives the way we do.

Deciding to Grow: Taking on the 5As

Despite from where we start out—at what level of developmental well-being we may find ourselves—we can embark on our practice toward self-development. It might be slow, it might be messy, and it might be challenging. But let's just start.

The 5As are a tremendously powerful process and are here to guide each of us through five sequential, powerful steps that foster self-awareness, self-agency, and self-mastery. To take them on, we need to engage these three initiatives:

1. Study and understand each of the five steps and what they ask of us.
2. Acknowledge the benefit of each step and experience it as we practice each one with patience, kindness, and self-compassion—over and over again.

3. Curiously and honestly come to recognize and understand what blocks each of us from any one or more of the steps.

I find it's less difficult to read over the 5As and see their benefit than it is to get honest and clear about what's blocking their implementation. Desiring the benefits is a good starting point, but that's only the first and most friendly part of this process. Encountering the resistances we have is where the bigger work resides and where our potential for change gets either ignited or derailed.

What Blocks Us?

While our comprehension may be high and our intentions dutifully in place, we will often find we run into a wall of some kind. A block. This block actually does just that: it blocks us from doing any or all of the steps for some *"What is this about?"* reason. While seemingly in the way, these blocks (resistances) are most likely there for some conscious or unconscious purpose.

They are often (almost always) organized to protect us from something—from getting overtaken, being seen as too soft or too difficult, not getting heard, being ignored, or to prevent us from losing time or losing the battle, to name a handful of examples. Or there's resistance in place to perceptibly gain something—as in power, dominance, self-assertion, righteousness, fairness, esteem, value, autonomy, or respect.

With each of the 5As, take a good look at how each of the five steps is beneficial, and—equally importantly—what each or any of the 5As' steps perceptively costs us if we follow them through.

> What do we think we'll lose as we follow each of the 5As?
> What, if any, resistances do we find we have now, just as we read over each of them?

Awareness: What Blocks Our Awareness and Gets in the Way of our Good Intentions

The fact is, prior to starting any kind of awareness practice, our thoughts and actions are pretty much on autopilot. Our lives are lived primarily on automatic, running—unbeknownst to us—habitual patterns of thinking, feeling, and behaving. This goes on until we decide to stop and take a look at it all "running."

Our habits of mind, our type structure's focus of attention and routines, our impulses and reactions, even our compulsions and defensiveness carry us day in and day out. To give nature a bit of credit here, these patterns do keep us from having to stop and think about every single thing, every single time—as if we've come at it for the first time. Phew! Imagine again how exhausting that might get and how little we'd ever accomplish!

The problem is that when we're on automatic, we don't know it because *automatic is all we know*. We don't know any different because we're not aware. We don't know that our own habits, routines, impulses, reactions, and forms of expression are all running on somewhat predictable patterns. In fact, we really don't control these patterns; they control us.

In contrast, if we've developed a capacity for self-awareness—and if we're doing our practice well—we will have come in contact with these patterns, engaged with them, and found them curiously interesting.

Thanks to the Enneagram, we've read about many of these patterns, which helps to spot them. Thanks to a mindful awareness practice, we've witnessed them up front and personal. It's at this point in the road that we take a pivotal turn, one that literally changes our lives. This is the point that we begin to become aware and start to have some say in the matter.

We Don't Know That We Don't Know

How do we come to *know* that we *don't know*? And why aren't *all* of us striving to become self-aware? Self-awareness really is one of today's highly promoted elixirs, grounded in research. It's touted as a key starting place for personal development, and it's the bedrock of countless stress-reduction mindfulness studies.

It's true, not everyone is actively pursuing this work, and, well, I wonder why. Perhaps there's disinterest or discomfort of some kind. Or perhaps it's because we struggle with a capacity deficit of some sort. What if it's because while we're *not* aware, we think we *are* already aware? If that's the case, then, being proactive about starting a practice to *become* aware won't be very high on our to-do list.

We've long normalized our patterns, and that's that. These patterns are familiar and comfortable. They are the *us* that we are used to, the *us* we have come to know and trust. Our patterns are all that we know, and we're easily fooled into thinking we're already aware of them, anyway.

Until we do the work of becoming aware, our habitual patterns will be who we are; they'll stay in place until we begin to awaken to and expand to *the vastness of self* behind the familiar and habituated self—the one awareness begins to challenge.

If we have not yet started an awareness process *of some kind*, chances are high that we're not much aware, which leads to our probably not being that much intra-personally aware or present either.

Chances are that we're more likely running habitual patterns right in line with our Enneagram type structure—doing its best with its level of developmental well-being, with little self-awareness of what's really running us. This is more often the case than not.

Self-awareness naïveté, a very human condition, is one of the key obstacles preventing us from a self-awareness practice becoming a part of our lives.

The Impact of Discomfort: A Good Sign

There is another challenge when developing our level of presence via a self-awareness practice to become self-aware, and that's the discomfort of self-awareness itself. We have often heard Enneagram author and master teacher Russ Hudson say: **"And how much presence can we actually tolerate?"**

Getting present takes courage and lots of practice, and it leads us to becoming aware of things we might not have wanted to acknowledge, let alone feel.

For instance, let's suppose we're an Enneagram Type 9 (the Mediator). Awareness might expose us to the fact that often when our partner asks us to do something, we feel a resistance, and we feel it in our body. It's a heavy, stubborn feeling of resistance. (Ugh!)

With more awareness practice, we come to realize, for example, that we're not happy all the way to being irritated that we're being asked to do something *right now* that we might not want to do *right now*. With further awareness practice, we realize that we feel overpowered by these kinds of requests and that they just make us feel tired.

After even more practice, we come to see that it's *our inability to say no* that's actually weighing the heaviest. While we do have the right to say no, we don't exercise it. We want to say no or not now, but our pattern to go with the flow takes over. At this stage of our awareness practice, we may start getting frustrated with ourselves, as in thinking, *Why am I like this? What's wrong with me? Other people say no all the time!*

This is the point at which many of us stop our practice. Who wants to commit to a practice that leads to feeling badly or to attacking oneself? Becoming aware without remedy, becoming aware without self-kindness, or seeing into ourselves only to trigger self-attack or self-dislike—as is what sometimes happens in the very beginning (well, a lot of the time!) on the personal development journey—can be distressful and highly unpleasant.

But if we don't give up at these fragile junctions, we're on our way! So, we practice again. And again. Slowly, we begin feeling into the frustration that we've directed at ourselves, but this time, we allow ourselves to go a step further.

Remaining *still* inside of ourselves, our next practice invites a new layer of awareness as we begin with more curiosity. *Why do I struggle to say no?* we now ask ourselves when our partner asks us yet again to take out the garbage *right now* while we just want to finish reading our book.

We now acceptingly observe that our well-hidden resistance is turning on like a faucet. Next—and gently—we come to realize a deeply held belief that we have that if we say no, our partner might not love us or want us anymore. And (ouch!) that feels awful. It feels dreadful, so much so that that belief is now pretty much controlling the show. It controls *us*.

So, as we watch ourselves yet again . . . We watch as we say nothing and go along with the request. We concur and do what we're asked. Our book goes down, and we take out the garbage. But our body, surprisingly, *isn't really* going along. It's holding all this *heaviness* (which we come to understand is an intrapersonal experience of our suppressed anger). This anger shows up as a felt resistance and acts its way out as a growing stubbornness. That can neither be good for us nor healthy.

But we are tuned in now to this resistance and heaviness. It's quite a normal feeling for us, actually, but we never questioned it before. It was "just me" and how it felt "to be me."

This kind of deep realization is what we're capable of getting in touch with as we commit ourselves to developing a truthful and accepting presence to the self, and by exercising this kind of self-awareness practice over time.

Awareness gets us more honest. It's also the catalyst to taking right action. This allows us to deal differently in the present moment, if we want to, with what's found inside of us. Awareness gives us a *choice*. In the example above, our habitual pattern of suppressing our no now has a chance to be addressed. We can coach ourselves to safely say no at times without succumbing to that dreadful feeling that we won't be loved if we do say no.

Thanks to awareness, we can now ask ourselves if we want to live out our lives with a body and psyche full of suppressed anger felt as resistance and heaviness. That heaviness is a form of Type 9 "emotional-somatic pain," the pain that tells us that if we don't do XYZ we won't be loved.

Each Enneagram type suffers its own kind of pain as it runs its own narrative that then follows up with—and acts out—particular make-sure-we'll-be-loved behaviors. This kind of pain runs each of our lives and then inadvertently expresses itself in our bodies.

Our Type 9's habitual pattern would have surely kept doing this to us: stuffing our healthy no and flooding us with unconscious resistance over and over again, no questions asked! But is that all there is for us as 9s? Or do we have more of a say as to how we might learn to relate to ourselves?

With awareness, we now have a chance to develop beyond that locked-down pattern. We can learn more about our fears of not being loved if we sometimes stand up and say, "I really don't want to . . ." And, in turn, we save our physical body a lifetime of emotional suppression that, in the end, might become detrimental to our health and well-being across our many years of life.

(This goes for Type 9 as well as the several other Enneagram types that are good at suppressing emotional discontent.)

Importantly, the feelings of discomfort, the cognitive-emotional doubt we may wrestle with as we take on new self-awareness initiatives, are signs that we are, in fact, growing. Just like the growing pains children experience when they are growing *physically*, so do we experience discomfort when growing *developmentally*. This kind of discomfort, though, is a good thing. Don't let the discomfort dissuade us. Instead, welcome it.

Distraction Has Its Beneficial or Destructive Purpose

Each Enneagram type's particular brand of cognitive-emotional pain is in large part what we prefer to avoid, and we set up significant obstacles to becoming self-aware as a result. As previously mentioned, the kind of data self-awareness gathers may be difficult to stomach at first, but it's part and parcel to the beginning and ongoing stages of a self-awareness practice.

What we might encounter as we start tuning in might be distressing. By not doing the work of self-awareness, though, we avoid facing this stuff, which means we avoid knowing ourselves. We avoid the many opportunities to develop ourselves, and we skip the chance to remedy our reactivity, defensiveness, or adaptive limitations.

By avoiding all of this, we proactively avoid our pain. (Well, isn't that convenient!) As we circumvent becoming aware, we circumvent ourselves, and we keep far enough away from any unwanted emotional pain. And *how* exactly, do we do this? Well, we've got a few maneuvers up our sleeves. We avoid personal development work, that's for sure! But another great technique is the mechanism we'll call "perfectly organized distraction."

It's amazing just how good we are at transporting our minds to some other time, place, or world when we don't like where we're at or what we're feeling. We'll take ourselves to places (either in our minds or in person) where we're emotionally safe and insulated from the pain of agitation, frustration, impatience, self-loathing, unwantedness, or a variety of other anxieties.

We all have ways of escaping the emotional discomfort of day-to-day life and how we show up (or not) when trying to deal with it. We might stare at our phones, obsess about the past, or dream up exciting futures. Or we over-schedule ourselves, fantasize about the next adventure, get lost in TV, bury ourselves in our work, make plans we may never keep. Or we simply ignore ourselves altogether; we go numb. Maybe we get high. Or maybe we eat, drink, and pursue people and things to dull the reality of our internal anguish.

Or we escape through books or movies, games or music, sex or shopping that carry us to another world where self-awareness realizations and cognitive-emotional pain don't exist—if only for a short time.

We seemingly and readily manufacture either peace of mind or neurotransmitter highs, all via well rationalized, self-protecting mental or physical escape and self-soothing activity.

While distracting ourselves can be useful and necessary *at times*, becoming more self-aware allows us to choose our distractions—*and* choose the time to distract ourselves. Growing in self-awareness also helps us recognize if our distractions are imprisoning us or freeing us.

We need to know *when* we're checking out and *why*. We need to know what's taking us away from others, our relationships, and from showing up in an authentic, all-in, present way. We need to know when we've lost contact with ourselves. We need to know the feelings we don't want to feel and any action we may inadvertently be avoiding.

> What do you find yourself distracted by?
> How often do you go someplace else in your mind other than staying present?
> How do you medicate, soothe, or get away from your cognitive-emotional pain?

The practices of growing in self-awareness, in presence, and in mindful awareness are all ways to get at the same thing: a simple, honest, witnessed recognition of where our mind goes, where our hearts get taken, and what our bodies are doing—including *when* and *why*. It's also about building the mental muscle we need to bring ourselves back to presence and tolerate it. We train ourselves to do this with focused intention and skillful determination.

Through self-awareness, we learn to *intentionally* place our attention on *what really is* at any given moment. Self-awareness, after all, is the pursuit of well-being. It's the pursuit of a more fulfilling life with ourselves and with others.

Acceptance: What Blocks Us from Accepting Self and Others?

Acceptance does not mean concurring, condoning, or capitulating. Acceptance is not resignation, either. It's not forgetting, and it's not about giving permission either. Acceptance in Enneagram speak is allowing—clearly, truthfully, and without censorship—*what is*. That's it.

We might not like or want what we see or have recognized, but at least we're not in the dark. Acceptance allows us to honestly stand there with it. Only then can we take appropriate action.

Acceptance allows us to shamelessly dive deeper in order to acknowledge and heal a hurting part of ourselves. Acceptance breaks the silence of the soul. We cannot heal when we do not accept that we are hurting. We cannot speak our truth when we really need to if we've not accepted our voice. We cannot stand for ourselves if we've not accepted that we're afraid we'll be ignored.

When acceptance is resisted, we are lost without a paddle, and suffering is incalculably extended. Non-acceptance only delays our development, puts obstacles in our way, and hinders our access to rightful action.

The acceptance piece seems to be the most difficult principle for most of us to grasp. It's hard to believe that acceptance itself won't derail us. It's almost felt as an oxymoron, as counterintuitive. Acceptance can feel like agreement. It tends to be more comfortable to be *against* what we don't like or don't want. It's as if by going against, by resisting, by *not accepting*, we'll have the best chance of making it go away.

I get that. But acceptance herein means seeing from a very receptive (welcoming) and non-judgmental place and in such a way that it invites truth and permits validation. It's only from truth that we come to make possible constructive change. It's only from truth and its cleansing alchemy that we make possible the resolution of buried shame, grievances, and difficulties.

It's hard to be honest with others if we're not first honest with ourselves, and we can't get honest with ourselves if we're in a non-accepting place with the truth of what is. Acceptance calls on us to be honest, and acceptance deconstructs denial.

Denial leaves us suspended in a form of resistance where we don't even know that we've fled from, from *what is*. Resistance and denial, non-acceptance and denial—either leave us astray or very vulnerable, with self-deceit as the only way out.

Being honest with ourselves can often include the owning of some difficult material. Like admitting, "I'm jealous." Or "I'm scared." Or "I'm feeling inferior," "I'm helpless," "I'm unlovable." Or "I'm being disrespected or harmed emotionally, and it's not what I want to acknowledge!" Or "I am deeply unhappy, even though I've been pretending for a long while that I am not."

These are vulnerable findings and vulnerable feelings. And for countless reasons, facing such delicate personal material is not how most of us enjoy seeing ourselves in our lives. Owning it and calling it out, we start there because taking action requires validating the simple truths of it. *This* is acceptance.

Being honest with ourselves requires the discipline and willpower to exercise a non-judgmental curiosity because curiosity fosters truthful emotional discovery and recognition. Curiosity is genuine and is what's needed for an honest assessment, one that's not afraid of what might surface. Acceptance is really hard when we succumb to not liking what we find and then judging it harshly.

When we are judgmental of someone—our partner, for instance—we'll find they often become defensive. They may even create elaborate rationalizations for what they are doing or feeling to get above being judged, just as we may do.

When we judge ourselves, our natural reaction is often also to justify and defend. But in this case, we do it *inside of ourselves*, because we are standing there attacking ourselves, and it hurts. Defendedness as a result of judgmentalness blocks presence, curtails openheartedness, and makes it much harder to accept the truth of ourselves or another.

None of these impacts foster intimacy. Without acceptance, awareness can create debilitating suffering, as is what the story of our Type 9 (as shared earlier) exposed. Without acceptance, we may block continued self-awareness practice if that practice leads us to feeling ashamed, mad at ourselves, or intra-personally agitated. Not to mention how much non-acceptance impedes us from taking appropriate action.

Thus, awareness must not get too far ahead of acceptance. Awareness must include that we open our hearts so that we can accept what awareness has brought forth to discover, learn from, and work with.

Awareness is curative, yes, but only when not punitive. It's a far rougher and harder—maybe impossible—road without acceptance.

The Present Moment

The present moment is all there is, ultimately. I know, we've heard that a million times, but it's true. Our lives are one long present moment, a gazillion of them strung together. Each of us, in the end, only ever has the present moment to work with. It goes without saying (but we'll still say it): within that moment, we can only work with who that we really are—cognitively, emotionally, and developmentally—and with the truth we dare to courageously peer into.

We are all in a different place in our own development, and that's OK. Some of us approaching this work might have already adopted a presence process, and our well-being has been developing for some time. Others might be starting from a place that lacks well-being, where there's immeasurable psychological suffering day in and day out.

We might be suffering so much inside we're using substances like alcohol, prescriptive medication, or even illegal drugs to help us cope. And, while harmful, it's critical that we see these choices for what they are. There's a reason why we need help coping, and we'll get to see into that once we start an awareness process.

What's important is that we start, and committing to a self-awareness practice is the start. Right now, today, in this very moment, we can start. And if we miss this moment? Guess what, there's another one right behind it, because it's always the present moment. (How glorious!)

An acceptance of the present moment is an acceptance of the power we truly have each second to own, direct, and show up fully for all of our so precious, so extraordinary human lives.

Appreciation: What Blocks Us from Appreciating Self and Others

Having a genuine appreciation for something we might not have wanted is a real art. In fact, it's an artful skill. Fortunately, it's a skill that can be cultivated. Appreciation is the close companion to gratitude, both of which are vibrationally powerful and key to how we energize—or de-energize—ourselves. According to Robert Emmons, PhD, professor of psychology at UC Davis and author of *Thanks! How the New Science of Gratitude Can Make You Happier*, appreciation—heartfelt gratitude—can make us feel so good that our blood pressure decreases, and our stress hormones are lowered. And when gratitude is a consistent part of our lives, it helps us develop a stronger immune system.

Appreciation generally leaves us happier and healthier. Appreciated employees give more. Appreciated partners and lovers feel that much more loved. And an appreciation for what we see in ourselves, regardless of the content, can lead to a level of self-acceptance that, in turn, fuels the will in us to not stay stuck but rather to grow and change—to potentiate our best self.

A lack of appreciation and gratitude, however, can leave us feeling locked in a never-ending cycle of dissatisfaction and self-recrimination—all the way to feelings of resignation and defeat.

So, where do we get blocked when landing on A3, the appreciation step of the UGP? Perhaps we fear that if we appreciate something that we do not like in ourselves or that we do not want to acknowledge, appreciation will leave us stuck in it. Or what if we fear that appreciation renders us lazy, resting on our laurels, entitled, or fate-tempting? Or do we struggle to appreciate something when we're ground down, grumpy, and just plain pissed off? What's there to appreciate when we're in this frame of mind?

I asked a colleague of mine when he's most apt to deny the appreciation step, and his response was this: "I have a hard time appreciating what I'm noticing in myself if what I'm noticing is that I'm being weak for any reason."

Well, that's interesting. Herein lies what might be the pivotal dilemma for the appreciation step: self-judgment (oh that again!), coupled with the refusal to accept and love certain aspects of our authentic, vulnerable selves.

Weakness or strength is just weakness or strength. They are what they are. We might see weakness in ourselves at some point, and at other times we may see strength. Does it matter *what* we see? Or does it matter *that* we simply *see*?

If the truth is that I'm showing up as weak, then the skill it takes to see *that* is worth appreciating. Because if that's me in this moment, my truth is that I have some reason for showing up as so-called *weak*.

What if I'm scared? What if I feel overpowered? What if I'm resisting what I really don't want to do but need to do? What if I want to say no but I know it will raise hell if I do? If I *won't allow myself* to acknowledge that I'm witnessing a "perceived weakness" in myself, then how am I going to go to the next step that gently inquires what that weakness is about?

What if that perceived weakness is, in fact, a benefit? And by taking a moment to honor that part of myself, I get to ask, "How is it that this perceived weakness might actually be serving me right now?" Can I accept that I see weakness and that it's there for some reason? And once I accept its presence, can I appreciate the fact that I'm now honest about it and engaged with it?

There's also the possibility that by having acknowledged my perceived weakness, I am now able to develop a new strength. By taking a moment to honor that part of myself, I get to ask, "How is this weakness *not* serving me right now?"

As I develop and allow appreciative gratitude for whatever it is that I discover in myself—thanks to my budding self-awareness processes—that discovery gets imbued with energy and with my attention, care, and curiosity. I now have a conscious and empowered chance to review and ascertain, understand, and develop as is desired and needed. That's certainly something to be appreciative of!

Considering how the UGP is structured, appreciation (A3) and acceptance (A2) work closely together. To experience appreciation, we must first allow and foster acceptance. This requires a ceasefire on any kind of judgmentalness, because judgmentalness doesn't allow us to accept, let alone follow with appreciation.

Action: What Blocks Us from Taking Conscious Action?

A little repeating here to make this next point. As you've surely heard me say, **"Awareness without action is not awareness at all."** What's the point of becoming aware—in particular, of a pattern that's gripped us, that's inhibiting our self-expression, damaging our connection to others or hurting us—and doing nothing with that awareness?

Insight is great, cognition is great, and accepting and appreciating what we find inside of ourselves is great. But without formulating our findings into some concretely formed outcome, we are missing a great opportunity—one that could, in fact, be a part of what changes our lives.

Awareness needs that fourth-A follow-up, which is the action step. Here's where we go from cognition to a conscious form of action. It's where we go from seeing to accepting, from appreciating to doing, with each step engendering self-empowerment and self-efficacy.

Here's where the rubber of awareness meets the road of reality, and where we can impact that reality consciously. This is where we experience our own intrapersonal shifts. These shifts then impact our commitment and resolve. From here, we begin to witness change unfold in our lives, and in relation to others and the world around us too.

What blocks our ability to take conscious, mindfully aware action? How much time do you have? (Just kidding!) What is it that gets in our way at the fourth step of the UGP process? Is it overwhelm? A fear of failure? A sudden burst of anxiety? Some form of negative self-talk or self-doubt? Feels like too much effort? Or is it a sudden bout of paralysis, being stuck between how we might have habitually taken action in the past and the desire to take a different action now? What if the new action feels a bit unsure and awkward? What about fearing that we won't take action well enough? Or that we won't do it right? Or what if it all backfires completely?

Taking action begins by first befriending imperfection. The action step is where we do our best to enact conscious right action but we give ourselves permission to fumble. Know that it's not going to be perfect—it might not be pretty at all. But we can allow ourselves to be OK with that, and be OK with others seeing that, if that's what's needed to occur.

Moving through these personal development steps by way of the 5As will surely be full of pitfalls, setbacks, missteps, getting them out of order, forgetting one or more of them—you name it. That's how it looks when we begin and that's just fine.

It's the practice, day in and day out—through trial and error, through struggle and repetition—that will eventually turn a lot of rough practice into seamless self-mastery. *Awareness* and recognition practiced over and over again leads us to the trust we need to *accept* and then to *appreciate*, which then leads to the taking of appropriate *action*, the ability to consciously conduct ourselves—loving and compassionately—in any given situation. That's the ultimate goal of the first four As of the UGP.

> How are you at taking action?
> Are you able to constructively challenge the habitual pattern of thoughts and feelings that get in the way of your taking the action you need or want?
> When behavioral change is called for, can you act on it?
> How do you respond when asked to take action on behalf of others?

The Anatomy of Taking Conscious Action

The Pause: We Need to Sort It Out

As we self-observe and recognize, accept and appreciate—whatever might be showing up in us, including importantly our reactivity—we are standing successfully in "the pause." We're now beautifully positioned to intentionally observe, collect our energy, and contain it. Not suppress or deny it, but contain it consciously, while fully and respectfully acknowledging it.

Pausing—getting grounded in our bodies and present to the now—allows us to delay responding, to delay an action, one that might not be a conscious one. This split-second pause gives us time to assess, decide, and emotionally recover so that a consciously thought-out action can be entertained and then mobilized. (Rest assured, it gets easier with practice!) This pause, which begins at the self-awareness step—the first A in the UGP—allows space for more of a 360-degree knowing to come into awareness.

The pause prevents us from mindlessly acting out our habitual patterns, particularly those dysfunctional, reactive behaviors that get ourselves and others in trouble. This is essential! It means we make space to consciously respond to our lives and everything happening in it. A key to the action step's success is all of what we need to do that precedes it, which is the self-awareness noticing, recognizing, accepting, and appreciating. This includes our honest recognition of our reactions, our upsets and distress, and especially, the recognition of our body's in-the-moment felt-sense, emotional-somatic experience.

Tuned in, which is what *practice* gifts us, we can literally feel our reactivity come on as it grips us every time in a familiar way someplace in our bodies. It is visceral. Tracking first the sensations and second noticing where they are located are critical steps in our developmental process.

Do we feel a lockdown in our throats? A churning in our stomach? A metaphorical knife in our solar plexus? A gripping contraction that seizes our heart? Dizziness or faintness? What is physically happening to us when we feel threatened (emotionally or physically) in any small or large way?

The somatic-felt sense of our bodies is oh-so important because the autonomic nervous system always reacts automatically, nanoseconds before any conscious cognition takes place.

Our physical, somatic responses are how *we feel into* ourselves. Our soma is full of valuable data, data in the form of sensations that tell us who we are and how we're doing. We need and deserve this somatic data to intimately understand ourselves deeply and authentically.

Father Time's hourglass may not register that nanosecond of space between our reactivity and our cognition, so we need to squeeze ourselves into it. Using our breath, inhale deeply, bring the air in and down into the gravitational center of our bodies. One oxygen-filled breath is all it takes to get us in there because oxygen diffuses cortisol—that very familiar stress hormone.

An action step that is consciously determined can only happen if we pause, wait (inhale), assess (exhale), and then decide. Compassionately harnessing our reactivity thanks to a mindfully aware pause is one of the most important skills we can hone on the path toward personal growth, on the path to our own peace and happiness.

While we are often not present to ourselves when reactivity takes off running, whipping us into doing something, into taking some sort of action, we need to be in sync with *all* of the reactivity, the whole kit and caboodle.

Reactivity is what triggers very intense (stress hormone) impulses, and those impulses may have us react in a way that may not serve us well—reactions that we may even regret. Let's *respond* instead of *reacting*. (That's a piece of advice that just keeps on giving!)

Let's learn to be intentional and conscious about our action or resolution rather than reacting from a place of preprogrammed adaptations or defensiveness, which prevents us from loving and living fully.

Deciding What to Do: Gentle Inquiry that Leads the Way

Once we're able to consciously *track* our reactivity as it takes hold, and once we've identified where in the body it seizes us, then we're ready to inquire what it's about. While *talking about* reactivity helps us begin the deconstruction of either the shame we feel or the need to rationalize our reactive behavior, reactivity tracking is no small task!

This is intense work that involves all our emotional resources and faculties. (Kudos to you reading this section with your reactivity compasses out and your "squeeze into that pause" climbing boots on!)

Reactivity doesn't show up for no reason. So, once we've called out our reactivity, the next step is to ask ourselves, "What is *driving* this reactivity?" From a place of grounded presence, which is the place that gave us the strength to contain the charge of the impulses and feelings and then pause in the first place, we can now practice a thoughtful and gentle inquiry.

Here's where we venture to discover, discern, and work with whatever the truth of the reactivity may be. First ask, "Did I get triggered from *within* (old stuff)? Or am I being violated in some way by someone or something *externally* that needs my earnest attention?"

Also pay attention to these questions: What are the emotions we felt (sadness or distress, frustration or anger, anxiety or fear), and what seems to be the underlying theme? What's the content that's upsetting, that's churning us up emotionally? What are the external factors?

And consider if it is possible we are misinterpreting something, like another's intentions or them being upset? Here once again, we can return to the wisdom of the Enneagram as it gives us a map. Each of the nine personality structures as it happens gets triggered by uncannily specific issues and challenges.

By studying the Enneagram, we are brought that much closer to recognizing our **triggers** and understanding them more deeply and far more quickly than struggling on our own to figure them out. Here are some of many simple examples of what may trigger sensitivities and reactivity in each of the nine Enneagram type structures:

Type 1s can get reactive when someone has dropped the ball, leaving them feeling unfairly responsible.

Type 2s can get reactive when they give and give yet not feel appreciated.

Type 3s can get reactive when they've worked themselves to a bone and a colleague gets recognized instead.

Type 4s can get reactive when something's less than what they expected, less than the ideal they've imagined or fantasized about.

Type 5s can get reactive when someone is not interested in the information they're about to share and instead wants to talk about something perceived as useless, too personal, or invasive.

Type 6s can get reactive when they think someone's untrustworthy or possibly taking advantage of their kindness and loyalty.

Type 7s can get reactive when they can't go and do what they want to, and when they feel trapped by something or someone.

Type 8s can get reactive when they're ignored or when they see someone who cannot protect themselves getting overpowered and bullied.

Type 9s can get reactive when pushed to do something they do not want to do, but they don't want to say no or don't find a way to do so.

Aside from the triggers found in each Enneagram type (and these type-specific examples could go on and on), there are universal triggers (not necessarily related to type) as well that beg for compassion.

These triggers that elicit a stress response are shared by all Enneagram types, all peoples, and are somewhat existential in nature. They may include but are not limited to the experiences of and fears around natural disasters; real threats to our physical safety; threats to a loved one's safety; blatant attacks to our dignity, personhood, or cultural norms (belonging); and threats that result in a great loss such as the death or pending death of a loved one or oneself due to disease or old age.

Curiosity: One of Our Greatest Resources

Curiosity is a profound friend. What an immense personal resource this is, and we come in with it. Curiosity is innate. It's akin to the seeking instinct. We are wired with it, and it gives us energy. Curiosity drives exploration, and exploration is the way our brain takes in the world (for assessing and processing) so it can grow and develop, seek and learn.

It is neutral and playful. Curiosity is the non-judgmental ticket to the greatest show on earth. That "show" is our drive to explore the world and the beauty, wonderment, and truth of all that we encounter. It is not childish, though it is childlike as it fills us with fascination, openness, and possibility.

Curiosity is an asset and one that needs our definitive reverence and consistent facilitation. Curiosity is a quality resourced readily in higher states of developmental well-being; it is also a quality we can lose contact with as we leave childhood behind and are domesticated into the rigors and responsibilities of adulthood.

Getting to the Bottom of It: Curiosity Meets Gentle Inquiry

Gentle inquiry is a life-changing, game-changing tool. It's a great internal mentor. It's a coaching mechanism that will guide us through probably the most important investigative challenges one might ever undergo: the investigation into self.

Gentle inquiry cares enough to not assume but to question. Gentle inquiry needs to show up full of heart and care about what's hurting, what's troubled, what's triggered, and what's been threatened. Curiosity goes hand in hand with gentle inquiry, as curiosity ensures that our inquiry is not a judgmental hunt, but a pleasing discovery.

Curiosity is not looking for logic, keep that in mind; it's more so looking inquisitively for what's there, what's really there. Curiosity is not picky either—it's neither liking what's there, nor *not* liking what's there. It's genuinely interested and it's neutral. It's not attached to the outcomes. It approaches everything as if it doesn't know yet.

Curiosity is open. It's free of agendas and expectations and has no language for criticism. Curiosity is what allows a gentle and caring personal inquiry to take place. Allow it and be still. Listen tenderly, with a genuine interest for the vulnerability that may arise.

Gentle inquiry allows an awareness of embarrassment, disappointment, and even dismay to be felt. It also allows for shame to reveal itself. Our inquiry may also expose pride, righteousness, arrogance, delusion, or rationalization.

Curiosity can be revelatory if we take full advantage of it. Allow a consciously curious, gentle inquiry process to consume us; let it work its magic and work on our behalf!

Mentoring the Self: Awareness that Leads to Action that Results in Conscious Conduct

Within each of us is an inner self-coach laying in waiting, ready to take a stand for us and support our higher good. With its own brand of self-discipline, motivation, and love, a deep care for ourselves and a desire to grow, our self-coach steps in to support us in going from automatic to conscious conduct.

Our self-coach is a thoughtful, supportive, non-judging voice of truth and honesty combined with encouragement, guidance, and mentorship. Self-coaching for self-mastery is a form of self-care and self-love. With the core beliefs of each of the nine Enneagram types comes the unique and extraordinary opportunity to challenge how those beliefs automatically run themselves, our lives, and, inadvertently, each of our interactions with ourselves and with others.

That said, it's right here that we—with great reverence for each of the nine Enneagram type's core beliefs—come to understand their respective highest intention. Going back to earlier chapters, remember that each of these core beliefs is fundamentally designed to ensure that we are lovable.

These core beliefs are also conjoined with our focus of attention, which contributes a much-needed something—a critical evolutionary something—to our collective survival. So, before we start battling with our core beliefs thinking they are what's at fault, let's instead coach ourselves into training a better, more effective, reverent application of them.

Doing this takes discipline, though. Self-mastery takes discipline—the discipline to practice beyond each failed attempt. It takes discipline to stay curious. It takes discipline to inhale and squeeze into that ridiculously tiny nanosecond of a pause. It takes discipline to try again after our last practice got us frustrated. And it's our discipline that must want this for ourselves and won't give up on us as this is what's called for. We can do this because we deserve it, because getting to live our lives and love ourselves more fully deserves it. (Go, coach!)

For example, let's take Type 1s. They bring a particular aptitude and wisdom to the world. Type 1s hope to inspire our goodness and our capacity to do the right thing for the higher good of all involved. They teach us to step up to our integrity, to stand in right alignment, personal accountability, and responsibility.

When these higher qualities of being get hijacked by a core belief that tells the Type 1 that **it will not be loved unless it is good, responsible, integral, accountable, mistake-free, and above condemnation**, then we go from self-mastery to self-punishment, from expansiveness to contraction.

Once hijacked in this way, we have moved from love to a conditional love, and conditional love triggers fear. We have moved from the expansiveness of our essence to the contraction of its unwanted and feared shadow.

When a Type 1 expresses their evolution-contributing qualities through reactivity, through self-righteousness, the highest intention of this type structure may not be realized or expressed fully, if at all.

Self-honoring and self-mastery feel good and are full of available life-force energy. Self-punishment and self-degradation that come from fear do not feel good and zap our source energy. Scolding is not inspiring. Correcting is most often not motivating. Finding fault does not engender greatness.

Here's where we need our self-coach to tell the difference: "On what side of my higher qualities am I? Am I expressing them vibrantly and expansively? Or am I expressing them scornfully and narrowly? Am I, or others, feeling good and dignified? Am I, or others, feeling badly or less than?"

Coaching ourselves toward self-mastery develops self-respect. It allows us to work with ourselves beyond the clutching of the hijacked-into-compulsions habits of our driving core beliefs and our need to thrust them onto the world, narrowly, bitterly, or righteously.

The question we want to pose is this: **How can we bring the talents and aptitudes that we have—those that are fundamentally organized around our core beliefs—to the world in the way they were best designed to be offered and expressed?**

In a way that contributes to our well-being, others' well-being, and to the well-being of our human family as a whole.

> As I run the impulses–all the way to compulsions–of my type structure's core beliefs, am I hurting myself or another?
> Am I honoring my core beliefs' higher gifts in a way that is supportive and helpful, inspiring, or bettering of another and of the world around me?
> How am I expressing my best self, the essential qualities of my higher self?

Self-coaching for self-mastery allows us to discern how we are using ourselves, expressing ourselves, and showing up in the world for ourselves and for others. It allows us to see our impact, not just our intention. It allows us to make choices— to selectively choose our most dignified response—rather than react to internal, on-automatic impulses or compulsions, ones that we haven't yet questioned or challenged, let alone understood or mastered.

Learning our Enneagram type structure opens up a garden of colorful insights about ourselves. Enneagram study gives us a vast amount of personalities-development information that we can utilize, and benefit from, in order to more succinctly enhance our lives, live better, and love more fully.

Adherence: What Blocks Us from Adherence, from Sticking to Our Process?

Let's start by asking what blocks us from commitment. Why is it often easier to falter on a commitment we make with ourselves than one we make with others? Adherence is synonymous with commitment. It's another form of discipline. And to share again, it's an expression of self-love and self-care.

Unfortunately, we may fail our commitments because we get too busy and lose steam, we get tired, forget, have something more pleasurable that distracts us, or we're not seeing the results quickly enough, so we lose interest. On and on go the excuses and challenges we face. All of these are well-known reasons we tell ourselves as to why we don't keep up with something we said we wanted to keep up with. But is there more?

Conflicting Parts of Self

What about a far more covert reason as to why we may struggle with adherence? As in, what else could be interfering with our adherence to a personal-development practice, one that might be life-changing and personally expansive? (Sure sounds like good stuff!)

But what if we're either (subconsciously) afraid of the changes we may bring forth, or we're apprehensive about any level of pain, personal revelation, or struggle that we may encounter as we do these awareness-inducing exercises and processes? Could that be impacting our adherence? Or what if we're not aware that deep down we're actually resistant to some of this development work because we are not sure who we're going to become if we do it? (Now, *that's* a challenge . . .)

For those reading this who are familiar with "parts of self," also known as Internal Family Systems (IFS), Dr. Richard Schwartz's groundbreaking work and his book, *Internal Family Systems Therapy*, you'll be aware of the following insights. While we may have the best of intentions when declaring, "We're gonna stick with that fifth A of adherence," those intentions might not be strong enough to override a part of self that fears letting go of some aspect of its fierce and defending, seemingly protective reactivity or habit of being.

For example, let's say I'm an Enneagram Type 4 who has always wanted to sing publicly. I really want to take my talent to the next level so I can live out this dream. For years, I've known I needed to take singing lessons. But years go by, and I never sign up for lessons. I've got lots of reasons, like being too busy, for instance. But what if, unbeknownst to me, there's another part of self that's operating whose role it is to protect me from embarrassment and failure?

If I put myself out there, starting with taking singing lessons, I might be shamed or I may learn that I can't really sing after all. Or I might go all the way to my first engagement and flop! Or what if I do so well and start traveling to sing all over the place and my boyfriend leaves me because of it?

These parts of self are strong-willed and are often there to protect us. They are in place thanks to years of environmental conditioning in response to psychological and emotional stressors (threats). They are our temperament's and our essence's best conjured-up solutions at a time when some sort of protective solution was needed.

These parts require understanding and compassion, and the role they play in our lives needs to be honestly encountered and deeply understood. They may very well be what's in control of our *not* adhering to something we seemingly want to adhere to.

To summarize with great respect the valuable contribution of Dr. Schwartz, IFS work allows the many disparate parts of self to surface into our consciousness where they can be felt, identified, spoken to, appreciated, and respected. From this point of recognition, we have the chance to integrate them back into the entirety of our personality system where they can no longer independently take over and unknowingly steer the course of our lives. Instead, they have a chance to be understood and redirected in a way that's coherent with the rest of our hopes, dreams, and desires.

Parts of Self and the Enneagram

While this book does not specifically explore the so-called parts of self from IFS—as in exiles and protectors, managers and firefighters—it's not lost on us to see that each of the Enneagram structures with their identifiable schemas are able to declare not random but patterned, recognizable, and very similar parts of self by Enneagram type. (That could be a very interesting thesis for someone to explore!)

Intention

As we embark on **adherence** (A5) and the highly rewarding process of personal development, it's equally important to connect with our intention. Intention creates a powerful kind of energy, one that drives action and outcomes as much as heartfelt desire, protective reactivity, even disruptive compulsions, for example. We want to ensure that our intention is known to us. Is the intention clear? And is it in line with our best interests?

To organize around our intention, start with an inventory of any possible resistance we may have to doing this work, including our habitual struggles with commitment and discipline as well as any deeply held parts of self that may not be down at all with personal change and the vulnerability that comes with it.

Once we've tackled those key stumbling blocks and have identified resistances, take some time to do a benefits inventory. Tune in to the promise of this work, which may include relief from cognitive-emotional pain, enhanced communication with ourselves and with others, more love and joy in our lives, less debilitating conflict, less hurt, and more personal freedom.

We may also see results that include better physical health as well as an always-desired increase in developmental well-being, our level of presence, and our level of expressed and experienced joy.

> How are you with adherence, with committing yourself to a regular practice, and with keeping commitments you make in your life?
>
> What do you find helps you keep your promises to yourself?
>
> What do you find most gets in your way? What resistances do you encounter doing this work?
>
> Are you better at follow-through with yourself? Or with others? Why do you think that's the case?

Adherence and Internalizing the Universal Growth Practice

We customarily take time to nourish our bodies and care for ourselves every day. Most of us sleep, eat food, and drink water on a regular, repetitive schedule. But there's more to us that needs attention and care.

Nourishing our emotional-spiritual health—our developmental well-being and how that impacts our relationships—we'd like to suggest be no different. And we get multiple chances a day to put this kind of adherence into practice.

Every single day, we go on automatic. We get reactive over and over again in both small and large ways, and we can count on it. Our lives provide us so thoughtfully with the best fodder ever to practice with! (How convenient!)

Adherence lies in waiting minute by minute. All we need to do is activate it! This is what I call "enlightenment on the hoof." Every upset and challenge faced daily calls up a chance to practice, which aligns with our commitment to this fifth A.

Through adherence, we can begin to internalize the UGP for Self-Mastery, which will foster an incredible amount of personal development and growth over time—growth that is far beyond just a nice cognitive idea. This is growth that gets embodied and is sustainable, developmentally giving, and life enhancing.

Adherence and Our Will

Adherence is demonstrative of our will. Our will is a power, an energy, and it is driven by the spirit within us. This is one of the driving energies fueling our adaptive strategies, protecting our soul from emotional harm, and it strives to serve us at all times. Our will is committed to meeting our basic needs for security, love and connection, and our autonomy and dignity. It's also a strong resource we call upon to stand for ourselves and resolve conflict. Our will drives our survival behaviors, as well as how each of us fights for the self within, for our sense of self.

Our will is the force behind our conscious and deliberate intentional action. Our will includes the power to choose our own actions and exercise discretion regarding how and where we apply ourselves.

Put differently, our will fuels the power to direct and act in accordance with those choices. And choice is key. When aligned with our free will, choice empowers our self-agency and our inner authority.

When our will is proactively, intentionally directed, it serves our purpose and is full of determination, volition, resoluteness, persistence, and free-flowing self-discipline. When we skillfully come from a place of grounded presence and awareness, our will drives intention and supports regulative, meaningful self-agency.

It is our will that determines and governs our success with the fifth A of adherence, and well, our overall success in life too.

CHAPTER 10

What Separates Us from One Another and from Ourselves: From Resistance to Development

What drives us apart? If I had the answer to this question, I might be able to save the world! While the question is simple, the dilemma is complex. I think it's safe to say that when entering any kind of relationship—be it with a newborn child, a potential best friend, a new boss or a new love—most of us go into it with an unspoken hope, confidence even, that we'll succeed.

We begin relationships with good intent, thinking that a connection will develop, that we'll get beyond our first introduction. But as we all know, relationships can struggle and go awry, and having that happen is not pleasant for anyone. In fact, in many cases—as in parent-child relationships—relational failure can be catastrophic. What caused our relationship to fail? What actually drove us apart?

There are countless big reasons why relationships fail. These are easy to see and comprehend. For instance: when one or both parties is dishonest; or there's betrayal leading to a breakdown in trust; or when there's damage or harm to our physical safety; or there's out-and-out disrespect and disregard; or there's emotional cruelty inflicted; or when there's undermining, back-stabbing, or blatant insincerity.

Having to deal with these kinds of relational damages will sabotage a relationship, almost always irreparably. But what about those relationships that seem to be going pretty well—as there are no great catastrophes, no huge breakdowns per se—but in the end, they don't make it either? What happened, this time, that simply drove us apart? It's time to question the subtle ways we derail our relationships. What are the ways we whittle away at our ability to build trust, mutual respect, and a deepening intimacy?

The Sabotage of Non-Acceptance

While it's impossible to cover every possible nuance of relationships-corrosion in this chapter, there are a couple of significant deal-breakers that while subtle, can have far-reaching, slow-boiling impact over time.

Non-acceptance of self or other has already been shared in a number of ways across this book, but it's important to reiterate in this context. Non-acceptance separates us from one another. It drives a wedge between us by burying our vulnerability under the "I'm hoping I'm acceptable" me, and "You're hoping you're acceptable" you.

When one or both of us feel that some part of us is not accepted by the other, we get mad, or we try to exile the anger by downplaying or suppressing it. Worse yet, we may take ourselves "offline" when in the presence of the other. (What a loss!) Or we may begin to live out that seemingly unacceptable part of ourselves in other ways—in secrecy perhaps. It's easy to predict how potentially or even profoundly problematic any of these compensations could be.

Non-acceptance of others is often an extension of simply not accepting ourselves (something we covered in greater detail in Chapter 9). The conditions we place on ourselves to ensure our acceptability and lovability inadvertently spill out as conditions we'll place on unassuming, innocent others as well—others that are, in turn, doing that very same thing to themselves and, inadvertently, to others in *their* lives.

Placing conditions on ourselves and others is an aspect of our more unconscious and limiting human nature. Unfortunately, the setting of conditions makes acceptance far more difficult. In fact, conditions and acceptance are at odds with one another.

But when acceptance is granted, it's unfortunately often only granted when our conditions have been satisfied. At that, that acceptance may still only be given partially at best. It's a wonder we figure out how to get along at all!

There's tremendous suffering when there's little acceptance of ourself or another in a relationship, just as there's great suffering when we feel that others do not accept us either.

Not feeling accepted can wreak havoc on our *self*-esteem and the esteem we hold of ourselves in *another's* eyes. This is particularly detrimental in parent-child dynamics where the child cannot meet the expectations—let alone garner the acceptance—of their parents. This can lead to immense damage to the child's developing self-system and, if not addressed, may continue to do so over a lifetime. It's also a significant issue for partnered romantic relationships.

Can we truly love each other if we really don't accept one another as we truly are?

To fully understand acceptance, let's acknowledge once again that acceptance does not mean concurring, condoning, or capitulating. There are times when situational non-acceptance has its place, and we'll touch on that in a moment.

What acceptance *does* mean though, is to see and then accept someone *as they actually are.* This means that we honor them—with their gifts and foibles—as they present themselves to us, and we do so with respect, reverence, and a caring discernment. The discernment called for here is not judgmentalness. Instead, it is clarity.

Discernment allows us to witness and understand our differences with neutrality. It then allows us to decide for ourselves what to do at any given moment. In particular, discernment guides us when we're struggling to understand one another, or when there's an incompatibility or incongruence that needs to be addressed. Discernment lets us peer into challenges in a healthy and constructive way. It allows all involved the chance to *see what really is* without condemnation or projection. Discernment functions to support us to see clearly, to make wise and sound decisions, and to pursue healthy relational choices.

Discernment also helps to steer us from the hard and frustrating work of trying to change someone so we can *accept them better.* It allows us to see another as they are rather than how we want them to be. The feeling of someone loving us *only if we change* (conditional love) is a tough pill to swallow and usually does the very same thing to our sense of self and esteem as did a conditional-love parent way back when.

As our self-esteem erodes under the watchful, critical eye of non-acceptance, so does our capacity to continue showing up with all of ourselves in a given relationship. Hence, non-acceptance puts the *relationship* at risk as well as one or both individuals' *self-esteem* too.

Situational non-acceptance is different from the non-acceptance of our partner or ourselves. It has its place in relationships as it allows for in-the-moment discernment, discrepancy resolution, and on-the-spot constructive right action.

An example is in the way we sometimes use words without integrity. When words spoken don't line up with the speaker's actions, we might sense that incongruence somatically or note it intellectually—that is, if we're tuned in enough to our inner cues. Situational non-acceptance allows for an in-the-moment authentic response to something being "off."

We can then choose to discuss or challenge, address and resolve. It honors an identified red flag and a chance to confront, in real time, something that's not acceptable, something that might be misleading, incoherent, inconsistent, or even deceitful—all of which can cause damage to our relationship if left unaddressed.

Whether situational or personal, non-acceptance can create a challenging dynamic between people. It can actually be felt (registered) even when not spoken or explained, and it can cause disturbances in our relationships, small or great.

When discussing our felt-sense, direct experience of non-acceptance, we cannot overlook or minimize nonverbal cues, a very important aspect of our communication. We communicate our love and acceptance of one another (or not) in many, many ways, including without words. In fact, the nonverbal data we pick up may be even more impactful than words spoken. Not being accepted can readily be felt in our soma (bodies) and can trigger emotional reactivity, which can lead directly to conflictual discord.

Our partner's upset or disapproval, which can trigger a lot of discomfort, is often seen in a facial expression or heard in a vocal tone, even if the words spoken say the opposite. Those nonverbals speak volumes, and we are cued into them as a metric of our minute-to-minute acceptability.

There are seven known nonverbal forms of communication that we as humans are sensitive to and dependent on. And these nonverbals are incalculably important—from infant on up—as children are masters at deciphering these inputs long before they have language at their disposal. These are: eye contact or lack thereof; facial expressions; tone; gestures; posture; timing; and intensity.

Finally, non-acceptance rubs up against our need to belong, our need to feel safe with each other, and our desire to feel protected by one another. Being accepted leads us to feeling liked, feeling "OK in the world," feeling viable, and feeling worthy. Acceptance is the foundation of our very sense of belonging. It's about survival.

Remember, those who were not accepted by the tribe a million years ago were tossed out and eaten by predators! (Not desirable!) So, to belong—a byproduct of being connected and accepted—is part of being human, and our Social Instinct dominants work hard at and are imbued with heaps of this survival intelligence, as we read about in Chapter 7.

The Sword of Judgmentalness: The Critical Mind

Understanding the impact of non-acceptance leads us to understanding the mechanisms in place that kick us into the non-acceptance spiral. Within each of us resides what I like to call the critical-judging mind, which is often referred to as the superego.

The superego is the ethical component of the personality and provides the moral standards by which the ego operates. The superego's criticisms, prohibitions, and inhibitions form a person's conscience, and its positive aspirations and ideals represent one's idealized self-image.

Within our self-system is a structure that organizes the ideals and standards regarding what we'll deem as acceptable, good, and reasonable for us—our superego. These constructs are formulated non-consciously and in early childhood—a combination of our own neural propensities meeting up with what's being recorded in our implicit (emotional-reactive-responsive) and explicit memory systems.

The critical-judging mind develops in response to the identification and subsequent internalization of the values, rules, and beliefs set forth *for us* and *by us*. These crystallize in response to the reward and punishment systems of our parents, authority figures, our societal culture, and the consequential ideology we then construct within. All of it is in accordance and compliance with our type structure and how it comes to believe it must conduct itself to ensure that we'll be accepted and loved—our core beliefs.

We need our critical-judging mind; it has positive functions in that it supports our personality structure by providing healthy guidance as to who *we need to be* and *may want to be.*

But the superego can also become a hard-to-break barrier to self-acceptance and other-acceptance, as it can become rigid, condemning, and inflexible. So much so, our critical-judging mind can interfere with our own inner knowing and can even block paradigm shifts in cognition and new levels of awareness from occurring.

This critical-judging mind, while the benevolent broker of our morals and values, also doles out criticism of another or connection-breaking *judgmentalness.* While sound judgment is a good thing, judgmentalness can significantly hinder relationships.

Judgmentalness, a far cry from discernment (thoughtful awareness that is differentiating and neutral), limits our capacity to *accept* and hence to *love* without conditions and without resistance.

While judgmentalness can disguise itself as helpful and protective, its energies do little of the kind when it comes to loving, human relating. Often our formulas for judgmentalness are based in the past as it attempts to preserve some idea of the status quo it has learned. It sets up conditions and inadvertently causes all sorts of rejections—of the self, of others, of our differences, of new ideas even. Its mere presence can diminish current and new experiences.

Judgmentalness is a joy buster and an intimacy inhibitor. Judgmentalness causes suffering because it's separating and isolating, and it can lead to undeniable and not-understood degrees of distress and discord.

It has been my experience that the critical-judging mind often presents as the most ubiquitous and difficult aspect of the second A of acceptance within the UGP, as it shows up over and over again in unbelievably subtle yet compelling, protective, receptivity-inhibiting ways.

What Really Gets in the Way of Intimacy

You'd think we'd all want to walk around with an open and loving, undefended heart in a receptive and curious state of mind, because isn't that such an overwhelmingly pleasant, euphoric state in which to find ourselves? Why would any of us choose anything different? Why, after reading the paragraph above, would any of us want to spend much time in critical judgmentalness? (Blech!)

Critical judgment—judgmentalness—is one of the big relationship breakers, which is why we've chosen to highlight it. It's only *one* example of what can get in our way and what drives us apart, but it's a big one. And here's how it works. (Use this example as a model to help you take "judgmentalness inventory" in your own psyche.)

Judgmentalness is the great splitter. It is a proclivity that splits things into black or white, right or wrong, good or bad, me versus you. And it does it *in an instant*. It separates us from the object we are judging and from that moment on, we're no longer connected to it. Instead, we're propped up in some type of polarity with only one winner.

As mentioned earlier, judgmentalness is not to be confused with healthy discernment—the neutral reception and acknowledgment of clarifying differentiations. Judgmentalness is the antithesis of neutral. It lacks neutrality because it's loaded with opinion. And opinion readily prevents acceptance, receptivity, and openness. Judgmentalness finds some sort of fault that then ignites some aggravating point of view, one that often gives us permission to either push against or pull away.

As a matter of fact, judgmentalness does to a loving relationship what a scratchy needle on vinyl does to John's Lennon's "Imagine." You're a blissful minute into Lennon's lyrics and "*screeeeeeech!*"—that bliss comes to a grinding halt and non-blissful irritation becomes your reality.

Judgmentalness turns "me and you" into "me can't align with you." With that, the interpretations that mindset induces get our fears running. Catapulted out of a beautiful melody and our union with it, judgmentalness finds us in a lonely place.

Once united, we're now separated. What happened in a split second may seem insignificant, but it's actually catastrophic and will greatly impact our relationships—especially our love relationships. In short, judgmentalness immediately jeopardizes our ability to stay there, *with* another, in loving connection.

Not only is judgmentalness one of the many connection saboteurs; it is also a self-harmer. And we critically judge others and ourselves in so many ways—instantly, unconsciously, and habitually.

Judging ourselves is just as separating and as disconnecting as judging others. In both cases, we split off from ourselves. The critical-judging mind becomes the almighty, and the self (or the other) becomes nothing more than an object needing correction or fixing, scolding, or rejecting.

It is salient to learn *how to identify* when we are being judgmental—whether to ourselves or to another—and then *how to intervene* (pause and contain) so as to not jettison ourselves out of bliss, out of connection and acceptance, and ultimately, out of sustainable, life-giving love.

Chances are, the more we find ourselves critically judging others, the more we are actually judging ourselves, which hurts everyone involved. And it gets tiresome.

The solution, of course, is to become present to what we're doing—that is, to incite awareness. Next, we can consciously allow the softening (relaxation) of our superego's pressurizing constrictions—constrictions caused by the stories we tell ourselves that invoke and allow us to justify setting ourselves apart from one another.

It's about paying attention to what our well-intentioned superego (the critical-judging mind) is demanding of us. What the conditions are we're being reminded of right now—you know, the ones that want to ensure that we're worthy of love. All of this is felt as a contraction, a huge scratch, if you will—one that screeches across the heart, cutting us off from so-desired connection and from love itself.

Coming out of judgmentalness is about softening these painful, separating contractions. It's about wanting more for ourselves. The cut of judgmentalness is abrupt, and it unknowingly hurts. It's time to start caring that we are doing this to ourselves. Realizing we can let this go—that it's not serving us—is a kind and validating big step toward self-love and our ability to love others.

Now, here's the kicker. Judgmentalness, as it turns out, is a very clever way for the superego to unwittingly protect us. But the way judgmentalness separates us from another also protects us from intimacy. It derails our vulnerability, which then keeps us distanced from that place where we're more exposed, where we might get hurt. Vulnerability is necessary for intimacy, though. It's what is at the heart of love itself. It's what is at the core of loving and of being loved.

What better solution then is there than to find something definitively wrong with another—our partner, in particular—in order to save ourselves from getting too close, from being vulnerable?

Judge them critically, and "Ahhh . . ." we can justifiably and righteously push against or pull away. We're none the wiser as we return safely to familiar, non-vulnerable, not-at-risk-but-disconnected territory.

A seemingly solid and believable critical judgment can keep the best of us from showing up. How safe is that? Very. How loving and intimate and life-giving is that? Not very. While we all want love so dearly, we are often masters at pulling ourselves right out of it. And so, we suffer, as do others. Because pulling away and standing against are truly an emotional loss for all involved.

Alleviating judgmentalness begins first with the deepest desire *not* to do this to ourselves anymore, not to cut ourselves off anymore from letting ourselves be known, from vulnerability, from lovingkindness, from intimacy. We don't have to be stuck there, though. We can decide to no longer allow ourselves to succumb to this kind of separation from the beauty, love, and connection that we are here on planet earth to cultivate and experience.

Using mindful awareness practice, let us set our intentions to investigate, "What's the critical-judging mind doing for us?" and "What's it giving us?" Also "What's it protecting?"

To alleviate destructive self-judgment, let's practice discernment more consciously, and from here, begin the even bigger process of forgiving ourselves for where we're not measuring up. (Despite how good the superego is at calling this stuff out!)

Importantly, let's instead turn self-judgment into curiosity and from that place of curiosity replace the harmful need to judge, punish, or self-edit with a loving and guiding urge to self-motivate. This is the intentional turn from critical judgment to healthy discernment. It puts us in a state of cognizant awareness where we can differentiate what's what with neutrality and sobriety.

Discernment is what clarifies for us what is the best thing, the right thing, the integral thing to do for self and, hopefully, for the highest good of all involved as well. It allows us to assess neutrally and make sound decisions. Discernment fosters thoughtful right action. It is non-blaming, self-accountable, and mindful.

In contrast, judgmentalness is a destructive mental preoccupation. It zaps our energy and focus. When left unexamined, judgmentalness prevents healthy, clarifying perceptions. And its rigidity can leave us separated from others and trapped in stages and places in our lives long beyond what was necessary or called for, let alone desired.

How Anger Impacts Our Relationships and Covers Shame and Guilt

Anger is one of the three aversive mammalian emotions wired in us to protect us. Anger is a vital emotion that erupts in response to the subjective as well as objective experience of violation.

In all its forms, anger alerts us to perceived personal threat—threats to our dignity, our values, our sense of self, our emotional safety, and perceived or real threats to our free will and autonomy. Anger shows up when we don't get what we want, aren't treated with respect, or when we're emotionally wounded, shamed, or pained. It also floods our system when issues of power or control (or being overpowered or controlled) come into question.

Anger can be triggered when circumstances or people stir feelings of powerlessness, helplessness, or inferiority. It rages when our freedom is taken, and is the emotion ignited when we perceive injustice, unfairness, or dishonesty. Physiologically, anger rises rapidly and often before cognition takes place.

In anger, many Enneagram types *move against*, meaning they become aggressive or passive aggressive. But in standing up for what we value and hold dear, we *move toward*. We become assertive, invested, and convicted. In hoping to negotiate, we contain the anger and when we do so, we become reconciling.

The aversive but positive-in-function emotion of anger goes back millions of years in mammalian evolution and has its critical place. As such, it is not to be shunned or suppressed but instead be understood and honored.

Anger is a vital, change-evoking, life-force energy that in many ways and for several reasons has gotten a bad rap. It is a big force and if used in a reckless way, it can get us into trouble. But when understood and expressed constructively, anger can bring about the changes we want to see in the world and in ourselves.

The necessary and intended function of anger is to get us what we want and to protect what we value. It's also used to obliterate (cover) feelings of humiliation and shame, and to deflect feelings of abandonment, loss of connection, or the perceived absence of love. In other words, anger can be the secondary emotion covering up the real primary feelings that are buried underneath.

Anger's more destructive uses—which can wound and dominate another, inflict pain, and destroy what we hoped would change—often hurt us and, sadly, often diminish our ability to get what we and another truly want, need, and value.

Correctly or incorrectly, anger ignites us, encouraging us to overcome a violation or escape a perceived threat. It activates the sympathetic part of the autonomic nervous system through what's called "biogenic amines," especially rallying norepinephrine and the secretion of cortisol.

The release of these stress hormones causes the heart to pound, blood flow to increase, neural excitability to surge, pupils to dilate, alertness to heighten, and muscles to tense up and strengthen in readiness. We are preparing to perceptively attack the object of upset (or, if also in fear, run from it, or freeze).

No wonder it's difficult for us to become receptive and reflective—and engage those 5As—when the chemistry of anger is coursing through our veins. It takes dedication and practice to hold the charge of this powerful emotional system long enough to determine what's going to be best for us. And thanks to the 5As, we have a methodical way to approach a healthy and viable expression of anger.

However, *explosive anger* without cognition does have its place in our evolutionary scheme. There are certainly times we need to act fast, like when we're staring a raging attacker in the face. At such a moment, the 5As are neither timely nor effective. Instead, activated rage is!

And when anger runs in our systems over time and with no engagement with it and no understanding of it (no resolution), it's called *chronic anger*. Chronic anger is the result of emotional upheaval and the building up of resentments that are unexpressed by either being *suppressed* ("I know I'm angry, but I stuff it for one reason or another") or *repressed* ("I don't even realize I'm angry . . . I lost contact with it long ago, but it's nevertheless brewing in me subconsciously").

Over time, chronic anger can manifest into serious health consequences. It can lead to long-term physical health disorders, such as high blood pressure, tension headaches, rigidity and stiffness, heart disease, ulcers, musculoskeletal disorders, even cancer and auto-immune disorders.

It can also lead to mental health disorders, such as ongoing irritability, disruptive defensiveness, frustration, oppositional defiance, impatience, complaining, blaming, withdrawing and withholding, even malicious, manipulative niceness and depression.

Furthermore, chronic anger creates tension thanks to anger, rage, and resentments that are not dealt with. And when we don't deal with anger, it can become pressurized beyond our capacity to contain it, being discharged into unexpected aggression, even violence.

John Gottman, an American psychological researcher on relationships and divorce at the Gottman Institute, claims that he can predict a relationship's success potential based on the presence of what he calls the Four Horsemen: contempt, criticism, defensiveness, and stonewalling.

Each of these coping behaviors is a result of some form of suppressed, repressed, or felt-sense anger. These ways of discharging unspoken, unresolved anger are detrimental not only to ourselves but also to the health of a relationship. These behaviors impact our ability to stay safely connected to one another and impair our ability to love freely and to feel loved.

The way anger is understood, handled, and dealt with is vital to the success of our vital, intimate relationships. This includes the constructive expression of anger leading to self-sovereignty and the setting of healthy boundaries. As such, it promotes dignified self-agency.

Such constructive expression of anger honors our authenticity and encourages that in another. And it prompts us to constructively confront behaviors and coping mechanisms that are destructive, confining, and detrimental to all involved.

How We Defend Our Deepest Hurt

In its rightful form, anger is a protective emotion. It's a vital energy that does its best to stand up for our rights, our dignity, our safety, and our autonomy. It's what stands up for and exercises our free will. And yet, it's a tricky emotion too in that it can be used to protect us from ourselves.

Anger is what often steps forward to defend an internal response to the unwanted feelings of hurt, humiliation, and degradation. It rises when we're being blamed or are feeling guilty, and most tenderly, it can be called upon to bury our shame. These are among the feelings that are so vulnerable, so sense-of-self-shaking, that to actually *feel* them challenges us.

By using anger, we can block these feelings from ourselves. Without a presence practice in place, feelings such as these can send us into debilitating despair or self-attack, so much so we may lose contact with our sense of personal power—even our vital life force. As a result, our love of life wanes, and our sense of self may greatly suffer.

Shame: Anger's Big Cover Up

What is shame? It's something systemic enough to trigger a blushing, reddening of the face or a nose-dive into inferiority. Shame lends us to hiding our faces from others or deflecting eye contact. Shame makes us just want to disappear. It's a painful personal response to feelings such as humiliation, degradation, or unwantedness.

Shame is experienced and felt not only by those who drive dominantly from the Heart Center of Intelligence but by all nine of the Enneagram types. How shame is *expressed* or *suppressed* by each of the nine types is worthy of observation as well, as each Enneagram type tends to formulate its own type-organized solution to detrimental, uncomfortable, shame-stirred feelings.

There's more than one kind of shame to observe, and I credit therapist and educator John Bradshaw's pivotal work—found in his book, *Healing the Shame That Binds You*—for bringing these valuable distinctions to our attention.

Healthy shame, as Bradshaw calls it, says we must not continue a behavior lest we be excluded and banished. This is the kind of shame that guides us toward tribal acceptance. Healthy shame provides us with the cues we need to ensure we maintain our belonging. It's the kind of shame that protects us from unwanted disapproval, from being thrown out of the group only to be eaten by lions or abducted by a warring tribe. Healthy shame helps us to socialize and fit in, accommodate group boundaries, and live successfully within the parameters of a given family or society.

But then there's toxic shame, and that's a different story. Toxic shame is shame felt not for something that we've *done*, but for something that we *are*. Toxic shame turns against the self and that renders us perceptively, shamefully, flawed, and utterly unworthy of love. This is not a book to go too deeply into this kind of shame and its origins and resolutions. But you can only imagine what this kind of shame does to a child, or to a relationship's potential—to our ability to be intimate and vulnerable—if one or both partners suffer it.

The distance we keep from ourselves as a result of shame is, inadvertently, the distance we will keep from others. Toxic shame keeps us from ourselves. It keeps us from accepting and loving ourselves fully, and it interferes with our ability to feel fully lovable by others.

Shame—particularly toxic shame—hurts as it can lead to varying degrees of self-rejection, which then distorts our capacity for vulnerable disclosure and intimacy with ourselves and, hence, with others.

Toxic shame along with the unwanted feelings of hurt, humiliation, and degradation is particularly hard to process directly and consciously, it is hard to tolerate and can render feelings of powerlessness and helplessness. This brings us back to anger's protective qualities over the pain beneath it.

Anger as a Secondary Emotional Expression

What we often see show up in place of these unwanted feelings is anger. Anger protects us from the debilitating pain and despondency of these hauntingly personalized, we-don't-want-them feelings. Anger mobilizes us and, for a bit, circumvents the intolerable, deeper hurts lurking below. Anger leaps up and leads the way as it attempts to resolve that which is too vulnerable and too difficult to deal with directly.

If, however, we're on the path to developing mindful awareness and we're practicing and committed, we may build up enough coherence to stay present to these feelings—to feel them, parent them, and respond to them—healthfully, effectively, thoughtfully, and compassionately. As a result, anger may no longer be the automatic, secondary emotion that covers up and attempts to ward off the deeper emotional pain we've not been able to absolve and integrate yet.

Shame that is covered with anger needs to be dealt with. Why is that? When left festering, it is undeniably corrosive to not only ourselves but also to our relationships. If not addressed and processed, anger will keep reoccurring, and the shame—the deeper hurt—will never surface consciously. Meanwhile, nothing will get resolved.

And guess who usually takes the brunt of this unresolved anger of covered-over shame? Our beloved partners, our children, our aging parents, our employees, our closest friends, or on a bad day, the unwitting customer service representative who isn't getting a problem solved for us.

Guilt is another emotion that may show up as anger. Anger fires up in self-defense, preventing us from the recriminating pain and angst associated with "I could have/should have" guilt.

Healthy guilt and healthy shame are both self-regulating feelings that help guide our participation with others and with society as a whole. Guilt is an internalized judgment, directed at the self and targeting a behavior that, if taken to extremes, could also potentially lead to exclusion or banishment (thrown from the tribe and our life threatened).

Shame and guilt are both destabilizing emotional experiences. Left unresolved, they can fester as irreconcilable sadness and lead to high levels of distress because these feelings are part of the system that warns us that vital connections needed to sustain our lives are being threatened. Shame and guilt are cognitive-emotional reactions geared at protecting our associations, our belonging, and our critical acceptability with others. Learning to work with these internalized emotional systems honestly and compassionately is an important part of our personal development.

Counter-Shame

While we're at it, let's cover counter-shame too. Like anger, counter-shame covers shame—our resistance to it and our fear of it. In this case, though, shame is diverted by focusing our attention outward and away from the self onto others or circumstances. Counter-shame is a mechanism built on well-constructed *denial.* Counter-shame sets out to present to the world an unashamed self by not consciously, yet cleverly, deflecting the shame that is painfully repressed within.

Some examples of this include showing off, running others down (either overtly or camouflaged as humor), acting on a sense of entitlement, or by acting audaciously, omnipotently, and invulnerably. All of these may be in direct contrast to the deeply subverted truth and the underlying shame driving the engines—and the countering behaviors—below.

Counter-shame is more complex as it's an attempt to feel good and look good when one feels really bad (though that is repressed). This is tricky to decipher, let alone address, because counter-shame presents itself as the opposite of what it really is.

Anger is, in many ways, simpler to deal with than counter-shame, as anger's presence is often a straight line to the issue at hand. Counter-shame can create a lot of indirect, unresolved conflict, harming ourselves and our relationships in the long run as what's being acted out gets farther and farther from our authentic experience (our deep hurt) and truth. It's best to confront counter-shame for what it is—well-hidden toxic shame.

Counter-shame strategies need to be dismantled in order that the self-loathing, self-disconnecting toxic shame can be honestly and caringly addressed. As difficult as it is, allowing shame to be felt and experienced along with the fear often associated with its exposure, allows it to be owned and processed, and then compassionately dissipated. This is better than having it covered up, acted out, and left to erode our self-system and destroy our intimate relationships, which it inadvertently just might do.

Anger and the Nine Enneagram Types

The Enneagram system, through the understanding of its various energetic triads, details for us how each type most typically expresses anger. Of course, depending on the circumstances, we're all capable of all forms of anger. But there are some identifiable type-specific patterns that can help us better recognize anger's various expressions by type.

Additionally, understanding *how* and *what* triggers our anger, by Enneagram type, is another incredibly valuable way to more readily see into ourselves and into those in our lives.

Importantly, let's first start to observe our own anger. Practicing mindful awareness, let's ask ourselves: "How often am I reacting angrily to perceived or real violations?" Or "Is my anger ever being activated to cover shame or guilt? Or "Is my anger often directed inward—toward myself or my own behavior?" Or "Is my anger being directed at the behaviors or qualities of others?"

These questions hope to invite some important personal reflection.

What Triggers Anger–and the Potential for Conflict–for Each Type?

Here are some examples of what may trigger each of the nine Enneagram types to get angry. These examples are all external triggers, those found in the environmental experience of others or the world:

Type 1 | Unfairness. Irresponsibility. Disorganization, disorder, messiness or mayhem. Things being done the wrong way. The flagrant ignoring or disobeying of sound rules. Being unjustly criticized. Being lied to, manipulated, tricked, or unjustly blamed.

Type 2 | Feeling unappreciated or uncared for. Not being thanked for all that is given. Feeling uncaringly controlled. Having unmet personal needs and wants when having given others so much. Being rejected. Treated as dispensable and unnecessary. Being blocked from giving.

Type 3 | Obstacles that get in the way of the goal. Anything or anyone that threatens or thwarts progress and our ability to get to completion. Indecisiveness. Inefficiency. Criticism. Not being recognized or applauded when recognition is due. An insult to the image that's been constructed and wanting to be projected to others. Failing.

Type 4 | People that disappoint us. People that let us down. People that leave us and leave us feeling abandoned. Feeling unheard, unseen, and unimportant. Feeling slighted, invisible, rejected, and unwanted. Feeling misunderstood and not enough. Phoniness. Insincerity. Meaninglessness. Ugliness.

Type 5 | Being considered factually incorrect or not smart. People not interested in the information that we have to share. Demands placed on us from others, especially emotional ones and those that infringe on our private time. An overloading of emotional input. Too much stimulation. Intrusions that might tire us. Needing time alone and that being disrupted. Not being able to restore our energy.

Type 6 | All failures of trust and untrustworthiness. Betrayal. Being cornered. Being controlled or feeling overpowered. Interactions with others that feel too unreliable or that feel unsafe. Discrepancies in other's speech or behavior and inconsistencies. Being accused of something unfairly or wrongfully. Others' lack of responsiveness. Giving others warnings and advice that they do not take seriously. Lack of respect or a lack of integrity as seen in others.

Type 7 | Constraints or limits that prevent us from getting or from doing what we want. People that get stuck, are unhappy, depressed, or others-blaming. Debbie Downer attitudes and those who lay guilt trips on us. Feeling trapped. Feeling restricted. Feeling beholden to others when we want to take off and be free. Getting bored. Things that are too tedious or a total hassle. Being told what to do. Being told, "You can't . . ."

Type 8 | Deceit. Manipulation. People who won't stand up for themselves. Indirectness or beating around the bush. Liars. People that we perceive as fake. People that don't have our backs. Weakness. Boundaries or rules that are too constraining. People abusing their power and that need to be put in their place. Injustice and unfairness.

Type 9 | Being treated as invisible or not important. Feeling controlled or pushed by others to do something. Being forced to face conflict, state an opinion we don't want to state, or feeling pushed to make decisions. Saying yes to something we really don't want to say yes to. Disharmony. Angry, mean, or pushy people. Confrontation and disruption.

The table below summarizes how anger tends to be expressed for each type.

Table 1: How Anger Tends to Be Expressed by Type

Type	Anger Manifestations by Type
1	Perfectionist	Resentment. Self-justification. Tension and tightness. Outbursts of indignation followed by the onset of remorse and guilt.
2	Giver	Intense, often sudden, emotional outbursts. Being accusatory. Crying. Anger that manifests as withdrawal and withholding.
3	Performer	Impatience. Irritability. The pressuring of others. Being demanding. Occasional outbursts of hostility.
4	Artist	Fiery outbursts of dissolving into tears. Lamenting or complaining. Moodiness, passive-aggressiveness, even depression.
5	Observer	Self-containment, withdrawing, and withholding. Tension, arrogance, and disapproval. Short bursts of temper followed by isolation.
6	Loyal Skeptic	Wit. Sarcasm. Biting remarks. Getting accusatory and blaming. Defensive lashing out, projections, subverted defiance.
7	Epicure	Becoming curt and dismissive. Being brief and to the point. Short-lived but intense. Episodic. Impetuous. Being demanding of others. Bitching.
8	Protector	Powerful anger expressed in a direct, confrontational style or an armored withdrawal. Balancing the books and getting revenge.
9	Mediator	Passive aggression, including stubbornness and outright but subverted resistance. Complaining. Occasionally boiling over and exploding.

Using the 5As to Constructively Honor Our Anger and that of Others

Anger has certainly gotten its fair share of negative press across various cultures, across gender norms, and in families too. I've worked with many who are afraid of their own anger, afraid of their partner's anger, or there are those who will not allow anger in their households at all, considering it too disruptive or destructive.

Children who grow up not allowed to express their anger are either forced to suppress it or repress it. This does not allow them to cultivate an ability to process their anger in healthy ways, let alone learn to speak to it confidently and effectively, with themselves or others, when it's actually called for.

Anger is a vital energy source that mobilizes us to take action against some perceived violation, to defend and protect, and to fight for our dignity and sense of self-worth.

"I matter because I exist" is the great tenet of being that anger stands for and expects us—provokes us—to honor.

Honoring the Anger in Others with a 5As Approach

Whether we express, suppress, or deny our anger, we still find ourselves up against trying our best to deal with the anger of others. Honoring our anger is one thing; honoring that emotion in others can be another challenge altogether, especially if we've not dealt in healthy and constructive ways with our own.

When anger is expressed *at us*, it can rapidly change our physiology from a state of peace to a state of stress. If someone begins speaking angrily at us or starts yelling at us for some reason—whether justified or not—it can change our biochemistry within seconds. It can raise our levels of cortisol and adrenaline and either put us on the defensive (reactively fighting back) or send us into withdrawal (consciously not responding). Some even feel a need to avoid and escape entirely! (Where are the 5As when you need them?)

Either way, when there's more than one person escalating, the chance for reasonable and thoughtful resolution diminishes while escalation peaks. Despite years of mindfulness practice, we can still find ourselves unraveling when facing someone else's anger, especially when we perceive it to be unjustified.

This becomes a test of sorts, as encountering another's anger is the kind of interaction that can grip our central nervous system and activate reactions within us before we even realize what has happened.

The million-dollar 5As question is: Can we hold ourselves through those surging shifts in our physiology—our soma—and stay present? And here's the next question on the self-awareness path: When we witness and receive the anger of another, can we stay present to what's happening *within us* as well as stay present to the other? Can we simultaneously feel into the other's experience of their upset as well as our own? That's a tall order, but it's doable.

Here's where understanding our mirror neurons comes in handy. While mirroring someone else's state of being—whatever that state may be—we can also begin to mirror another's *emotional* state, taking on the other party's anger, for example. That tends to happen without us often even noticing. But if we consciously stay present to it all, and if we add *compassion* and *empathy* to what we're witnessing and receiving, it opens the door for us to get curious rather than reactive. And when we're curious as to what's happening to the other person and offer up compassion and empathy, we can keep ourselves from mirroring their anger.

This takes a conscious sprint through the first four of the 5As, holding ourselves all the way from that so critical, awareness-harnessing pause to thoughtful conscious conduct. Herein lies the chance to honor (**accept** and **appreciate**) someone's anger without rallying or interjecting our own.

Caring deeply for the state of another as can be mirrored and felt by us is a whole new way to be in the presence of someone else's anger. And getting curious is a whole new way to divert our reactive defendedness. The possibility for a new kind of interaction, one that may lead to a more positive resolution, is now upon us.

Curiosity and "Tell Me More..."

"Tell me more..." is a communications tool I've used for years when working with couples. It's a great way to respond to any situation with genuine curiosity. It also sets us up for understanding, which can lead to empathy. "Tell me more..." has to be one of the most compassionate and caring approaches we can take when in the face of someone's upset, particularly that of a partner or a child.

Instead of fighting back and going on the defensive (does this sound familiar?), this question invites more sharing, more explanation. It's an immediate way to take an interest in the not-so-pleasant grievances that have arisen in another. "Tell me more..." is the spoken invitation we can choose to extend when faced with another's upheaval.

It's also a good question to lean into to enable a pause—one that can support our 5As journey toward undefendedness. In a split second, we can go from *reacting* to *reflecting*, from *resisting* to *listening* actively and curiously.

"Tell me more..." creates a pause that becomes an invitation to learn something—and whether we agree with it or not, we can benefit from learning more about the other person and often about ourselves too. Whatever is said in response is most likely something that needs to be heard, wants to be heard, and deserves to be dealt with, especially when in partnership. This is our chance to learn more about the other person and why they are upset.

"Tell me more . . ." demonstrates care because it invites the other to verbalize their anger, and we receive their words without interruption. This does not necessarily mean we capitulate, condone, or are in agreement with what's said. We may, in fact, have another point of view to share that is just as important.

But *receiving* the response to the invitation to tell us more means we allow another's grievance to be heard and felt, listened to and considered. It's about paying attention to their perspective, their point of view. And as we hear the needs and upset of another—whatever those may be—we have a chance to learn something.

Pausing to ask, "Tell me more . . ." is not easy. It takes self-mastery to bring this to the table. It takes discipline along with self-love (great care for ourselves) as well as empathy for another. And it takes heartfelt curiosity.

I have witnessed how remembering to ask the other to tell us more when a critical exchange is underway can have quite an astounding impact on all involved. It's one of the most effective ways of diffusing anger respectfully, and it can get us to the truth of a need that needs to be met or something else that needs attention. But it takes having a mindful awareness practice in place and an ongoing commitment to taking conscious **action** and to ongoing **adherence**.

Honoring each other's upset in a stabilizing 5As way can build intimacy, clarity, and vulnerability. It's an effective communications tool that turns curiosity into sharing and the chance for understanding. This is what moves us consciously toward connection rather than defensively toward separation.

> Forgive others. Not because another deserves forgiveness, but because we deserve peace.
>
> ~ Jonathan Lockwood Huie

A Tidbit on Forgiveness

Thriving relationships—especially those that are longer term, like a 62-year-long marriage—have most likely had to work through some form of forgiveness. Simply defined, **forgiveness is the pardoning of offenses accompanied by a letting go of ongoing resentments**. Forgiveness has all sorts of benefits, but it can be hard.

Since an "unforgiven something" usually involves offenses that violate our beliefs, values, or personal identifications, it makes forgiving difficult—*really* difficult. The unforgiven something almost always violates something we believe to be fundamental to our personhood or overall well-being. At times, though, when peering into the issue from the outside, it might not seem exceptionally important, violating, or obviously offensive.

In the ways we may struggle with acceptance, we may also struggle with forgiveness. For many of us, forgiveness translates as condoning, capitulating, concurring, and even the giving of permission, like we're welcoming it to happen again. (Yikes!)

But forgiveness does not at all mean that we're condoning, capitulating, or concurring. (Let's get that off our chests and out of our psyches right now and from here on out!) Believing that greatly complicates and inhibits forgiveness.

One of the tremendous insights gained by studying the Enneagram is that it allows us to correlate with clarity what is fundamental to our type structure with what we're trying to protect of our self-esteem and personal boundaries.

I remember a Type 4 woman who just wouldn't forgive her father. He had passed away 18 years earlier, but she was still full of resentment toward him. Why was she still holding so much unforgiven resentment toward her father? She shared that she felt fundamentally violated by his dominating behavior and his seeming refusal to understand her. She felt that he never made her feel special nor took the time to attend to her emotionally. He was tough on her and never let up. Years later, this remained her perception of her father.

Given her type structure and the fact that a child's experience of its parents is often blamed on themselves rather than on the parent, I found that she had internalized his behavior, translating it to mean that she was deficient in some way. And *this* was what hurt her the most. Her being deficient is what rendered her unlovable in his eyes, or so she fundamentally believed, as a Type 4.

Through studying the Enneagram, she came to understand that her father's behavior was true to his type. He was acting out his own Enneagram structure—a somewhat unevolved, lower level of developmental well-being Type 8.

Soon, she began to shift some of her perceptions of her father. It wasn't that he refused to love her or refused to love her the way she had so wanted and needed as a Type 4. It was an issue of his lack of developmental capacity and his inability and propensity to express his love for her in other ways—ways that she may not have received or perceived at all as love.

This more educated perspective of his being a Type 8 freed her considerably. She came to forgive her father for being unable to love her in ways she needed. And she forgave herself for feeling she was unlovable in response to her father's personality style and limitations.

She also became aware of how her father was trying to express his love to her in other ways, albeit coming at her in his very much Type 8 way—as in his domineering restrictive style, or at times demanding that she "man up." After a lifetime of not appreciating her father, she began appreciating aspects of him— reinterpreting his over-protectiveness as his way of caring.

> Forgive one another as we know not what we do, *until we come to know.* In the knowing comes understanding, compassion, and healing.
>
> ~ Aurelie Suzanne Dion

Forgiveness, Anger, and the Critical-judging Mind

It's important to realize how ruthless the critical-judging mind can be when we begin a forgiveness process, and how it may have closed our hearts. Closing our hearts is actually the worst and most tragic outcome of anything we may have endured. It closes us off from the fullness (the fullest potential) of ourselves and the experience of our lives.

For this reason, we urge everyone to consider the cost of not forgiving alongside the benefits. Forgiveness, when all is said and done, is an inside job. It's our own process and one that is necessary to free up our own divine life force, freeing us from the confines of vengeance, contempt, feelings of having been overpowered or harmed, and all the feelings that go into *not* feeling loved, respected, or honored.

Extending and receiving forgiveness is an energetic choice that frees our entire being from carrying the toxic emotional waste produced by enduring and not resolving an unforgiven something.

For example, chronically held anger in the form of resentment or vengeance associated with unforgiveness is deleterious to our physical health and our mental and spiritual well-being. Thoughts of vengeance can take up valuable real estate in our minds, are immensely preoccupying, and take us away from the life we would rather be designing and creating—not to mention the pain of not being able to forgive ourselves for how we got ourselves in a given situation (our part in it). Resentment can drain us and usurp our ability to honestly self-reflect, missing out on valuable insights that could help us take the better action in the future.

In deciding to move toward forgiveness, we proactively free ourselves from emotional toxins that may accumulate and become spiritually harmful. And in so doing, we reopen our own hearts. We do this *for ourselves* and for the benefit of our own lives.

Within just this process, we begin to heal ourselves because we're letting go of the simmering suffering that was occurring in our being. In turn, this frees up our formerly trapped vital energies, allowing us to regenerate our cognitive, emotional, somatic, and spiritual health. We become more available to the joy of creating our own positive future and to the love within us that forgiveness creates space for.

Importantly, it is a process. We forgive not by brushing over what has happened or by ignoring its impact but by seeing clearly who was responsible for what, what our role was in any aspect of what had happened, and then, by grieving what needs to be grieved.

We acknowledge the situation from a 360-degree perspective. We then grieve fully, and we do so with compassion, honesty, and awareness—sober as to what has taken place, what has been lost, and what is needed to repair or redeem, if possible.

Forgiveness Bypass

I've witnessed something I'll call "forgiveness bypass," where we forgive hastily and without the due diligence needed to really bring forth authentic forgiveness. It is a way of circumventing a lot of the unprocessed pain we just don't want to deal with (consciously or unconsciously), like our rage, our deeper hurt, or our repressed self-blame and shame.

We can also get a lot of kudos for claiming we've forgiven someone. We can look rather altruistic, so loving, by jumping swiftly to forgiveness. But perhaps that is premature. Maybe it's our way of sidestepping the actual hurt or anger felt altogether, keeping us from facing appropriate right action or pursuing proper remediation.

Forgiveness bypass occurs on the surface of ourselves and avoids grieving the pain and loss we have endured. It's often slapped in place without fully engaging the truth of what happened to us, sometimes without taking right action and nicely avoiding unwanted conflict, or without doing the work needed to authentically reopen our own hurting hearts in the aftermath.

Unburdening (reopening) our own hearts is what we deserve for our own lives and future relationships. Bypassing to get to the much-wanted forgiveness endpoint will not get us there; it can actually leave us seething or suffering endlessly and in silence.

Tips for Working with the Critical-Judging Mind, Anger, and Forgiveness

First, work with the UGP—the Universal Growth Process for Self-Mastery—that we've been discussing. Personally, it has changed my way of dealing with myself and others. It has helped me tremendously in working with my life and relationship issues, with integrating the higher essential qualities of faith and courage into my life and relationships (the attributes of transformation for a Type 6), and with freeing myself as often as possible from running on automatic.

I believe that transformative results are attainable for all of us. Practicing the UGP's process of 5As helps us deal far more constructively with anger, shame, our negative superegos, and even our struggles with forgiveness.

In return, the UGP assists with softening the powerful grip of many of these difficult-to-process emotional states and lessens the ways in which they habitually want to act themselves out.

Recognize that the critical-judging mind (our negative superego) is almost always involved when we have personal reactivity, discernable via sensations such as tension, constriction, explosion, or anxiety. Reactivity plays itself out somatically. It is *felt* physically and may be *expressed* verbally or behaviorally. Practice reflecting on this. With awareness, practice sensing reactivity in the body and observe the intensity and flow along with the escalation or suppression of it.

Know that the body, the felt-sense experience of it, is a resource. Reactivity is trackable. It's visceral and its sensations are, in fact, locatable. Know that without a conscious awareness of its sensations (reactivity) rising in the body, we will mostly act out the reactivity again and again, as our reactivity is our way of fending off what's happening in our bodies, that which is too uncomfortable, too unmanageable, and hard to tolerate.

Recognize there's usually something fundamental underneath our personal reactivity—under our reaction to a perceived wrongdoing or an unforgiven something. This means our upset almost always points to some deeper threat to our well-being, to our type's adaptive strategies, and to what we are identified with.

This then takes us to working with the underlying themes and issues associated with our center of intelligence, our Enneagram type, and our dominant instinctual drive. This is what can help us locate the internal source of these deeper triggers and perceived violations.

We actually need to starve out the negative voice of the superego, which means to not feed it by obeying it, trying to slay it, or by defying it. Instead, we can quiet our critical-judging mind by delaying action—by pausing and breathing, inhaling deep into our bellies—in order to do our curiosity-filled inquiry, foster discernment, and facilitate conscious conduct.

This is the process, once again, that effectuates the dismantling of reactivity's emotional grip, which in turn, alleviates the on-automatic defenses that habitually follow.

Developing ourselves beyond the critical-judging mind calls us to open our hearts (a conscious act) and be kind to ourselves as best we can in the turbulence of reactivity. An open heart is what allows our awareness to be followed by acceptance, which is crucial. An open heart is the key to forgiveness too, as the anger and resentment associated with the unforgiven something can own us— mind, body, and soul—causing our hearts to harden with defenses and bitterness.

As we release ourselves from the liability of our more negative core beliefs and misunderstandings and as we open our hearts to love and its powerful way of understanding things, even the unforgiven something abates and finds its way to being perceived differently, learnedly.

When in the throes of difficulty, give ourselves permission to remember the positives in our lives, especially those times of genuine kindness and joy, and to give thanks for the things for which we are grateful. At times of anger and distress, recall what we are appreciative of. Then, as we respond, pay attention to how that appreciation makes us feel, giving ample time to sense it in our bodies.

Shifting to another feeling state, a positive one, can open our hearts, both to ourselves and to others. Take note of the fact that lovingkindness is at the core of our well-being. Fostering it is one of the smartest and most powerful things we can do for ourselves, especially in moments of challenge and difficulty, and to enhance and sustain our connections to others.

> ❝
>
> Hatred can never cease by hatred. Hatred can only cease by love.
>
> ~ The Buddha, on opening the heart to love in relationship
>
> ❞

The Ultimate Trap and the Ultimate Avoidance of Each Enneagram Type Structure

Each Enneagram type structure's core belief about what is necessary to be fulfilled and loved also becomes the ultimate trap in their life. The core belief, which imbues us with particular sensitivities and aptitudes can, if overused or turned against us, go from mildly interfering to downright compulsive and relationships destroying. This may be the case for most of us until we take the time to study these mechanisms and understand both their positive and negative impacts.

The traps and avoidances of our Enneagram type structure do, in fact, become the bane of our most intimate and important relationships, particularly for our partners and our children. They can suffer a lot in response to our core beliefs running amuck without our knowing it. This especially happens when we have not done our own deeper work to self-understand, self-nourish, and self-develop.

Each type's core fear (deepest concern) about what would be its undoing becomes its ultimate avoidance. Our deepest concerns and ultimate avoidance pinpoint the source of what triggers most of our reactivity—that is, the reactions that take us into conflict with ourselves and with others.

The Ultimate Trap: Also known in Jungian terms as "The Idealized Self," I coined this phrase to refer to the core beliefs we hold about ourselves and who we believe we must be. These beliefs are deeply ingrained.

The Ultimate Avoidance: Also known in Jungian terms as "The Shadow Self," I coined this phrase to refer to our deepest concerns for ourselves, what we fear the very most and who we believe we cannot be.

The core belief (trap) and deepest concern (avoidance) conspire together as opposite sides of the same coin (the same core theme). Our core beliefs serve to keep our type's adaptive strategy in place, as does the avoidance of the core concern or fear. They collude, working in tandem to guide us, if you will, inadvertently showing us the inherent and intrinsic sources of our type-based, type-triggering reactivity.

This is the stuff that brings unrest, upset, miscommunication, and discord into relationships. And our relationships are the foundational glue of our lives.

With curiosity and honesty, take time to inquire and explore the true nature of your Enneagram type's reactivity based on your core beliefs (trap) and deepest concerns (avoidance).

For clarification, I'd like to add: We tend to believe that these core beliefs are predominately lodged in *implicit memory*, are held deep in our soma, and were formed in large part before cognition was developed. As we started out in life and certain aspects of our needs were not met (like that first pang of gnawing hunger and no one coming to feed us), these core beliefs formed a story, their own particular type-correlated story, their perception, as to why we were not being satisfied.

Our Essential Strengths Drive Our Solutions

Something within us formed these perceptions. And to cope, something within us formed solutions. That goes to deduce that our core beliefs, driven by our neural wiring, are what formulate our particular solutions.

Our neural propensities with their inherent strengths, particular focus of attention, and contributory aptitudes are called upon to come up with a solution for our flourishing or eroding sense of self, for the pursuit of a satisfactory existence, and for our survival in the tribe and in the greater world.

From the slight of an unmet need all the way to the impact of severe trauma, our neural propensities organized as an Enneagram type formed an adaptive solution to protect our essence.

How we either contract and defend or expand and potentiate is not random. Rather, our solutions are intelligently patterned and organized coping mechanisms. And from a perhaps unique progressive Enneagram perspective, they are not solely determined and orchestrated by our environment or the people in it; they're something more deterministically constructed from within.

The Enneagram's core beliefs are fundamental adaptations formulated in great part by our neural wiring and how we were and are predisposed to forming a particular perception of ourselves in the world.

And when all of this is going down, the virtue of our type—our essential qualities of being, our definitive preciousness—protectively goes into the background. To a greater or lesser degree, we seemingly lose contact with the truth of the higher aspects of ourselves while struggling to make sense of the world and what's happening to us within it.

In Chapter 4, we outlined the Basic Propositions for each type. Below, we've listed the originating core belief (trap) for each Enneagram type and its deepest concern (avoidance), with each of the virtues (essential qualities) that go into the background as a result of unmet needs, our childhood's best shot at development, and the structural dilemma of forming each of these particular personality structures.

Table 2: The Basic Propositions' Core Beliefs and Deepest Concerns, and the Essential Qualities Lost by Type

Type	Core Belief (Trap)	Deepest Concern (Avoidance)	Essential Quality Lost
1	I must be good and right.	I must not be intrinsically bad or wrong.	In the process, the serenity that comes with the acceptance and appreciation of myself and others–of our differences and unique contributions–goes into the background.
2	I must be giving and useful.	I must not be intrinsically needy, selfish, or useless	In the process, the reciprocal flow of giving and receiving that imbues humility goes into the background.
3	I must be doing and succeeding.	I must not be intrinsically unable to do or succeed.	In the process, the veracity of my own true feelings goes into the background.
4	I must be special and complete.	I must not be inherently deficient or incomplete.	In the process, the equanimity that comes from acceptance and from appreciating all that actually is as is goes into the background.
5	I must be self-sufficient and autonomous.	I must not be subjected to being depleted or drained.	In the process, the non-attachment that remediates the avarice I feel in a world that takes too much goes into the background.

6	I must be certain and self-sustaining.	I must not be inherently helpless or dependent.	In the process, the courage to move forward associated with having faith in myself and others goes into the background.
7	I must keep life upbeat, stimulating, and optimistic.	I must not be inherently limited, a Debbie Downer, or suffering.	In the process, the steadiness of presence and a willingness to take in both joy and sadness, called sobriety or constancy, goes into the background.
8	I must be powerful and strong.	I must not be inherently powerless or weak.	In the process, the capability associated with coming freshly with innocence to each situation, without asserting my own agenda or power, goes into the background.
9	I must blend in and seek significance by yielding and conforming.	I must not be causing conflict or differentiation from others.	In the process, the right action of honoring self and showing up as equal to all others goes into the background.

Virtues or Essential Qualities as Experienced by Each Enneagram Type

The **serenity** of **Type 1** is when everything around them is seemingly perfect; there is nothing for them to do, to improve, or complete. They are free. They can finally feel their feelings, let go, and enjoy. They are serene.

The **humility** of **Type 2** is when they are no longer driven to seek ingratiation. They are giving because they love to be. They are free to allow others to give to them, allowing them to feel good about it too. They are not more giving than others and don't have to see themselves that way. They are free. They are humble.

The **veracity** of **Type 3** is when they have come to feel that they are more than just their performance. There is a real person inside with feelings and preferences and a need to slack off sometimes too. They can be more truthful about their needs, and they no longer fear people won't like them if their needs conflict with the image they've projected. They are free. They are honest.

The **equanimity** of **Type 4** is when they no longer place themselves above (superior) or below (inferior) other people, a situation, or their surroundings. They can be equal, accepting, and belonging. They are no longer attaching their identity to specialness, disappointment, defiance, or melancholy. They are free. They allow—even welcome—the bliss of equanimity.

The **non-attachment** of **Type 5** is when they can let go of clutching at what they absolutely believe they need to know and must figure out. As in, if they don't intellectually protect themselves, something exhausting or disrupting will happen to them that they may not easily recover from. They are free. They can go with the flow. They can live life fully and will be fine.

The **courage** of **Type 6** is when they allow themselves to stop the whirring, whizzing mind that takes them back and forth across what-if scenarios. Instead, they allow themselves to know that they will courageously handle it, that they *can* handle whatever they are dealt, and that nothing bad will happen to them if they stop over-worrying, over-doubting, or over-thinking. They are free. They are safe.

The **sobriety** of **Type 7** is when that impulse to get up and go, go, go ceases to grip their every waking moment, and they can be still. They can take things in. They can deal with things they need to deal with. They can focus and stay present as they relax the anxiousness that arises and pulls the trigger to amp up again or move on to something else—something more interesting or less frustrating. They are free. They are constant, and they can handle it.

The **truth** of **Type 8** is when they allow themselves to tap into not only their truth, but the truth of others who stand before them as well. There's an innocence to each of us, and they see that. Innocence is not weakness, it is core to our essence, and it is vital to our tenderness. They are free. They are all of the energies within them, both strong *and* vulnerable.

The **right action** of **Type 9** is when the impulse within them to speak up for themselves or take care of their own life, as is needed, is not repressed. Instead, it's alive within them and they act on it as is required and called for and at the moment when it's needed. They are free. They are here and they also matter. They take care of and honor themselves as they take care of and honor others.

Applying the 5As to Work with Reactivity and Type-Based Resistances to Love

Daily, we want to practice cultivating self-awareness. How about several times each day? How about every moment? (Yes!) How about this? Practice cultivating awareness as often as our reactivity comes up. Reactivity is always driven, in some way, by issues related to our type's core belief (the ultimate trap) and our deepest concern around what makes us lovable or not (the ultimate avoidance).

It is our unresolved type-based reactivity coupled with our level of developmental well-being that hinders and diminishes our ability to fully love, to receive love, and to *be love,* as is our truest nature. Managing our reactivity is the number one way we emotionally evolve and is probably also the number one way that we can heal a relationship.

Fortunately, there are universal principles for this process that apply to all nine Enneagram types.

Sound the Alarm Bell: The Great Pause

The moment we feel our reactivity coming on—our anger, distress, or fear—sound the alarm bell. It's time to pause. It's time to take a deep breath and dive into our subjective world where we get to connect with ourselves in the privacy and sanctity of our own minds, hearts, and somas.

Here's where we can feel and observe—honestly, kindly, and with curiosity—what is happening to us, what we may be doing to ourselves, how it's making us feel, and what we may be doing to others too.

As we witness, recognize, and become aware, we grow for a moment in our ability to contain the impulse to react. Using our breath, we can come to hold (contain) the viscerally felt physical charge or impulse—one that might be really strong at this point—and gently but firmly suspend the reactivity.

This suspension is not to deny our reactivity, force it to be something else, or suppress it either. Rather, it's to allow it, see it, and be with it. Being with it means without our being enslaved to responding to it immediately. This is the beginning of what we've been calling self-mastery.

Gentle Inquiry into What's Really Needed

Once we have successfully engaged a pause, we follow it with gentle inquiry. It might look like this: "What's really needed here from me?" "What are my most vulnerable feelings around this?" "What's the best way to accomplish what's called for?" "Can I do what I need to do without so much unwanted tension?" Or "Can I get to what's needed without having to disconnect from another, from love?"

Without good processes in place—like that of the 5As—reactivity covers our upset and throws us into automatic. Reactivity follows having become triggered (our emotional buttons got pushed), and it does not feel pleasant. If our tendency to run on automatic is left unattended, it runs willy-nilly across our central nervous system and catalyzes its familiar pattern. It hinders our ability to stay present to ourselves, and it's often loaded with conditions too—conditions that get us attached to particular outcomes.

On-automatic reactivity also hinders our ability to love others without those same conditions being met. It literally prevents us from staying present to others. Even if someone makes changes (shifts) right in front of us, chances are we won't see it. If we somehow *do* notice, we won't be able to shift alongside them, because unbridled reactivity lacks presence, and presence is necessary for shifting to occur.

Without a conscious awareness practice in place, interrupting reactivity patterns is tremendously difficult as its midway point is fueled with emotional momentum, momentum that is protective, quite possibly righteous, and energetically charged.

The Conditional Love of the Nine Enneagram Types

Each of the nine Enneagram type structures has conditions when it comes to love. These conditions are based on each type's respective core belief. The core beliefs, named the Basic Propositions (discussed in Chapter 4), are what we must fulfill and abide in order to love ourselves and to feel lovable.

What we'll come to see as we gain an understanding of each of the Enneagram types, is how we have conditioned ourselves into assuming, projecting, and expecting, "My rules for me are my rules for you! And my conditions for me are yours too." We do this even if we've never explicitly stated these rules and conditions to ourselves; we simply formulate this from our Enneagram type.

Without doing the work of cultivating mindful self-awareness and self-acceptance, when conditions aren't met, we may inadvertently pass our refusal to love ourselves (and the discomfort of it) onto others. Or we'll *not* love others either when they do not meet our standards or the conditional beliefs that we are beholden to within ourselves. Finally, allowing ourselves to be loved—to receive love when our conditions for ourselves aren't met—is stifled as well. We simply won't feel worthy of love.

It's important to all nine types to come to realize that our respective core beliefs (Basic Propositions), when left unquestioned, will run their course across our lives. While working hard to keep us on track, doing what they feel *we should be doing* in the world in order to be loved and satisfied, they will interfere with and diminish our full expression of unconditional love and our capacity for vulnerability and intimacy with ourselves. They will also limit our ability and willingness to have intimate, unconditionally loving experiences with others.

With that said, we are not typically aware of this working in us in the background, let alone the potential sabotage of it.

For love to be expressed fully, it needs to be protected and held dear by all aspects of ourselves and by all parties involved. While we cannot control another, we can surely begin with ourselves. Each one of us can begin our own journey toward love by learning, first, how we cut ourselves off from love by not loving ourselves.

The Enneagram system is one of the best possible maps for providing the incisive information we need to help us look into just that. How is it that we only love ourselves when certain conditions are met? Sounds harsh, but this is what we unknowingly do.

To put it another way, each Enneagram type's core beliefs write the rules for how we need to be. Only then do we feel safe, acceptable, and lovable. *This* is the set-up.

And there you have it: the trap. But the trap doesn't stop there. Just as we unknowingly and unconsciously do this to ourselves, we do the same thing to others.

Love is not an accident. It is not random. Love is a practiced state of mind and an intentional opening of the heart. It is expressed in many loving actions that flow from our state of mind and the condition of our heart. It is the basis of all higher states of well-being. Love at its purest is imbued with free will. Most truthfully, it is expressed in states of free will. Love is generated from within us, willfully and conscientiously, without conditions or expectations. It is what we are at the very core of our being. Love is inducible and accessible with awareness, intent, and grace.

Hearing for decades that *we cannot love another before we first love ourselves* always made me think, "Well, yeah, that makes sense. I get it." But, in truth, it's only *now* that I really get it, thanks to the fundamental mechanisms laid forth in this chapter. Because that statement also points us to the critical truth that *how* we love ourselves (or not), is also how we will love others (or not).

Looking at the ways we only conditionally love ourselves provides us with a guid to how we will in turn only conditionally love others. To know love, we must be love. Quite contrary to the notion that love is something we find "out there," in some acquisition or in another person who will bring it to us.

To express love, we must engage with it fully and freely. We must confront the conditions that prevent us from loving, that prevent us from showing up lovingly. We must understand how we create love for ourselves (or not), and how the *not* translates to our inability or refusal to love others due to conditions not having been met.

Type 1 | The Perfectionist | Conditional Love

Sit comfortably upright in a quiet place, allowing your body to soften and yourself to breathe in and down into your belly. Do so several times. Read this core reflection, then close your eyes and go inward to compassionately experience this aspect of Type 1.

As Type 1s, when we find ourselves getting upset or reactive with someone we're in a relationship with, chances are we've just launched ourselves into some kind of judgmentalness. Judgmentalness tends to be unrelenting and unforgiving, absolute, and rife with conviction. It most likely concerns what is wrong that needs mentioning and correcting, or it might have to do with unfairness, a lack of accountability, or irresponsibility.

Our reaction is further fueled by a subtle to not-so-subtle tension, an erectness and tightness felt in the face and in the body. At its core, this tension is suppressed anger (an emotion) and resentment (a feeling).

This is how we diminish our expression and experience of love as Type 1s. Tension and resentment—a result of passing an automatic, inflexible judgment—separate us from others. It inadvertently places us in a seemingly superior role, and another in an inferior one. Where in most cases, our feelings and those of the other are not much on our radar as we take on a constricted, rigid stance and feel justified doing so.

As Type 1s, we need to accept and then integrate our personal desires and pleasures into our lives alongside our conscientiousness, dutifulness, high standards, and responsibilities. This not only enhances our lives but also the lives of all who love us and interact with us. Becoming more tolerant is a virtue worth developing as it can ease much destructive and unnecessary tension.

We will also want to learn to discern if what we judge to be errors or wrongdoings are actually simply differences that come from our fundamentally different aptitudes and talents—not necessarily violations that need addressing. Without being judgmental but instead being appreciative, respectful, and grateful, we can allow ourselves to recognize others' preferences and choices.

As we feel our Type 1 reactivity take hold, sound the alarm bell. It's time to pause. Ignite the pause that lovingly and respectfully acknowledges our reactive, triggered energy by breathing deeply down into our bellies, realizing that this reactivity and how we handle it this time can either hinder or enhance our ability to love. Using the breath, hold (contain) the viscerally felt, physical charge–that impulse that might be really strong at this point–then gently but firmly suspend the reactivity. In this tender place, we are ready for gentle inquiry, reflection, and the formulation of a conscious action, as is needed.

As Type 1s, we believe we must be right and good, above recrimination, and a model of integrity. We must be responsible. These are at the core of what Type 1s believe they must be to be worthy, secure in the world, and lovable. Our Type 1 structure tells us that we must avoid being wrong for whatever reason to avoid feeling inferior all the way to wretched, insecure, and full of fault, any of which renders us unacceptable and unlovable.

Without doing the work of self-awareness and development, we will inadvertently pass onto others our refusal to love ourselves whenever our Type 1 conditions for ourselves aren't met. We will conditionally turn on others in the same way that we conditionally turn on ourselves.

We will tend not to love others when they do not meet our standards or when we feel they do not honor the beliefs we are beholden to within ourselves. For example, as we do not tend to take liberties for ourselves—let alone take a break—all in the name of "having responsibilities," we will struggle to love and accept our partner when they take liberties. (Who could we be if we allowed the unallowable for ourselves?)

It's important for Type 1s—as it is for all nine types—to come to realize that our core belief when left unquestioned will automatically run us. While working hard to keep us on track, dutiful, responsible, and committed to doing good in the world, these conditions for ourselves can interfere with and diminish our full expression of unconditional love and our capacity for vulnerability and intimacy with ourselves. They can also limit our agility, even our willingness, to have intimate, unconditionally loving experiences with others.

Type 2 | The Giver | Conditional Love

Sit comfortably upright in a quiet place, allowing your body to soften and yourself to breathe in and down into your belly. Do so several times. Read this core reflection, then close your eyes and go inward to compassionately experience this aspect of Type 2.

As Type 2s, when we find ourselves getting upset or reactive with someone we're in a relationship with, chances are we've just launched ourselves into some kind of frustration that's impeding our desire to help. Or we're feeling unappreciated. Or we're engulfed in that good feeling we get when "we know best" what's needed, except something is in our way. Or we are not feeling appreciated for all that we give and do.

Our reactivity is also fueled by pride ("I am a caring person") and our need to feel indispensable. These feelings diminish our expression of love because they set us up as superior in a way and that can feel ingratiating, invasive, and disingenuous to others.

Additionally, our giving-to-get approach can often be sensed by others, even though we may not realize that they are onto this nor are we consciously aware that's what we're doing either. Our reaction is further fueled by tightness and anxiety in our chests—a contracting heart that is, at its core, the expression of distress (an emotion) and unappreciatedness (a feeling). This is how, as Type 2s, we diminish our expression and experience of love.

Distress and a kind of heartfelt anxiety, the result of coming up against a recurring and inflexible frustration and hurt, separate us from others. Pridefulness inadvertently places us as a superior of sorts, and another as an inferior.

We feel justified reacting when finally calling on the other person to meet our needs and wants as we've met theirs. When at this point, the feelings of the other are not on our screens. Instead, *our* hurt and *our* needs are. We feel justified feeling this way and expressing it, after all, it's their fault, the result of their failings. We've done so much already.

> As we feel our Type 2 reactivity take hold, sound the alarm bell. It's time to pause. Ignite the pause that lovingly and respectfully acknowledges our reactive, triggered energy by breathing deeply down into our bellies, realizing that this reactivity and how we handle it this time can either hinder or enhance our ability to love. Using the breath, hold (contain) the viscerally felt, physical charge–that impulse that might be really strong at this point– then gently but firmly suspend the reactivity. In this tender place, we are ready for gentle inquiry, reflection, and the formulation of a conscious action, as is needed.

As Type 2s, we believe that we must fulfill the needs of others in order to be loved and to have love come to us, to show up for us. We avoid feeling useless, unappreciated, and dispensable. These sentiments are at the core of what Type 2s believe they *must counter* to be worthy, secure in the world, and lovable.

Our Type 2 structure tells us that we must avoid being selfish and uncaring and that in order to be loved, we have to step up and give love, and care, and whatever else we can to ingratiate ourselves to others and become indispensable. If we don't comply, love will not come our way. If we are not giving, we'll be seen as selfish, uncaring, even mean; feeling useless and helpless to others is not an option for us, as it would render us unacceptable and unlovable. These are our conditions for self-love and for feeling worthy of the love of others.

Without doing the work of self-awareness and development, we will inadvertently pass onto others our refusal to love ourselves whenever our Type 2 conditions for ourselves are not met. We will conditionally turn on others in the same way that we conditionally turn on ourselves.

We will tend not to love others when they do not meet our standards or adhere to the beliefs that we are beholden to within ourselves. For example, as we will not tend to say no to others, regardless of what is asked of us, we will struggle to love and accept our partner when they say no to us after all we have done and given. (Who could we be if we allowed a no for ourselves?)

Keep in mind that as Type 2s, we can gently coach ourselves into letting go of what we covertly expect from others. This will come from knowing that in relationships, thanks to the law of divine reciprocity, both giving *and* receiving are active forces and equal in value.

As we unhook the expectations we place on others to meet *our* needs, in turn we empower ourselves willfully to meet our own needs and care for ourselves without feeling that as we do so, we are uncaring of others, unavailable, or worse yet, selfish.

It's important for Type 2s—as it is for all nine types—to realize that these core beliefs, when left unquestioned, will automatically run us. While working hard to keep us on track as someone so caring and giving and unselfish, these conditions for ourselves can interfere with and diminish our full expression of unconditional love, our capacity for vulnerability and the intimacy we can cultivate with ourselves. These conditions can limit our humility, even our willingness, to have intimate, unconditionally loving experiences with others.

Type 3 | The Performer | Conditional Love

> Sit comfortably upright in a quiet place, allowing your body to soften and yourself to breathe in and down into your belly. Do so several times. Read this core reflection, then close your eyes and go inward to compassionately experience this aspect of Type 3.

As Type 3s, when we find ourselves getting upset or reactive with someone we're in a relationship with, chances are we've just launched ourselves into some kind of impatience, agitation, or frustration. There's something in the way of our accomplishing our tasks and goals. Or there could be some problem getting approval or admiration for what we're doing. Or the image we're wanting to project isn't working with someone, for some reason.

These upsets are fueled by our image-driven, go-ahead energy that suspends our heartfelt feelings. This triggers reactivity that diminishes our expression of love. Love gets bottlenecked behind our broadly self-oriented, competitive, outcome- and results-orientation. Our reactivity is fueled by an angst and impatience that are felt in our chests—an anxious heart response, which is, at its core, the expression of distress (an emotion) and "unapproved-of-ness" (a feeling).

This is how we, as Type 3s, diminish our expression and experience of love. Distress and a kind of impatient anxiety, a result of coming up against an automatic, inflexible sense of urgency separate us from others.

Because of what we are trying to accomplish or because how we need to be seen by others feels of paramount importance, we push harder and faster and with more tenacity to either gain approval or get it done. In most cases, the feelings of another, let alone our own, are not much on our screens.

> As we feel our Type 3 reactivity take hold, sound the alarm bell. It's time to pause. Ignite the pause that lovingly and respectfully acknowledges our reactive, triggered energy by breathing deeply down into our bellies, realizing that this reactivity and how we handle it this time can either hinder or enhance our ability to love. Using the breath, hold (contain) the viscerally felt, physical charge–that impulse that might be really strong at this point–then gently but firmly suspend the reactivity. In this tender place, we are ready for gentle inquiry, reflection, and the formulation of a conscious action, as is needed.

As a Type 3, we believe that we must succeed, accomplish, and present an image that will be acceptable, approved of, and admirable. We cannot fail and must avoid at all costs the inability to perform. We must perform well. These sentiments are at the core of what a Type 3 believes it must be and do to be worthy, secure in the world, acceptable, and lovable.

Our Type 3 structure tells us that we must avoid failure, laziness, or the inability to accomplish. We must present a particular image to others in order to be deemed worthy. Who we are deep down might even be different from the person we're projecting onto the world. And that's not a concern.

If we don't comply with our internal conditions for acceptability, love will not come our way—*nothing* will come our way because we'll be seen as nothing. We'll have no worthwhile identity, no role, and no importance. This is not an option for us and would render us unlovable. These are our conditions for self-love, and for feeling worthy of the love of others.

Without doing the work of self-awareness and development, we will inadvertently pass onto others our refusal to love ourselves whenever our Type 3 conditions for ourselves aren't met. We will conditionally turn on others in the same way that we conditionally turn on ourselves.

We will tend to not love others when they do not meet or concur with our standards or hold up the beliefs that we are beholden to within ourselves. For example, as we tend to expect and demand much of ourselves in the name of achievement, we will struggle to love and accept our partner when they don't pursue their goals or leave things unfinished. (Who could we be if we allowed this for ourselves?)

Keep in mind that as Type 3s, we can gently coach ourselves into letting go of the way we need others to respond to us. This will come from knowing that in relationships, veracity—the habitual practice of being true to ourselves and others—is the deepest form of success. Veracity begins first within ourselves, and then veracity with others can ensue.

We will benefit from allowing ourselves to take in that our beingness (our presence) is, in fact, what others desire most in us, much more than our "doing-ness," much more than the image we hope to present to others, the image we've deemed is acceptable and worthwhile. May we even notice our pace and slow it down in order to let others in. Let our hearts be still so that it can *feel*. Open ourselves to the welcoming feeling of receptivity, which allows our own true (not contrived or suppressed) feelings to emerge, and those of others to be received.

It's important for Type 3s—as it is for all nine types—to realize that our core beliefs, when left unquestioned, will run away with us. While working hard to keep us on track as someone so successful, accomplished, and worth admiring, these conditions for ourselves can interfere with and diminish our full expression of unconditional love and our capacity for vulnerability and intimacy with ourselves. They can also limit our ability, even our willingness, to open ourselves enough to have intimate, unconditionally loving experiences with others.

Type 4 | The Romantic | Conditional Love

Sit comfortably upright in a quiet place, allowing your body to soften and yourself to breathe in and down into your belly. Do so several times. Read this core reflection, then close your eyes and go inward to compassionately experience this aspect of Type 4.

As Type 4s, when we find ourselves getting upset or reactive with someone we're in a relationship with, chances are we've just launched ourselves into some kind of disappointment. We may be feeling something is missing or not enough, is lacking or incomplete. We may be feeling unheard, unimportant, offensively disregarded, or overlooked.

This disappointment is fueled by our deep longing, even envy for what others seem to have that we don't, all of which diminishes our experience and expression of love. We tend to be seemingly insatiable, suffer emotional shifts and mood swings, and tend to express our too-familiar disappointment, either vocally, sometimes explosively, or passive-aggressively and in withdrawal.

As we feel our Type 4 reactivity take hold, sound the alarm bell. It's time to pause. Ignite the pause that lovingly and respectfully acknowledges our reactive, triggered energy by breathing deeply down into our bellies, realizing that this reactivity and how we handle it this time can either hinder or enhance our ability to love. Using the breath, hold (contain) the viscerally felt, physical charge—that impulse that might be really strong at this point—then gently but firmly suspend the reactivity. In this tender place, we are ready for gentle inquiry, reflection, and the formulation of a conscious action, as is needed.

As a Type 4, we believe we must obtain the ideal love or ideal situation, and we must be the most special person—unique and different—in order to be worthy of being loved, worthy of being heard, seen, felt, and worthy of being desired and wanted. We cannot bear the feeling that we are lacking in something, that we're just like everyone else—mediocre and average. Or that we are in any way deficient.

We strive for superiority or extraordinariness *in something*, to be above average and special, to create something that might make a difference, touch someone, or bring meaning. In some way, we hope to overcome the daunting fear that we just might not be enough. If we're not superior, we may spiral into inferiority, comparing ourselves to others (comparison trauma). And in such a painful way, we end up cascading to the bottom, while others who are *more* of something rise to the top. These are our conditions for self-love, and for feeling worthy of the love of others.

Without doing the work of self-awareness and development, we will inadvertently pass onto others our refusal to love ourselves whenever our Type 4 conditions for ourselves aren't met. We will conditionally turn on others in the same way that we conditionally turn on ourselves.

We will tend not to love others when they do not meet our standards or hold dear the beliefs and requirements that we are beholden to within ourselves. For example, as we will tend to expect idealized experiences, intensity, and special treatment, we will struggle to love and accept our partner when they don't seem to be bothered or don't put in the effort. (Who could we be if we allowed this for ourselves?)

Accepting others *as they are* is commensurate to our accepting ourselves *as we are*. Fulfilling relationships require a reciprocated acceptance of one another as we actually are, not as we want each other to be.

As we work toward acceptance, we can make a commitment to gently coach ourselves into letting go of our attachment to the intrusive thoughts and energetic spirals of disappointment, and the savoring of sadness we hold onto. We will benefit from remembering to turn to what is in the here and now because it's also ripe with gifts and enough-ness, beauty, and meaning. If we will only allow ourselves to see it, accept it, and experience it in the moment we are actually living it.

We can coach ourselves to take our innate tendency and desire for intensity and apply it to everyday experiences as they actually are and as we actually are. Life can be felt just as fully when in equilibrium, in equanimity, and in the conscious reverence of enough-ness.

It's important for Type 4s—as it is for all nine types—to realize that our core beliefs, when left unquestioned, will take over. While working hard to keep us on track as someone so special, unique, intense, and authentic, these conditions for ourselves can interfere with and diminish our full expression of unconditional love and our capacity for vulnerability and intimacy with ourselves. They can also limit our reception, even our willingness, to allow intimate, unconditionally loving experiences with others.

Type 5 | The Observer | Conditional Love

> Sit comfortably upright in a quiet place, allowing your body to soften and yourself to breathe in and down into your belly. Do so several times. Read this core reflection, then close your eyes and go inward to compassionately experience this aspect of Type 5.

As Type 5s, when we find ourselves getting upset or reactive with someone we're in a relationship with, chances are we've just launched ourselves into some kind of concern of being invaded or put upon. We may have encountered obstacles or challenges to our need to protect ourselves from intrusions, or to our need for a bit of privacy. Or we may be feeling other's emotional demands, ones we do not feel up to meeting. Or we may be feeling irritated by another's disinterest in the diligently acquired knowledge we have and want to share, which is akin to our being personally rejected.

Our reactivity often shows up as the need to detach (pull away from others altogether), a shutdown of our feelings, and as a demand for private time to regroup. This is all fueled by an overwhelming feeling of shrinking into ourselves.

It's a contraction of sorts that gets coupled with a clutching avarice for what we just can't *do without* in that moment or in life. Our withholding, unavailability, and resistance to others' needs, including their need for affection, time, or attention, greatly diminish our expression and experience of love.

> As we feel our Type 5 reactivity take hold, sound the alarm bell. It's time to pause. Ignite the pause that lovingly and respectfully acknowledges our reactive, triggered energy by breathing deeply down into our bellies, realizing that this reactivity and how we handle it this time can either hinder or enhance our ability to love. Using the breath, hold (contain) the viscerally felt, physical charge–that impulse that might be really strong at this point–then gently but firmly suspend the reactivity. In this tender place, we are ready for gentle inquiry, reflection, and the formulation of a conscious action, as is needed.

As Type 5s, we believe that we must protect ourselves from a world that demands too much and gives too little. We have to guard ourselves and our energy in order to assure our survival, our security in the world, and our fear of impotence. We must avoid being drained of life energy.

We ask that we are knowledgeable and studied, and we expect ourselves to acquire knowledge and mental competencies. These are our conditions for self-love and self-sustenance, and for feeling worthy of, and capable to receive, the love of others. When conditions aren't met, we struggle to love ourselves and feel safe in the world and will struggle, in turn, to love others.

Without doing the work of self-awareness and development, we will inadvertently pass our refusal to love ourselves whenever our Type 5 conditions for ourselves are not met. We will conditionally turn on others in the same way that we conditionally turn on ourselves.

We will tend to not love others when they do not meet our standards or lack respect for the beliefs that we are beholden to within ourselves. For example, as we value the acquisition of knowledge and greater knowing and are willing to put in the time and effort to attain it, we will struggle to love and accept our partner when they don't seem interested in learning something new, applying themselves intellectually, or focusing on figuring things out. (Who could we be if we allowed this for ourselves?)

Loving others when they need us, when they want something from us, when they are asking for our feelings and for our attention is an expression of care and love. Opening our hearts to the source within each of us is how we'll fuel our capacity to meet these needs and our own needs as well. That source is what props us up and boosts our vitality, day in and day out. It's there and it's real and it's an energy we can count on.

Can we allow ourselves to trust in this? Can we reorganize our perceptions in such a way that we will no longer perceive that we are being depleted when interacting fully with others and with life? There is a flow to life, and it provides ample energy for each of us to fully engage in it, to pursue our wants and desires, to have our feelings, and to show up in those relationships that sustain us.

Keep in mind that as Type 5s, we can gently coach ourselves into allowing more go-toward energy than that of moving away, and to do so in such a way that is respectful and giving, mutually supportive and engaging, to our relationships and ourselves. Operating from this fundamental premise, we are now using and refueling, nurturing and honoring, both our heads *and* our hearts.

It's important for Type 5s—as it is for all nine types—to realize that our core beliefs, when left unquestioned, will run our lives. While working hard to keep us on track as someone unobtrusive, smart, and knowledgeable, measured and private, these conditions for ourselves can interfere with and diminish our full expression of unconditional love, our capacity for vulnerability and intimacy with ourselves. And they can limit our ability, let alone our willingness, to have intimate, unconditionally loving experiences with others.

Type 6 | The Loyal Skeptic | Conditional Love

> Sit comfortably upright in a quiet place, allowing your body to soften and yourself to breathe in and down into your belly. Do so several times. Read this core reflection, then close your eyes and go inward to compassionately experience this aspect of Type 6.

As Type 6s, when we find ourselves getting upset or reactive with someone we're in a relationship with, chances are we've just launched ourselves into some kind of over-focused magnification of something—of hazards ahead, of doubting what and who we can count on, on discrepancies or incongruencies, on pessimistic scenarios, or on a perceived or real lack of preparedness.

Our reactivity is fueled by an underlying angst—driven by a whirring preoccupation—that is experienced as hypervigilance, anxiousness, edgy-ness, and an adrenalized physicality, which can often present on the sharp edge of seething frustration.

This reactive state of being diminishes our expression and experience of love. The energy and outward expression of our reactivity generate a sense of mistrust, cautiousness; and sometimes we are other-provoking and testing, as well as accusatory, even controlling.

> As we feel our Type 6 reactivity take hold, sound the alarm bell. It's time to pause. Ignite the pause that lovingly and respectfully acknowledges our reactive, triggered energy by breathing deeply down into our bellies, realizing that this reactivity and how we handle it this time can either hinder or enhance our ability to love. Using the breath, hold (contain) the viscerally felt, physical charge–that impulse that might be really strong at this point–then gently but firmly suspend the reactivity. In this tender place, we are ready for gentle inquiry, reflection, and the formulation of a conscious action, as is needed.

If we're a counter-fear Type 6, also called a counter-phobic 6, we'll tend to address our fears and apprehensions head-on rather than feel paralyzed by them. We are more dispositionally wired to go toward, assert with contrary or tyrannical, oppositional thinking—confront and deal with. Challenging can feel much better than waiting, stewing, and whirring.

As a Type 6, we believe we must seek certainty, trustworthiness, and security in what we believe to be a hazardous and unpredictable—often dangerous—world. We must avoid becoming utterly helpless and dependent on others or anything that we cannot control, especially *in this kind* of world. We must be vigilant, don't-miss-a-thing observant, and cognizant of all that surrounds us in order to protect ourselves and our loved ones. These are our conditions for self-love and for feeling worthy of the love of others.

Without doing the work of self-awareness and development, we will inadvertently pass our refusal to love ourselves whenever our Type 6 conditions for ourselves are not met. We will conditionally turn on others in the same way that we conditionally turn on ourselves.

We will tend to not love others when they do not meet our standards or fail to fall in line with the same beliefs that we are beholden to within ourselves. For example, as trustworthiness is readily demonstrated by keeping one's word, we will struggle to love and accept our partner when they do not keep their word or sometimes change their mind, for *any* reason. (Who could we be if we allowed this for ourselves?)

As we tend to sense danger coming, as Type 6s we give our love by predicting trouble before it occurs and by warning others or giving advice. On this one, we can gently coach ourselves into allowing others to receive our warnings as *they* are willing even when we feel compelled to give our love in this manner. It needs to make sense *to them*, which may differ from *our need* to give them our (sometimes) unsolicited inputs.

Furthermore, we can coach ourselves to not take personally their seeming lack of appreciation for our heads-up or their inability or refusal to heed our advice. Either way, their response to our caring warnings is not necessarily an indicator that we are respected, trusted, or loved.

We can benefit from allowing ourselves to transcend the need for evidence, proof, and certainty by tuning in to the power of faith and to the untold mysteries we have access to within and that make up so many of our intuitive capacities. Learn to allow ourselves to express a faith and trust in the capacities and intuitive divinity of others too.

May we allow the agility of our extraordinary imagination to see into our own and others' greatness rather than using it to magnify a more doubtful, negative spin on people and on life.

Through self-coaching, we can train that same imaginative capacity to see clearly into potential, in the positives, and into constructive and discerning troubleshooting and preparing rather than catastrophizing. As we bring the power of faith into our lives and into our relationships, so do we bring the greatest capacity for love's unbridled, endearing unfoldment.

It's important for Type 6s—as it is for all nine types—to realize that our core beliefs, when left unquestioned, will take control and run off with us like a wild horse. While working hard to keep us on track as someone loyal, trustworthy, dependency-averse, and real, these conditions for ourselves can interfere with and diminish our full expression of unconditional love and our capacity for vulnerability and intimacy with ourselves. They can also limit our ability, even our willingness, to become safe enough to allow intimate, unconditionally loving experiences with others.

Type 7 | The Epicure | Conditional Love

> Sit comfortably upright in a quiet place, allowing your body to soften and yourself to breathe in and down into your belly. Do so several times. Read this core reflection, then close your eyes and go inward to compassionately experience this aspect of Type 7.

As Type 7s, when we find ourselves getting upset or reactive with someone we're in a relationship with, chances are we've just launched ourselves into a reaction to an unwanted feeling, unwanted reality, or a perceived limitation. Something's infringing on our freedom—our free will and our excitation—and our desire to keep life upbeat, flowing in positivity and possibilities.

Our reactivity may also be in response to another's feelings and how they're expressing them to us, feelings we do not welcome nor engage with. We do not want to get stuck in heaviness, sadness, helplessness, or boredom. Our reactivity is fueled by any restriction to our gluttony for all things epicurean in nature, including any restriction to a gluttony of the mind that might impede visionary thinking, more ideas, positive options, endless opportunities, and the planning of new and stimulating adventures.

Our intense response to restriction is felt as an anxious frustration, a contraction in the solar plexus, and a wind-up of titillating energy. Heat is felt in the body as it adrenalizes and readies itself for flight, for escape. Our reactivity diminishes both our expression and experience of love as our undeniable, self-centric focus and personalized view of life leave little room for others. It renders us often without constancy, without reliability, or stability. And the experience of us, felt by others, can sometimes be that of an immature shallowness or superficiality.

As we feel our Type 7 reactivity take hold, sound the alarm bell. It's time to pause. Ignite the pause that lovingly and respectfully acknowledges our reactive, triggered energy by breathing deeply down into our bellies, realizing that this reactivity and how we handle it this time can either hinder or enhance our ability to love. Using the breath, hold (contain) the viscerally felt, physical charge—that impulse that might be really strong at this point—then gently but firmly suspend the reactivity. In this tender place, we are ready for gentle inquiry, reflection, and the formulation of a conscious action, as is needed.

As Type 7s, we believe that we must keep life pumping, open to limitless possibilities, and free from suffering or boredom. We must keep moving and be stimulated in order to have a happy life worth living, one that does not leave us trapped, perceptively limited, or stuck in any kind of pain we cannot get out of. These are our conditions for self-love, and for feeling worthy of the love of others.

Without doing the work of self-awareness and development, we will inadvertently pass onto others our refusal to love ourselves whenever our Type 7 conditions for ourselves are not met. We will conditionally turn on others in the same way that we conditionally turn on ourselves. We will tend not to love others when they do not meet our standards or fail to live up to the beliefs that we are beholden to within ourselves.

For example, as we tend to look on the brighter side of life and steer clear from getting mired in difficulty, we will struggle to love and accept our partner when they tend to practicalities and responsibilities and can't join us. (Who could we be if we tended to these practicalities for ourselves?)

Keep in mind that as Type 7s, we can gently coach ourselves into allowing a broader view of human life, one that comes to know, with confidence, that we will not get trapped in suffering if we slow down, feel all of our emotional lives and that of others, and allow the good-or-bad truth of any given situation to emerge freely. At times, life may include a lack of stimulation, feelings of sadness, time spent in inactivity, or the tending to mundane tasks that support our lives as well as that of our loved ones.

As we coach ourselves further, we can gain the sobriety to let go of our intense resistance and apprehension to getting trapped and limited. Life does, at times, include limitations, psychological pain and challenge, sorrow, and even grief. Life also includes immense pleasure and stimulation, joy and excitation, and countless waiting-to-be-discovered possibilities.

Opening ourselves compassionately to what our reactivity is trying to protect (save) us from, we can relax our reactivity's automatic take-over and choose our responses wisely and consciously. And we can do this in collaboration with others and their needs, hopes, and aspirations as well, holding them in our hearts as much as we hold ourselves.

It's important for Type 7s—as it is for all nine types—to realize that our core beliefs, when left unquestioned, will run away with us. While working hard to keep us on track as someone so exciting, adventurous, free-wheeling, and fun to be around, these conditions for ourselves can interfere with and diminish our full expression of unconditional love and our capacity for vulnerability and intimacy with ourselves. They can also limit our ability, even our willingness, to surrender into intimate, unconditionally loving experiences with others.

Type 8 | The Protector | Conditional Love

> Sit comfortably upright in a quiet place, allowing your body to soften and yourself to breathe in and down into your belly. Do so several times. Read this core reflection, then close your eyes and go inward to compassionately experience this aspect of Type 8.

As Type 8s, when we find ourselves getting upset or reactive with someone we're in a relationship with, chances are we've just launched ourselves into a perceived violation to our sense of truth, fairness, and justice. What may have also triggered us is an issue of power and control, someone trying to overpower us or another, or someone not doing what they're supposed to be doing. Or someone has overstepped our or another's boundaries, and they need to be put back in line.

Our reactivity is fueled by our exuberant, sometimes excessively vibrant energy, which is felt physically as a rush of heat and vitality that floods our system in seconds. Fire! Ready? Aim. This highly impulsive charge is intense, and it diminishes our expression and experience of love as we can become immediately dominating, and without tenderness or kindness. We can be intimidating and insistent on only one way—our way! Where does that leave the other?

> As we feel our Type 8 reactivity take hold, sound the alarm bell. It's time to pause. Ignite the pause that lovingly and respectfully acknowledges our reactive, triggered energy by breathing deeply down into our bellies, realizing that this reactivity and how we handle it this time can either hinder or enhance our ability to love. Using the breath, hold (contain) the viscerally felt, physical charge–that impulse that might be really strong at this point–then gently but firmly suspend the reactivity. In this tender place,

we are ready for gentle inquiry, reflection, and the formulation of a conscious action, as is needed.

As a Type 8, we believe that we must be strong, powerful, dominating, and truthful in order to secure our place in the world. We believe that we cannot be taken advantage of, and that we must protect ourselves and others from being overpowered, manipulated, or used. We must be in control and avoid becoming weak and powerless—let alone helpless—at all costs. These are our conditions for self-love and for feeling worthy of the love of others.

Without doing the work of self-awareness and development, we will inadvertently pass onto others our refusal to love ourselves whenever our Type 8 conditions for ourselves are not met. We will conditionally turn on others in the same way that we conditionally turn on ourselves.

We will tend to not love others when they do not meet our standards or fail to stand up with us to protect the beliefs that we are beholden to within ourselves. For example, as we tend to not shy away from conflict, that is, addressing in real time the elephant in the room, we will struggle to love and accept our partner when they do not cop to what's really happening or if they avoid what needs confronting in the here and now. (Who could we be if we allowed non-confrontation or avoidance for ourselves?)

Keep in mind that as Type 8s, we can gently coach ourselves into allowing that powerful urge to be felt and understood, but not always acted out, especially with such fierce intensity. Conscious conduct is called for with such exuberance on the line. For Type 8s, the pause-and-contain process is of paramount importance. Learning to hold such an intense physiological charge in the body takes perseverance, capacity, practice, and patience.

Our will and our way are not always conducive to the needs and free will of others. Can we see that? Can we accept that we would most likely resist being overtaken by another, but it's what we often tend to do to others?

As our reactivity leaps forward to take charge, it imposes our sense of truth or justice on another. Remember that this is just *our version* of the truth. This is the way we protect our own innocence and vulnerability, which are qualities we readily sniff out in others, sometimes to their detriment and our gain. As we won't allow vulnerability in ourselves, we won't allow it in another either. We often challenge it, even step on it, as we readily see it as weakness.

As Type 8s, we will not tolerate weakness in ourselves or others until we do our personal development work and utterly redefine its meaning and imagined consequences. Our reactivity prevents us from being vulnerable, from being impacted, and from allowing our gentile self to show up. It prevents us as well from the experience of another's truth, their sense of self-worth, and the ways in which they might want to express their power and dignity in our presence.

It's important for Type 8s—as it is for all types—to realize that our core beliefs, when left unquestioned, will take over and run every relational transaction of our lives. While working hard to keep us on track as someone so strong, intense, and protective, these conditions for ourselves can interfere with and diminish our full expression of unconditional love, our capacity for vulnerability and intimacy with ourselves. They can also limit our ability to tenderly and innocently show ourselves in intimate, unconditionally loving experiences with others.

Type 9 | The Mediator | Conditional Love

> Sit comfortably upright in a quiet place, allowing your body to soften and yourself to breathe in and down into your belly. Do so several times. Read this core reflection, then close your eyes and go inward to compassionately experience this aspect of Type 9.

As Type 9s, when we find ourselves getting upset or reactive with someone we're in a relationship with, chances are we've just launched ourselves into some form of resistance; we might feel that we're being pushed into action or forced into conflict, neither of which we want. Or our reactivity may be due to something that is important to us being ignored. Or we are feeling ignored or overlooked—again, with no one else seeming to notice or care that this has happened.

Our reactivity is fueled by our own inertia, an inertia of the self that results from the fact that *it's us* who actually ignore and diminish ourselves, our priorities, and our needs. It's *us* who inhibit our stepping up to be included, counted, and heard. This is felt in our physicality as an emotional as well as somatic heaviness, a kind of weighted despair as a result of conciliatory defeat, the defeat and sublimation of the vibrant, individuated self that we were born to express.

All of this diminishes our expression and experience of love as we default without a fight to seeking psychological, emotional, and physical comforts first. We defer as a habit; we are not aware that we are doing this, nor is it easy for us to access our own deepest desires and sense of worthiness when acquiescing to others.

Showing up authentically is difficult as it might risk our uninterrupted connection, something we are profoundly sensitive to maintaining. But all the while, others do—in truth—want to know and engage with *all of who* we truly and really are.

As we feel our Type 9 reactivity take hold, sound the alarm bell. It's time to pause. Ignite the pause that lovingly and respectfully acknowledges our reactive, triggered energy by breathing deeply down into our bellies, realizing that this reactivity and how we handle it this time can either hinder or enhance our ability to love. Using the breath, hold (contain) the viscerally felt, physical charge—that impulse that might be really strong at this point—then gently but firmly suspend the reactivity. In this tender place, we are ready for gentle inquiry, reflection, and the formulation of a conscious action, as is needed.

As Type 9s, we believe that we must not exert our importance, that we must not be too much trouble, and that to love and to be loved, we need not differentiate ourselves. Therefore, we must align with others. With a propensity *to merge* energetically with another, any difference between us could impede the desire to merge. We become one with the other and can easily subjugate ourselves to do so. We go along and get along, which prevents us from the exposure of standing apart, not being liked, or feeling potentially valueless or insignificant when differentiated. These are our conditions for self-love, and for feeling worthy of the love of others.

Without doing the work of self-awareness and development, we will inadvertently pass onto others our refusal to love ourselves whenever our Type 9 conditions for ourselves are not met. We will conditionally turn on others in the same way that we conditionally turn on ourselves.

We will tend to not love others when they do not meet our standards or when they try to push us beyond the core beliefs that we are beholden to within ourselves. For example, as we tend to avoid conflict and keep the peace at all costs, we will struggle to love and accept our partner when they create conflict, even demand a confrontation that is uncomfortable. (Who could we be if we allowed this for ourselves?)

Importantly, as Type 9s we can gently coach ourselves into permitting a differentiated-from-others self. As we do, we begin to express our worthwhile personal value. Our unique existence *is* of value, and it's wanted by the world. We *can* individuate and *still be connected*, deeply connected, with others. In fact, it's an equally felt connection we're so desperately seeking.

Through self-coaching, we learn that others need us to show up in our own personal glory, in our own power, and in our truth—as that's what stimulates others too. As we share our true selves, others are inspired to do so as well.

Within any vital relationship, there are two differentiated energies. Each brings something to the other, including challenge, the potential for learning, camaraderie, and the gift, God willing, of mutual developmental growth. We come to learn that denying others our differentiated self is a disservice, because they too miss out on much when we do not show up fully.

As we allow ourselves to stand up and be seen, we risk the safety of invisibility, yet acquire the stomach for accountability and self-agency. We too have boundaries and limits. They are important. And as we allow ourselves to be seen, those boundaries and limits may be challenged by others. Can we handle it? Are we ready? While perhaps uncomfortable at first, these are experiences we need to welcome—for our own growth and development. We innately deprive ourselves of such growth when trapped in a Type 9's more typical strategies.

It's important for Type 9s—as it is for all nine types—to realize that our core beliefs, when left unquestioned, will be the over-a-lifetime experience that we have of ourselves and others. While working hard to keep us on track as someone so kind, deferential, accommodating, and pleasant, these conditions for ourselves can interfere with and diminish our full expression of unconditional love, our capacity for vulnerability and intimacy with ourselves. They can also limit our capacity to authentically show up for intimate, unconditionally loving experiences with others.

The Enneagram Brings Us Back Together

It's fair to say that, fundamentally, we all want to love and be loved. We most often enter into all sorts of relationships with the highest of hopes and greatest of expectations. For certain, in personal and significant intimate relationships, we start out having met high on life, filled with joy, happiness, and excitement. We are full of hope and anticipation. We are open to love. We feel it seemingly coming at us and running through us. We are ecstatic, perhaps. We bask in its beauty and life-altering chemistry. Without much thought, we let it play itself out.

Some of us fear that the end of a blissful first few months or year is simply inevitable. Others try to squelch our unadulterated joy to minimize the letdown that we fear will only come over time. And why is that? Why does it have to change so much? And why do we almost expect it to do so? As a relationship takes shape and we get to know one another better, why does it so often seem to get harder instead of more loving?

Learning how it is that we do not love ourselves—or more succinctly, how we tend to love ourselves *with conditions*—allows us to learn how we will also make it difficult to love any other. Conditional love for ourselves ends up as conditional love for others too, for our partners and our children, our family members, and even coworkers.

Whether those unmet conditions are expressed as judgments, as a lack of acceptance, or as unfulfilled expectations being placed on the unsuspecting other, it's amazing that our relationships are as sustaining as they are half the time.

By understanding how our type structure sets up conditions for love and acceptance, we can take a new journey. While this journey starts with ourselves, it's one that can lead to a fascinating and rewarding discovery with others. How we condition ourselves right out of loving, self-acceptance is how we'll inevitably play out that same non-acceptance, at some point, on our partners, children— on all of our loved ones.

But we have a choice. An incisive study as to what we're doing to ourselves allows us to see what we may be doing to another. Using the 5As of the UGP, we have a method that guides us through the unconscious terrain of polarizing, conditional love and reactivity—those places where defenses show up and loving connection falls away. These love-depleting struggles don't have to be a given.

Take your time going back over this chapter. Delve into your type structure's conditions and resistances to self-love first, then those of your partner. This is probably one of the most important reflections we may ever do for ourselves *and* for our beloveds.

As we see into the conditions we have set for love, consider the impact they've had on us and then on those closest to us. With compassion, consider how to expand your willingness to love beyond the conditions and start the extraordinary process of *allowing love,* at every turn and in every moment.

> Take a moment to reflect on one of the conditions you've set for yourself in order to accept and love yourself.
>
> How does this condition affect your ability to love your partner?
>
> Take a moment to reflect on one of the conditions you've felt you must abide in order to be loved (as you perceive) by your partner?
>
> How does this perceived condition affect you?
>
> How do you think it affects your partner?

PART 3

The Enneagram, Love, and Intimacy

" Openhearted communication stirs our emotions, which opens us up to sharing and receiving vulnerably. "

— *David Daniels, M.D.*

CHAPTER 11

Intimacy and Sexuality

There's no doubt, *intimacy* and *sexuality* are powerful words. And while they go together beautifully, they can also be mutually exclusive, which is a big topic. We can't really write a book about how critical love and relationships are to our well-being without also talking about emotional intimacy, physical intimacy, and sexual intimacy. (Notice the calling out of both physical and sexual intimacy—we'll come back to that.)

These aspects of human life are highly complex and there's much to explore. And as personal as this topic is, it's a discussion worth having.

Our Dilemma

Intimacy in all of its forms along with sexuality impacts us, whether or not we're conscious of it and actively pursuing it. For many, intimacy can be a struggle. As for sexuality, it often suffers the wrath of shame, guilt, or repression thanks to our upbringing, restrictive religious dogma, or countless many other influences, notwithstanding sexual trauma.

In working with couples, I often marveled at how little discussion so many had about their sexuality, the sexual experience of one another, and physical and sexual intimacy overall—all of which could have organically brought more intimacy within the relationship.

I also often when couples did talk about their sex lives and emotional intimacy, including addressing vulnerability and ways they could open their hearts to one another, it wasn't the hottest of topics. Instead, these delicate conversations are often resisted or flat-out avoided.

It is often when a relationship has gone awry that a couple would attempt to "spice things up" sexually or increase the frequency of sexual intimacy. But while that's one place to start, I found many skipped right over developing a vocabulary around physical intimacy and the importance of it. (This includes physical affection and touch—touch that is supportive, kind, and caring, touch that is sensuous and connecting, and touch that is stimulating, sexual, and erotic.)

As for physical intimacy—in all its forms it is a way of relating. It's a way of expressing love and care, and a way to intercourse itself, to lovemaking.

Regardless of the type of intimacy we're talking about, intimate banter could bring a couple closer, especially since opening up conversation about physical connection isn't always that easy. And bringing up unmet needs or sensitivities—emotional, physical, or sexual—is vulnerable stuff, not to mention that couples often lack the experience or confidence to address, let alone articulate these personal issues and vulnerabilities of intimacy.

Intimate, vulnerable conversations around physicality and sexuality most often do not happen among newly dating couples prior to their first highly anticipated sexual encounter. I guess good sex—however that's defined by each participant—is something we're supposed to be proficient at, connected with, and attuned to without saying much first. It's like we're supposed to have a sixth sense about each other to make sex amazing.

When we find ourselves attracted to someone and them to us, from there it's almost expected that emotional or physical intimacy will happen thanks to us simply having sex.

However, given the right conditions, sex is and can be its own form of profound communication, one that needs neither words nor explanation. At its instinctual and spiritual best, it's a mutual unfoldment that is precious, sensory, highly intuitive, and love-giving.

My point here is this: What promotes and fosters deep intimacy and great sex is the development of our self-awareness of course, but coupled with that is a special kind of communication made possible when we open our hearts (receptive and neutral) without agenda, expectation, or judgmentalness.

This kind of communication might include openly gazing at each other, listening and sharing with one another with delight, caring, and curiosity, and genuinely wanting the best for one another—openhearted communication that builds trust alongside a sense of closeness, safety, and reverence.

Openhearted communication stirs our emotions, which opens us up to vulnerably sharing and receiving. We begin to "feel" the other and "feel into" ourselves. From here, physical intimacy—including gestures of affection, care, interest, and tenderness—begins to come naturally and is highly nurturing as well as stimulating.

This might lead to sexual union, or it might not. But what is certain is that we don't simply meander our way to a deliciously symbiotic, magical union—one that is wildly fulfilling, deeply trusting, and honoring of all parties. Getting to *that* place requires that we explore our desires and that we expressly, personally, and vulnerably communicate them with one another.

Intimacy Itself

It's easy to focus on the sex side of the duet of intimacy and sexuality because it's straightforward to identify when we first had sex but harder to identify exactly when we became intimate. After all, what is intimacy?

Intimacy is a state of authentic, unguarded closeness. At its best, intimacy is shameless, revealing, and vulnerable. It is what allows us to come to know ourselves deeply, richly, and fully—the things we love about ourselves and the aspects we struggle with too. As such, intimacy can also be described as "in to see me." It's a good description, in my opinion, reflecting the openhearted seeing into *ourselves* and the openhearted seeing into *another*.

As we *accept* and *honor* what we see, we get in touch with *intimate substance*, including aspects of each other's true nature. We come close to what is authentic, real, and meaningful, that which we desire to share and be held sacred. It is bonding.

Through intimacy is how fulfilling self-knowing is honed and developed and how fulfilling attachment is formed in adulthood. Intimacy is the gateway to our precious uniqueness and to the uniqueness of others. It allows us to encounter and offer up what's tender and uncertain, sensitive and quirky, idiosyncratic and peculiar, beautiful and fierce, tiny and vulnerable.

Intimacy is possible only once self-acceptance and self-compassion are in full bloom and shame and judgmentalness have lost their isolating grip. Intimacy leads us to exposing who we and others truly are and to what we each hold dear. It also invites us to share those deeper sentiments with those we lovingly choose.

It's much harder for us to ask succinctly for intimacy when we sense *a lack* of intimacy—particularly emotional intimacy—as it's very tender to confront the deep needs and longings that may arise around its absence. Plus, it's a rather complex journey to develop the capacity for emotional intimacy.

A lack of sex in a relationship can lead to frustration as well as physical discomfort or agitation, especially for men. (I hope I don't get in trouble for saying that!) But for both men and women, a lack of *emotional intimacy* tends to lead to feelings of loneliness and isolation—a gnawing, felt longing for real connection. It inadvertently shows up as an "ache without a name," which might include the need to be emotionally felt and touched, heard, listened to, and cared for, or as an ache to be acknowledged, included, and valued. It may also show up as an ache to feel seen—*deeply* seen and known—as well as a need to be wanted, trusted, and needed.

This kind of ache is harder to put our finger on, and we may have a less developed vocabulary to describe it. So, these aches are often expressed as anger for what's not, projection and blame for what the other isn't giving, or as shame that can escalate when fearing the reason for this ache is that we might not actually be worthy of anything more . . .

Allow us to define intimacy in its many forms—including emotional, physical, and that which can lead to sexual intimacy.

Definition Intimacy: Intra- and interpersonal disclosure is authentic and emotionally vulnerable. It is caring and attentive, honest and tender, receptive and unguarded, honoring of self and the other, and it is compassionate toward self and the other.

This might all sound wonderful, but what we're really after is *developing* the capacity for intimacy. While it's not easy to get to such a place of greater capacity for intimacy, it is possible. It just takes conscious devotion, commitment, and practice. The road to greater capacity for intimacy is quite *simple* but not *easy* as it requires vulnerability.

Capacity happens when we've done our development work and set the intent to develop our capacity to share ourselves authentically, vulnerably, and personally. From developing self-awareness to fostering self-intimacy, it's about getting us to the point where we dismantle our defenses and sabotaging habitual patterns—the ones that lead us time and again to a sense of separateness and struggle.

Greater capacity for intimacy is within our grasp. Once we're on that road, it sets us up, as best as possible, to come to our relationships with a receptive, open, and undefended heart. Such a heart creates fertile ground needed for emotional, physical, and sexual intimacy to flourish.

Sex and Sexuality

Sex is many things to many people. For some, it is procreation, an activity with a very specific biological purpose. For others, it's a service exchanged for money, opportunity, or power. For some, it's an extraordinarily intimate act that engenders closeness and connection. And yet for others it's something too shameful to enjoy fully (or at all). For some, it's used to harm and control. For others, it's about pleasure and fun.

What have we enhanced it to be or diminished it into? How present are we to the sensory experience of sex itself? Do we experience physical, pleasurable liberation, or do we shudder secretively in shame and just get through it?

Do we expose our desires for arousal openly to our partner, or do we keep those hidden? Or do we go along to get along and not be a fuss or expect much? Do we focus only on our own gratification and struggle to tune in to the other? Or do we make it all about our partner's experience? Or maybe we hide inside of ourselves where we're safer from rejection.

Daily, we are inundated with sexual impressions. Sexual desirability is exploited, and sex is often presented as little more than a physical act. Men are pressurized to believe it's a performance or a conquest, while women are often shamed, led to believe that sex is a measure of her value or her reputation and thus a source of shame.

Meanwhile, sex is also used to market products thanks to longstanding research that says sex sells. Such research was initiated by renowned psychotherapist Sigmund Freud and well presented in the 2002 BBC documentary, "Century of the Self."

While our culture has developed a great interest in sexual positions, toys, and techniques, far less is said about intimacy—the kind of intimacy that stretches far beyond nudity and intercourse but instead touches us emotionally, psychologically, spiritually, *and* physically.

Intimacy of this kind opens our hearts and expands our sense of self. It takes us to moments where we relinquish control and surrender. It's the kind of intimacy that exposes us to another and challenges us to fully and uninhibitedly show up.

When, if ever, was your heart so open it felt scary?

Our sexuality does, in fact, have the potential to take us to profound kinds of intimacy. Awaiting us is the potential for a deeply felt, intra- and inter-personal, highly integral experience—one that integrates the senses of the body, the feelings of the emotional system, and the awareness of the mind with the consciousness of the spirit. Importantly and not often mentioned, it's the way we experience sex and our sexuality with and within ourselves first. *That* is what co-creates the sexual experience with another.

It is this fundamental approach that we want to share and that is so profoundly important, one that is worthy of discovery and exploration. This is the foundational starting place of what makes shared intimacy possible. It's also fair to say that the way we experience sex within ourselves has a tremendous impact on our partner's experience too.

Understanding our intrapersonal sexual experience is the key to enhancing our interpersonal sexual experiences. It is worth exploring how to first cultivate our sexual presence and personal sexual attunement; and then to cultivate the integration of our sensory physicality as it interacts with our subjective experience—with what is happening in our cognitive-emotional, spiritual selves, our inner worlds, our minds.

In this state, the intimacy we allow—that we have cultivated through awareness, presence, and practice—opens the doors of vulnerability, allowing us to be truly intimate with another.

So, to gain that understanding of ourselves so we can share ourselves more vulnerably, physically, and sensuously, we start with a genuine curiosity to explore this within ourselves. And perhaps, the first thing to address is what keeps getting in our way of this kind of self-connection—the kind of self-connection that leads to connection with others.

> We're all in this together, because we all have and struggle with various patterns, many of which are in common. And as it turns out, they inhibit us greatly and get in the way of what we truly want, particularly in matters of intimacy.
>
> ~ J.D. Daniels, PhD

Does Our Enneagram Type Affect Intimacy?

What, if any, is our Enneagram type's impact on intimacy and our sexual experiences? Pondering this question and sharing what I've discovered have been the work of many years. What we found through study is that our Enneagram type contributes to specific patterns that get in the way, ones that are infringing on people's intimacy and sex lives.

The way in which these patterns correlate with our Enneagram type structure's propensities alerted me years ago, and it is one of the reasons I wanted to write this book.

Our Enneagram structure—including its focus of attention, habit of mind, and core beliefs system and how it invokes its particular brand of personal suffering—both enhances as well as interferes with our sexual experiences. And after closer study and time spent talking to people, I concluded, "How could it not?"

In Chapter 14, I share a multitude of case stories that boldly highlight both the enhancements and diminishments we bring to our sexual experiences according to type. These recognizable type patterns are far reaching, as the impact on our relationships goes all the way into our bedrooms. How they either *enhance* our intimacy and sexual experiences or *get in our way* is an application of the Enneagram I have long hoped to bring to the table.

Back to intimacy and sexuality, while distinctively different they are distinctively connected; they can exist independently of one another as much as they can be gloriously enmeshed. When brought together consciously, proactively, and when integrated, it can lead to extraordinary levels of not only pleasure and excitation but also profound nurturance, deep connectivity, and utter fulfillment.

Cultivating Self-Intimacy

Our case in point is that the intimacy we have—that we allow, that we cultivate through awareness, presence, and practice with ourselves first—is what opens the doors of self-vulnerability. And that then allows us to be truly vulnerable, truly intimate—physically and beyond—with another.

Self-intimacy opens us up to other-intimacy. The same intense care and deep interest we take in ourselves catalyze a deep care and intense interest to be taken in another.

And here's the clincher. *Most of us don't know that we aren't intimate with ourselves*—not until we do the work of cultivating presence, until we come to some level of intrapersonal self-disclosure and honesty, until we are done manipulating our unwanted feelings or discarding them, until we are done hiding the parts of ourselves we feel are unlovable.

In the end, we only know the experience of the self that we know. It's hard to set out to develop something in ourselves that we haven't even considered was missing. So, to cultivate it, we start at the beginning. Assume nothing. Commit to becoming present and aware. Be willing to tune in and inquire. Be willing to want it all for ourselves—and be courageous too. It might get uncomfortable at times—vulnerability isn't a walk in the park. What's unfamiliar can be daunting.

But, most of all, know that we will, in fact, be OK as we pursue personal vulnerability and self-intimacy.

Invite the chance to grow, even if it's uncomfortable at times.

Cultivating Shared Intimacy

To add to our definition of intimacy: it is the cultivation of a fully receptive presence to each other, characterized by expressing our deepest nature safely and unashamedly. This opens the door for all kinds of intimacy to be developed. This foundation becomes *a state of being* with each other, and one that is developed over time as a result of presence, commitment, and trust.

Love and bonding foster healthy development, as we discussed earlier. Love and bonding in our early development foster self-intimacy, which is the basis for fostering intimacies with others later on. Without the presence of these experiences in childhood, we may have more of a struggle to develop intimacy capacities healthfully, and fully, in adulthood.

For some of us, reparenting ourselves beyond what was lacking in childhood might need to become part of our process from the get-go in order to pursue healthy self- and other-intimacy. This is a pursuit that is surely worth the extra effort and commitment.

Love and Intimacy

Love is something that comes from our being. It's a sign of personal integration tied to the Enneagram's three centers of intelligence. Love shows up as thoughtfulness (from our Head Center), kindness (our Heart Center), and gentleness (our Gut/Body Center). *All three centers of intelligence are involved in the full expression of love*, and it is divinely expressed when we've attained non-judgmental presence and are in a state of free will.

With the presence of love, we can focus on the experience of both emotional and physical intimacy in conjunction with the expression of our sexuality. Our capacity for intimacy and our sexual expression can either foster our experience of love or diminish it.

It is something that I have come to believe is so important to explore, as the very nature of our potential for intimacy and our expression of our sexuality represent a vital aspect of most couples' relationships and their potential for deep fulfillment or tremendous disappointment.

Fundamentals of Sex and Sexuality

In the dictionary, *sex* is defined as the sum of the structural, functional, and behavioral characteristics of living beings or organisms that subserve reproduction. That's a pretty pragmatic, somewhat boring description, if you ask me. Sexuality is the state of being sexual, ranging from sexual appeal to the many varieties of sexual expression.

There are three fundamental levels of sexuality in all human beings. The first is simply desire for sexual satisfaction expressed by the words *lust* and *sensuality*, meaning, the gratification and indulgence of the senses. This level, of course, can be quite enjoyable so long as it is consensual and doesn't violate anyone. Much of this level resides in the brain stem or reptilian brain (hypothalamus) and includes hormonal influences and connections to the sex organs, limbic system, and even the cerebral cortex.

At the second level, sexuality is the expression of attraction as well as the expression of care and bonding. It is essentially love-based and associated especially with the limbic system, but it also involves the cerebral cortex. The word *sensuous* means that the senses are being affected in a pleasing way, that is, pleasantness, attractiveness, and that which is appealing.

In a significant way, these are all aspects of what produces feelings that potentiate physical and sexual pleasure. This is related to the interweaving of both lust (sexual desire) and care, one of the demonstrated emotional states shared by all mammals. This combination of sexual desire and care constitutes a biological imperative, meaning it's necessary for our lives and well-being. This even accounts for the preoccupation with another, often associated with "falling in love."

The third level—and perhaps the deepest impact of sex and sexuality—is that of soulful union, which is often attained in association with commitment and especially involves the cerebral cortex alongside the limbic system and the entirety of our being and our life force. It can result in a divine spiritual experience.

As defined by neuroscientist, Jaak Panksepp, **"At its best, intercourse is the pleasurable interpenetration of two souls."** This naturally allows for spiritual experience. This experience of sex and sexuality not only satisfies the biological imperative; it is the basis for deep emotional and spiritual intimacy and a profound, life-impacting connection.

Full sensuous or sexual experience includes all three areas of the brain (the hindbrain or reptilian brain, limbic or mammalian brain, and forebrain or cerebral cortex) and all three centers of human intelligence (mental or Head Center, emotional or Heart Center, and instinctual/physical or Gut/Body Center).

Grounded, receptive awareness and acceptance integrated with attunement and resonance makes room for empathy and compassion to spontaneously emerge. This allows each of us to release the grip of our often distracting and limiting habits of mind, which then allows us to truly connect and intimately enjoy one another.

Here again lies the importance of utilizing the UGP and its five steps for our development—the 5As of awareness, acceptance, appreciation, action, and adherence.

At the same time, our habitual focus of attention, our habit of mind, our hurtful conditioning, our triggered reactivity, our lack of intrapersonal integration, our shame, and our non-self-acceptance—all of these aspects of self—do not dismiss themselves when we want to be intimate, when we try to love another, or when we try to bond and connect.

It's only with concerted determination and practice that we develop our capacity to transcend the limiting aspects of self that diminish our experience of love and intimacy. As we allow for self- and other-awareness, we allow for presence, unconditional self-love, and self-intimacy. All of this makes possible—let alone enhances—our capacity for intimacy, sexual expression, and unbridled love for another.

Sexuality and Spiritual Experience

So many of us tend to doubt the spiritual aspect of sex, often discounting it because of our biases that say, "How can something so carnal, so physical, like sex, be a spiritual experience?" Those of us who have already experienced a spiritual connection in our own sexual love life are smiling right now as we are way beyond this doubt.

For those who are doubting that sex could be all that and more, for those who have struggled with sex in their lives for countless reasons—some of which may even be hard to discuss or is a part of one's life in need of deep healing—there *is* this possibility.

When sensuousness is integrated with sexuality, a sublime joyful union (a spiritual connection) takes place when accompanied with our full presence in the moment. Arriving here, what we'll find is an experience free of the habitual constraints, the chaos or the rigidity, of a not-consciously-developed personality structure that can readily keep us from the full experience of life itself as well as our sex lives.

For spiritual union, the presence of **high receptivity** and **uninhibited expressiveness** is called for. The experience turns spiritual when it is genuinely caring and imbued with our essential qualities.

Spirit and sexuality join when sexuality communicates *love* energy, the vibration of love, which unto itself catalyzes an intensely emotive, deeply connecting felt-sense of the life-giving energy of the self and that of another. This connection then rises to that of spiritual, one that is flooded with sensuousness, a highly sexual physicality, and inevitably, a kind of surrender that culminates in oneness, having become one with the other to the point of undeniable, deeply felt union and inseparability.

Our deepest nature, our true spirit, is full of love—*is* love—and is intrinsically radiant, unencumbered, and free. It includes the energies of both the divine feminine and divine masculine, which, in turn, create two distinctive polarities as they interact, igniting one another. These polarities form an arc of energy not unlike the formation of the arc of energy that generates electricity (a negative and positive ground), forming a spark unto itself.

Feminine energy grows spiritually by allowing itself to love openly and expansively in a state of full receptivity, going far beyond just longing for it or hoping to attain it.

Masculine energy grows spiritually by learning to focus generously and gently with no target except for a union with the heart, body, and spirit of the partner. When developed, it has gotten beyond its assertive energy, which can get locked into performance and, when at its worst, perhaps, is not attuned, is negligent, or feeds an insensitive need for domination.

Spiritually-Felt Sexuality

Spiritually felt sexuality includes a willingness to surrender control of our body and its performance. It's the courage to surrender defenses and expose ourselves more organically, allowing one another to see beyond the guarded walls of the self that seemingly protect us and keep us safe.

This type of sexuality allows another to receptively receive us and *our* essential qualities, and us *theirs*. It includes the expression of both masculine and feminine divinity and its interplay.

Spiritually felt sexuality is where oneness and a sense of selfless union occurs. Bring to that a devotional component—a sanctified commitment to self and partner that supports a mutually held-dear relationship (irrespective of contractual circumstances)—one that gives rise to a precious honoring.

This is the experience of a shared divinity. It is sacred, respecting, and trusting, and is what creates a palpable holding space for all levels of intimacy and sexual experience to tenderly and naturally unfold and potentiate.

Intimacy and Sexuality

Discussing intimacy and sexuality is in no part a small task, but one that felt necessary to address as we tackle the Enneagram's application to bettering relationships—romantic relationships in particular.

Devoting ourselves to developing our intimacy-capacity is where we need to begin, as it's this capacity that is the gateway to all levels of intimacy with another, be it emotional, sexual, or spiritual.

"Allowing" intimacy is not necessarily a given. With intimacy comes vulnerability, and with vulnerability comes real and perceived risk. Protecting ourselves from the vulnerabilities involved with sharing ourselves authentically—with ourselves or with others—started long before we were making choices on "how to be." Our capacity for intimacy began early on as we were encouraged to either express ourselves freely or learned adaptively to shut ourselves down safely.

With intimacy comes the chance to fully love and to be fully loved. Hiding from ourselves only leads to hiding ourselves from others, preventing us from intimacy. Developing our capacity for it begins with self-knowing and self-disclosure. The vulnerability that follows takes a concerted effort, the fundamental desire for more of ourselves and for richer, more meaningful experiences.

It takes a committed devotion to break free from the countless impositions, conditioned loss of authenticity, and limitations that keep us from ourselves and keep us distanced from one another.

This is an exploration that takes us back to the innocence and self-acceptingness of our true nature. We just have to be willing to do—and actually *do*—the work, because it's so profoundly worth it. Every incremental step of it.

Personal development work takes us back to the undefended, animated, more readily vulnerable and available self, a self we'll be more open to share freely and uninhibitedly. This work is what returns us to our authenticity—to our tenderness and our sweetness, to our wildness and our fierceness, and to our hopes and aspirations.

Doing this work potentiates our fulfillment and returns us to love.

CHAPTER 12

Obstacles and Misunderstandings: What's Impacting Our Intimacy?

There are many misunderstandings, a lot of disconnect, and many detrimental teachings about our sexuality and its role in intimacy. Sexuality can play a beautiful, powerful role in our significant, romantic partnerships, if we so desire it and allow it. Humans, like all mammals, are sexual, and particularly for humans, sex leads to far more than procreation.

Our sexuality is a natural process driven by multiple instincts. It's a biological imperative that's wired into our beings. In its purest state, it entices us, makes us feel desired, empowered, loved, and feels tremendously good. It also fosters many physiological benefits as well as connects us intimately with one another. Our sexuality also has the potential to connect us more deeply to ourselves—our bodies and our spirits—and is a very potent aspect of our life force.

Striving to enhance our sexuality and our sex lives is a worthy endeavor. So, where do we start? Often, many begin this journey focused on new sex toys or new positions or different (even *more*) partners. But we have another suggestion.

We'd like to break down what interferes with our sexuality, our sex lives, and our intimacy-potential. Taking the time to examine how some of the most common myths, obstacles, and deeply held beliefs about sex itself and our own sexuality have impacted us can do us wonders.

We cannot work with what's impeding our experience of sexuality and intimacy, for instance, if we can't recognize we're struggling or don't know what's in the way. If we haven't tapped into what we really think or what we really feel when being sexual or intimate, it's easy to simply normalize what we have been taught to think and feel about sex and sexuality, without giving it much reflection, inquiry, or challenge.

But we do have a choice here. We can take our sexuality and our consciousness of it for our own well-being and satisfaction into our own hands. Not so surprisingly, we all share much in common with what's defeating us sexually or

271

impairing our capacity for sexual intimacy. And, also not surprisingly, we struggle individually with unique-to-us issues too, ones that we alone are contending with.

Becoming aware of our internal obstacles affords us the opportunity to compassionately lessen, even remove, those obstacles. Once the obstacles are addressed, the ability and capacity to expand and develop sexually are opened up considerably.

So, let's get curious. Let's take some time to investigate, grasp, and examine our subjective views, then open up and discuss our sexual selves with our beloved partners. Let's move toward more receptivity and understanding, compassion and vulnerability, willingness and exploration. Doing so will get us that much closer to shared liberation and uninhibitedness.

Navigating the Sexual Diminishments Obstacle Course

While there are countless ways each of us may be struggling with sexual expression, sexual and emotional intimacy, and sexual desire, there are some common themes regarding what's in our way and how we're impacted. We'd like to categorize them as follows to assist us to address each:

- Issues and impacts based in our personality structures—our center of intelligence, our dominant instinct, and our Enneagram type, including our level of developmental well-being and presence
- Issues and impacts related to our acculturation, including societal, religious, familial, and historical beliefs
- Issues and impacts related to our biology, our upbringing, and our psyche

The Impact of Our Enneagram Type on Our Compatibility and Expression

Our Enneagram type structure—meaning our habit of mind, focus of attention, and cognitive-emotional pattern, particularly our type's core beliefs about itself and its place in the world—has great impact on our sexual expression.

Our as-developed personality is a labyrinth of complexities that manages our deepest concerns about ourselves and our lives. It is run by what we believe we need to do to be loved (our core belief), and it is where we hide the ways we suffer disconnectedness from our true selves. It also drives the workings of our inner critic, our level of defendedness, and our ability or inability to contain and modulate our emotional reactivity.

How flexibly and proactively are we responding to our lives, or not? Our personality (type structure) also includes how much presence and vulnerability we can tolerate, if any at all. Each of these character-structure components significantly influences and impacts our capacity to express ourselves, let alone express ourselves sexually and intimately.

What's also important to take into account are our views about and experiences of sex, including our libido, our arousal and sensuousness, our openness and our tenderness, and our capacity to initiate and lead as well as surrender and submit.

These core attributes of our sexuality result in what I have come to term the Enneagram's sexual enhancements and diminishments.

Using the Enneagram as the extraordinary map that it is, we can use our understanding of type structure and level of developmental well-being to understand our sexuality and its expression that much more. We can also understand that of others.

How each developed type structure deals with respect and trust, shame and openness, over-giving and selfishness, dominance, and control, submission and surrender, presence and vulnerability (or not) are all critical components of how we will relate sexually and intimately.

These are some of the many aspects of our as-developed personalities that have an impact on our sexuality and its expression and that are key to our own self-knowing process.

Beyond the impact of our type structure on our sexual expression, we've got another big consideration here: our level of developmental well-being.

All nine Enneagram types have the potential to be highly present, adaptable, responsively flexible, loving and caring, undefended and enlightened, if you will. Which means, when healthy, when in a higher state of well-being, we have tremendous capacity to love and explore heightened states of consciousness, and sexual intimacy too, if that's so desired. That said, any of the nine Enneagram type structures with a lower level of developmental well-being can suffer moderately, all the way to tremendously, with intimacy and sexual expression.

And back to this fundamental question for a moment: What causes us to fall somewhere on the lower side of the spectrum of developmental well-being? Referencing, in large part, the research findings of the ACE studies, a lack of nurturance, neglect, or traumas and abuses when young are among the indisputable ways to get us there. Trauma—all manner of unresolved trauma and abuse, emotional, physical, as well as sexual trauma—that occurs from childhood all the way up to approximately age 30 (the age until when our personality's development is still malleable and impressionable) is a well-known culprit.

Add to that trauma the experience of abandonment, or one or more parents struggling with addictive, behavioral, or mood disorders. Add also our own addictive disorders and our ability or inability to form and maintain coherent and healthy cognitive-emotional stability. It is no surprise then that basic well-being becomes a harder-than-ever struggle—one that's compounded greatly if we do not pursue our own healing at some point.

It's important to note that well-meaning parenting caregivers face all sorts of stresses while we are growing up, not to mention the many stressors that impacted their early lives and their own developmental well-being. Their cognitive-emotional health greatly impacts their ability to connect with us, nurture us, and support our healthy development (or not).

All of this contributes to the many possible causes of developmental stress that leads to a child suffering a lower level of developmental well-being by the time they (*we*) enter adulthood. Any of these noted circumstances (and many more not listed) may lessen our level of developmental well-being, and a life-sentence of loss-of-self adaptations and defenses ensues.

Compatibility

So, this brings us to talking about compatibility again. Our level of developmental well-being is a key factor in a couple getting along and building a sustaining, loving, long-term relationship. It's a bigger issue than what Enneagram type gets along best with what Enneagram type. As Enneagram teachers, we've been asked this a lot: "Given my type, what type should I date?" "What Enneagram type am I most compatible with?"

To these questions, my answer is always: "A developmentally healthy one!"

Remember this; it's critical! The higher the level of developmental well-being of each individual, the higher the chance of compatibility. Developmental well-being is something that's gifted us in many ways by conscious and attuned parenting caregivers, the ones with whom we've securely attached and with whom we've been able to develop fully and potentiate. But if we didn't get this kind of start—by some stroke of cosmic unluckiness, if you will—we can, as adults, develop well-being in ourselves, step-by-step.

The reparenting process that is necessary to raise our level of developmental well-being happens as a result of our own mindful awareness practice and a commitment to developmental healing. (Refer back to Chapter 2.)

Compatibility and the Three Instinctual Drives

The other significant impact on longer-term, sustainable compatibility is how synched up we are (or not) in our expression of the three instinctual drives. (Refer back to Chapter 7.) Further to this insight, even when both individuals in a relationship are operating at a high level of developmental well-being, a misunderstanding can still occur when they suffer disparities in their instinctual drives.

When the drive that mobilizes a lot of our behavior gets acted out—when and where and why—it affects our partner. And because these drives tend to greatly influence our love language as well, a misunderstanding can occur and can cause varying degrees of conflict, even deep and lasting hurt, and even between a couple who otherwise interacts very well.

Here's a story that really drives this point home. An upwardly mobile, educated, engaged couple came in for support as they were beginning to struggle with ongoing hurts they couldn't seem to overcome. They wanted to resolve these issues before taking that big, contractual step of marriage.

The couple had taken a weekend trip to a little town named Sonoma. "Gina" had in mind romance all weekend long. As they awoke their first morning at the bed and breakfast, Gina whispered to "William," her fiancé, "Good morning, darling. Breakfast, or bed?" (That is, sex.)

Unbeknownst to either of them at the time, William drives from the Self-Preservation Instinct (he'll most likely make a great provider), and Gina drives from the Sexual/One-to-One Instinct. So, we have two people with very different mobilizing energies and priorities.

When William chose breakfast, Gina's heart sank. She felt utterly rejected, undesirable even, and beyond puzzled. It took her hours of their beautiful sightseeing day to recover. Meanwhile, William didn't understand what all the fuss was about. As always, he was hungry when he woke up and figured they could find another time for romance.

Without understanding the critical way these instincts can drive our motivations and are at the core of what gets us up and moving—active in the world and producing—the misunderstandings here can be catastrophic. This doesn't mean we have to have the same dominant instinct to make it together. But for couples whose primary instinctual drives are at odds with one another— meaning, they are not in sync—communication is of paramount importance.

In the case of William and Gina, had they understood their instincts, they might have laughed at this incidence, talked about it, and had fun with their differences. They could have worked it out more happily and without the lingering hurt.

And without understanding each other's instincts, their cognitive-emotional response to this incidence and others like it will most likely be met with confusion, feelings of rejection, or defensiveness. In their case, that's exactly what happened.

Mental Preoccupations

Here's another big issue. What are we thinking about right when we're sexually intimate with our partner? How long can we actually stay present to each other before jumping out of the sensory experience, our mind's having gone someplace else?

As we do the work of self-inquiry and developing awareness, we'll often find our minds have fled to type-related mental preoccupations. These preoccupations are strong, they are habit of mind after all, and will run on automatic if we don't get conscious and self-aware.

Thinking about the dishes that still need washing or our boss and his harsh feedback the day before takes us from our sensory-feeling-emoting body and drops us into our very busy heads, which is an instant diminishment. For most of us, neither washing dishes nor agitations with our boss would stir up sexual arousal—let alone keep that connection alive and in sync with that of our partner.

What we also need to realize is that our succumbing to countless mental distractions can be felt by our partner, which becomes diminishing for not only *one* of us but *both* of us. Unrelenting stress, life-management concerns, even daydreaming of being someplace other than with our beloved definitely diminish our relational, sexual experience—especially our sensuous experience.

It's unfortunate but true that our joyful and loving sexual expression can disappear in a nanosecond if we do not tune in consciously to what's happening, to where we've placed our attention, and then consciously and thoughtfully—willfully—bring ourselves back if we find that we've strayed from the present moment and the person we're with.

Sexual Openness and Growth, a Willingness to Share and Explore

Ponder this: What are the things you're most proud of in your life up to this point? Whatever is your answer, it's something you probably had to work hard for, something you most likely put a lot of time into. So, why do we think having a beautiful love life would be any different? It's also something that needs to be cultivated, that needs concerted amounts of devoted time and attention.

Like anything else of great value in our lives, a great relationship requires great input, care, and our intentional focus too. A big part of enhancing our relational mutuality, vulnerability, and intimate sexual experiences is through open exploration and a non-judgmental curiosity in one another's arousal and desires.

It calls for a willingness to share ourselves, our needs, and our deeply personal whims with one another. This allows us to more thoughtfully show up for each other's experience as well as try new or never-thought-of ways to play sexually with and for each other.

Of course, we need to add the caveat that this kind of openness and exploration are not recommended if they include any kind of unwanted or nonconsensual pain, humiliation, or force.

Gentleness Needed

Now, before we go any further, allow us to highlight the fact that this is tender material. Communicating in this manner can bring up all sorts of insecurities, fears of inadequacy or embarrassment, or fears of being rejected. Fears of being compared to others and fears of not being enough, for example, are a couple of the bigger ones that can lead to sharing-apprehension. Openness at this level before we've reached inside ourselves and have done the work to elucidate our sexual obstacles and diminishments can leave us not feeling excited but shut down.

We surely need to have compassion for each other and take great care as we begin to communicate at this level. Here, readiness is an inside job. Share with your beloved partner your reticence about any or all of this subject matter and be incredibly kind, non-judgmental, and genuinely committed to hold space for each other's fears and insecurities (if any) along the way.

What is OK? Along the lines of sexual exploration, what is deemed acceptable (or not) is either at the center of many couples' most intimate conversations or their greatest frustrations. Particularly, when desires and fantasies don't line up and one or the other in the relationship is deemed wrong, unacceptable, or—at worst—perverted, both individuals suffer.

It's also worth sharing that pathologizing sexual exploration and adventure in the bedroom was an issue of state law in the United States not too long ago. (For instance, all the way into the 1970s, oral sex was considered criminal and grounds for divorce in California.)

The Sexual Crucible by David Schnarch presents the radical idea that good sex is not reducible to a technical intervention based on anxiety reduction or ingrained stipulations on "what's normal." Rather, it is a function of personal development.

"**Most couples end up with left-over sex**," Schnarch says. By left-over sex, he means the kind of sex both can tolerate, where nothing is brought in that one or the other has outlawed out of fear or disgust.

Sharing our sexuality, our unique arousal systems, and our deeply private sexual desires is vulnerable stuff. It's not easy, because as we risk sharing ourselves, we risk rejection. We risk turning our partner off, even, which is an enormous fear when vulnerably and personally sharing this material. But in *not* sharing this level of vulnerability, honesty, and intimacy, we risk the relationship itself.

Hiding aspects of self—the sexual self, in particular—often leads to immense frustration and resentment, or the need to find other outlets for sexual expression without one's intimate partner. This, of course, can lead to immense consequences, which, in most if not all cases, will *not* result in a positive outcome.

For instance, the damage to the relationship one has with one's intimate partner as result of betrayal can be catastrophic and, more often than not, irreparable. But full-blown betrayal aside (and for countless possible reasons), much intimacy is either lost or never attained when we are not sharing, not being self-disclosing or honest, or when not attuning to the expressed needs of our partners. This too, over time, can be catastrophic. It's *another form* of betrayal, a withholding, and maybe not be overtly identifiable.

This lack of disclosure and vulnerability is more of a slow drip toward dissolution, disconnection, and disappointment, all of which put our intimate relationship in jeopardy, but in a different way.

Sexual Compatibility
Herein lies a next and very important conversation around fundamental sexual compatibility: How much do we underrate this critical component of an intimate relationship? How often do we *not* at all check in with it?

It seems quite common that we just hope for the best, or we tell ourselves we can become what another wants us to become, and that'll take care of it. Or not to worry, we can change our partner over time, and that'll work! But in truth, this may leave one or both of us starving inside and struggling over time to find an outlet that may not fit the relationship we've put ourselves into.

Sexual compatibility begins with an honest conversation with oneself. We can't be honest with another if we are not first honest with ourselves. (There's that self-intimacy thing again!)

We're all in this together, because we all have and struggle with various patterns, many of which are in common. And, as it turns out, they inhibit us greatly and get in the way of what we truly want, particularly in matters of intimacy.

In the upcoming sections, we'll reflect on how our biology impacts our sexuality. We'll learn about hormones, the power of touch, and the necessity of attraction.

The Impact of Our Differentiating Biology and Hormones

Our biological make-up impacts our sexuality. Physically and hormonally, men and women are different. For example, the hormone testosterone is found in both women and men but in differing amounts. It tends to govern sexual desire, sexual assertiveness, and a preoccupation with sex in general. Typically, adult men have seven to eight times more testosterone in their systems than adult women.

With that much more testosterone, the chance that men will have a much stronger sex drive than women is highly possible and can often be the source of many challenges in an intimate heterosexual relationship.

Sex drive, which, for starters, includes sexual frequency, tends to be an important aspect of relational compatibility and is undoubtedly a great source of frustration, disappointment, and hurt for couples when frequency compatibility is not in sync. There are, of course, couples where the woman's sex drive may be higher than her male partner's. And surely, the same frustrations and challenges may arise.

While testosterone is known to be one of the definitive sex-drive chemicals and supplements are sometimes prescribed for men with low testosterone levels, it's not been widely successful in enhancing sex drive in women. It goes to say that for women, testosterone levels are simply not the only ingredient of sex drive. Researchers continue to study how to increase a woman's sex drive; however, it's still somewhat of a mystery.

Referring again to David Schnarch's work with couples and sexuality, sexual frequency in an intimate relationship often defaults, much to one partner's dismay, to the partner who presents with the *lowest* sex drive. Left to settle as such and without discussion, frustration can mount and, over time, this discrepancy can become detrimental to the relationship. Feelings of rejection, unwantedness, and unfulfillment are some of the ways the couple may suffer when sexual drive is not compatible.

Not enough sex for one partner and always being solicited for sex felt by the other may become frustrating, very difficult to unbearable, depending on each partner's perspectives and how they're interpreting the situation. Again, the issue of sexual compatibility arises. Being in sync or out of sync on the sex-drive issue can be a real deal-breaker for some couples if good communication and an understanding of each other are not established.

On a positive note, there's more to this story than just hormonal science. Despite less testosterone than men, human females are and can be sexual their entire ovulatory cycle and not just when ovulating one or two days per month like most other mammals. (Bonobos, also called pygmy chimpanzees, are like humans in this regard.)

So, what does this mean to us? It means that across each 30-day period we humans are more apt to be sexually expressive and intimate with each other and with greater frequency than for just procreation. This provides us with far more opportunities for intimacy to occur with one another over time.

A case comes to mind from my years in practice. It's the story of a commitment a couple made to mutually enhancing their sexual expression and the desire for it without depending solely on biological chemistry to light the fire first, so to speak. In the end, they were great exemplars that we can consciously decide to be sexual and from that, arousal follows. We can willfully drive our own sensuousness and openness to each other, deciding for ourselves how much we want to so do in a given month.

Sexual expression can also be driven by our desire for closeness and intimacy. There was another couple who was struggling with a massive change to their sex lives. The man, "Bob," suffered prostate cancer and had undergone surgery to save his life. Prior to this surgery, the couple had a very active and fulfilling sex life. Post-surgery, Bob could no longer get an erection.

This couple faced a choice: either give up their sex life entirely, or adjust their sex life based on their new reality. While this was not easy at first, this couple was committed to continued sexual sharing and the intimacy generated by sharing their bodies. They were committed to sensuousness, emotional intimacy, reciprocated affection, and shared sensations.

What happened, thanks to their commitment, was an even more enhanced and fulfilling way of relating sexually. They opened up to new and creative, playful ways of arousing each other and, in the end, found their sexual satisfaction had not diminished.

The Energetic Impact of Touch on Our Biology and Psyche

It's important to call out that all manner of touch is *felt*. We often hear, "You've touched my heart." This is the emotional touch of deep sentiment. It may have begun with a loving gaze, with gestures of lovingkindness, so much so that it opened our hearts and we received.

Then there's physical touch and all of what it brings—from nurturance to affection, to care, and to arousal. We are nurtured through touch. Touch is bonding. And physical touch doesn't have to be but surely *can* be erotic. All forms of touch can be arousing, be it emotional or physical. As we touch another, whether emotionally or physically, *we are touched*. We are impacted.

And yet, another level of fulfillment still awaits, as in, when our touch is received. It feels good to experience that our touch has been received and felt, perhaps as much as it feels good to touch. There's a reciprocity to touch when at its best. And there are developmentally necessary life-enhancing chemicals released in us when we are appropriately and caringly touched. This can leave us feeling cared for, nurtured, and attended to.

Human touch can trigger oxytocin (the cuddle, bonding, and connection neurohormone) and dopamine (the pleasure, motivational, also addiction-triggering, reward-system neurotransmitter). These are the fundamental neurochemicals that fuel the joy, love, and happiness we are designed to experience across our lives. They are critically important.

How we interact with each other, including the intentions we hold, the energies we bring, and the kind of touch we offer up are all part of the equation too. For example, wires can get crossed when aggression is mistaken by one or both for assertiveness or when assertiveness is mistaken for aggression.

Confusion and disconnect can also take place when passivity—just going along but not actually engaged—is taken for the active and definitive state of receptivity, desire, and openness.

How We Approach Each Other: Energetic Polarities

For fulfilling sexual encounters, let's circle back to the need for presence as well as the impactful interaction of both feminine and masculine polarities. This is not to say that a woman won't take the masculine polarity at times and the man won't take the feminine polarity at times. Both sexes can play either role at any given moment, and exploring these two polarities consciously and constructively can enhance sexual arousal and intimacy.

What Is Assertiveness?

As we consider assertiveness, we want to appreciate the masculine polarity. This is the dynamic of leading, guiding, declaring, and expressing outwardly and toward our partner and on behalf of our mutual enjoyment. Aggression, however, is different from assertiveness. Aggression can be taking, insisting, forcing and dominating, and may leave little room for a partner to object or suggest something different.

Aggression is often not met with mutuality or a concern for the other. We may also see assertiveness being confused with aggression. This confusion, of course, is based on interpretation. Our interpretations go hand in hand with our type structure, our level of developmental well-being, and our level of presence.

Often, our interpretations are colored as a result of unresolved trauma, a fear of being vulnerable, and shame around aspects of surrender or submissiveness, also when we suffer an inability to trust anyone else but ourselves being in control.

What Is Receptivity?

Receptiveness is where we'll come to appreciate the feminine polarity. Receptivity is not passivity, but the two are often confused as they might look the same when viewing from the outside. We can appear receptive when what we really are is vacant. But from the outside, we're seemingly with it and agreeable. Passivity can lead to just going through the motions.

While in a state of seeming non-resistance—maybe even covert apathy—passivity's outward appearance can be misleading. It can look like free will. It can even be misread as agreement or desire. This is *not* receptivity.

We might feel easy to get along with when passive, but are we really? What is really going on with us when we silently opt out of showing up yet pretend to? This could be a result of trauma, early neglect, perhaps extreme introversion, aspects of our temperament (our Enneagram type), or various other reasons worth exploring.

Receptiveness is an *active force*; it is not passive. It is decidedly present, invitational, and attuned. Receptivity is active willingness. It receives and it desires to actively receive.

Touch that mutually arouses the senses requires a reciprocity-rich active force. The one who is giving *touches*, and the one who is receiving *feels*. This exchange is then shared in a multitude of ways, resulting in an exchange of "I touch you, I feel you; you feel me, you touch me." Such an exchange may escalate in intensity and sensuousness and become deeply fulfilling on many levels and in many ways.

Reactions to Touch

While we've espoused the many benefits and qualities of touch, touch might also be a challenge. Some of us may like a lot of physical touch. Others may not. Some of us may not have grown up with much physical touch and affection even though we were loved, yet that love was expressed in other ways. Others of us may have been touched abusively or inappropriately when young, which has led to discomfort, fear, or shame, even being repelled by touch.

> What does the paragraph about the different reactions to touch bring up for you, if anything?

I once worked with "George," (a Type 7, the Epicure). While he had a highly active and interesting childhood, it was very traditional, stoic even. Affection was not expressed. His mom was not a hugger or a cuddler, nor was his dad, for that matter.

George's wife "Frankie," (a Type 2, the Giver) grew up in an Italian household full of affection, family meals, lots of emotional conversation, and countless kisses. When they came to see me, George and Frankie's relationship was at an impasse as George couldn't understand why his wife wanted and needed so much affection. He described her needs as, well, "so needy."

Huge frustration was mounting as Frankie was increasingly feeling unloved. Since George hadn't developed comfort with much touch, George avoided countless opportunities for him and Frankie to touch each other, and Frankie found it unbearable. George's activity-driven way of expressing his love with exotic holidays each summer wasn't cutting it for her. She felt ignored.

Here was a case where building a *capacity* for touch by developing *receptors* for touch could remedy a couple's growing dilemma. Learning more about the impact of each other's childhoods on their expression of affection helped them both depersonalize some of the struggle and raise their compassion for each other.

We designed exercises that had the couple hug, for example, twice a day, heart-to-heart, for an extended amount of time "till it felt a bit uncomfortable." This began opening George's tolerance to touch and affection. He slowly went from tolerating touch to enjoying it, and then to appreciating touch. And he and Frankie, thanks to their mutual willingness, developed an entirely new pattern of successful touch-relating that had not existed for them before.

The Necessity of Attraction

What is attraction? It's the action or power of *evoking interest, pleasure, or the liking of someone or something* for particular reasons. Some of those reasons are conscious and tangible, some are not.

But why is attraction particularly important in our romantic partnerships? We decided this was a worthwhile question that deserved some concerted thought, as attraction is probably more important than we tend to admit. We considered two kinds of attraction relevant to the journey of romantic partnership: physical and emotional-spiritual.

Physical attraction is based on how much a person's physical features aesthetically please us—features that we find handsome, beautiful, or pleasing in some way. Physical attraction is directly linked to sexual attractiveness and desirability.

Emotional-spiritual attraction is incited when we look into the eyes of another, something is seen and registered, and it's intoxicating. It's what we feel in another with our hearts, and it's what we hear in the words and attitudes of another as they speak.

Emotional-spiritual attraction includes being drawn to someone's true essence—their higher self or Buddha nature, their mind and spirit—and finding it's compatible with our own. This may include the wisdom, values, beliefs, developmental well-being, and dignities imbued in someone's personhood that we are receptive to when in their presence.

The fact is, physical attraction—no matter how shallow we've tried to tell ourselves this is—is most likely a highly sophisticated phenomenon that meets up with our survival strategies and what we subconsciously want for our future offspring. This is probably activated on some very deep, evolutionary as well as instinctual level.

Physical attraction seems to me the "all systems go" springboard for emotional-spiritual attraction to unfold and explode into our psyches and spirits in simulcast. The "love at first sight" encounter—widely popularized in media and film—along with the personal stories of so many most likely resonates with these multiple levels of attraction being seemingly present and felt on a rather subconscious as well as instinctual level right from the get-go.

Romantic partnerships that have the best chance of thriving over time are composed of both physical attraction as well as emotional-spiritual attraction.

Physical attraction alone can lead to exciting and enticing romances, but it can be short-lived when emotional-spiritual attraction is not concurrent, never developed, or when it's not compatible and can't be cultivated despite the physical attraction being high.

It's also worth stating that both kinds of attraction—physical plus emotional-spiritual—are needed to be understood, hopefully garnered and honored, for the entirety of romantic partnerships to unfold uninhibitedly and be sustainable. If either or both of these attractions to one another change over time—at worst, change significantly, particularly the emotional-spiritual—the relationship may be jeopardized and potentially fall apart.

Tuning in to what truly attracts each one of us to someone else is also an important piece of this puzzle. Media and advertising inundate us with images of whom we should be attracted to and of what is considered most desirable. That said, marketers and advertisers don't take into account our individual and unique aesthetics, let alone personal brand of emotional-spiritual attractiveness. And while we may be taught that this or that is what we *ought to be* attracted to, it may not be for us.

It's important to listen to our personal cues, signals, and responses rather than that of advertising dogma. Knowing what it is that turns us on, rocks our own hearts, and genuinely moves our spirits is part of our divine palate—and deservedly so.

The Impact of History, Culture, and Gender Norms

At different times in history, gender constructs of the day greatly influenced how we viewed sex as well as how it uniquely pertained to men and women.

Historical Gender Norms for Women

It was not that long ago in the West that cultural gender norms viewed women as overly sexual and seductive. This led to society's espousing that female sexuality be resigned to obligatory reproduction and overtly expressed sexual desire be deemed inappropriate and unladylike.

In some other cultures, virtuous women are separated metaphorically from sexually active women, as in a "Madonna" or a "whore." This way of differentiating women into two distinctive categories splits men's capacity to see both possibilities in one woman. This leads to all sorts of societal prejudices and a potential breakdown in partner intimacy that include—but are not limited to— the social status of a woman and limited options, degradation, and mistreatment, or a virtuous wife at home and a prostitute after work. ("Never the twain shall meet!")

Intimacies are split, as what is shared conservatively with the virtuous wife is far from what is shared debaucherously with the whore.

In truth, women are sexual beings, as are men. This fundamental truth needs to be appreciated and understood, as it would allow *both* sexes to seek and enjoy sex intimately and fully with each other, and for each to do so without condemnation, shame, splitting, or suppression.

Historical Gender Norms for Men

Throughout history—at least since the development of agricultural societies—men have generally dominated relationships, with women being viewed as property, a symbol of status, or as a means for gaining power. This led to the view of men as either protectors or oppressors.

Love-based marriage for sexual companionship, child-rearing, and a division-of-labor partnership is novel, beginning only 100 years or so ago with the industrial age. We can easily grow up to believe that marriage had always been love-based, but this concept is still evolving today.

Especially in Western cultures, this shift has contributed greatly to the liberation of women and the dismay of men, and to the liberation of any conjoined-in-marriage couple, for that matter. And what has since evolved is an attitude that if you no longer love your partner, there's no basis to stay married.

While this has solved some of the aches of the heart with people toughing it out in loveless marriages, it has churned up a host of interesting challenges with traditional family structure and complications with child-rearing and splitting property and wealth.

But this shift to love- and choices-based marriages continues today. It represents uncharted territory as women express more independence and empowerment, and men adjust. These cultural shifts too have greatly impacted both male and female sexual expression, including how we court, how we approach each other, and how we resolve a relationship that's no longer wanted by one or both parties.

From Sacred to Sinful: Cultural and Religious Norms

Sex and sexual expression have either been elevated as sacred or denigrated as sinful. We treat sexuality as worthy of reverence and veneration or as deviant, dirty, and bad. These polarities significantly affect our sexual experiences, because after all, they are oppositional views, and perhaps to some degree, mutually exclusive. What do we do with that?

What we've seen is that sexual expression gets deified or demonized, expressed or suppressed. These intensely polarizing expressions can obscure the vast possibilities of delightful and pleasing, exploratory and intimate, sexual interactions—ranging from the ordinary to the extraordinary. Our sexual views are really worth a good bit of self-inquiry.

For many, sexual shame is off the charts and potentially harmful to our cognitive-emotional psyches. We are human and we are, in fact, sexual. We want to procreate on some very primitive level, and we want to bond on an emotional-instinctual level.

While procreation is necessary to the survival of our species and we're readily given the sexual green light when having babies, fulfilling our sexual expression often gets caught on that, "Do I stop or do I floor it?" yellow.

What do I allow for myself sexually, and what do I not? How do we negotiate this contrasting duality? Whether deemed sacred or sinful, how we view sexuality and work with those views are fundamental to how we engage with it.

CHAPTER 13

Insights and Suggestions for Consciously Impacting Our Intimacy

How fulfilled we tend to feel in a relationship has quite a bit to do with how connected we feel to our partners. While our ability to connect with another begins with our attachment experience in early childhood—something we are learning we can resolve as adults, if we so desire—it also has to do with our ability and willingness to develop self-intimacy.

Self-intimacy is a strong, practiced, familiar, and vulnerable connection to self. And self-intimacy in the form of self-connection is the foundation of every other connection we may hope to successfully make in our lives.

Using the Enneagram system as a compassionate basis for self-awareness and self-intimacy, we have an excellent chance at cultivating what we need on our end to have a relationship that's built on shared intimacy, mutuality, tender vulnerability, and fulfillment.

So, how do we create such a bond with a romantic partner? Success in this area is far less about our or our partner's Enneagram type. Instead, it's about our level of developmental well-being and how much we understand our type structure—its gifts as well as its liabilities.

What's the key then to becoming part of something heartfelt and beautiful, open and receptive, mutually life-giving and love-generating? What can help us go from the infatuation stage of new love (which can last up to three years) to something still passionate but also deeply loving, committed, and sustaining over time?

There are a few fundamental ingredients to be considered and explored, and they have everything to do with how we verbally express what's on our minds and in our hearts (*what* we say—expressions of love, appreciation, and sensuality), as well as all the many nonverbal communications too (*how* we say it—the tone, facial expressions, as in gestures, and more). Both the verbal and nonverbal greatly affect how we feel in each other's presence and how close (connected) and safe we feel to each other.

In the end, what creates meaningful and delightful intimacy—shared sensuousness, a deep connection, and a fulfilling sexual experience—is how we show up for ourselves, how our partners show up for themselves, and how we collaboratively show up for one another.

Six Insights to Greater Intimacy

If we were asked what's most important in this book besides all the Enneagram teachings, we'd say *intimacy* and *cultivating it*. What follows are six universal insights—ways we can show up for ourselves and one another in order to experience greater intimacy and fulfillment in our romantic partnerships.

Insight 1: The Importance of a Unique and Independent, Individuated Self

While becoming one with our beloved partner is highly desired and an utterly beautiful experience, we best conjoin as one only when we have first developed as an individuated, autonomous self who can meet another with presence, sovereignty, and personal dignity. This in turn gives rise to our partner's presence, sovereignty, and dignity to be cultivated and honored as well.

It's only when both of us are fully present that we are able to experience a deep and soulful connection with one another, one that is equally and mutually respectful, attuned to one another's needs and desires, and one that is mindful of our experience alongside that of our partner.

In fact, we might even say that **the capacity for self-love *is* the foundation and the capacity to love.** This foundation is what then lends itself to sharing and connecting, honoring and adoring. But importantly, it does so without possessing or becoming clingingly dependent as that reduces the partner to an object, someone to possess and love—or else . . .

Without our self-developed capacities to love, there's a risk of becoming addicted to the other, which is a form of externalized compulsive escape from self-abandonment and its agonizing internal emptiness.

The kind of self-love we are talking about here is not ego-driven, and it certainly is not narcissism either. As Suzanne would share with many of her incarcerated students, **"Self-absorption is not to be confused with self-love."** Instead, self-love is a *deep care* or compassion for oneself. Self-love leads to self-sovereignty and a healthy sense of one's own dignified personhood.

Developing individuated self-sovereignty and a healthy sense of personhood is an inside job, one we ought to take on before we enter into romantic partnerships and magical unions. It begins with a mindful awareness practice, self-inquiry and curiosity, and the desire to personally develop and potentiate.

Insight 2: Creating Fulfilling Sexual Expression Is About Cultivating Presence During the Actual Experience

Satisfying sexual expression is about fully showing up. It's to bring our receptive self into full engagement with another. It's to consciously bring our presence first to ourselves and then equally to our partners. Our presence is our soulful, awake, self-witnessing, attuned-to-self and attuned-to-other state. It's about really being in it. Sensorily. Emotionally. Physically. Mindfully. And caringly.

Satisfying lovemaking is not about performance; it's not about judgments that dictate what is "normal" and "right" or what is "weird" or "bad." It's not about an end goal (orgasm), nor is it about measuring our worth or validity. In fact, a preoccupation with performance, validation, an end goal, or various inhibiting judgments are all ways we take ourselves out of presence and diminish our experience.

Insight 3: Communicating Our Deepest Desires

This is a step I often found was skipped by couples. Perhaps we feel shy or embarrassed, or we might feel we shouldn't have to spell this out for one another, all of which lead us to avoid this opportunity for intimacy-building.

This kind of deeply personal communication requires a non-judgmental exchange, one that is honoring, self- and other-respecting, and deeply caring. We have to come at it with an open and tender heart, a curious heart, and a lion's heart—one that will not take offense at another's needs or feel inadequate or inexperienced as our partner shares their desires.

To show up for each other with the purest of intentions is to take great care to express a genuine interest in bringing a sensuous, fulfilling sexual experience to one another. While the communication may feel awkward at first, it's one of the most profound ways to develop a tender intimacy and vulnerability together.

Insight 4: Understanding Our and Our Partner's Struggles to Stay Present During Sexual Experiences

What is diminishing our sexual experience? Can we articulate it? And how about for our partner? In the next chapter, we'll detail various ways each of the Enneagram type structures innately brings enhancements to sexual experience as well as how their type structure diminishes—pulls them out of—sexual experience.

What hinders each type's respective ability to stay present when sexual? These are conversations often never had, yet are ones that make possible precious, support-generating intimacy with one another. This kind of sharing encourages each partner to hold space for the other, allowing for working together so that the sexual experience can consciously and proactively be co-created.

Herein, we decide to no longer have an experience where each partner is doing our best (hopefully) to show up for the other but we're still struggling to stay with it, neither being any the wiser. Instead, we set it up as a mutual endeavor where each other is held and acknowledged and guided toward presence, and with enough care to ward off shame, inhibition, self-consciousness, or judgment.

Insight 5: Integrating the Three Life Forces with the Sexual Experience

What this means is that we're bringing forth all three of the great life-force energies when making love. These are the three energies:

- Receptive (also called internalizing or withdrawn) energy
- Active (also called assertive) energy
- Reconciling (also called balancing) energy

To understand these three energies as depicted in Figure 5, it would be good to understand the Law of Three (also known as the Law of Creation). This law teaches us that for anything to be created or for any event to materialize—a decision, action, or situation—three forces *must* be present. *All* three must be present and are equally important.

Each of the nine Enneagram types expresses these energies in one way or another, but each type tends to express one of these energies more innately and readily.

- Receptive energy | Types 4, 5, and 9
- Active energy | Types 3, 7, and 8
- Balancing energy | Types 1, 2, and 6

(See Figure 5 on the next page.)

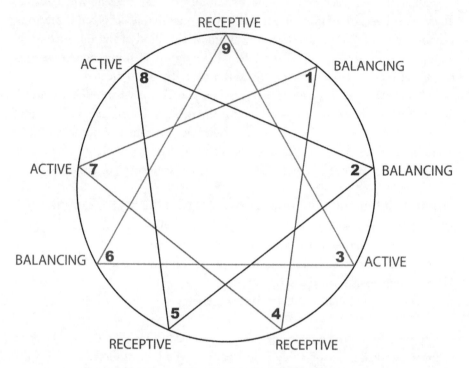

Figure 5: The Three Life-Force Energies Innately Expressed by Type

Receptive energy—also called internalizing or withdrawn—naturally flows into oneself as a feeling of introspection and inward-first orientation. It's an active form of welcoming and inviting without expectation or judgmentalness.

This receptive energy is not passive, in fact, quite the contrary. It's conscious and engaged. It is felt by another as engaged presence, an expressed flexibility, willingness, and acceptance. It's actuated, alive, and vibrant. But if receptive energy gets shut down, for whatever many reasons this can happen, we contract, which leads to withdrawal, avoidance, disappearance, and inertia.

Active energy—also called assertive—naturally flows outward as directed and decisive action. It feels unrestricted, unencumbered, and expansive. It can also manifest as a highly alert stillness or presence. When active energies get shut down, we contract, and while still focused outward, it's focused in a way that is felt by others as an aggressive, unrestrained, forceful action rather than an assertive, intentional action or powerful yet quiet alertness.

Balancing energy—also called reconciling or compliant—naturally equalizes and harmonizes receptive and active energies. When our balancing energies get shut down, again our systems contract, and then balancing energy collapses into narrow, amplifying rigidity.

Harmonizing and integrating all three energies within the sexual experience is, in my opinion, the ultimate energetic process to consciously achieving mutual sexual fulfillment.

Insight 6: Desire for Arousal Doesn't Need to Come Before Actual Arousal

Centering ourselves in our bodies, being present, breathing deeply, grounding our hearts, and stabilizing our presence to all that's within and outside of us—each of these steps prepares us for intimacy. So, why wait for *arousal* to initiate *intimacy*? Willingly and purposefully opening ourselves into a receptive state ignites our connection to another. By sharing words of affection and showing interest in each other, we further open up to that connection and open the gateway for an intimate exchange to unfold.

Connection can be sought and manifested by a loving gaze. We can open up a conversation that engages one another, choosing content to talk about that is intimate and feelings-oriented. We can open ourselves to touch and being touched, which often leads to arousal and, furthermore, to sexual excitement.

Just beginning some form of engagement with another can ignite the possibility for connection, which can escalate to sexual arousal. Start with messages of reassurance, affirmations of attraction, or nonverbal communications, such as a wink or a longing smile. Perhaps, start with a light and affectionate touch, a gentle and loving inhale that is felt, all the way to slowly introducing recognizable sexual foreplay that will then actually trigger sexual desire and arousal, especially in women.

While realizing that touching and caressing, connecting and responding can stimulate a sexual response in our partner, it's always important that we are attuned to both our partner's sexual and non-sexual needs, and attuned to what's needed and ultimately desired in any given moment.

CHAPTER 14

Sexual Expression and the Nine Enneagram Types

Across my many years working with the Enneagram leading panels and listening carefully to the various—often very disclosing—narratives, I found myself thoughtfully taken by each type's expression of the most tender of their human challenges and sensitivities.

I found myself paying close attention to how each of the Enneagram types found and described themselves when most vulnerable. For me, that might have included when people were emotionally exposed, dependent on others, when ill and/or facing death, when grieving, when needing nurturance, and even, when sexually intimate.

In times of vulnerability, we—each of us an Enneagram type—stand on the precipice of our greatest potential for opening that which can bring forth self-revelation and life-changing developmental shifts in well-being. Of all the places we may find ourselves vulnerable across our lives, what I found to be universally true was this: we find ourselves particularly vulnerable when struggling with and striving for significant relationships and whatever levels of intimacy we can tolerate.

Self-intimacy takes immense courage, brutal honesty, a lot of compassion, and devotion. But intimacy with another tends to exacerbate every insecurity we suffer (not one of us seems to escape this!) as it pushes up against two immense fears: that of rejection and that of being alone. Relational interactions and sexual intimacy surely confront both. So important are our intimate, significant partner relationships that when they're not doing well, we don't do well either.

When our communication skills are not developed, our relationships suffer. When our self-intimacy skills are not developed, our relationships inadvertently suffer. And when our sexual self is not developed, our intimate, more sensuous relationships suffer.

Exploring this rather new application of the Enneagram, it is my wish to open us up to communicate the harder-to-communicate sensitivities between us— particularly those issues relating to sex, deepening connection, and sensuality.

It is my hope to see the Enneagram's incisive grasp on our fundamental core beliefs—and how they condition us—alongside our focuses of attention be applied to freeing us up to connect more, feel more, and express more.

I believe that by using the Enneagram to peer into ourselves that we're gifted the best possible chance to share our greater vulnerabilities as they no doubt put us face-to-face with some of our greater relational fears. And I hope to help us expand our sensitivity to each other's sexual experience and gain further compassion for one another in a way that supports these tender objectives. As a result, may we come to attain deeper connections and deeper intimacy—emotional, sexual, all the way to spiritual—with one another.

Sexuality: Enrichments and Diminishments Expressed by Each of the Nine Types

I have come to understand that each Enneagram type's unique core beliefs, neural propensities, focus of attention and way of relating to the world greatly show up everywhere, even in sexual experience. Each type's innate qualities catalyze enrichments or stir up diminishments. The ways each of the nine type structures addresses sexuality—respective desires and struggles—open our hearts and minds to our much-shared commonalities as well as to our unique and powerful differentiations.

There is so much to learn from each other—from each Enneagram type. This learning can lead us to new ways of stepping up and better supporting one another's sexual selves and experience, and to do so when facing this most tender part of our lives. This is where non-judgmental, openhearted, loving support is most needed, but is what we so often *don't ask for*. This is where we don't share ourselves so freely, don't venture to request, and where we may protect ourselves most from the possibility of rejection.

Enhanced sexuality and sexual expression ask that we infuse the sexual relationship with presence and receptiveness. It is presence and our commitment to cultivating it during lovemaking that opens us up to our sexual-relational development. To know our true nature beyond just the physical brings forth our wholeness. When our intimate inner life meets with the physical and meets with presence, the body activates the spirit and its expression. Sexuality that is infused with spirit is felt differently than when not—it is felt with love.

"Love is the capacity to 'become one with,'" says author David Deida in his book, *Enlightened Sex, Finding Freedom and Fullness Through Sexual Union.*

Spirit is what infuses our physical being with light, with a vibrational frequency that fills us with feelings of connection, of oneness.

Feelings of separation that occur at any given time in our lives is not the experience of love, but that of "un-love"—the absence of love. Deida goes on to say that when our sexuality is infused with love, when it is sensuous and "one with" another, we have accessed the capacity for sexual-spiritual union.

In preparing for this book, I worked closely with individuals of the nine Enneagram types. I explored their ideas and struggles with love, partnering, and sexual expression. Included herein are each type's own words as they discussed their sexual experiences, covering both diminishments and enrichments. All of these disclosing exemplars have considerable life experience and are well versed in the Enneagram as well. I'd like to express deep gratitude to Rochelle Wald, for much of the descriptive material shared that follows is based on her groundbreaking thesis, "The Enneagram Types: Nine Style of Expressing Sexuality."

In the overview for each Enneagram type, we focus on the nature of the type's essential qualities, how these go into the background with personality development, and how they can eventually be reintegrated back into our character structures and our expression of our lives, through practice.

These vital integration practices actually return us to unity, where our developed personality and our essential qualities can be interwoven into one cognitive-emotional fabric. These practices are intimacy-building and very important as they challenge us to loving better and living more fully.

The fundamentals of these practices can profoundly influence all vital relationships. It is not necessary to know your Enneagram type to participate. Take the time to reflect on each Enneagram type presented, as each will expand our understanding, acceptance, and appreciation of others as well as of ourselves.

In the upcoming sections on each type, allow yourself five or so minutes to reflect on how this particular aspect of this type's structure affects intimacy, including its sexuality and its higher essential qualities. This can be done in silence on your own or with a partner. If with a partner, consider taking a few additional minutes from an openhearted, non-judgmental, self-accepting stance to share your experience and thoughts with one another.

Type 1 | The Perfectionist | Sexual Fulfillment

Overview and Ultimate Fulfillment for Type 1

Recall that as Perfectionists, we believe that to assure our lovability, self-worth (dignity), and security in the world, we must be good and right, according to the mandates of the judging mind. We cannot be found to be wrong or bad in a world that we experience harshly judges and condemns us.

In the process of personality formation, what goes into the background is the original, undivided oneness of all that is at the core of our being; it's what's rightfully within when we are free of judgmentalness. This gets experienced in the body as a serene and calm abiding, coupled with an appreciation of each of our many unique and valuable differences. In this state, we experience the virtue of serenity.

Also going into the background is the preciousness of our idealism, unrestricted and uninhibited personal expression, and our ability to be in the undivided, accepting state of oneness in the moment. These qualities would have naturally enriched both our sensuousness as well as our sexual experience because of our proclivity toward intensity and passion, stemming from our deep commitment to be the strived-for best self we can be.

When fully present during intimacy, our heart opens with unconditional goodness, joy, and a felt-sense of the sacred. Herein lies utter self- and other-acceptance, a blissful dignity, and our unquestioned sense of self-worth.

As young children, our **Type 1 temperament was innately imbued with "rhythmicity, regularity, and predictability"** over time. A higher expression of sensuous sexuality, however, becomes muted when judgments of the critical mind affect and impact—interfere with—the sensual-sexual experience. Not having the "right" conditions or appearance can diminish our sensual experience. There's often a theme of restriction and a suppression of desire/arousal.

Our Type 1 anger—often in the form of tension, irritation, and compressed resentments—interferes with sensual-sexual responsiveness as well as formulates negative self-comparisons and feelings of unworthiness, shame, and guilt, all of which are powerful deterrents. Moreover, the Type 1's partner may need to be perfect in some particular way. Many "shoulds" can adversely influence responsiveness, arousal, and desire. Judging the partner as well as the self also occurs since the partner too must strive to improve and meet the idealistic standards of our Type 1's critical-judging mind.

Lastly, some Type 1s will have formed an internal standard that dictates that sexual expression "is good," in which case, it can also be fodder for judgmentalness. As this standard unfolds, it leads to judgmental assessments, as in, one may conclude that the partner is just not sexual enough, one way or another. Judgments of this nature, of any nature for that matter, can adversely affect sexual expression and sexual experience and the connection felt and allowed with another. Judgmentalness is separating and inhibits the possibility of experiencing oneness, full stop.

What Type 1s Have to Say about Their Sexual Diminishments

On Being Correct and Right and Dominated by the Judging Mind

Sue puts the need for "right" sex this way: "For me it used to be, am I doing this [sex] right? Is this the right thing to do? I feared making a mistake in touching the 'wrong place' in the wrong way. I needed to be washed and clean to have sex."

According to **Tom**, "Before awakening, I thought that a desirable sexual partner would be 'perfect' in every way. This preoccupation made fantasy and media-saturated sexual images more desirable than someone more available. I even had periods of sexual inactivity, resulting from my perceived need for perfection."

Arnold reports needing to be correct as, "At a younger age, I thought it was bad to be sexually excited. Some older friends wanted to teach me to masturbate. I went away thinking it was not right to fondle one's penis—to be sexually aroused was already sinful enough."

And **Martha** expresses correctness and its limiting expression as follows: "My fantasies used to be about perfection, having a freshly bathed body and crisp laundered linen. My partner needed to be well mannered, well dressed, and physically exquisite. And so would I. I wanted every detail to be right and even small flaws would put me off. Now I shudder when I realize how limiting this was."

On the Driving Emotions of Anger, Shame, and Guilt

Molly expresses, "My tremendous, suppressed anger toward my partner came out as a total lack of desire for sex with him."

Ross puts the anger over his partner's bad behavior this way: "I would feel angry at myself for not being good enough in bed, and then shameful about having sexual feelings for other women. I got angry with my wife because she remained overweight; she was no longer slim and attractive. I would become aware of bodily tension felt in my head, neck, shoulders, and arms. This tension resulted from anger that I had internalized. Thanks much for the Enneagram, which provided understandings that so helped my release."

Ruth's anger was turned inward, "I feared penetration; I would contract, experience pain, and then berate myself for being such an inadequate spouse. This took all the joy out of lovemaking."

And about her criticalness, **Heidi** says, "With sex, I lived by the injunction that 'I would rather be right than happy.' How stupid of me."

On the Underlying Deepest Concerns: Being Wrong and Unworthy of Love

Lynn says, "Feeling unworthy was the basis for accepting less than I would have hoped for. I wanted the whole sexuality issue to die completely so I could relate mind-to-mind and heart-to-heart, without the indignity of physical fumblings."

Gale states her past deepest concern as this: "My naked body gave me huge feelings of worthlessness. In the past, with boyfriends, I was never able to stand in front of them nude with the lights on."

And **Thomas** puts unworthiness this way: "Before the Enneagram, I seemed to have failed in my attempt to have a close, intimate, and sexually fulfilling relationship with my wife."

Doug expresses the core concern of unworthiness this way: "Argh! That truly was my worst fear, that underneath everything, I am unworthy—I don't deserve to have a sexually fulfilling relationship. Guilt and shame were the main fuels for this fire."

***

In all of these instances, we have the chance to grasp the powerful impact of type on the expression of intimacy and sexual experience.

> Take a few minutes to reflect on how Type 1s diminish sensuous/sexual experience and interfere with the integration of their higher qualities of being into their sexual experience, and their lives in general.

Path of Development for Type 1

For Type 1, the path of development involves becoming receptive, accepting, and self-aware. The need to relax the judging mind is paramount. Type 1 does have the innate capacity to reflect, strive for, and exemplify "perfection" in and for all that is, as is, in the present moment. This is often experienced as an undivided state of oneness, a kind of bliss.

Gentleness and permission being given from the partner facilitates the process along with giving oneself an aesthetically pleasing environment. Most importantly, the path for Type 1 encompasses the experience of accepting ourselves as we are and, ultimately, allowing the expansion into serenity that comes from accepting our sensuousness as it is, as it spontaneously wants to express itself, and without comparison to other experiences or idealized standards or situations.

A Type 1's path is the path of acceptance. And that acceptance must be permitted without judgmentalness or conditions; allow without censorship the natural ups and downs of intimacy, and of sexual experience. Allow it to unfold spontaneously—be it messy, silly, engaging, as uninhibited and as raw as it will. The path for Type 1 serves to create and allow delight, arousing pleasure, connection, sensuousness, and a deeply loving and freed-up sexuality.

> Take a few minutes to reflect on and absorb what Type 1s need to develop within themselves in order to allow fulfilling intimate relationships, including unconditional acceptance that leads to **the higher quality of serenity**.

What 1s Have to Say about Sexual Experiences on the Path to Fulfillment

Betty expresses the path as follows: "When I feel confident with my lover, I can let go completely and lose myself in the sex act—then the commentary in my head fades and 'correctness' does not matter!"

Arthur puts fulfillment this way: "As I follow my breath, I am able to thank God for the desire to become sexual, knowing that through my being sexual, I can relate with others and be intimate with them."

Arlene says, "To me, serenity is a cessation of putting conditions on the nature of my experience. I can allow orgasm to flow through me and accept the joy without placing conditions on it. I now can recognize and accept my own body's physical needs and responses to stimulation. I am free to respond or actually take the lead when I am in serenity without judgment. I forget that my belly is soft and I am getting wrinkles. There is no separation of self and body."

Matt puts the path this way: "As I follow my breath, I am able to thank God for the gift of my sexuality, knowing that through my sexuality, I can relate more fully with my partner in an intimate way. I share my ideals and my joys and pains. I'm much more present thanks to understanding the power of sensuous presence."

***

You can see in these responses just how deep and rich sexually intimate experiences can be when we are fully present, non-condemning, self- and other-accepting, and in a state of openhearted lovingkindness.

> Take a few minutes to reflect on how Type 1s have expressed how they enhance their sensuous/sexual experience and how they can foster the integration of their higher qualities of being into their sexual experience, and their lives in general.

David's Work with Type 1 | The Perfectionist

David's commentary: It often gets assumed that Type 1 struggles with many inhibitions and restrictions when it comes to sexual expression. However, the content of their internal standards can vary across the entire spectrum of what is desirable and acceptable to a given Type 1. Here we have an example of a family where the bodily expression of love is the standard by which to live.

Sandra: I know I'm a Type 1 because I'm always making things perfect.

David: How do you know when something is perfect?

Sandra [with precision]: I feel resentful when things aren't right. I can just tell the way things ought to be. Well, that is until I discovered the Enneagram and learned that there are many different right ways to do and see things. This took quite a lot of work with myself, especially with my anger, to realize that my way was just one right way. At first, I didn't even know I was angry. Now I go, "Oh, there's my anger again!" So often these days, I can just breathe deeply and let go, realizing that this is just my old stuff.

David [with warmth]: So, I want to go now to what is love for you as a Type 1?

Sandra: For me, love is something very huge in my life. It's a bodily, very physical experience. It is strong, big, and joyful. It means caring for both myself and for another. In my family, that was expected. I would wonder what was wrong with other families.

David: Your expression of love and its bodily expression sound delightful. So, when it comes to the physical expression of love, what is that for you?

Sandra [stated quite clearly]: Now I love sex. It is a huge expression for me. I love to play. I love to dance. I'm a dancer. I've always known that sex is OK. I enjoy it. I let my sensual self come out.

David [said with a bit of surprise]: Delight in sex combined with love can make life wonderful! Some Type 1s have an internal standard that says that sex is really OK, important. Many 1s, however, have powerful injunctions regarding sexual expression. So, what would you say are your sexual diminishments?

Sandra: Having too much to do and too many things to get right can take me away from being present to my husband. I would feel there just wasn't time for sex, or we would hurry through it.

David [said gently but emphatically]: When we're too busy, it can take away from the experience, from our delicate and even divine sensuousness, which being fully present really allows. Slowing down and taking time really allows us to get receptive. Notice how your attention can go to what work or duties await you, what you feel needs to be done. Then, taking some slow breaths, you can allow yourself to come back to just being present to your gentle, more tender feelings of sensuousness. This lets all of us expand the joy, not just Type 1s, but all of us. Thank you, Sandra.

> Take a few minutes to reflect on how this example of Type 1 illustrates the work we need to do to increase our developmental well-being on the path to wholeness.

Type 2 | The Giver | Sexual Fulfillment

Overview and Ultimate Fulfillment

Recall that as a Giver, we believe that to assure our lovability, self-worth (dignity), and security in the world, we must give perpetually to others in order to have our own needs met, and we cannot be deemed totally useless in a world that we experience mainly rewards generosity and being at the service of others.

In the process of personality formation, what goes into the background is our fundamental freedom to be in the state of innocent, heartfelt and unrestricted giving, receiving, and responsiveness—termed humility. Humility naturally enriches the sensual/sexual experience through a shared awareness, reciprocity, and the gift of receiving equal to the gift of giving, which ultimately is what becomes the joy in fulfilling union.

In the state of presence and humility, as a Type 2 we experience openheartedness toward self and others and a genuine connectedness that supports both the self and the partner. As both of us feel appreciated, gratitude flows through us both, without the superiority or the immodesty often associated with prideful giving. These higher expressions of sensuous sexuality become adversely impacted by the Type 2's focus on the pleasures and needs of others and by the concurrent difficulty knowing what gives the self pleasure and satisfaction.

As young children, **the Type 2's temperament showed a "positive approach-response to new stimuli, a 'socially contactful' style to being received by others."** Since 2s so need the partner to be satisfied, they automatically monitor the thoughts and feelings of the partner and may not experience their own actual sensualness or arousal. This other-referenced focus of attention and energy often result in the experience and manifestation of "I don't even have needs."

Partly because 2s are so intently tuned in to their partner's very different needs and desires, the range of experience for 2s can be quite variable. Additionally, because it's now outside of their awareness, 2s do have desires and needs, but they go undetected and unexpressed. They can become emotional, clingy, and paradoxically demanding of attention and appreciation when their needs go too long without being recognized.

This orientation of not wanting to be self-referenced, because of the repression of their own needs, then leads to sensual/sexual diminishment for both, and the potential for resentment.

What 2s Have to Say about Their Sexual Diminishments

On Focusing Attention on the Other's Needs and Desires

Rachael says, "In the past, it was never that I could say no to a partner who wants intercourse. I got pleasure from pleasing the partner, much more than receiving."

Likewise, **Anna** states this outward focus on others as, "I had difficulty enjoying my own sexual experiences as my mind was too much focused on the other. It was even hard for me to know what gives me pleasure and, especially, how to ask for it?"

Oliver puts it this way: "Before I embraced the Enneagram's understandings, I got sexual gratification both alone and with my wife when I imagined that I was giving her great pleasure so that I could have enjoyment too."

Sophia reports, "My attention went to my partner. I enticed him, but I almost never initiated sex. Sexual feelings were in my lower body, and love filled my heart center. I could be very loving during sex; however, because of my focus on him, I was not really experiencing my own sexual arousal."

And for **Kristine**, this focus on others' needs and desires meant, "I felt turned on by turning my partner on, by pleasing him. I needed him to be turned on for me to feel turned on, to feel sexy and desirable. Without him losing himself in the experience, it became difficult to relax into and receive pleasure for myself."

On the Driving Feelings of Being Prideful and Indispensable

Says **Mia**: "When I was younger, I felt I was indispensable as a sexual partner. I was likely to be willing because I cared about being loved and included."

About the theme of pride **William** declares, "I felt that I knew it all and I was able to provide what was needed and wanted. I just knew how to make the other feel good, drive her crazy, and be the best at satisfying."

Robb puts pride this way: "I am still attending to all of their sexual needs—but also to how much I'm needed; how much they can't do without me. I'm feeling 'all full up' with how good a job I'm doing giving my love, my goodness."

For **Judy** the power of pride got expressed this way: "I just knew that I'm the cause of my partner's happiness and that my actions were bringing him to the point of ecstasy and that he could not achieve it on his own. What pride."

On the Underlying Deepest Concern: Being Useless to Others, and Dispensable

Roseanne expresses this theme like this: "For the first 10 years of my marriage, I would never have refused sex—didn't even know this was an option. I could allay my worst fear of being dispensable by being desired. When I feared being worthless, I would initiate sex to waylay the fear."

Jennifer states this concern about being useless as, "I felt when I was young that I wouldn't be included, or worse, I'd be rejected if I didn't fulfill the sexual pleasures of my partner."

Roger says, "I liked the belief that no one could be as satisfied as they were with me. There's some sadness that I'm dispensable, but believing I was indispensable created a lot of obligations. I would stay in relationships that weren't what I really wanted."

And **Nancy** puts her former concern as, "I feared being dispensable, which encouraged me too often to be in my imagination with sexual fantasy. It was safer as I worried about not satisfying my partner. I imagined that I was wanted for all that I do and give."

***

Here again in all of these themes/issues, type structure powerfully influences and limits sexual expression and intimacy in general.

> Take a few minutes to reflect on how Type 2 diminishes sensuous/sexual experience, thus interfering with the integration of their higher qualities into their sexual experience, and their lives in general.

Path of Development for Type 2

For 2s, this involves noticing their active, even intrusive, energy and slowing the pace of this active energy. Type 2s need to become more grounded in self, becoming receptive to themselves, which will foster an awareness of this tendency.

Directing attention inward as well as outward, and then over time, allowing the reciprocal flow of giving and receiving to occur, with grace and love. This generates the development of sensuousness along with the experience of humility, the quality of modesty that comes with the freedom felt when giving and receiving without conditions.

It helps 2s to be in a calm, receptive, and aesthetically pleasing state in order to share (not only give) in the delights of sensuousness and loving, caring sexuality. Because of a Type 2's concerns with dispensability, at first this state can create varying degrees of anxiety that need relaxing.

> Take a few minutes to reflect on and absorb what Type 2 needs to develop in order to have a fulfilling intimate relationship that integrates **the higher quality of humility**. This means, the capacity to allow an unconditional flow of both giving and receiving, that which is shared with one another.

What 2s Have to Say about Sexual Experiences on the Path to Fulfillment

Jennifer says, "I learned that humility is a receptive state that truly allows me to be touched. So, when I'm in that state, I can be honest about my needs. I can take risks. There is also the experience of not having to carry the whole thing. The quality of the sexual encounter is about how it unfolds between the two of us rather than my responsibility to make sure it goes well. I have more freedom of expression because I'm not tied to the outcome. I find that now as I'm more able to verbalize my own needs this actually is a turn-on."

Gale states, "Now after 20 years of marriage and being nearly 45 years old and having worked with my type, I feel much greater freedom to show up authentically. I can ask for sex or deny it. I can fantasize or not."

Berry puts the path to fulfillment this way: "Now, I honestly am not finding it difficult to say what I want in a sexual-pleasure sense. This way, I am both giving and receiving freely. This is what I want most of all. This in not pride speaking, it is for me a genuine desire to freely give and receive."

And **Kim** says, "When I move into humility, I can talk about my thoughts and fantasies. I am far more available for intimacy and my husband feels safer, closer to me. Control of feelings has dissolved, and I am my body and my climax, beautiful high energy in my body leads to multi- climaxes, then to peace, gratitude, and love flows."

***

We, as in all of the Enneagram types, need to realize how universal the flow of giving and receiving actually is and how the impairment of this flow diminishes intimacy experience in all of us, not just in Type 2.

> Take a few minutes to reflect on and absorb how Type 2 enhances their sensuous/sexual experience, thus, fostering the integration of their higher qualities of being into their sexual experience, and their lives in general.

David's Work with Type 2 | The Giver

David's commentary: Here is a heartfelt example of doing the work of becoming whole, of personal integration. Richard, a young man in his 20s, expresses the path for Type 2 as discovering his own needs and desires and in the process, finding himself on the road to more organic, unconditional giving and receiving, to himself as well as to others—both of which are gifts. This level of development is inspiring.

Richard: I know I'm a Type 2 because I'm helping, and helping is a way to be. To be honest with you, that's it!

David [smiling]: That's concise. So then, what is love to you?

Richard: To be with somebody and to just be appreciated.

David: Say a little more; what does being appreciated mean to you?

Richard: It is the longing for connection. To be appreciated for who I am so that I don't have to explain myself or even, I won't have to keep doing more to feel accepted.

I'm always helping people in terms of asking, "How are you?" or "How can I make you smile today?" I'm really there for the other and I expect that back too, I really do. But I don't want to say that every time. I want this back with my wife though.

David *[with concern]: That is treacherous territory because she doesn't think the way you do as a Type 2. She may love you deeply but doesn't operate from the same habit of mind. While as a Type 2, you go out of your way to notice what another needs; others won't necessarily be doing that for you. You may need to tell her what you want and need.*

Richard *[laughing]: I may need a course in how to ask the right questions!*

David *[lightly yet emphatically]: She may need to take your course and you hers. But seriously, true love is being in a natural flow of giving and receiving, which is an unconditional flow. It's a process where both shows up willfully and within their own volition, with their own freewill. It goes beyond any course that has us trying to ask the right questions, as useful as that can be.*

Richard *[speaking seriously]: What stops me is not knowing myself. To me, sex was always something difficult because I was giving something that I hadn't given myself, but I didn't know it at the time. So, to really make sex not a "doing for someone else," thing by slowing down and just being present—I didn't have any grasp of that.*

David*: Yes, it means being there "for you." You have never put attention there. You beautifully describe the path; I can just sense your depth of understanding. The key theme for you is to have your heart actually opening to yourself. This means, continuing to practice. Come back to your own feelings, sensations, and desires every time you practice. So, while you are waking up to this, what can be the difficulties in your sexual expression?*

Richard *[said tenderly, kindly]: I thought and was often confused, is there something wrong with me or with her? The answer is that I was missing being there for myself. [pauses] Now I'm finding me from the inside, which is different.*

David *[said warmly with a few tears]: Process is the path for all of us. You are on the path and that is a gift you are giving yourself. It is very moving. Thank you, Richard.*

Take a few minutes to reflect on and absorb how this example of Type 2 illustrates the work of development on the path to wholeness.

Type 3 | The Performer | Sexual Fulfillment

Overview and Ultimate Fulfillment

Recall that as Performers, we believe that to assure our lovability, self-worth (dignity), and security in the world, we must accomplish and succeed and not be totally unable to do or accomplish. In other words, we must not be a failure in a world that we believe rewards what we accomplish and deems us valueless when not achieving.

In the process of personality formation, what goes into the background in Type 3 is our innate ability for a go-head sustained focus *and* the veracity of deep care, receptive presence, and a pace that is naturally-kind-to-self slower. We need to trust in the contribution of the other, which naturally enriches the sensuous/sexual experience. This all involves flow, or even alert stillness, beyond self-conscientiousness and effort.

In a state of presence during intimacy, there is an inner knowing that love stems from the qualities of being, with a heartfelt care for both self and partner. In the process, being and doing harmoniously blend together as do feelings and action.

As young children, **Type 3s' temperament displays "high activity levels in the motor sphere," which readily busies them**, taking 3s away from their more authentic feelings and more personal and true-to-themselves interior terrain. Non-consciously, sensual/sexual activity is about success, competing and winning, e.g., "I can do that or be that or get that," and by demonstrating competence.

Worse yet, Type 3s may even avoid sexual activity, fearing incompetence, especially since a feeling of shame can accompany any sense of incompetence. Therefore, sex could even be felt as nothing of value without performance as the goal. At the very least, ambivalence occurs around the honest expression of one's non-image-consistent true feelings and when taking more time to slow the pace.

For a Type 3, higher expressions of sensuous sexuality become adversely affected by the fast pace, focus on performance, and the concern with maintaining a good image in the partner's eyes. When these occur, Type 3s' sexual experience diminishes as they can begin to "perform" in the bedroom rather than "be" with the experience of it.

Type 3s can get absorbed in tasks or self-images, and as a result, experience difficulty getting to their own feelings and sometimes their bodily/somatic experiences. Even orgasm can become a goal-directed activity.

What 3s Have to Say about Their Sexual Diminishments

On Being Competent and Successful While Maintaining a Good Image

Before working with the Enneagram, **Carla** said this about performance: "I tended to see a relationship as a job to be worked at and controlled. My feelings could be far from my awareness. My thoughts were along the line of, 'How am I being perceived?'"

As **Chip** puts it: "I used to be more focused on my sexual performance and orgasm than on all else."

Robin sums it up this way: "My tasks and goals typically got in the way of good sex. Sex was just another thing to do."

And **Russ** simply states his preoccupation with success as, "In my younger, days, I would set goals around pleasing my partner. I did not feel much because I was so connected to outcomes and my partner's experience, and, yes, to my image too."

On the Driving, Go-Ahead Impulse that Leads to Deceiving the Self about One's True Feelings

Wendy exemplifies this preoccupation as this: "In the past, my self-deception would show itself as I would compete to win a man by being attractive; the goal would be to get him in bed. I would perform to please my partner. I was not connected to my bodily feelings."

Kirby puts former self-deception associated with the go-ahead energy this way: "I was an incorrigible flirt! I loved women and I loved sex and would synchronize myself with a woman's personality to be attractive to her, with the goal of having sex. My feelings mattered little."

For **Doreen** sex was as follows: "Me often being in a role with my sexuality, performing in a way I thought was expected, watching myself through the eyes of the other person with my feelings suspended."

And **Nan** simply puts it this way: "I have trouble knowing what I'm feeling during sex."

On the Underlying Deepest Concerns: Incompetence and Failure

About this, **Julie** says, "If I did not attain the goal of making my partner feel great, I would feel shame and that my image was tarnished. Sadly, I would cut off this partner and might never see him again because of my fear of failure."

Similarly, regarding the incompetence theme, **Madeline** says, "I used to project an image of being sexy and together, but in reality, I feared I was not a competent lover. I feared that I would disappoint in bed and be rejected."

Edward puts it this way: "Before the Enneagram understandings, I had a deep fear of not being attractive to women in the future, as I age. Getting older and wrinkled is very scary and depressing. Being unattractive to women was like death."

And **Quinn** succinctly says, "Failure means being impotent and losing sexual desire."

***

In each of these descriptions, concerning the diminishments associated with type, the powerful restriction type has upon intimacy and sexual experience is evident. These Type 3 examples show how vital presence is to self and other, regardless of type.

> Take a few minutes to reflect on how Type 3 diminishes their sensuous/sexual experience and interferes with the integration of their higher qualities into their sexual experience, and their lives in general.

Path of Development for Type 3

For 3s, this involves becoming receptive and aware. This process also involves slowing the pace and allowing in the natural flow of energy beyond active effort and a destination. This means knowing that the fast, go-ahead energy will always be there when needed. And this means releasing concerns about inadequacies that may arise. Once "here," the natural range of feelings occurs, all of which are simply part of the flow of life along with the deep, natural care about doing well—both of which enrich the sensual/sexual experience.

In the process of relaxing into just being present to self and other, the experience of being appreciated and loved, separate from doing and accomplishing, occurs. Then Type 3s come to realize that love really is felt deeply for the qualities of being, not solely for the outcomes of doing, as in worldly accomplishments.

> Take a few minutes to reflect on and absorb what Type 3 needs to develop in order to have a fulfilling intimate relationship that integrates the higher quality of truly being present to the self's heart-felt feelings and that of others. This quality is named **the higher quality of veracity**.

What 3s Have to Say about Sexual Experiences on the Path to Fulfillment

Madeline expresses the path this way: "I am working at being more honest and true within myself—not just performing sexually."

Van says, "I like to honestly know what my partner wants and will ask her what she likes best. When I'm being honest with myself with my own true feelings, I experience a deep inner contentment."

Elaine puts fulfillment this way: "Over time I have been able to own my pleasurable, sexual feelings and experiences—to acknowledge them to myself and my partner. We were among the first few thousand same-sex couples to be married."

Brittany states, "I now let go of tasks and goals and relax completely into being myself. I don't need to be on guard or anticipate any possible misunderstanding of what I do. I feel safe, loved, and cared for and also much more loving."

And **Monica** sums up the path this way: "I am working with being more honest within myself—not over-giving sexually just to have another success."

***

In these responses you can realize how deep and rich our intimate experience can be when we are not focused on performance and "successful sex" as an end-goal. For all of us, this means the realization that we are loved for being—not just for doing.

> Take a few minutes to reflect on and absorb how Type 3s enhance their sensuous/sexual experience by slowing their pace and, in the process, by fostering the integration of their higher qualities of being into their sexual experience, and their lives in general.

David's Work with Type 3 | The Performer

David's commentary: Here we experience how type structure often determines how we express ourselves in both love and sexual expression. The fast pace of Type 3 can be satisfying but can also leave one blind to deeper feelings and unavailable for true union with intimates. Furthermore, it is important with 3s to not make sexual enhancement another task to accomplish.

Jeanette: Well, what tells me I'm a Type 3 is that feelings make it hard to get things done. I get impatient with people who keep me from getting things accomplished. With the Enneagram, I learned that Type 3s' love language involves doing and accomplishing for their loved ones. This has always been true for me.

David: *Then, how does your Type 3 structure impact your expression of love?*

Jeanette *[with fast pace]: My husband is busy too. We do things for each other. We don't stop much. I support his work and he supports mine. We get a lot done and support each other's agendas and complement each other.*

David *[slowly]: The process for 3s is being able to expand your pace by also being able to slow it down, by breathing in fully and exhaling fully. Slow it down and just notice all of your active energy, which is a great thing; but it's not a great thing when you cannot access or express other energies within you. Allow more receptive energy, as both active and receptive energies are needed for life and for love. So, what are the enhancements and hindrances to a really satisfying physical relationship?*

Jeanette *[slowing her pace]: Well, I keep thinking even sex is something that has to be done. We enjoy each other physically, but I don't know if we are really fully there. He wants to go fast and that was always fine with me.*

David: *Well, you both care and going fast is fine too if that's what both wants. Still, the benefit for him in slowing your pace is that he will likely slow his pace and then you can both be present to your own deeper, more tender feelings during lovemaking. When we slow our pace, we can more fully open our hearts and feel ourselves and someone else too.*

Jeanette *[with intensity]: Yes, when we slow down, we appreciate each other more. I've always loved him. He is full of energy and has an adventuresome spirit.*

David *[said resolutely]: Remember, we can only be where we are, on our path, at any given time. Lovemaking isn't something to accomplish; it is something to simply be present to, with yourself and with your partner.*

> Take a few minutes to reflect on and absorb how this example of Type 3 illustrates the work of development on the path to wholeness.

Type 4 | The Romantic | Sexual Fulfillment

Overview and Ultimate Fulfillment

Recall that as Romantics, we believe that to assure our lovability, self-worth (dignity), and security in the world, we must be special, unique, and complete. We must not be deficient or flawed in a world that we experience will eventually abandon us because of it.

In the process of personality formation, what goes into the background is an appreciation of *what is* and our own authentic connection to it. This is what promotes a present-moment "as is" respect for ourselves as well as for others.

"As is" acceptance and respect naturally enrich the sensual/sexual experience through an unwavering and devoted presence, through an open heart to that of self and other, and through embracing the full spectrum of *what is as is*—what is real—here and now, with a deep and abiding gratitude.

Inner peace abounds when realizing that nothing of substance is really missing. This is what leads to inner equanimity. Equanimity means that we are neither above nor below, neither superior nor inferior. We are in balance and emotionally stabilized. During intimacy, we can return to our original, complete sense of connection, provided we are in the present moment, held reverently with all there is, and experiencing depth, beauty, and wholeness—with nothing of substance perceived missing and consequently, without suffering habitual disappointment.

Wanting *and expecting* enriched experiences all the time, however, diminish the higher expression of sensuous sexuality, as expectation can lead to disappointment, a lack of fulfillment, and a partner who may be left feeling as if they are failing or not enough.

Type 4s' early childhood temperament is observed as "labile quality of mood," meaning, there is much emotionally expressed behavior that is both positive and negative. This can magnify the experience of missing out on something special, or of being deprived or let down sexually, all the while also magnifying and romanticizing idealized sensual/sexual experience. All of this can leave actual sexual experience feeling flat and disappointing, resulting in devalued sensual experiences and furthering sexual diminishment.

Because attention goes to the ideal and to *what is not* present, we can miss what is there in the sexual experience. This stance is fueled by longing for what isn't but could be. Not wanting the experience to end also leads to diminishing the experience. Longing takes away from the here and now. There may also be a sense of being lacking or inadequate or worrying about being less than. Shame over what is insufficient in oneself also adversely affects our sexual experience and capacity for intimacy with another.

What 4s Have to Say about Their Sexual Diminishments

On Being the Ultimate Ideal While Focusing on What Is Missing, Disappointing, or Lacking from This Ideal

Haywood puts lack or deficiency this way: "In the past, I felt there was always another area of sexual behavior to explore, and I was missing out on some aspect of my sexuality by being monogamous. It left me feeling deprived, restricted, and confined."

Likewise, **Sue** says, "I used to romanticize sexual experiences to such a high degree that it sometimes left the real experience flat or boring. Masturbation could then be more fulfilling."

Zale expresses the same theme about what's missing as, "I read widely to understand the female body and female sexual responsiveness, out of both a curiosity and a desire to feel what a woman feels, which might be missing from my own experience!"

Ali expresses focus on what is missing as follows: "Before becoming aware, I used to fantasize about ideal sexual acts and was often disappointed. I like the intensity of sex and orgasm, but noticed what I didn't do and what they didn't do. It was never quite the right time."

And **Jana** says, "I focused on what was missing while with my partner—wanting a different position than he wanted, wanting to postpone orgasm to make it more delicious, but still feeling cheated when we did because it was all over too soon. I'm so grateful that I woke up to this. Now I focus more on what is and on just being present."

On the Driving Emotions of Longing and Envy

Hayward expresses longing this way: "Even now, I still want the kind of sex that I imagine other people have. I have a longing to belong with my partner sexually and feel inadequate when I'm not."

Sue puts it this way: "In the past, I longed for romantic lovemaking as in films. I envied women with beautiful bodies. I liked to have a partner who was away a lot. Then I could feel close without having to deal with the disappointment of feeling others had better sex than me."

Bert says, "Before I brought the Enneagram into my life, I never got as much sex as I desired. The longing and envy for more or different sexual partners virtually precluded any long-term monogamous relationship. I'm so grateful that that has changed thanks to the Enneagram."

And **Holly** sums it up this way: "Envy took me away from the here and now and sometimes still does. If I'm fantasizing about the sex being more passionate, I'm not in the experience. Envy can still enter my feelings about orgasm. If I don't have an intense one, I may long for one and feel slightly deprived."

On the Deepest Concerns: Being Deficient and Lacking

While **Sue** puts concern with deficiency this way: "I did not initiate sex because of this fear of deficiency and abandonment."

Says **Cynthia**, "I used to worry about not being the best sexual partner."

Jim says, "I used to have a number of fantasies about inadequacy, like needing to grow a larger penis and not being able to make a woman come continuously for ten minutes or more. How self-degrading those thoughts were."

Jason expresses, "I restrained my over-the-top sex drive for fear of rejection in society. Fortunately, I'm a decent-looking fellow. Otherwise, my deficiency feelings would be much worse."

And lastly, **Mary** puts the former fear of lacking this way: "In the past, if I was not the perfect lover, filling your every fantasy, want, and desire then you would see me as deficient. I would see me as deficient, and you would abandon me and I would abandon me. Put simply, why would you want my body with its stretch marks, baby belly, varicose veins, and aging? I am so delighted that all this has changed through allowing myself to focus on what's there, not what's missing or flawed."

***

In these areas of diminishments, we can experience how type structure can painfully and powerfully impact intimacy and the manifestation of love for oneself and for that of another.

> Take a few minutes to reflect on how Type 4 diminishes sensuous/sexual experience and interferes with the integration of their higher qualities of being into their sexual experience, and their lives in general.

Path of Development for Type 4

For 4s, development calls for becoming receptive and aware and then allowing in, simply, what is present in the moment, without judging what is lacking, disappointing, or deficient. Returning attention to *what is present*, rather than focusing on *what is missing*, paradoxically allows for sensuous experience to naturally deepen and expand, even into the experience that what is present *truly* is whole and complete, as is.

This encompasses the experience of being loved, as we are, perceived deficiencies and all, with gratitude and equanimity. This permits multifaceted feelings and the desire for a deep and authentic connection that will naturally enrich the sensuous/sexual experience, thanks to a heart that is open and satisfied and expressed as such for both self and other.

> Take a few minutes to reflect on and absorb what Type 4s need to develop in order to have a fulfilling intimate relationship that integrates **the higher quality of equanimity**, and an acceptance and appreciation for what is, as is.

What 4s Have to Say about Sexual Experiences on the Path to Fulfillment

For **Max** the path involves, "Having balance in my sex life combined with a strong sense of boundaries."

While **Gerald** puts development this way: "I allow myself to experience my feelings and fantasies regardless of where they go, but I observe them. This has helped me keep in balance because I value the authentic truth more than whether I like or don't like the truth. I would never want most of my fantasies to really happen."

Emily puts fulfillment this way: "I have learned to give equal attention to my partner's pleasure as to my own. I appreciate what we have, what is there in the present moment."

Mary expresses the path as, "I experience deep love and connectedness when I release the envy. I have learned to be neutral and in the here and now. I am unselfconscious about my body and enjoy the feeling of earthiness."

Mia sums up development as follows: "To not over-think or over-fantasize leads to excellent sexual experience and being present in the moment. When balanced, my natural sexual drive is stronger, more fulfilling, and flowing."

And **Joseph** states his path simply as, "My sense of balance and equanimity come in when I accept and love another, as they are."

***

As we reflect on this, let's do our best to realize how deep and rich our intimate experience can be when we are not lamenting over what is missing and lacking. Allow ourselves instead to feel that we are lovable and loved for who and what we are, as is, and we can express this to our partner as well.

Take a few minutes to reflect on and absorb how Type 4s enhance their sensuous/sexual experience, fostering the integration of their higher qualities into their sexual experience, and their lives in general.

David's Work with Type 4 | The Romantic

David's commentary: Here we experience the deep longing for the ultimate ideal that can dominate a Type 4's life and that can profoundly affect the ability to love freely as well as can affect their lovemaking experiences. In the process, this longing can take Type 4s away from what is present and positive. Katherine's awareness is ahead of her ability to keep her heart open to herself; she's still learning and allowing herself to be receptive to what is positive in the moment. This is her next step toward integration and wholeness.

Katherine: My 4-ness shows up as I always find something missing in my life. I'm always seeking something, longing for more of what I feel is important. It is my life story.

David: The sadness to me in Type 4 is not in the seeking of quality itself, which is lovely, but that you are never enough, others are not enough, and you don't appreciate all that you are, or that others are. So, tell me, what is love to you?

Katherine: A lot of energy goes into this seeking, getting disappointed, and never feeling enough. I once had a true love, but he left me [tears come up]. I have never found that love again.

David [with intensity]: This left you in a state of longing, which is core to your work of development. [pausing] Keep working on noticing this focus of attention—on what you feel is not enough, and let that be a reminder to go to what you appreciate in yourself and life instead.

Katherine: To me, it is just holding on to what is positive in both me and another person.

David: It means more than holding on, it means staying present to what is, not what isn't in either you or the other. There is even a definition of love that goes, "Love is appreciating differences."

Katherine: I need to feel that what he gives me is fine and there's not something better or more he should have done. It's so disappointing to the point I cannot enjoy what's there and being given, at all. I know I need to just hold on and stay present.

David: And paradoxically, truly loving and appreciating yourself, is what will allow you to truly love and appreciate another. What you are doing to another is what you are doing to yourself, deep within. This work goes beyond just holding on. This is the work of awareness. This is the work of self-acceptance. So, how does all this show up for when it comes to your sexual expression?

Katherine: I like to be truly there, present in the moment. All what you say about love for me is the same in my physical relationship with a partner. I just need to be there, appreciating what is and express it as a desire, though it's not an actuality. I find myself struggling.

David [with warmth and definiteness]: Can you notice how you express this as an idealization? This is an awareness of the mechanism you are using to engage with another. That is different than simply being there present in the moment with acceptance for self and other. You have much awareness, so much so, you can see how you are actually trying to cope. I urge you to use this to become aware of the deep longing that takes you away from what is present and real and there for you. Let that be the key to being kinder to yourself. Learning how to come back to what is there in your love life, and when lovemaking, that's real; this is your practice. I urge you to take some time to reflect on this work you have just done and absorb its developmental potential for you. Thank you, Katherine.

> Take a few minutes to reflect on and absorb how this example of Type 4 illustrates the work of development on the path to wholeness.

Type 5 | The Observer | Sexual Fulfillment

Overview and Ultimate Fulfillment

Recall that as an Observer, we believe that to assure our lovability, self-worth (dignity), and security in the world, we must become self-sufficient, independent, and knowledgeable and not be totally depleted of energy in a world we experience demands too much and/or gives too little.

In the process of personality formation, what goes into the background is our original calm-abiding presence, ability to freely give to the world, and to match the energy of others in such a way that we naturally enrich our own and others' energy and hence, our sensuous/sexual experience. This is made possible as we allow a free, unrestricted flow of energy between another and ourselves. From a grounded and centered self, and with an open heart, we—our partner and our self—can both give and receive attention and nurturance.

Being willing to be present to intimacy, the heart as well as the mind opens. This allows a flow of nurturance; consciousness is clear and illuminated. Inner knowing knows that the mind alone is not what savors direct experience, because the body and heart are where it's at. As we allow all centers of intelligence to participate, we are both connected as well as still separate, allowing us to blissfully and safely surrender to an energetic quality of non-attachment.

These higher expressions of sensuous sexuality, however, become affected by the protective detachment and retraction of Type 5, **as these are the young children whose temperament showed a "low threshold of responsiveness,"** meaning, they were very sensitive to external stimuli and needed little to react or express discomfort. These sensitivities are at the root of how detachment and retraction occur. Responsiveness and full experience are diminished when we, as Type 5s, escape into thought and consequently experience sex too mentally and even as too much effort. There is a splitting off of the Head Center from the body and heart, therefore limiting responsiveness and full-bodied presence.

As 5s, we may keep thoughts private. We do not always communicate fully as we are often "unwilling to share inner life." Concerns around depletion and feelings of inferiority can also diminish spontaneity.

Energy concerns may lead to the experience of limitation and then sometimes lead to the need for extra stimulation. Still, we can and do have the capacity to release into the physical and heartfelt experience of sensuousness, allowing our authentic urges and deep yearnings, despite the overwhelm protected by our ingrained hesitations.

What 5s Have to Say about Their Sexual Diminishments

On Being Private, Wary about Intrusion, and Detaching into the Mind

Evelyn expresses how privacy and wariness used to be as, "The sexual act did not involve 'me.' Sex to me was just a physical release."

For **Blake**, privacy in sex manifested this way: "Withholding my thoughts during and about our sexual experience, I had a lot of hesitancy and fear about suggesting something new. I was very protective about my feelings."

Connor puts it this way: "When too many problems, fears, and thoughts were running around in my head, it was hard to adequately drop into sexual feelings. Spontaneity was and sometimes still is hard."

For **Melinda**, detaching means, "Sex was a mental experience. Even now I must remind myself to stay in my body, breathe, and notice the tactile experiences. Formerly, the thought of sex would be much sexier than sex."

Nichole states her concerns about privacy and intrusion as, "The most emotionally satisfying sexual experiences are also the most private. I limit public displays of affection."

And succinctly put by **Evan**, "The most emotionally satisfying sexual experiences are still when we really can be alone together in our private world."

On the Driving Need to Pull Back, a Kind of Avarice for Time, Space, and Self-Containment

In **Pauline's** words: "In my past, I could be very selfish sexually. If I was not interested in having sex myself, I selfishly withheld myself and didn't even try very hard to let my body get aroused. It just seemed like too much work most of the time. Yet sometimes I could be greedy for my own orgasm and for him to be done so that I could retreat into myself."

Herb says, about the avarice of pulling back, "I like sex. I want sex. But I don't want to have to pay the price of giving up information about myself in conversations."

Molly puts past holding back this way: "I was unwilling to share my inner life. I never was completely open and vulnerable. It was easier to receive than to give massage and caresses, etc."

For **John**, this energy of pulling back manifested as, "Sex was my affair and I shared it when I felt like it. I didn't want to have sex with my partner because she expected it."

And **Tanya** simply expresses the self-containment theme as, "When I was angry or tired, I held back from my partner. I just wished to be left alone. But sometimes the urge for sexual expression would override other considerations."

On the Deepest Concerns: Being Depleted of Energy and Resources

Trudy expresses the former fear of depletion as, "I wanted sexual encounters to be meaningful experiences. So, I had to put what seemed like a great deal of energy into keeping my partner going. This could be really tiring. I feared being drained of energy."

For **Ed**, depletion is, "Before awareness and self-understanding, I just didn't have much energy for much sex. It made me feel like withdrawing to protect myself from depletion."

Jeanine says, "In the past, I feared having a lack of resources sexually. It's like there was just nothing there regardless of stimulus or loving attention from my partner. Even in orgasm, I experienced a sense of never being able to absorb enough pleasure or hold onto it long enough, even in the midst of ecstasy."

And **Herb** puts the depletion theme this way: "I feared not having the energy to please my partner, of being a poor lover. Then I would lose my spontaneity and desire. That was awful. Thanks to the Enneagram that has changed."

And for **Lori,** the concern with depletion sounds like this: "I wanted to meet my partner's desires and needs, but I feared not having enough energy to do this. Just these recurrent thoughts tended to drain me."

***

Here too for Type 5 we can experience how type structure can create painful and diminished sexual experience.

> Take a few minutes to reflect on how Type 5s diminish their sensuous/sexual experience and the integration of the higher qualities into their sexual experience, and their lives in general.

Path of Development for Type 5

For 5s, this involves becoming receptive and aware. This process also involves relaxing into connection and trusting the source of life energy. When the alleged "protective" energy of retraction occurs, it becomes vital to breathe fully, inhale and exhale, returning attention to the body and the heart and away from the mind. As a Type 5, we need to recognize the contraction-energy, especially as it's felt in the chest area; it used to serve a purpose, but now it seems more to actually drain us. This means we need to release the upper-body contraction and open the heart—allow it to receive and be impacted. This allows in an embodied experience of source energy.

Releasing that heartfelt contraction results in the experience of staying engaged and connected to the security and support systems that are real and that are a part of life. Love itself provides. Love can be, and is, a kind of vibrational nurturance for a Type 5's hungry mind. With love there's a sense of abundance, curiosity, and joy, all of which naturally enrich sensuous/sexual experience.

> Take a few minutes to reflect on and absorb what Type 5s need to develop in order to have a fulfilling intimate relationship that integrates **the higher quality of non-attachment**, which means allowing the free flow of vital, life-giving energy as it is being shared and readily available, without being consumed by the fear of being drained by it.

What 5s Have to Say about Sexual Experiences on the Path to Fulfillment

Richard states the path this way: "When I become relaxed, light-hearted, and humorous, I allow sex to take on an appropriate place in the universal scheme of things. Then my head, heart, and gut are in balance and are in pretty good tune."

For **Liz**, sex flourishes when, "I become unattached to outcome. Sex is more fun if orgasm is not a goal and when touch and exploration of our bodies in the here and now are the focus."

And **Timothy** expresses it this way: "Now being in the flow operates pretty well. This happens when I interrupt that tendency to pull back to protect myself. I just accept that what will be, will be, and I'm OK."

Daniela poignantly expresses the path to fulfillment this way: "Sex was such an effort, when I realized that my pulling back, contracting away even in the presence of desire was what actually drained me. Once I released into just being there in my body and heart with my loving partner, everything changed. What a joy."

For **Molly**, the fulfillment means, "Allowing myself to be in the flow of energy, just present in the moment with no attachment to outcome."

***

Here with Type 5, we can sense the release from the "protective" habit of mind into the flow of a natural, receptive presence with each other; note how this flow exemplifies the essential quality of non-attachment being integrated into the intimate experience.

> Take a few minutes to reflect on and absorb how Type 5s enhance their sensuous/sexual experience by fostering the integration of the higher qualities into their sexual experience, and their lives in general.

David's Work with Type 5 | The Observer

David's commentary: Here we can experience Holly's intellectual understanding and see her work at letting go of her retraction away from others that diminishes her love and sexual experience. When a Type 5 releases from the seemingly protective contraction and realizes that love and its physical expression nurture and not drain us, life energy can fully flow.

Holly: Well, I know I'm a Type 5 because I believe life is something that must be understood. I need to know things. I'm unable to live life just to live life. I first have to understand what to do before doing something.

David [with curiosity]: So, this means you believe that you need to observe and know first before engaging in a relationship, for instance?

Holly: Actually no. At least I think love means the opportunity to be myself with somebody else. And it means the opportunity for the other person to be himself or herself with me.

David: That's beautiful. Yet, it needs to be more than a good idea. So, when it comes to physical expression, how is that for you?

Holly [in a quiet voice]: It is a bit hard. It is hard accepting myself physically, to think I'm enough.

David: You know, when you go to a grocery story and see all the women's magazines displayed by the checkout stand, they all have feature articles about the secrets of sexual happiness. There can be a lot of pressure from these on all of us.

Holly: Well, I get stubborn. [laughs] I want the freedom to do what I value. I want to be me and when we have privacy and there are no disruptions, I can be very intense.

David: Given your Enneagram type, what have you found to be one or more of the diminishments in your sexual expression?

Holly: I have to be really into it. Let go of the detachment.

David [said emphatically]: Yes, true. It is not in the literature, but the greatest blind spot for Type 5 is how the seemingly protective detachment actually drains you of energy, can keep you from really being "in" the physical expression of lovemaking. Notice this in the felt-sense awareness of your body, usually it's in your chest, and let yourself know that you won't be drained. You can breathe fully, inhaling and exhaling, and release into the experience of abundance. You can even say, "May I allow myself to just be here in my body, heart, and mind." There is much evidence that the sexual experience is very nourishing to both partners.

Holly [with earnestness]: I know, I know, sometimes the contraction stops me. Thank you.

> Take a few minutes to reflect on and absorb how this example of Type 5 illustrates the work of development on the path to wholeness.

Type 6 | The Loyal Skeptic | Sexual Fulfillment

Overview and Ultimate Fulfillment

Recall that as Loyal Skeptics, we believe that to assure our lovability, self-worth (dignity), and security in the world, we must sustain ourselves, question what could go wrong, and gain certainty in a world we experience as hazardous and unpredictable; it's a world we just cannot trust. We must not be rendered totally helpless, dependent, or unable to cope in such a world.

In the process of personality formation, what goes into the background is our original, trustful presence and a flowing and easy-going openness, which can naturally enrich sensuous/sexual experience through uncompromised, trusting union, one that trusts in the self and another, which includes an openhearted groundedness and a presence in the body. In the presence of intimacy, we, as Type 6s, can hold ourselves in wakefulness and with courage, while free of doubt and uncertainty, experiencing the self and partner fully, safely, and powerfully, in the moment.

Faith abounds, bringing unwavering love and intimate touch to sexual union. However, these higher expressions of sensuous sexuality can get diminished due to our anxiety, uncertainty, doubt, and our tendency to magnify worst-case scenarios. This includes when a fear of betrayal, exposure, being taken advantage of or abandoned seizes us and gets amplified.

As young children, **our Type 6 temperament showed "attention span and persistence,"** meaning, sticking with and attending to, even in the face of obstacles. Simply put, it's a proclivity for rigorous vigilance. Because we 6s can have trouble trusting, sex can be used as reassurance and proof of the impact and influence we have on our partner, especially in the more counter-phobic 6 stance. Therefore, sex temporarily provides a sense of security and proof—evidence that we are impacting and affecting our partner, and that we are loved. While this can mitigate feelings of helplessness and dependency, genuine presence becomes muted.

We 6s often have concerns regarding hazards, such as pregnancy and sexually transmitted diseases. All these concerns may interfere with the ability to relax into a sensual/sexual experience and its expression.

What 6s Have to Say about Their Sexual Diminishments

On Not Being Dependent and Dealing with Hazards in a World You Just Can't Trust

A more fearful 6 such as **Sophia** expresses, "Before the Enneagram, I was afraid of becoming pregnant and of sexual diseases. So, I either avoided sex or I didn't much look forward to sex. But now that I have trust in myself and a trusting connection with my partner, I love sex."

And **Ella** says about trust, "I avoided sex until I felt trust, which hardly ever happened until I developed some faith in myself. With this trust in my own capacities, I can relax my vigilance and my response can be intensely sexual. I even play with the hazard element as an enhancement of sexual experience, like having sex on the beach."

It was hard for **Jim** to be sexual without being in control of the situation. He says, "I couldn't engage or even get excited if I didn't feel trust. I needed to have sex in a safe, comfortable place, because otherwise potential hazards distracted me, making it hard for me to focus and enjoy."

And **Madeline** says, "I worried about the risks, especially sexual disease, and before having a tubal ligation to prevent pregnancy. I'm still careful about safe sex, communicating risks, and getting annual checkups. But when I stopped worrying about hazards, I began to enjoy sex more and now take pleasure and give it too."

On the Driving Emotion of Fear and Its Associated Doubt

Carol simply puts it this way: "I always had thoughts and doubts about my ability to affect my partner sexually."

Serena expresses how fear influenced her sexuality, "I early on had this fear of being used and abandoned or betrayed if I didn't perform, enjoy, or wasn't sexy enough. Once I was in relationship, I still was terrified that he would leave because I trusted him with myself, my body, and my sexuality."

For **Charlie**, this inner fear manifested this way: "I did not easily initiate sex because I had a lot of doubt and uncertainty. I needed a lot of reassurance. If my partner was passive or undemonstrative, I imagined all the things that can go or were wrong. Made it really difficult."

Don, a more counter-phobic 6, differed this way and embraced the challenge. "I love sex with my partner of many years and can really romance her, turn her on, satisfy her and myself in the process. Feels very satisfying. I only worried about climaxing too soon and not satisfying her. This could really dampen the joy."

Similarly, **Ruby** says, "I could turn him on anytime, and before marriage, anyone I was with. I would really get going too, holding nothing back. This was and still is so reassuring. I was a proof-junkie, so to speak. And to some degree, I still am."

On the Deepest Concerns: Being Dependent and Unable to Cope

Here, experiences reveal this fear and ways of coping to overcome it. For example, **Carol** says, "When I was younger, I doubted my abilities to satisfy my partner sexually. I was unable to really relax and enjoy sex until I learned to masturbate. Then I felt safe enough to experience the physical sensations and learn about my body and sexuality."

For **Pat**, the deepest concern before awakening was, "To be feeling boring sexually. So, I gave him more sex than I would personally need, fearing my husband would be unsatisfied, even though our agreement has always been to have sexual mutuality. One way to overcome the fear is to embrace it."

Virginia puts it this way: "A recurring fantasy for me was of being bound and helpless. Feeling helpless while still trusting my partner is thrilling."

Ruby expresses more of the counter-phobic style, "I've always just sensed what my partner wants and I could satisfy him."

Likewise, **Donald** says, "When I got older and despite a lot of desire and a history of confidence, I started to fear losing my erection. This could consume me until I let myself relax into trusting whatever the outcome would be with my loving partner."

***

Here, type concerns and issues clearly impact the sexual experience, and in the process, diminish it. With development, these deep concerns abate, allowing more presence and pleasure.

> Take a few minutes to reflect on how a Type 6 diminishes sensuous/sexual experience and interferes with the integration of the higher qualities into their sexual experience, and their lives in general.

Path of Development for Type 6

For 6s, this involves becoming receptive and aware, noticing when fear and anxiety arise about a variety of hazards, such as pregnancy, venereal disease, and being taken advantage of. When this shows up, breathe fully, inhale and exhale, and allow a sense of trust to fill the body, beyond getting proof or certainty.

This trust in self and others, before and beyond getting proof, depends upon the power of receptive energy. "May I just trust in myself and the other." This also means not testing the other's love and care for us with questions, accusations, or challenges. Finally, all of this encompass the experience of being trustworthy, assured, and confident in the love-enduring and flourishing that accompanies a trust in self, another, and the universe.

Most all 6s have had times of trust and confidence in some aspects of life. The felt-sense of these experiences can be recalled with faith and courage and can be activated at will to enhance sexual experience.

> Take a few minutes to reflect on and absorb what a Type 6 needs to develop in order to have a fulfilling intimate relationship that integrates **the higher quality of courage** (to surrender control and the need for certainty) and step fully into the experience with a trust in oneself and others.

What 6s Have to Say about Sexual Experiences on the Path to Fulfillment

For **Jim**, this integration of faith into sexual experience is expressed this way: "As I have connected to faith and courage, I've become a much better lover. Now I can be present to my partner and myself in the moment and even fully open to long, slow, exquisite lovemaking."

For **Donald** this means, "Being so present that I release from all cognition and concerns. Sometimes orgasm together is even a spiritual experience of loving oneness between us. Then I need to not try to repeat this rapturous experience, just allow it."

Counter-phobic **Ruby** voices faith this way: "When I realized there was much ego reassurance in my active sex life, I let go and allowed myself to be much more receptive. At first, my underlying fear of being taken advantage of appeared. As I released from this, I experienced my whole body, skin and bone and muscle, not just genitally. And I am truly there for both of us."

For **Rose,** faith is, "The courage to go along with my husband's fantasies—like making love in the open countryside—has been important."

For **Hailey** courage sound like this: "I ask for what I want and share my worst fears. This new trust is transforming."

And **Carole** says, "Courage is the move through fear, first by trusting and then allowing, and then it's just about being present. "I feel irresistible."

***

In reflecting on the path to fulfillment for Type 6s, notice how transforming the integration of the essential qualities of courage, along with trust and faith, truly is and can be.

> Take a few minutes to reflect on and absorb how a Type 6 can enhance their sensuous/ sexual experience and foster the integration of the higher qualities of being into their sexual experience, and their lives in general.

David's Work with Type 6 | The Loyal Skeptic

David's commentary: Type 6s can lean toward a more phobic (fearful) stance or a more counter-phobic (against fear) stance. Vicky manifests some of both. She welcomes intimacy yet fears speaking up for herself. She tends to magnify what might go wrong yet embraces sexuality and the work of development. To me, her attitude and success inspire hope for all of us on the path of development.

Vicky: I know I'm a Type 6 and it's OK, but I have a lot of fear. It makes my life difficult as this is my reality and there is so much to worry about.

David: Well, you know that is coming from your structure's core belief, the way you are organized, your habit of mind. It's doing that about 90% of the time. [both chuckle]

Vicky: I was with this man for 25 years, very loyal, but I never could satisfy him. When I discovered the Enneagram, it helped free me from the worry that I just had to put up with this repeated sense of disappointing him. And then we broke up.

David: One thing about the Enneagram is that when one person in a couple goes on the path of development and the other doesn't, it can destabilize the relationship, which can lead to separation. For this reason, I have always urged couples to commit to this development work together.

Vicky [with earnestness]: Well now, I'm married to a new man and I'm very happy. He truly is there for me so I needed to develop myself. I had to learn I'm OK and safe as a separate person, which was prompted by being courageous enough to leave my former relationship.

David [also earnestly]: Yes, it is really important for us Type 6s to develop faith in ourselves first so that we can be there for the other. So, for you now, when it comes to the sexual relationship, what are your blessings?

Vicky [said candidly]: Well, I have always liked sexual things. And my husband, he also is physical. It is very reassuring to me that we have this closeness.

David: Yes, the physical is a very important part of an intimate partner relationship. It has always mattered to me too. What do you find can get in the way and diminish your sexual experience?

Vicky: Sometimes [pauses] my fear can get in the way. I can still question if he loves me. This can really dampen my expression, or, I will tend to claim too much from him, wanting more expressiveness from him as proof of love.

David [said reassuringly]: When these doubts come up, just briefly pause, notice where in your body you experience the fear, then do your best to come back to more faith in yourself, saying to yourself, "May I have more trust in myself and our love for each other . . . "Then become aware and consciously present and become awake to the experience. And do so while knowing that you are loved, and that you also love. Know that you both are flourishing. Doing this work can really liberate our spirit.

Vicky: Thank you, David.

> Take a few minutes to reflect on and absorb how this example of a Type 6 on the path illustrates the work of development toward greater wholeness.

Type 7 | The Epicure | Sexual Fulfillment

Overview and Ultimate Fulfillment

Recall that as Epicures, we believe that to assure our lovability, self-worth (dignity), and security in the world, we must keep life upbeat, full of possibility, and stimulating and *not be* limited by obstacles, mundane tedium, and suffering in a world we experience as painful, frustrating, and potentially limiting.

In the process of personality formation, what goes into the background is our original ability to hold focus and interest on what is present and in front of us and on the whole range of possibility, which naturally enriches sensual/sexual experience. Fully present to self and other, we are curious and joyful when experiencing the full spectrum of life's possibilities as they arise, and having embodied the delight of welcoming—through receptivity—even moments of vulnerability. Our vulnerability might include feelings of sadness, limitations, and boredom as well as a greater depth of feeling when joyful, stimulated, and expansive.

When presence is brought to intimacy, we as Type 7s can experience the freedom to feel it all, the entire range of emotional ups and downs. We readily express joy and interest in whatever takes place and do so without running away from what is challenging or difficult or emotionally deep. The ultimate freedom of being in the moment fully with oneself and one's partner is called sobriety.

Higher expressions of sensuous sexuality, however, become diminished by our well-practiced need to escape from limitation, frustration, and perceived suffering. This results in a wide range of "mind chatter" and the seeking of diversionary stimulation, both of which adversely affect our depth of experience.

All the associative thinking, the escape from reality into fantasies, and future-tripping to more exciting options take us away from the now. As invigorating as we may feel to others, we are often not in the present moment. While an experiences-junkie at heart, the experiences themselves are often missed as we are already off *to the next*, mentally. We tend to not stay long with reality as it's unfolding in the present.

Type 7s' temperament style is referred to as "distractibility," meaning, extraneous environmental stimuli, altering the direction of behavior. Preoccupation with losing autonomy as well as getting trapped and/or limited paradoxically limits the sensuous/sexual experience and we oddly get trapped in variety without depth. Even as little children, we 7s were easily distracted by all sorts of readily available experiences or "Oh, look!" stimuli that kept us moving.

While we can be highly experimental, this virtual gluttony for experience can also diminish the depth of experience. Relationships can be short term, which also limits the degrees of intimacy sought and experienced. In trying to satisfy hungers, we 7s may indulge in a quest for new experiences and a fascination with variety, e.g., "I want to try it all," and "It's hard to focus on one person at a time."

This actually limits the depth of experience and connection of anyone, leaving us on the surface of life once again, starving for "something new" stimulation and the hope for satisfaction.

What 7s Have to Say about Sexual Diminishments

On Being Unlimited and Wanting an Abundance of Options and Opportunities

For **Kelsey**, options mean, "When things with my partner are not going well, I catch myself fantasizing about males in my workout group. I imagine what it would be like to be with them. This can even lift me out of an emotional slump. But it takes away from my presence to my partner."

Or as **Paige** puts it: "Before becoming aware of my habit of mind, fantasies with explicit sexual action were often better than the reality. Letting go of the mind and just being there was so difficult."

About wanting an abundance of opportunities, **George** says, "I love lots of options and variety with my lover. The intensity of these can really set me off."

Marge expresses limitlessness this way: "In the past, I definitely was attracted to multiple options, like a variety of positions and fantasies about different men. Now with my husband, I work at just being in love and present."

Roland comments on opportunities this way: "All the possibilities make being gay easy since I feel open to expressing my sexuality and to alternative sexual practices. But I often forget where my partner is."

For **Betty**, options mean, "The mind is the finest aphrodisiac. My self-restraint is strictly based upon concern for others rather than for fear of the unknown or of violating taboos."

Linda states the downside of options as follows: "I couldn't let go of thinking. I always had other brain chatter going on during times of intimacy. I even relied on fantasies about others while with my partner."

On the Driving Need for Pleasureful Gluttony, Especially of the Mind

Kelsey simply puts this excess of pleasureful thought like this: "I always wanted to try sex in different positions and places, try new ways to give and receive pleasure, and just go ahead with it, almost always saying yes irrespective of my partner's desires."

For **Sue**, this gluttonous pleasure was, "I wanted to try it all. I wanted a lot of sexual play, touching, tasting, smelling, fantasizing, and intimate talk. And I would lose track of what my partner wanted."

George puts it this way: "I still have an endless imagination of sex acts with a substantial number of women. I do not pursue them in real life. But it's so fun to think about them."

Gluttonous pleasure for **Betty** before awakening was, "Fascination over sexual variety, especially the mental stimulation through fantasies and talking about fantasies during sex—that owned me."

Roseanne says, "I used to be very promiscuous in an attempt to satisfy some endless hunger for the ultimate sexual experience. I didn't realize I was missing the greatest delight of just being present with my partner in the moment."

And **Roland** sums it up as, "I thought of so many pleasureful options to explore. I felt that I needed an endless variety of sexual expression or I would feel very confined."

On the Deepest Concerns: Being Totally Limited and Trapped in Suffering

For **Betty**, suffering meant, "My fear of painful negative thoughts associated with my partner led me to fantasize about other men or to idealize my own attractiveness. When I didn't feel like being close with my partner, I even rationalized having sex with him just to feel good in myself."

Likewise, about being limited, **Gabe** says, "I didn't like feeling trapped in my marriage. I hated it. So, I would escape into my fantasies of other women even while having sex with my beloved. Now thankfully I am there for her."

For **Marge**, the poignant fear has been, "Losing my partner and being all alone. So, I still sometimes try to accommodate him by faking an orgasm when he isn't up to a long session in order to make him feel powerful and that he's able to fulfill my needs."

Vividly put by **Hanna**: "I truly feared coming into the present moment; I feared he would see the whole me with all my negative feelings, like anger, helplessness, and sadness, and that would be unacceptable to him. I thought, 'How could he want me then?'"

As for **Roland**, he said, "I felt like my freedom would be limited if I was forced to fit into a mold of sexuality. Limitation seemed like death. I definitely thought I needed to have a variety of sexual experiences to have a good life."

***

Here, regarding Type 7s' diminishments, we can see the tendency to escape unwanted anxieties disguised as boredom, to move toward positive possibilities and options that prevent us from getting trapped, limited, or unstimulated.

> Take a few minutes to reflect on and absorb how Type 7s diminish their sensuous/
> sexual experience and interfere with the integration of their higher qualities of being
> into their sexual experience, and their lives in general.

Path of Development for Type 7

For us 7s, this involves becoming receptive to others and aware of others by breathing deeply, inhaling and exhaling, grounding ourselves in the present moment and by committing to coming back to this groundedness of being, over and over as needed. This entails allowing in the infinity of the present moment, through holding on and staying with it, with a gentle persistence. This allows for the felt-sense experience of steadiness in the body, where impulses can be held, and presence is not left behind.

With an open heart that is accepting of whatever is to be had in the experience—as in the full range of honest feelings, from joy to sorrow, delight to disappointment—the present moment can be more fully lived.

With this openhearted presence, our partner's sensuous/sexual joys and longings receive equal attention and importance to that of our own. In the process, presence paradoxically welcomes in all that has been skipped over by us going off into our imagination, the future, or various other forms of distraction and stimulation.

Cultivating presence nurtures both ourselves and the other's sensuous/sexual experience. Presence and sobriety do not take away from the pleasure of possibility or the spice of variety. Presence is actually what brings that so-desired vibrancy to the experiences of life.

> Take a few minutes to reflect on and absorb what Type 7 needs to develop in order to have a fulfilling intimate relationship that integrates **the higher quality of sobriety.** In this case it means the capacity to stay present in the moment with what is and engage with it fully, without diverting attention to something else that is equally or more stimulating.

What 7s Have to Say about Sexual Experiences on the Path to Fulfillment

For **Jan**, this involves the following: "I am now focusing on being present with my partner, sexual pleasure or pleasuring, instead of my getting worried about being bored. I'm in my body, relaxed, open and slowed down—not so manic or racing ahead in my mind. I'm connected with our souls and the universe."

Gabe states the new experience of fulfillment as, "No matter how strong my sexual juice is, I do not lose my connection with my partner. I'm blessed with experiencing a wide range of feelings, not just fantasy but raw sensation."

Simply stated by **Mary**, "When I'm now calm and not in my head, the feelings are of unconditional love, both expressed and received. What more could I ask for."

Now **Roland** experiences fulfillment in this way: "Through practicing presence in the moment, I'm able to have a deeper connection with my partner. I'm able to experience full sexual engagement with him."

***

In these responses you can realize how deep and rich our intimate experience can be when we are focused on presence. Presence *is* how we experience the joy and richness of intimacy, and it does not hinder variety.

> Take a few minutes to reflect on and absorb how Type 7s enhance their sensuous/sexual experience and foster the integration of their higher qualities of being into their sexual experience, and their lives in general.

David's Work with Type 7 | The Epicure

David's commentary: This example represents the enhancements and diminishments for Type 7s in love and sexuality. Paul espouses the spontaneity and playfulness but also the need to stay in the moment and be equally present for the other as well as himself. This is part of his path of integration on the journey to wholeness in both life and love.

Paul: I know I'm a Type 7 as I have so many ideas and ideals. I see all the positives and many alternatives. Life is full of possibilities.

David: So, how does your type structure with its focus on positives and possibilities impact your expression of love for better and, yes, for worse?

Paul [with enthusiasm]: Well, it changes. I want to experience everything with her that we haven't experienced before.

David: Well, how does this affect your sexual experience?

Paul [more earnestly]: It has to do with the fascination. I'm always intrigued by what can happen. I love adventure. When I started doing some inner work, I became more quiet. She says, "I find you fun now that you are more balanced, you are more there for me." But, finding that balance is hard for me.

David [slowly with dispassion]: Well, this is part of the path of integration, bringing some balance between her desires and needs, and yours, and for you to learn to be equally present for her as you are for yourself.

Paul [again earnestly]: It has changed from play to more inner acceptance of what is there. I am starting to look for love by connecting to others. I feel now that I'm more connected to others, more present. I even have found in the last year, how much love I have of nature, just being more in the flow of things. I don't always have to be doing something.

David: Wonderful, but let's get back to intimate expression and sexual expression, what is best for you?

Paul: Oh [gently laughing] having fun, celebrating life. But my downside was in finding out that I was so enthusiastic, so expressive, that she would pull back. I know that with my "monkey mind," I can very readily shift to something else, something new and different, which leaves others feeling unattended to, in my close relationships and particularly, when sexual with my wife. This really hurts her, even turns her off. And I always wondered why.

David [with some zest]: That's where the growth is. It's in calming the racing mind and in noticing with felt-sense awareness what your body's impulses are; this is what your beloved experiences as too much enthusiasm, she feels you're twisting and shifting. Then you can come back and breathe slowly and deeply and coach your heart to fully open to her. This actually increases your own joy and paradoxically, expands your own fuller experience of love. And of course, it takes practice and patience, neither of which are a Type 7's stronger points.

Paul: Yes, I know this is my path.

> Take a few minutes to reflect on and absorb how this example of Type 7 illustrates the work of development on the path to wholeness.

Type 8 | The Protector | Sexual Fulfillment

Overview and Ultimate Fulfillment

Recall that as Protectors, we believe that to assure our lovability, self-worth (dignity), and security in the world, we must be strong and just in a world where we experience the powerful taking advantage and the weak being victimized. We cannot be powerless and weak.

In the process of personality formation, what goes into the background is our original innocence, which is what allows us to come freshly to life and each intimate contact without excess, our own agenda, or domination. Our original innocence naturally enriches mutuality and sensual/sexual experience, as it is a loving, so-available presence, one that is accompanied by the abundance of energy we innately bring to the table.

Experiencing the other's as well as one's own truth, together, is intimacy. In the presence of intimacy, we are empowered with openhearted tenderness and the sweetness of innocence in the present moment, which thanks to our 8-ness get combined with passionate, exuberant action. This creates a fully receptive presence to the other.

There's tenderheartedness without any power agenda. However, these higher expressions of sensuous sexuality become affected by our theme of power, excess, strong desires, and assertiveness, which are felt by others as we sexually express ourselves. Expression is easily unrestrained (and possibly not pleasing) rather than unrestricted—a key difference.

In young children of this temperament—of this Enneagram type— unrestrained was described as "intensity of response," meaning, the level of response is strong, irrespective of its quality or direction or the stimuli. We 8s also may unintentionally express a control theme, e.g., "My feelings of power in sex seem to be to an extreme," or "I am turned on by sexual power over a partner." The opposite, which looks and feels like the release of control, can occur when a sense of being safe and protected is allowed and cultivated, and not shamed or prohibited in any way.

Sexuality for 8s can also be expressed by endurance and intensity, physical expression taking precedence over emotional connection; a "bulldozing" with 8s can possibly be experienced as too much. We 8s can mistake vulnerability for weakness, which often results in difficulty letting go and being receptive because of our underlying fears of feeling vulnerable and powerless.

This difficulty concerning vulnerability, mistaken as weakness, together with the excess of lustful exuberance and domination, often diminishes the sensual/sexual experience.

What 8s Have to Say about Sexual Diminishments

On Being Powerful, Impactful, and Expressing a Sense of Fairness and Truth

Claire expresses the theme of power and impact as, "I have a heightened sense of myself as a sexually powerful woman. Sexual power over a man turns me on. In my younger days, I even found it fun to make a man uncomfortable with my directness and strong sense of lustiness."

For **Josephine**, power gets expressed this way: "In the past, I felt a strong control over my lover. I wanted a guy who could respond to my sexual desires. I have learned to share fairly by giving rather than taking."

Jim simply says, "I enjoy the power of sex. Giving my partner an orgasm ignites me. But I have learned to be more thoughtful of my partner."

Lauren says, "I still have a high sexual drive, which delights and appalls my husband who started out much more inhibited and even avoidant."

Jack combines the power and fairness theme as, "While I lust for sexual experiences with different women, I'm true to my wife of 38 years and I'm protective of her. This satisfies my values by being true to my commitments."

Judy puts her truth this way: "Justice and power to me got expressed in my marrying a handicapped man and really caring for him. I always have wanted to empower him and I feel a sense of coming home when we relate sexually. But I still have fantasies of both over-powering *and* submitting to him."

On the Driving Energies of Exuberance and Associated Lust

Exuberance for **Henry** means that, "Even at age 68, my strong sense of lust is present. I desire more sex, but moderately. This is based on respect for my long-term partner."

Josephine puts exuberance sexually, like this: "Lust is a constant struggle for me. I hear that an average sex life is two times per week. We always have to exceed that. To me, lust means desire for sex, for orgasms, and for uninhibited lovemaking. I guess I'm just a bad girl."

Jacqueline describes sexual exuberance this way: "I'm totally into sex. In the past, one orgasm was never enough. Unfortunately, most of the time sex became a matter of quantity and quality, rather than that of emotional connection. Sometimes I was just too much for my husband."

And **Max** puts sexual exuberance like this: "When I was young and single, my thoughts and fantasies would heat up very quickly and go into excess when in the presence of a gal I considered very hot. We would go to bed as soon as I could get her to. But while sex needs to be an arena to express big life-force energy, I realized that such sexual exuberance could throw me off course and imbalance my relationships."

On the Deepest Concerns: Being Powerless and Weak and Mistaking Vulnerability as Weakness

Here again, **Max** felt that, "Before completing a lot of inner work and recognizing my vulnerability as a strength, I could never surrender to my wife. Now that I can allow in vulnerability and be receptive to my wife, the intensity of my orgasms is even greater."

Barbara puts being powerless this way: "In the past, my worst fear would be that when I'm vulnerable, I would be hurt. But now after an argument, when we receive each other and vulnerability envelops me, sex is even better. I feel protected, safe, and loved."

For **Ed**, being vulnerable is still difficult. He says, "It's a challenge to surrender. I fear powerlessness and that I'm losing control. I would love to feel safe just totally surrendering to sexual pleasure. Now I realize that this is not the same as grounded, receptive presence."

Elizabeth puts powerlessness this way: "It used to be that I could easily have casual sex with a partner and avoid any issues with vulnerability. I exercised my sexual power and felt nothing. Sex was easy, and love was hard."

And **Grace** says, "I still sometimes don't feel safe when my partner initiates sex. I feel exposed, not ready, and vulnerable. I can even shut down and I have little lubrication. But when I release from control, I become comfortable and even sometimes cry after orgasm because I am so full of emotion and gratitude."

***

For Type 8, the power of this type structure and issues impacting intimate experience can greatly diminish and distort the more intimate sexual experience. Releasing from the habit of mind of domination into receptivity both enriches and empowers the intimacy experience—both that of love and that of sex.

> Take a few minutes to reflect on and absorb how Type 8s diminish their sensuous sexual experience and interfere with the integration of their higher qualities of being into their sexual experience, and their lives in general.

Path of Development for Type 8

For 8s, this involves becoming receptive and aware, then allowing in the innocence of each moment without a personal agenda. This includes surrendering into union and experiencing the innocence and wonderment with which children come into this world. There can be much resistance to innocence, wonderment, and openhearted receptivity since these bring up vulnerability.

Gentleness for Type 8s is often experienced as weakness and avoided. We must pay attention to where in our body is the felt-sense of getting triggered that leads to our overpowering style of reactivity. Where does this feeling reside? We must breathe deeply and do our best to actively *allow* receptivity. Know that the receptive force along with its ability to welcome vulnerability is a strength. Let's not so readily define it as a weakness. This is our growth path.

Development toward wholeness encompasses the experience of being vulnerable, impacted, and trustingly connected to another. We must allow ourselves to sense reality innocently, purely, just as it comes to us, and know that our exuberance will always be there—and will always be there to protect us when needed.

Intensity without a personal agenda, when complemented with childlike innocence in the moment, allows us to surrender into a shared union, one that paradoxically magnifies our power, exuberance, and magnanimity.

> Take a few minutes to reflect on and absorb what Type 8 needs to develop in order to have a fulfilling intimate relationship that integrates **the higher quality of inno-cence.** In this case, it means coming freshly (without agenda) to a situation with an open heart, with vulnerability, and with a non-judgmental, open-to-others mind.

What 8s Have to Say about Sexual Fulfillment on the Path to Fulfillment

For **Jacqueline**, this involves the following: "Allowing myself to become soft and gentle and quiet. When I slow down, pay attention, enjoy the moment and engage my partner, all kinds of titillating exchanges occur. What a blessing receptivity has been for me, actually for both of us."

For **Cody**, the path to innocence in the moment is, "My not getting into a power struggle. Then, I can be the most delightful, spontaneous, creative, and fun partner to my sweetheart. I innately have an innocent curiosity, which lets me relax the big instinctual energy and just be."

The path to fulfillment for **Sara** is to, "Just breathe deeply, knowing this allows me to be present. This leads to openness, trust, surrender, and joy, taking in the pleasure this gives to both of us. To me, this is the innocence associated with no agenda, no expectation."

Max puts it this way: "I now meet my beloved partner sexually without any preconceived notions. It's freedom—it's childlike in a way. How would I have grasped this without knowing the strength and power of receptivity?"

And lastly, **Mark** says, "I approach lovemaking time as a new experience—no expectations or preconceived power scenarios. We are like two innocents at play."

***

As you reflect on these comments, allow yourself to experience the power of personal development and the freedom it provides us. We can even observe transformation in ourselves and in others if we look closely.

> Take a few minutes to reflect on and absorb how Type 8s enhance their sensuous/sexual experience, fostering the integration of their higher qualities of being into their sexual experience, and their lives in general.

David's Work with Type 8 | The Protector

David's commentary: Type 8s' big energy, little pause, and impactfulness can be just too much for others. The move to action can be so fast that there is little notice of where the other's state may be. Slowing down, becoming more receptive, and allowing in the more tender feelings can benefit both the expression of love and lovemaking.

Hector [expressed with big energy]: I'm an 8. I take charge "knowing" that I can change things. I just express myself, often I am not aware of my over-impact on others, sounding like I must do things my way or else. But to me, I feel like I'm just helping the other.

David [much softer]: How can this be challenging to those others in your life, when with you in love relationships and lovemaking?

Hector: They feel it is criticism, threatening, like I'm just too much. If I'm physically with you, I pay attention to you, and I help you with your agenda; then you know I love you. In lovemaking, I have a big appetite and my partner knows I'm with her. From my point of view, there is a lot of respect. From her point of view, I can just be too much and not really with her at all.

David [said firmly]: Yes, your impact, which feels so natural to you, can be experienced as too much active even aggressive energy to others. What then are your diminishments in lovemaking?

Hector [expressed more slowly, softly]: I create a sense that she is not OK and I'm just too much. I'm learning to be more still and more receptive. I used to think of stillness and receptivity as weakness or passivity.

David: Yes, this is the path, not just in lovemaking, but also in life. Practice noticing the big energy, pause and breathe deeply, inhale and exhale, so that you can allow yourself to get more receptive; welcome in the soft and tender feelings like you would when holding a small child. Remember, vulnerability is a huge strength and not a weakness. Then, your big, exuberant active energy is a blessing when interwoven with your softer, gentler, receptive energy.

Hector [with a sigh]: Yes, I now know this is my path. Sometimes now, we are finding true union in our lovemaking.

> Take a few minutes to reflect on and absorb how this example of Type 8 illustrates the work of development on the path to wholeness.

Type 9 | The Mediator | Sexual Fulfillment

Overview and Ultimate Fulfillment

Recall that as Mediators, we believe that to assure our basic needs for self-worth (dignity), love, and security, we must go along to get along in a world that we experience requires us to blend in and not be too much trouble for anyone. We do this by removing our differentiation from the other, by not being seen *as not aligned*, and by not standing out which can render us rejected in any small or large way and can leave us feeling unworthy of love.

In the process of personality formation, what goes into the background is our original ability to simply be present to our own personhood. The self is an equal to another—sometimes different, sometimes the same, and both are OK. With receptive energy, our presence can naturally enrich sensual/sexual experiences thanks to our propensity for flexibility, responsiveness, and harmoniousness in receiving, initiating compliance and acquiescence, and spacious bodily and emotional presence. In the presence of intimacy, our whole-hearted engagement results in grounded beingness, expansiveness, and a unity felt with the partner.

Love of self is equal to love of other—not more than or less than—and the self can differentiate from the other without feeling at risk. These higher expressions of sensuous sexuality become adversely impacted by our personality structure as the many environmental claims on our attention can lead to losing self-agency, a dispersion of one's energy, passiveness, and going along so as to not stand out or differentiate. These proclivities then prevent true receptivity to both ourselves and others.

This is the child whose temperament displays "high adaptability to any environmental, external claims placed on them," which is what leads to an innate ability—a talent—to accommodate, not be a fuss, and be seamless with others.

Sexual expression is often about arousal, occurring when one partner is assertive, for example, "taking the lead." Then, given time to get aroused, sexual responsiveness does occur with presence given to the experience. As Type 9s, our driving inertia toward ourselves can get expressed as tiredness, shutting down, wanting comfortable routine, and a lack of directed energy. We can readily feel not enough, invisible, and disregarded, yet it's most often not expressed.

Diminishment, when it occurs, results from an other-referencing loss of self or non-availability (as other's claims have been placed on our time and energy) and an inattention or inertia toward ourselves, while not so much toward others. This can cause difficulty over time.

What 9s Have to Say about Their Sexual Diminishments

About Going along to Get along and Being Pulled by all the External Claims

For **Cathy**, getting pulled by external demands gets expressed this way: "Before awakening with the Enneagram, when music was on during lovemaking, I could be distracted by the lyrics. Outside noises, like lawnmowers or cars also distract me. And especially, all the tasks I still have on my list sidetrack me. It was hard for me to get sexually responsive. It still may take time."

Shannon puts external claims this way: "Sexual responsiveness became a hurdle, especially after the first two children were born."

And for **John**, "I used to be paying attention to my work and other aspects of my life. I could become distracted and lose myself, not stay present."

The pull of external claims affected **Whitney** too. She says, "I just waited for my husband to take the lead before I felt OK being sexual or allowing my erotic energy to show. Most of my attention was on him. I even did things I didn't really enjoy."

Similarly, **Monica** says, "It used to be all about him, almost obsessively. I thought about him; I wanted to be with him. Sex was more about his orgasm than my own. I felt empty and full at the same time. I poured myself out so when he was not with me, I (could) feel connected and one with him."

And for **George**, this going along meant, "I always focused my attention outward to what the other wanted. Yes, I always tried to match to my partner's needs and desires. Then I just wouldn't get what I want."

On the Driving Resignation into Inertia toward Self, of Numbing Out and Seeking Comfort Instead of Engaging with One's Real Desires

Holly states numbing out to new adventure and wanting comfort as, "I really enjoy sex with my long-term partner and almost always climax with him. However, before waking up to my own deepest expression, I only liked the pleasureful routine of the tried-and-true so to speak. He can really excite me with his desire for me. Now I can take the lead too and really excite him."

Similarly, for **Dana**, "I so liked routine. I liked the comfort of doing it the way we always did it. And I still feel right at home going along with what he wants to do. The difficulty is I'm cheating us out of deep satisfaction."

For **Tim**, the comfort of numbing out manifested as, "I used to put off initiating sex. I felt inadequate, like I was going to do something wrong, so it was better to do nothing than get in trouble. It was easier for me to masturbate than risk the possibility of painful disagreement."

Lastly, here **Jake** says, "I followed the easy-does-it approach. I didn't want to push too hard and work too much for sex. Its enjoyable, especially when my partner takes the initiative. Now our sex life is more balanced, enriched."

On the Deepest Concerns: Being So Insignificant that You Would Be Dismissed and Rejected

Whitney expresses the core fear of being dismissed simply as, "It (rejection) used to be a great fear for me, sexually and in every other area of my life. It prevented me from taking the initiative sexually on most occasions, except the few times when I felt confident. Now I've learned to appreciate myself and to speak up for my desires."

Likewise for **Joan**, dismissal was a key theme: "When I felt dismissed, my sex drive went out the window. I would feel the anger, which meant a shutdown would happen in my body and I'd be 'gone.' I now participate in order to feel heard, respected, and honored; I am more likely now to be sexually present."

Victor puts past concerns with dismissal this way: "If my wife seemed dismissive, I got angry, and sex would never follow. But when she was responsive, sex could be really satisfying. She needed me to take more initiative."

Joan puts the dilemma about insignificance simply as, "I still worry about being dismissed, so I work at being a good lover by being sensitive to what's needed—to make it feel good for him first, and only then for me."

And lastly, **Jonathan** puts insignificance this way: "I used to really worry that I'm not enough for my partner, that I am just too ordinary and not exciting. And of course, that would just diminish lovemaking and my sense of my own sexuality, for sure."

> Take a few minutes to reflect on how Type 9s diminish sensuous/sexual experience, interfering with the integration of their higher qualities of being into their sexual experience, and their lives in general.

Path of Development for Type 9

For us 9s, this involves becoming receptive and aware, placing our attention as equally on ourselves as we do on the other. In the process, there is a reclaiming of one's openness. This is now proactive, rather than a pseudo receptivity that is really a non-presence to the self, which is, to a greater or lesser degree, inadvertently felt by the other.

With an active receptiveness to ourselves—which does take practice as our receptivity is often a self-forgetting attunement to the other—coupled with our innate ability to merge, what could be better? Here an unconditional, all-in blissful union can take place that flows to and from our grown-into independent and differentiated self and with that of the other.

This engenders flexibility and a harmonious connection that nurture each individual. We all need a good seeker-self (an independent self). Meaning, we are differentiated, we show up in the world, and we pursue our dreams. We interact as our own person, and we take right action for our own higher good. As such, others can feel us and know us.

We also need a good merger-self (a self that aligns with others). Meaning, we allow ourselves to merge but without our differentiation intact. We resonate with others and empathize with their subjective experience of themselves. As such, we can experience becoming "one" with another. Both are beautiful capacities and fulfilling human experiences.

Take a few minutes to reflect on and absorb what Type 9s need to develop in order to have a fulfilling intimate relationship that integrates **the higher quality of right action**. In this case it means taking a present-moment stance that acknowledges the self as equal to others and one's actions reflect this fundamental stance.

What 9s Have to Say about Sexual Experiences on the Path to Fulfillment

Ryan puts the path to growth this way: "Now I allow myself to be sexual, sensual, and feel strong. I'm much more present to what I want and need. I prepare myself by getting grounded, taking some deep breaths, and paying attention to what my body, heart, and mind are telling me and by not getting distracted with less important aspects of my life."

Joan expresses fulfillment as, "I'm in right action, which to me is being my truly passionate self—being adventurous, creative, playful, energized, kinky, fun, and being alive in my body, not numbed out. I now feel easily aroused and experience more sensations. Even simple kisses can turn me on to him."

For **Anita**, the journey to wholeness is, "Becoming an active participant in initiating what we try. I'm in a more actively giving, loving, and creative place than the passive and merged mental self I used to be. I feel more freedom and less inertia to do what my intuition tells me to do, both giving *and* taking."

For **Jonathan**, fulfillment means the following: "I'm better able now to know what I want and can articulate it. It's certainly better for me, but also for my partner, as it has increased his enjoyment."

Lastly, **Molly** expresses fulfillment as presence, "I'm now so directly responsive to his touch; I'm just there for it, moaning in delight, and when I touch him, I experience a similar joy."

***

As you contemplate, notice how important being present for both self and other is in truly fulfilling, intimate sexual experiences, regardless of type. The capacity for presence and merging as one with another is often so beautifully expressed by Type 9.

Take a few minutes to reflect on and absorb how Type 9s enhance their sensuous/sexual experience, fostering the integration of their higher qualities of being into their sexual experience, and their lives in general.

David's Work with Type 9 | The Mediator

David's commentary: This example with a Type 9 clearly shows the connection of our sexual expression to our type, to the rest of our lives, and to the path of development. Here, Emily is truly doing the work of integrating her own importance with the importance of others. She exemplifies this in her metaphor about the breath. She needs to be kinder and more compassionate toward herself in this process.

Emily: *I know I'm a 9 because it is so hard for me to know why I'm doing what I do and what I'm thinking.*

David: *So then, what does love mean to you?*

Emily *[said quietly with warmth]:* *I sense the heartbeat of the world and of the other, but not my own. This makes lovemaking hard for me. I sense my partner's heartbeat, but not mine. Then I get anxious, and my heartbeat gets so fast, so different than my partner's. I'm just not present when lovemaking.*

David *[said gently and with firmness]:* *You pay attention to your partner's heartbeat, wonderful, but not to your own heartbeat. Deep love pays attention to both, in both life and in sex. This is the core of the path for Type 9.*

Emily: *If I pay attention to my own heartbeat, it feels like a very lonely place.*

David: *Yes, this is the core fear of Type 9, "If I pay attention to my own heartbeat, I will lose my connection to the heartbeat of the other." [Pause] Where are you now?*

Emily *[tearfully]:* *I'm now trying to take care of myself more and pay attention to my own loving feelings. But to get to my own heartbeat, I have to go through loneliness.*

David *[said with presence]:* *Again, this is your core concern; I will lose the world if I'm present for myself. When that fear of loneliness comes up, do your best to just notice where it is in your body, your felt-sense of it, and pause, so that you can do the work of inquiry. And this is just as true in lovemaking as it is in life. You will discover that this is stemming from your core belief, which is underlying your Type 9's structure. Just do your best to come back to yourself. You will never lose the other. And your lovemaking will flourish when you are there for both your partner and you.*

Emily *[said softly but with firmness]:* *I know now this is my path.*

> Take a few minutes to reflect on and absorb how this example of Type 9 illustrates the work of development on the path to wholeness.

Sexual Expression and Fulfillment with Enneagram Knowledge

How interesting is the impact of each of the nine type structures on sexuality and how differently each brings themselves to sex and lovemaking. Love, when expressed through the intimacies of the body, through sexual physicality, opens the doors to sharing some of our greatest vulnerabilities.

Our sexuality exposes us to each other. It's where losing control, receiving, and surrendering to one another, are made possible and can be practiced. It's also where we can assert ourselves or learn to demonstrate our desire and hunger for another.

Lovemaking is a place where little can be hidden and where very private, personal sensitivities and needs have a chance to be expressed, shared, and explored, though this may take courage, some self-inventory, and practice.

Deep sexual intimacy takes self-knowing and other-trusting, a genuine interest to connect in more deeply intimate ways, and the willingness to work through the obstacles and diminishments of our own type structure as well as that of our partner's.

In the end, we hope to be given permission and to be needed by one another for support. We hope to be accepted and loved, as well as nurtured and encouraged. Intimacy calls us to show up fully, honestly, uninhibitedly, and spiritually.

Let this application of the Enneagram and its wisdom assist us to do just that.

Understanding One Another Leads to Loving Better and Living More Fully

This is what I know to be true and the reason we decided to write this book. I was compelled. Loving better is what we crave, living more fully is what we need and deserve. Contributing to our developmental well-being and improving our experience of ourselves, and of each other, have been on my heart and Suzanne's for a very long time.

> All nine Enneagram types have the potential to be highly present, adaptable, responsively flexible, loving and caring, undefended and enlightened...
>
> — David Daniels, MD and Suzanne Dion

Understanding One Another and the Enneagram

Awareness is where we begin. Understanding is where we go with it. Connection is what happens. Love is what's made possible. Because love *is*, at our very core, who and what we truly are. Love is what we are seeking and searching for, every time, in ourselves and in another. Living more fully allows us to express that *love* every day, in every way, and with everyone we encounter.

We start as potentiated love. We thrive in its presence, and we shrivel in its absence. To reiterate, 17th-century philosopher John Locke popularized the theory of *tabula rasa* or a "blank slate." We now know, thanks to contemporary research, that the (human) mind, a human being, at birth is *not* a blank slate. To the contrary, we are born with an organizing system for processing data. The flow of life-force energy and our inherent qualities of being human are already there. Both our spiritual and biological inheritance are in place and meet our external environment from the moment we are born.

The Enneagram reveals that we come in, already prepared, predisposed in some very intelligent way, to respond in certain and particular ways. Our emotional-instinctual bodies actually respond as best as they possibly can for us, long before we are consciously making our own "response" choices.

Honoring our innate disposition—our neural propensities, as Dr. Dan Siegel calls them, along with our higher spiritual qualities—gives us permission and the tremendous opportunity to study for ourselves three aspects of our becoming: First, and this is the more mysterious part of our *story of becoming*, are the essential qualities of being that "celestially, perhaps" inform the very fabric of our beingness from the get-go. These are the qualities of being that are always there with us as we evolve and emerge into the wholeness of who we truly are, and of what we leave behind.

Second is our innate temperament, which is our predisposed way of self-organizing information and energy as they flow within us into particular developmental pathways that then structure our personalities. Third is the what and whom we are given to deal with, to experience and respond to, including the parenting-caregiving relationships we are dependent on, from the very first day of our lives, all the way into young adulthood, our peer groups and expanding social networks, and numerous life events (both traumatic and life-giving).

Committing to understanding this, both with compassion and reverence, is sacred work. It's the profound work of personal development. It's the incalculable journey toward personal freedom; the personal freedom that liberates us from the confines of our habitual focus of attention, our conditioned hurt and its corresponding defenses, and the often-narrowing limits of our level of developmental well-being and its impact on our particular character structure.

Personal development is what can take us beyond the defendedness and judgmentalness that separate us *from everything* and can begin to restore the many possible losses of self that have cut us off from ourselves inside, and from love. It's the work that takes us to loving better. It's the work of getting to live far more fully, within *and with* ourselves and within *and with* each of our relationships.

Through psychological, emotional, and somatic work, we have the capacity to heal our emotional wounds, the ones that happened in relationships with others—starting with our earliest caregivers. This we do by working on deepening our relationship to ourselves first (have we mentioned this enough yet?), and by entering sacred-witnessing, loving relationships with others who are on the path of taking this journey to self-love and self-knowing, right alongside of us. We have these capacities. We only need to exercise the intelligences within us—to activate them—and to reparent ourselves enough in order to move forward and into our fullest potential. We *really can* do this.

To begin to study our temperament—our differentiating biological propensities and aptitudes—we need look no further than the Enneagram. My studies of the Enneagram and fascination with its nine type structures only deepened decade after decade.

I continued to marvel at the vastness of this map of understanding and its many applications. It's one of the most proficient models for self-understanding and self-assessment I have ever come across. And how the Enneagram benefitted my clients in private practice and the countless others I have had the chance to work with cannot be over-expressed.

The intelligence of the Enneagram system points us at the highly complex way we as individuals—and as a human community—are designed and organized to support each other and survive. With a name based on two Greek words and depicted as a nine-pointed diagram, the Enneagram garners its fair share of apprehensive attention. However, the symbol itself is based on sophisticated mathematical patterns and the sciences are now just touching the surface of what can be known from its study and the complexities for healing and development contained within it.

In the field of psychology, the Enneagram offers us an incisive and reliable understanding of our human nature over and over again, in country after country, and culture after culture. It reveals how we are uniquely—even neurobiologically—differentiated from one another, as well as extraordinarily interconnected and interdependent. No other typology system known or studied today does this.

Within its framework comes our chance to know ourselves and each other reverently and intimately. This is where our deep need for each other—for our interconnectedness and our interdependence—stands out to me and is of critical importance. In understanding our inner connectedness, we come to understand our divine nature.

It has always been my belief that personal development requires not only psychological work but also spiritual work. We all have access to the Enneagram's nine Holy Ideas, which are associated with our higher mental capacities—perfection, will, hope, origin, omniscience, faith, constancy, truth, and love.

Through the study and contemplation of the nine fundamental Basic Propositions, we can learn to reconnect with our own. We can also reconnect with each of their essential strengths to work more effectively with how they drive our focus of attention, our solutions to life's challenges and our coping strategies.

We also have access to the nine higher emotional *qualities of being* revealed in the Enneagram: serenity, humility, veracity, equanimity, non-attachment, courage, sobriety, innocence, and right action.

And through mindful awareness and spiritual growth practices—such as the 5As of the Universal Growth Process—we can return to these higher mental and emotional qualities of our being. They are always there, simply waiting for us.

Relationships, Intimacy, and the Enneagram

A book about relationships, intimacy, and the Enneagram was a big ask. There are countless directions to have taken the material and countless aspects of intimacy cultivation that could have been explored.

We decided to direct this book to some of the deeper and more sensitive issues around intimacy that I saw time and time again cause immense disconnect and deeply personal suffering. Our fear of rejection and our fear of being alone are front and center as we try to relate to and love one another. These same fears haunt us as well as we struggle to love ourselves.

There is no doubt that most of us do our very best to bring all that we have to the proverbial table of each relationship we encounter, before our intrapersonal fears and personality liabilities start to get in our way and create the countless difficulties we are all too familiar with.

We decided to courageously go for it as we wrote this, hoping to move us toward the delicate issues that I saw couples and intimates struggle to address with each other, as well as struggle with inside of themselves. We wanted to open up a dialogue that would help each of us talk more openly and constructively with one another. To do that, we had to start with a very close look at personal intimacy—that of intimacy with self. This is the relationship we struggle with inside.

How do we cultivate self-intimacy healthfully, honestly, and fully? It's critical to take this on, as our relationship to self—the quality of it—is where any level of true and lasting intimacy begins and ends with others.

With the starting point being that of self-intimacy, this book ventured to take on the most intimate of intimacies—our sexuality. Our sexuality, along with how we connect in this realm, is something that touches our physical as well as mental, emotional, and spiritual well-being. Yes, our sexuality is driven in great part by our physical body. However, it's more than that as our physicality is one of the great sources and drivers of our overall well-being—and it's the temple that holds our essential selves. It is what holds and guides, manifests and reveals *our spirit*—our life force. Sexuality is also the kind of intimacy that leads to procreation, the creation of life itself, and to spiritual union, if we are so fortunate.

It is our hope to see the Enneagram be used as it's designed to be used— to free us up to connect more, feel more, create more, and express more. This extraordinary system for self-awareness development and self-understanding offers countless learnings, including an incisive grasp on our fundamental and specific core beliefs, our individual differences, and the habits of mind that drive our rather specified *focus of attention*.

From these understandings, we can grow much and love so much more. We hope that by using the Enneagram to peer into ourselves we're given the best possible chance to access our own tender vulnerabilities—those that are held deeply within—and that we dare bravely to share those vulnerabilities more sacredly and intimately with those closest to us.

We know in our hearts that the Enneagram can help us do this work. That mindful awareness training and practice—such as the 5As—can help us do this work. We know that the many ways this book encourages us to examine and come to know ourselves through gentle inquiry can help us do this work. That the many chapters herein that challenge our habitual ways of seeing the world and interacting with it along with seeing and interacting with each other . . . can all help us do this work.

It is our hope that the thoughts shared in this book may touch us all, most endearingly and supportively. May the insights shared be available to us in those moments inside of ourselves when we may feel very alone or overwhelmed, inadequate or disconnected or when we simply want to evolve—to love and live more fully. The Enneagram—any comprehensive and compassionate application of it—gives rise to this possibility.

Our great hope is that we come to attain deeper connections and intimacies— psychological and emotional, sexual all the way to spiritual—with ourselves and with others. Couples have a lot to share with each other, and when they do, intimacy develops. We invite each and every one of us to take this on—the quest for intimacy—with a heartfelt sincerity and copious amounts of devotion, gusto, and passion.

We encourage every one of you reading this book who are currently in a relationship to make time and space for all manner of sharing curiously with each other in order to develop many of the real-life intimacies shared herein and beyond.

May we curiously pursue *our being* fully and in its entirety. May we accept the mission that seeks and cultivates our own divine personhood, allowing it to potentiate and manifest as it was so designed to do—unhindered and unencumbered. And to the shear will it takes for each of us to find and express our love-ability and our wholeness, we salute our courage and the spirit within us as we boldly walk this path.

In reverence and with tremendous gratitude for all that we are and can become, for ourselves and for others, we hope you have enjoyed this read. May we rise to the occasion—to loving better and living more fully—for the higher good of all.

May we devote ourselves to the work of personal discovery for the benefit of all of life itself, for all of humanity, and for all of our beautiful planet.

That is my ultimate vision.

" There is nothing
more important than
self-awareness
and self-understanding
to bringing peace
and compassion
to our relationships
and to our world. "

—David Daniels, M.D.

ABOUT THE AUTHORS

David N. Daniels

David N. Daniels, MD, (August 30, 1934–May 26, 2017) was a world-renowned Enneagram and personal development teacher, Clinical Professor of Psychiatry and Behavioral Sciences at Stanford University School of Medicine, and a leading developer of the Enneagram system of nine personality types, including co-founding of The International Enneagram Association and The Narrative Enneagram.

David is the first author of *The Essential Enneagram: The Definitive Personality Test and Self-Discovery Guide* (Harper Collins, 2000, with a 25th anniversary coming out in 2025). This bestseller includes the only scientifically validated Enneagram personality test. He is a second author with best-selling author, Daniel Siegel of *Personality and Wholeness in Therapy: Integrating Nine Patterns of Developmental Pathways.*

In private practice for over 40 years, David taught the nine Enneagram types and system at Stanford University, in his community, and internationally to thousands of therapists, teachers, healers, coaches, and individuals worldwide. With his gentle and loving openheartedness, David also brought his knowledge of the nine Enneagram types to individuals, couples, and groups, and to a wide range of applications in clinical practice, the workplace, and to those incarcerated.

Together with author and teacher Helen Palmer, David founded the Enneagram Studies in the Narrative Tradition (now called The Narrative Enneagram) and The Palmer-Daniels Enneagram Professional Training Program. He was also one of the key founders of the International Enneagram Association.

David was a big believer in the personal liberation found in self-assessment and self-help practices, and he developed many simple personal development methods and practices to use daily, including the Universal Growth Process for Self-Mastery.

In the last seven years of his life, David devoted much of his time and heartfelt passion to writing this book with Suzanne Dion. It brings together the power of the Enneagram, relationship mindfulness, and a deep understanding of the nine Enneagram personality types to transform relationships from conflictual and struggling to harmonious and thriving.

He always believed that understanding our differentiating personality types was the key to instilling far more compassion for one another and in the end, healing world conflict. If we could come to truly understand ourselves and others, acceptance and love would follow, and world peace would eventually prevail.

Likewise, it was David's great hope that *this* book would share an insightful body of wisdom that would in turn help us all to heal the world.

David's work is archived and carried forth at drdaviddaniels.com.

Suzanne Dion

Suzanne is an Enneagram-informed transformational coach and trainer that works with individuals, couples, teens, families, and small companies. She co-authored this book with her mentor David Daniels, MD., a book that marries the wisdom of the Enneagram and David Daniels' years of experience with Dr. Daniel J. Siegel's research on mindful awareness, attachment, and interpersonal neurobiology.

As Suzanne carries David's compassionate approach forward, her focus is the bettering of human relationships through intrapersonal healing first, followed by the development of cognitive-emotional somatic capacity, emotional literacy, as well as defense system relaxation for the deepening of intimacy—with both self and other.

A teacher, writer, and educator of the Enneagram system for personal and professional self-awareness, Suzanne is currently an Enneagram consultant at the Deep Coaching Institute and the Creative Director for Marion Gilbert's Somatic Enneagram™ Training School. Suzanne is also one of the founders of T.A.P.P., The Attuned Parent Program—Parenting to Heal the World.

In 2008, Suzanne completed her teacher certification with the Palmer-Daniels Enneagram Professional Training Program, now called The Narrative Enneagram (TNE). She completed the Advanced Coaching 2.0 program with

The Enneagram in Business, designed by Ginger Lapid-Bodga, PhD, and has trained with Life-centered Therapy, designed and developed by Dr. Andy Hahn.

She was one of the founding board members of the Enneagram Prison Project (2012–2017) and spent several years developing course content and curricula as well as teaching a trauma-informed, addiction-informed Enneagram to incarcerated men and women in Northern California jails and the San Quentin State Prison.

Learn more about Suzanne at suzannedion.com

DAVID'S ACKNOWLEDGMENTS

This book is a summary of my decades immersed in teaching and practicing the Enneagram as well as providing therapy to couples. I have made several notes here to honor my colleagues who have contributed to the ideas, knowledge, and wisdom in this book. I am grateful to . . .

Colleagues of The Narrative Enneagram: I am grateful to all my fellow faculty of The Narrative Enneagram for what they have taught me and continued to teach me throughout the years and continue to teach so many—Helen Palmer, Terry Saracino, Peter O'Hanrahan, Marion Gilbert, and Renee Rosario.

Students of The Narrative Enneagram: I am grateful for all the students and teachers who have studied with us, who have taught with me, who have shared their knowledge with me, and who have served on type panels across the years.

Arthur Hastings: I am grateful to Arthur Hastings and his teachings. Before his passing in 2014, he explored sexuality and the spiritual experience in his teachings at the Institute of Transpersonal Psychology (now Sofia University) in Palo Alto, CA.

Terry Saracino: I am grateful for the contributions of Terry Saracino of The Narrative Enneagram, on the judging mind and the superego. Together, we also developed essential practices for relationship development based on our over 25 years of experience developed through our Enneagram Studies in the Narrative Tradition (ESNT) trainings. We employed these relationship principles for many years. With Terry Saracino, I developed the name the Universal Growth Process or UGP and the 5As.

Marion Gilbert and Peter O'Hanrahan: I am grateful for the groundbreaking somatic work and teachings of Marion Gilbert as well as that of Peter O'Hanrahan, they both have added enormously to the somatic work of the Enneagram.

Rochelle Wald: I am grateful for the groundbreaking work of Rochelle Wald. We have published her 2005 dissertation in Chapter 14, which was written for the Institute for Advanced Study of Human Sexuality in San Francisco, *The Enneagram Types: Nine Styles of Expressing Sexuality*.

Daniel J. Siegel: I am grateful for the work of Dan Siegel. The neuroscience studies in this book are based largely on the work of Dr. Daniel J. Siegel, especially from his book, *Mindsight: The New Science of Personal Transformation*.

Ron Levine: I am grateful for the work of Dr. Ron Levine, clinical psychologist in Van Nuys, California who teaches human sexuality extensively, exploring the three domains of sexual expression and their neurobiological connections. He participated in the Human Sexuality Training Program at UCLA's Neuropsychiatric Institute. He also is a licensed Rabbi. He is the author of numerous articles including *Mindful Teenage Sexuality: An Integrated Approach to Teaching Teenagers About Human Sexuality*.

Harry Harlow: I am grateful to the work of Harry Harlow (and to the Rhesus monkeys he studied). His work revealed the amazing power of bonding, connection, social contact, and love, for example, "Total Social Isolation in Monkeys," in *Proceedings of the National Academy of Science* from 1965.

WEBSITE RESOURCES

We invite you to the drdaviddaniels.com website to explore, learn, and interact with additional resources on The Enneagram, Relationships, and Intimacy. On Dr. David Daniels' website you will find:

Resources for Practicing and Developing Your Relationship(s)
- *The Enneagram, Relationships, and Intimacy Workbook*
- David's **"Weekly Reflections"** by Type, by Season
- The **Fundamental Breath Practice** developed by Dr. David Daniels

Resources for Self and Relationship Discovery
- The **Essential Enneagram Test**, a scientifically-validated Enneagram test based on a research study at Stanford University developed by Dr. David Daniels and Dr. Virginia Price
- The "Levels of Developmental Well-Being" **Worksheet**
- The **"Enneagram Relationships Matrix"** of all 45 type combinations
- The **Enneagram Triads** from David, including:
  o The Three Great Life Forces
  o The Emotional Regulation Styles
  o The Harmony Triads

Resources for Training, Workshops, and Coaching
- Enroll in **courses with The Narrative Enneagram**, co-founded by Dr. David Daniels and Helen Palmer
- Explore **working with Suzanne Dion, an Enneagram Certified Teacher and Coach**
  o Enneagram "Self-Discovery" Typing Sessions
  o Enneagram Individual, Couples, and Parenting Coaching
  o Enneagram and Relationship Based Workshops

REFERENCES

Almaas, A. (2014) *The Power of Divine Eros*, Boulder, CO: Sounds True

Altman, D. (2014) *The Mindfulness Toolbox*, Eau Claire, WI: PESI Publishing & Media

Assagioli, R. (1974) *The Act of Will*, New York: Penguin Books

Borys, A. (2013) *Effortless Mind: Meditate with Ease Calm Your Mind, Connect with Your Heart, and Revitalize Your Life*, Novato, CA: New World Library

Bradshaw, J. (2005) *Healing the Shame That Binds You*, Deerfield, FL: Health Communications

Brizendine, L. (2006) *The Female Brain*, New York: Morgan Road Books

Brizendine, L. (2010) *The Male Brain*, New York: Broadway Books

Catto, J. (2014) *Breaking the Approval Addiction and Expressing Our Creative Gifts*, Boulder, CO: Sounds True

Chestnut, B. (2013) *The Complete Enneagram*, Berkeley, CA: She Writes Press

Coontz, S. (2005) *Marriage, a History: How Love Conquered Marriage*, New York: Penguin Group

Daniels, D. and Price, V. (2000, 2009, 2025) *The Essential Enneagram: The Definitive Personality Test and Self-Discovery Guide*, San Francisco: Harper

Damasio, A. R. (2005) *Descartes' Error: Emotion, Reason, and the Human Brain*, New York: Penguin

Davidson, R. and Begley, S. (2012) *The Emotional Life of Your Brain*, London, UK: Hudson Street Press

Deida, D. (2007) *Enlightened Sex, Finding Freedom and Fullness Through Sexual Union*, Boulder, CO: Sounds True

Durant, W. and Durant, A. (1968) *The Lessons of History*, New York: Simon and Schuster

Eisley, L. (1959) *The Immense Journey: An Imaginative Naturalist Explores the Mysteries of Man and Nature*, New York: Random House

Emmons, R. A. (2007) *Thanks!: How the New Science of Gratitude Can Make You Happier*, New York: Houghton Mifflin Harcourt

Felitti, V., Anda, R., Nordenberg, D., Williamson, D., Spitz, A., Edwards, V., Koss, M. and Marks, J. (1998) "Relationship of Childhood Abuse and Household Dysfunction to Many of the Leading Causes of Death in Adults," *American Journal of Preventive Medicine*, 14 (4), 245–258

Feuerstein, G. (1996) *A Little Book for Lovers*, Boulder, CO: Sounds True

Fisher, H. (2005) *Why We Love: The Nature and Chemistry of Romantic Love*, New York: St. Martin's Press

Fisher, H. (2010) *Why Him? Why Her?: How to Find and Keep Lasting Love*, New York: Holt Paperbacks

Frankl, V. (1959) *Man's Search for Meaning*, Boston, MA: Beacon Press

Gottman, J. (1995) *Why Marriages Succeed or Fail: And How You Can Make Yours Last*, New York: Simon and Schuster

Gray, J. (1992) *Men Are from Mars, Women Are from Venus*, New York: Harper Collins

Gunaratana, B. (2002) *Mindfulness in Plain English*, Somerville, MA: Wisdom Publications

Hanson, R. (2013) *Hardwiring Happiness*, New York: Harmony Books, Crown Publishing Group

Harley, W. (2001) *Fall in Love, Stay in Love*, Grand Rapids, MI: Baker Publishing Group

Hawkins, J. (2004) *On Intelligence*, New York: Henry Holt

Harlow, H. (1965) "Total Social Isolation in Monkeys," Harry Harlow et al. in *Proceedings of the National Academy of Science*, U S A. Jul 1965; 54(1): pgs. 90–97

Horstman, J. (2011) *The Scientific American Book of Love, Sex, and the Brain*, San Francisco, CA: Jossey-Bass

Kabot-Zinn, J. (2003) "Mindfulness-based Interventions in Context: Past, Present, and Future," *Clinical Psychology: Science and Practice*, 10(2), 144–156

Keltner, D. (2009) *Born to Be Good*, New York: W.W. Norton

Killen, J. (2009) "Toward the Neurobiology of the Enneagram," *International Enneagram Association Journal*, Volume II

Kornfield, J. (2008) *Meditation for Beginners*, Boulder, CO: Sounds True

Lama, The Dalai and Cutler, H. (1998) *The Art of Happiness*, New York: Riverhead Press

Lederach, J. P. (2005) *The Moral Imagination: The Art and Soul of Building Peace*, Oxford: Oxford University Press

Lewis, T., Amini, F., and Lannon, R. (2001) *A General Theory of Love*, New York: Random House

Locke, J. (1850) *An Essay Concerning Human Understanding*, Philadelphia, T.E.

Maté, G. (2010) *In the Realm of Hungry Ghosts, Close Encounters with Addiction*, Berkeley, CA: North Atlantic Books

Money, J. (1955) *Gendermaps: Social Constructionism Feminism and Sexosophical History*, New York: Continuum Intl Pub Group

Neufeld, G. and Maté, G. (2006) *Hold on to Your Kids, Why Parents Matter More than Peers*, New York: Ballantine Books-Random House

Osho (2001) *Love, Freedom, Aloneness: The Koan of Relationship*, New York: Osho International Foundation

Palmer, H. (1998) *The Enneagram in Love and Work: Understanding Your Intimate and Business Relationships*, San Francisco: Chronicle

Panksepp, J. (1998) *Affective Neuroscience: The Foundations of Human and Animal Emotions*, Oxford: Oxford Press

Riso, D. and Hudson, R. (1999) *The Wisdom of the Enneagram*, New York: Bantam Books

Robert A. E. (2007) *Thanks! How the New Science of Gratitude Can Make You Happier*, Boston, MA: Houghton Mifflin

Rogers, C. (1951) *Client-centered Therapy: Its Current Practice, Implications and Theory*, London, UK: Constable

Roth, G. (n.d.) *Gabrielle Roth's 5Rhythms*, New York: 5Rhythms.

Salzberg, S. (2002) *Lovingkindness: The Revolutionary Art of Kindness*, Boston, MA: Shambhala Publications

Sax, L. (2007) *Boys Adrift: The Five Factors Driving the Growing Epidemic of Unmotivated Boys and Underachieving Young Men*, New York: Basic Books

Schafer, W. (2010) *Roaming Free Inside the Cage: A Daoist Approach to the Enneagram and Spiritual Transformation*, Bloomington, IN: iUniverse

Schnarch, D. (1991) *Constructing the Sexual Crucible: An Integration of Sexual and Marital Therapy*, New York: WW Norton

Schwartz, M. and Cohn, L. (2015) *Sexual Abuse and Eating Disorders*, New York: Routledge

Schwartz, R. C. (1995) *Internal Family Systems Therapy*, New York: The Guilford Press

Siegel, D. J. (2007) *The Mindful Brain: Reflection and Attunement in the Cultivation of Well-Being*, New York: W.W. Norton

Siegel, D. J. (2010) *Mindsight: The Science of Personal Transformation*, New York: Bantum

Siegel, D. J. (2010) *The Mindful Therapist*, New York: W.W. Norton

Siegel, D. J. (2012) *Pocket Guide to Interpersonal Neurobiology*, New York: W.W. Norton

Siegel, D. J. (2018) *Aware*, New York: Tarcher Perigee

Soosalu, G. and Oka, M. (2012) *mBraining: Using Your Multiple Brains to Do Cool Stuff*, Bellevue, WA: mBit International Pty Ltd

Sukel, K. (2012) *Dirty Minds: How our Brains Influence Love, Sex and Relationships*, New York: Free Press

Tannen, D. (2007) *You Just Don't Understand: Women and Men in Conversation*, New York, NY: Harper Collins

Thomas, A. and Chess, S. (1977, 1990) *Temperament and Development*, New York, NY: Brunner/Mazel

Trayser, J. R. (2016) *The ACEs Revolution: The Impact of Adverse Childhood Experiences*, Bellevue, WA: CreateSpace Independent Publishing Platform

Wagner, J. (2010) *Nine Lenses on the World*, Evanston, IL: Nine Lenses Press

Wilber, K. (2000) *Sex, Ecology, Spirituality*, Boston, MA: Shambhala Publications

Wilber, K. (2003) *Kosmic Consciousness* (DVD), Boulder, CO: Sounds True

INDEX

D

E

F

G

A free ebook edition is available with the purchase of this book.

To claim your free ebook edition:

1. Visit MorganJamesBOGO.com
2. Sign your name CLEARLY in the space
3. Complete the form and submit a photo of the entire copyright page
4. You or your friend can download the ebook to your preferred device

Print & Digital Together Forever.

Snap a photo

Free ebook

Read anywhere